Opera Companies of the World

OPERA COMPANIES OF THE WORLD

SELECTED PROFILES

Edited by
ROBERT H. COWDEN

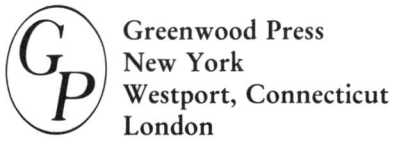

Greenwood Press
New York
Westport, Connecticut
London

Library of Congress Cataloging-in-Publication Data

Opera companies of the world : selected profiles / edited by Robert H. Cowden.
   p. cm.
   Includes bibliographical references and index.
   ISBN 0-313-26220-9
   1. Opera companies—Directories. I. Cowden, Robert H.
ML12.063   1992
782.5′02′95—dc20   91-24186

British Library Cataloguing in Publication Data is available.

Copyright © 1992 by Robert H. Cowden

All rights reserved. No portion of this book may be reproduced, by any process or technique, without the express written consent of the publisher.

Library of Congress Catalog Card Number: 91-24186
ISBN: 0-313-26220-9

First published in 1992

Greenwood Press, 88 Post Road West, Westport, CT 06881
An imprint of Greenwood Publishing Group, Inc.

Printed in the United States of America

The paper used in this book complies with the
Permanent Paper Standard issued by the National
Information Standards Organization (Z39.48–1984).

10 9 8 7 6 5 4 3 2 1

Every reasonable effort has been made to trace the translators of material in this book, but in some instances this has proven impossible. The author and publisher will be glad to receive information leading to more complete acknowledgments in subsequent printings of this volume and in the meantime extend their apologies for any omissions.

To the unsung heroes of opera companies and musical organizations, the technicians, and most especially, Larry and Ed

Contents

Acknowledgments	xix
Introduction	xxiii
Opera Companies of the World	
ARGENTINA	
Buenos Aires	
Teatro Colón	1
AUSTRALIA	
Adelaide	
The State Opera of South Australia	4
Melbourne	
Victoria State Opera	5
Sydney	
The Australian Opera	7
AUSTRIA	
Bregenz	
Bregenzer Festspiele	11
Graz	
Vereinigte Bühnen	12
Linz	
Landestheater Linz	13

Salzburg
    Salzburger Festspiele   14
Vienna
    Wiener Staatsoper   16
    Wiener Volksoper   20

BELGIUM
Brussels
    Théâtre Royal de la Monnaie   22

BRAZIL
Rio de Janeiro
    Teatro Municipal   25

BULGARIA
Sofia
    Sofiyska Narodna Opera (Sofia National Opera)   27
    State Musical Theater "Stefan Makedonski"   28

CANADA
Edmonton
    Edmonton Opera   31
Montréal
    L'Opéra de Montréal   32
Ottawa
    National Arts Centre/Centre national des arts   33
Toronto
    Canadian Opera Company   36
Vancouver
    Vancouver Opera   39

CHILE
Santiago
    Opera del Teatro Municipal   41

PEOPLE'S REPUBLIC OF CHINA
Beijing
    Central Opera Theater   43
Shanghai
    Shanghai Opera House   45

Contents

CZECHOSLOVAKIA
Bratislava
Slovenské Národné Divadlo (Slovak National Theater) — 46
Brno
Janáček's Opera Brno — 48
Prague
Národní Divadlo Prague (National Theater Prague) — 49

DENMARK
Copenhagen
Det Kongelige Teater og Kapel — 53

ESTONIA
Tartu
Teatre Vanemuine — 55

FINLAND
Helsinki
Finnish National Opera — 57
Savonlinna
Savonlinna Opera Festival — 59

FRANCE
Lyon
Opéra de Lyon — 61
Marseille
Opéra de Marseille — 62
Nancy
Opéra de Nancy et de Lorraine — 64
Nice
Opéra de Nice — 65
Paris
Théâtre National de L'Opéra de Paris — 66
Rouen
Théâtre des Arts — 69
Strasbourg
Opéra du Rhin — 70

GERMANY

Augsburg
Städtische Bühnen — 73
Bayreuth
Bayreuther Festspiele — 73
Berlin
Deutsche Oper Berlin — 75
Deutsche Staatsoper Berlin (Unter den Linden) — 83
Komische Oper — 89
Darmstadt
Staatstheater — 92
Dortmund
Städtische Bühnen — 94
Dresden
Staatsoper Dresden (Semperoper) — 96
Düsseldorf-Duisburg
Deutsche Oper am Rhein — 98
Essen
Theater und Philharmonie Essen — 100
Frankfurt am Main
Städtische Bühnen — 100
Hamburg
Hamburgische Staatsoper — 101
Hannover
Niedersächsische Staatstheater — 105
Karlsruhe
Badisches Staatstheater — 107
Kassel
Staatstheater — 109
Köln
Opera der Stadt Köln — 110
Leipzig
Opernhaus — 116
Mannheim
Nationaltheater — 117

Contents

München
    Bayerische Staatsoper — 119
Nürnberg
    Städtische Bühnen — 123
Stuttgart
    Staatstheater Stuttgart — 124

GREECE
Athens
    National Opera of Greece — 126

HUNGARY
Budapest
    Magyar Állami Operaház (Royal Hungarian Opera House) — 127

REPUBLIC OF IRELAND
Wexford
    Wexford Festival Opera — 132

ISRAEL
Tel Aviv
    The New Israeli Opera — 136

ITALY
Bologna
    Teatro Comunale di Bologna — 138
Florence
    Teatro Comunale di Firenze — 139
Genoa
    Teatro Carlo Felice — 142
Milan
    Teatro alla Scala — 143
Naples
    Real Teatro di San Carlo — 146
Palermo
    Teatro Massimo — 148
Parma
    Teatro Regio — 151

Rome
    Teatro dell'Opera   154
Trieste
    Teatro Giuseppe Verdi   155
Turin
    Teatro Regio di Torino   156
Venice
    Teatro La Fenice di Venezia   157
Verona
    Arena di Verona   158

JAPAN
Tokyo
    Nihon Opera Shinkokai (The Japan Opera Foundation)   159

LITHUANIA
Vilnius
    Lietuvos Operos ir Baleto teatras   161

MONACO
Monte Carlo
    Opéra de Monte-Carlo   164

NEW ZEALAND
Wellington
    Wellington City Opera   166

NORWAY
Oslo
    Den Norske Opera   168

POLAND
Gdańsk
    Państwowa Opera i Filharmonia Bałtycka   170
Kraków
    Krakowski Teatr Muzyczny   172
Lodz
    Teatr Wielki W Lodzi   172
Poznań
    Teatr Wielki   174

Contents xiii

Warsaw
    Teatr Wielki   176
Wroclaw
    Opery Wroclaws   183

PORTUGAL
Lisbon
    Companhia de Opera do Teatro São Carlos   184

ROMANIA
Bucharest
    Opera Română (Romanian Opera)   185

REPUBLIC OF SOUTH AFRICA
Cape Town
    Opera of the Cape Performing Arts Council (CAPAB)   188
Johannesburg and Pretoria
    Performing Arts Council of Transvaal (PACT)   189

SPAIN
Barcelona
    Consorci del Gran Teatre del Liceu   191
Madrid
    Asociación Amigos de la Opera de Madrid   192

SWEDEN
Stockholm
    Drottningholms Slottsteater   194
    Kungliga Teatern (Royal Opera)   196

SWITZERLAND
Bern
    Stadttheater Bern   200
Geneva
    Grand Théâtre de Genève   201
Luzern
    Stadttheater Luzern   203
Zürich
    Opernhaus Zürich   204

TURKEY

Ankara

Ankara Devlet Opera ve Balesi (The Ankara State Opera and Ballet) — 206

Istanbul

Istanbul Devlet Opera ve Balesi (The Istanbul State Opera and Ballet) — 208

Izmir

Izmir Devlet Opera ve Balesi (The Izmir State Opera and Ballet) — 209

UNION OF SOVIET SOCIALIST REPUBLICS

Kiev

Taras Shevchenko Academic Opera and Ballet Theater — 210

Moscow

Bolshoi Opera Theater of the USSR — 212

UNITED KINGDOM

Belfast, Northern Ireland

Opera Northern Ireland — 216

Cardiff, Wales

Welsh National Opera — 217

Glasgow, Scotland

Scottish Opera — 220

Glyndebourne, England

Glyndebourne Festival Opera — 221

London, England

English National Opera — 223

Royal Opera House Covent Garden — 225

UNITED STATES OF AMERICA

Baltimore, Maryland

Baltimore Opera Company — 233

Boston, Massachusetts

Boston Lyric Opera Company — 234

Central City, Colorado

Central City Opera — 237

Chautauqua, New York

Chautauqua Opera Association — 238

Chicago, Illinois
    Lyric Opera of Chicago   240
Cincinnati, Ohio
    The Cincinnati Opera   242
Dallas, Texas
    The Dallas Opera   244
Denver, Colorado
    Opera Colorado   248
Detroit, Michigan
    Michigan Opera Theatre   249
Fort Worth, Texas
    Fort Worth Opera Association   250
Honolulu, Hawaii
    Hawaii Opera Theater   251
Houston, Texas
    Houston Grand Opera   254
Louisville, Kentucky
    Kentucky Opera   256
Miami, Florida
    Greater Miami Opera   258
Minneapolis and St. Paul, Minnesota
    The Minnesota Opera   258
New Orleans, Louisiana
    New Orleans Opera Association   260
New York City, New York
    Metropolitan Opera Association   264
    New York City Opera   270
Omaha, Nebraska
    Opera/Omaha   272
Philadelphia, Pennsylvania
    Opera Company of Philadelphia   273
Pittsburgh, Pennsylvania
    Pittsburgh Opera   277
Portland, Oregon
    Portland Opera   280

Richmond, Virginia
    The Virginia Opera   282
Saint Louis, Missouri
    Opera Theatre of Saint Louis   283
San Diego, California
    San Diego Opera   285
San Francisco, California
    San Francisco Opera   286
Santa Fe, New Mexico
    The Santa Fe Opera   289
Seattle, Washington
    Seattle Opera   291
Vienna, Virginia
    Wolf Trap Opera Company   293
Washington, D.C.
    The Washington Opera   294

YUGOSLAVIA

Belgrade
    Opera Narodnog Pozorista u Beogradu (Belgrade National Opera)   301
Zagreb
    Opera of the Hrvatsko Narodno Kazalište (Croatian National Opera)   302

Appendix: Additional Opera Companies

Belgium
    Vlaamse Kameropera, Antwerp   305
    Opera voor Vlaandern, Ghent   305
    Opera Royal de Wallonie, Liège   305
Egypt
    Egyptian Opera House, Cairo   306
France
    Aix-en-Provence International Festival   306
    Opéra de Bordeaux   307
    Opéra de Lille   307
    Théâtre du Capitole, Toulouse   307

Index	327
About the Editor and Contributors	333

Acknowledgments

What began as a rather low-key search for information that I assumed was simply waiting to be gathered, ended up as a major involvement in letter writing, telephoning, and faxing urgent messages to all parts of the globe. Given a project of this scope, the participation of numerous individuals, both friends and strangers, was critical to its completion. I discovered patient secretaries and staff personnel all over the world, and I shall never forget the expressions of enthusiasm and endorsement that came repeatedly from so many people in the opera business. It was clear from the beginning that the need for this compilation was real; very few professionals had more than a hint of what other companies were doing and, indeed, very few had much of a grasp of the complicated history of their own organizations. Opera is a "now" operation. Once the curtain closes on the last performance, once the books are closed for the past season, all thoughts turn to the future. All the more thanks, then, to those many individuals who made this all possible:

Marilyn Brownstein, who was so supportive of my recent series of bibliographic compilations about performers, was the initiator of this book as a companion to Robert Craven's volumes on symphony orchestras, which she also masterminded. I know she understands the trials and frustrations of the journey—may she also share in the joys and satisfaction now that the destination has been reached.

My chairman at San José State University, Dr. Ted Lucas, as well as the Dean of the College of Humanities and the Arts, Dr. Jack Crane, who granted my sabbatical leave request and provided classroom release time, computer equipment, and telephone, fax, and mailing services—in short, all those scholarly necessities that make projects such as this one possible.

My faculty colleagues and professional friends who offered advice and consolation during those long months when the task seemed so frustratingly impossible.

Those opera company administrators who eased the path by identifying an official contact.

The individuals who so graciously assembled company profiles who are identified at the end of their individual contributions.

The talented linguists who provided translations, including Marc Änders, who is a law student at the University of Santa Clara; Eva Beaudet, who has been an opera singer in Germany, Italy, and North America; Charlene Chadwick, who was a principal artist with the Deutsche Oper am Rhein in Düsseldorf/Duisburg, Germany; Peter Kalev, who is an exchange student from Bulgaria; Professor Alex Liniecki at San José State University; Jonathan Muir, who is completing a doctorate at Yale University; Delfina Sabogal-Tori; Renée Schmuki, who translated for the Allies after World War II and is now retired; Astrid Sundelöf, who is a retired actress and theater director; and Loreta Kirnaite and Katarzyna Petryuniak.

And finally, those individuals who supplied information about their respective companies, information without which I could not have compiled the profiles: Dr. Victor Bouilly, Assistant to the General Director of the Teatro Colón in Buenos Aires, Argentina; Atul Joshi, Director of Marketing, The State Opera of South Australia, Adelaide, Australia; Dion Faulkner, Publicity Assistant of the Victoria State Opera, Fitzroy/Victoria, Australia; Press Office of the Salzburg Festival, Austria; Ingeborg Mosnička, Assistant to the Program Director, Staatsoper, Vienna, Austria; The Belgian Institute for Information and Documentation; Maureen Eley-Round, Communications Coordinator, Edmonton Opera, Canada; Francine Labelle, Public Relations Coordinator, L'Opéra de Montréal, Canada; Karen Lynch, Director of Public Relations, Canadian Opera Company, Toronto, Canada; Matias Perez, General Coordinator, Teatro Municipal, Santiago, Chile; Kuo-Chung Su, Assistant to the Dean, The Central Opera College, Beijing, China; Eva Dolečková, Foreign Department, National Theater, Prague, Czechoslovakia; Marketta Kussipalo and Leena Salakari of the Finnish Music Information Centre in Helsinki, Finland; Jean-Pierre Brossmann, General Director of the Opéra de Lyon, France; Agnes Pierron, Music Historian in Paris, France, for information on the Opéra de Nancy et de Lorraine; Albrecht Faasch, Dramaturg of the Staatstheater Darmstadt, Germany; Günther W. Weißenborn, Dramaturg of the Deutsche Oper am Rhein, Düsseldorf, Germany; Hans-Gerhard Marschalt of the Theater and Philharmonie Essen, Germany; Petra Hofmann-Paczkowski, Press Officer for the Badisches Staatstheater in Karlsruhe, Germany; Ina Iffert, Secretary to the General Musik Direktor (GMD), Staatstheater Kassel, Germany; Dr. Wolfgang Mika, Musikdramaturg of the Theater Krefeld/Mönchengladbach, Germany; Barbara Wagner-Galdea, Assistant to the Press Officer, Bayrische Staatsoper, Munich, Germany; Anja Weigmann, Musikdramaturgin of the Städische Bühnen, Nürnberg, Germany; Heike Weckend, Operndramaturg, Wuppertaler Bühnen, Germany; Hanna Munitz, Assistant Managing Director, The New Israeli Opera, Tel Aviv, Israel; Egidio Saracino, Capo Ufficio Stampa e P.R., the Teatro Comunale Maggio Musicale Fiorentino in Florence,

Acknowledgments

Italy; Yuko Egamo of The Japan Opera Foundation, Tokyo, Japan; Gillian Manolis, General Manager of the Wellington City Opera, New Zealand; Ana Torrents of the Gran Teatre del Leceu, Barcelona, Spain; José Luis Martín de Bustamente, President of the Asociacion de Amigos de la Opera de Madrid, Spain; Ursina Barandun, Public Relations, Stadttheater, Bern, Switzerland; Philippe Girard, attaché de presse, Grand Théâtre de Genève, Switzerland; Markus Wörl, Dramaturg, Stadttheater Luzern, Switzerland; Erol Gömürgen, General Director of the Ankara State Opera and Ballet, Turkey; Sergey Selivanov, Head of the International Department, Bolshoi Theater, Moscow, USSR; Randall Shannon, General Manager of Opera Northern Ireland, Belfast; Maggie Sedwards, Director of Publicity of the Scottish Opera, Glasgow, Scotland; Helen O'Neill, Head of Press and Public Relations of the Glyndebourne Festival Opera, Great Britain; Henrietta Bredin of the English National Opera, London, England; John Moriarty, Artistic Director of Central City Opera, Colorado; Carleen Roeper, Public Relations and Marketing Department of the Lyric Opera of Chicago, Illinois; Charlotte L. Shockley, Archivist of the Cincinnati Opera, Ohio; Gerald E. Farrar, Director of Public Relations of the Kentucky Opera in Louisville, Kentucky; Maria Scheverri of the Greater Miami Opera, Florida; David M. Reuben, Director of Press and Public Relations of the Metropolian Opera Association, New York; Barbara Zarlengo, Director of Development of the New York City Opera, New York; Michael Ching, Assistant to the Director, The Virginia Opera, Norfolk, Virginia; Dan Naumann, Public Relations, Opera/ Omaha, Nebraska; Brenda Hughes, Director of Marketing and Public Relations of the San Diego Opera, California; Koraljka Lockhart, Publications Editor of the San Francisco Opera, California; Mary Lou Falcone, Public Relations, The Sante Fe Opera, New Mexico; Jim Bailey, Director of Marketing of the Seattle Opera Association, Washington; Peter Russell, Administrative Director of the Wolf Trap Foundation for the Performing Arts, Vienna, Virginia; and Suzanne Stephens, Public Relations Director, The Washington Opera, Washington, D.C.

Introduction

Given the social, aesthetic, and financial politics of the operatic world, I simply could not resist the opportunity to edit a volume that would assemble profiles of the world's major opera companies. As a former opera singer and stage director myself, I was curious about the response I might receive as well as the tone and validity of the information. Opera, is, after all, a wonderful, magical world in which appearances sometimes mask a more intriguing story behind the scenes. My intent was to avoid compiling a series of statistical overviews. This meant that the challenge was to provide interesting and insightful historical précis without revealing house secrets or indulging some positive or negative prejudice vis-à-vis administrations or policies; this proved to be a fine line indeed, and I leave it to the discerning reader to decide whether my contributors have succeeded in their delicate task. From my perspective, suffice it to say that this has been a marvelous journey, coming as it did during a seminal period in Western history when the cold war was ending, when Eastern Europe was tasting the first morsels of freedom, when the Soviet Union itself was looking inward to its own multicultural ethnic fabric, and when more opera companies than ever before were experimenting with the ancient *Dramma per musica* which was invented almost four hundred years ago by the Italian Camerata and realized by the first genius of the new genre, Claudio Monteverdi. Caught up in the changing drama of our times, this project was also influenced weekly by the major alterations in opera company administrations and addresses, which seemed to shift with alarming frequency. The question often had to be asked, "Who is in charge of what, and how can they be contacted?" Had I known several years ago just what sort of a journey I was undertaking, I might well have graciously turned down Marilyn Brownstein's offer. However, then I would not have established such productive correspondence with opera aficionados all over the world.

Nothing remotely like this volume has ever existed in the world of opera, and, although most of the people whom I initially contacted were most enthusiastic and supportive, the problem was to obtain from each company a firm commitment to support the idea. I would like to say that we achieved 100 percent, but, given the state of the business, that is never likely to happen. What did happen was that 139 companies provided profiles, press releases, or some materials from which a valid entry could be made. There was statistical information available for another 28 organizations. When one considers that an additional 20 of the companies that I initially contacted are either out of business or do not primarily produce opera, my response and inclusion rate was, frankly, marvelous. It is my hope that some future edition will not only update, revise, and improve the present profiles; but will also include those few opera companies that did not provide materials for whatever reason. My professional thinking is that such a regular update would be of immense service both to the public and to the profession, and, with this in mind, I would encourage all readers to forward any and all corrections and additions to me in care of the publisher.

SCOPE AND PURPOSE

The purpose of this book was to assemble profiles of all 184 of the world's major opera companies so that the general reader would have a convenient and authoritative source for their current status (including address, phone, and fax information), historical background, typical repertoire, responsible artistic and administrative personnel, and perceived cultural impact. Given the number of organizations involved, it should come as no surprise that the profiles vary considerably as to length, specific content, critical and valuative observation, and general style. Profiles were authored by contributors from very diverse backgrounds: professional archivists, historians, press and media information officers, and even administrative and artistic heads of companies. Thus, the resulting entries are varied in length, content, and focus. That was my intention from the beginning. Each opera company has its own personality, and, hopefully, the profiles reflect that individuality. Occasionally I have added information to the entries; this material is contained in brackets and is entirely my responsibility.

Companies were selected because of their historical importance, geographical diversity, and artistic contributions to the art form. Many, such as the Metropolitan Opera, La Scala, Covent Garden, and the Berlin Staatsoper, are household words far beyond the boundaries of their own countries. Others, such as the Bayreuth, Glyndebourne, and Salzburg festivals, have been in the forefront of operatic excellence and experimentation for decades. Berlin's Komische Oper as well as the Deutsche Oper Berlin inherited the experimental energies of Hans Gregor's Komische Oper and the Krolloper, both originally in Berlin and neither one is in existence today. It was apparent early on that the list of opera companies would be considerably shorter than Robert Craven's compilations assembled for orchestras in the United States and his companion volume of orchestras of the world. Opera is a very expensive proposition. Indeed, an excellent orchestra is only the beginning, and many of the orchestras that support companies listed here engage in concert seasons of their own. Beginning with the theater or performance hall, an orchestra primarily needs a platform. In contrast, an opera company needs a pit; a fully equipped stage; set and costume shops, and storage for the fruits of these labors; and, finally, an ensemble of highly trained singers. As individual singers become more famous, they command higher fees and perform with a number of companies; this is quite different from an orchestra, where the principal instrumentalists remain at their desks over many seasons earning substantial but not exorbitant wages.

Some of the profiles were not authored by a contributor. In that case, the text is identified as being written "[From materials supplied by . . .]," which indicates that I have assembled the information from programs, press releases, and other materials that were sent to me. Few permanent opera companies outside Germany have a full-time staff member who is trained and authorized to author profiles of the sort found in this book. Press and public representatives were most helpful, but their obligations lay in providing an appropriate image of the company to journalists and the press. Most of them had neither the time nor the inclination to author material of a historical and policy nature. More power to those many individuals, then, who went out of their way to dig up information that would be useful. They are credited under the acknowledgments. Regardless of who authored the profile, however, the reader is advised that any judgments or observations emanate from the source and are not those of the editor-in-chief; nor, in some cases, of the company itself.

ORGANIZATION

When it was possible to obtain complete information regarding a specific opera company, that information is listed in the following order: (1) city with current population; (2) précis about the company; (3) chronological listing of directors/ managers/administrators; (4) bibliography; and (5) name of the company, with administrator(s), address, and telephone and fax numbers.

SOURCES

The greater percentage of the profiles have a short bibliography at the end. A sincere effort was made to include only the most recent titles, works that should be available at least in the country in question. Please note that many of these books are not mentioned in any other compilation, dictionary, or encyclopedia, and thus represent a valuable resource. Important operatic endeavors are consistently covered by such periodicals as *Opera News* (New York, 1936–present), *Opera* (London, 1950–present), and *Opernwelt* (Velber bei Hannover, Germany, 1960–present). Another fine source of historical information is *The Record Collector* (Chelmsford, England, 1948–present). Readers who desire specific current information about any of the companies or artists included here should refer to one or more of these outstanding periodicals. In addition, there exist a number of opera histories, both general and specific, as well as specialized dictionaries and encyclopedias covering opera. Most of these titles will be found in the excellent compilations of Vincent H. Duckles and Michael A. Keller (*Music Reference and Research Materials: An Annotated Bibliography*, 4th ed., New York, 1988) and Guy A. Marco (*Opera: A Research and Information Guide*, New York, 1984).

During the initial discussions with Marilyn Brownstein, it was assumed that a current discography for each company would represent an important resource. For a number of reasons, that has turned out to be impractical. The main problem has been the frustrations of many contributors in assembling representative, not to mention comprehensive, discographies for a particular company. The simple fact is that permanent opera companies do not release many complete opera recordings. A variety of individuals and organizations normally put together a package of soloists, conductor, and chorus, and then market the final product as representing a particular opera company. Unless the company itself is in charge of all the artistic matters, the recording is not really representative of its work. Notable exceptions exist, such as the recordings of the Bayreuth Festival, and live broadcasts, as well as studio productions, from the Metropolitan Opera, but most of these are no longer available. In the case of the Metropolitan Opera, Frederick P. Fellers did document the commercial recordings in *The Metropolitan Opera on Record* (Westport, CT, 1984). Another major problem stems from the fact that all LPs have been deleted from most catalogues and record stores, making a listing of such materials more a historical curiosity than a relevant guide to current materials. Of particular concern in this regard is the high probability that only a fraction of the operas recorded over the past half century will ever be rereleased on compact discs or whatever technology may be available at some future date. Unfortunately, financial considerations are paramount in the recording industry, as elsewhere in the world of business. If the market is large enough, the recording may reappear, but this is of little consolation to the small opera company or to the ensemble that recorded a work with major historical ramifications but little popular appeal. For those readers who relish the challenge of research, back issues of *The Gramophone* (London, 1923–present), *High Fidelity* (New York, 1951–present), and *HiFi/Stereo Review* (New York, 1958–present) all offer reviews of operatic releases. For these reasons, a selective, annotated research bibliography is included at the end of this book. Needless to say, a number of comprehensive discographies and indices to record reviews are included.

As a final note, the reader is urged to keep in mind that the rapidly changing political situation brought about by the restructuting of the Soviet Union suggests that some of the companies may have or will have acquired a new national status by the time this volume appears in print. The final editing was done during the early fall of 1991, and every effort was made to assure that the information was current at that time. With revised and expanded editions a future possibility, readers are encouraged to forward any corrections or additions to me in care of the publisher.

Opera Companies of the World

Argentina

BUENOS AIRES (metro 12,604,018)

Teatro Colón

Colonized by the Spanish, who were seeking a buffer state against the Portuguese in Brazil, the city of Buenos Aires was established in 1580. Independence resulted from Napoleon's invasion of Spain in 1808, which allowed the city to set up an autonomous government in 1810, followed by the provinces in 1816. Modern Argentina dates from 1862, when Bartolomé Mitre was elected the country's first constitutional president. Since that time all the arts have waxed and waned depending on the incumbent civilian or military national leadership. The first complete opera performed in Buenos Aires was Rossini's *Il Barbiere di Siviglia* in 1825, featuring the Spanish tenor Mariano Pablo Rosquellas and conducted by Santiago Massoni. Between 1830 and 1848 there is no record of a complete opera performance in Buenos Aires, but by the 1850s, French and Italian touring companies had returned. The original 2,500-seat Teatro Colón, which was built in 1856, opened the following year with *La Traviata*, featuring Sofia Lorini and Enrico Tamberlick. This first Teatro Colón mounted a final season in 1888 featuring Adelina Patti and Francesco Tamagno. Just one year after Tamagno had created the role of Otello at La Scala, he repeated his triumph in Buenos Aires, and shortly thereafter, the theater was demolished. The Teatro de la Opera, which opened in 1872 with Verdi's *Il Trovatore*, and the Teatro Politeama, which featured Meyerbeer's *Les Huguenots* at its opening night were among the many other local theaters that catered to the public with opera performed by French, German, and Italian touring companies. Arturo Beruti's first opera on a national subject, *Pampa*, was premiered on July 27, 1897. It was based on the well-known gaucho drama *Juan Moreira* by Juan José Podestá. The composer's *Yupanky*, which premiered July 25, 1899, was based on an Inca legend and featured Enrico Caruso in the title role. His last opera, *Los Héros*,

Germany
- Bühnen der Stadt Bielefeld — 308
- Oper der Stadt Bonn — 308
- Staatstheater/Groβes Haus Braunschweig — 308
- Theater am Goetheplatz, Bremen — 308
- Bühnen der Landeshauptstadt, Kiel — 309
- Vereinigte Städtische Bühnen, Krefeld/Mönchengladbach — 309
- Staatstheater am Gärtnerplatz, München — 309
- Opernhaus, Wuppertal — 310

Iceland
- Iceland Opera, Reykjavík — 310

Italy
- Teatro Massimo Bellini, Catania — 310
- Festival dei Due Mondi, Spoleto — 310

Mexico
- Opera Nacional, México, D.F. — 311

Netherlands
- De Nederlandse Opera, Amsterdam — 311

Spain
- Teatro de la Maestranza, Seville — 311

Sweden
- Stora Theatern Kungsparken, Göteborg — 312

Switzerland
- Stadttheater Basel — 312

Union of Soviet Socialist Republics
- Kirov Opera House, Leningrad — 313

United States of America
- Connecticut Opera, Hartford — 313
- Tulsa Opera — 313

Venezuela
- Opera de Caracas — 314

Chronology of Foundings for Opera Companies Profiled — 315

Selected Annotated Bibliography — 321

opened on August 23, 1919, at the new Teatro Colón, and it continued his preoccupation with indigenous Argentinean subjects.

Although the foundation stone for the new opera house was laid in 1889, some nineteen years were to pass before the new Teatro Colón opened its doors. Fortunately, the Teatro de la Opera was still available to serve as a cultural center for the city. The new Teatro Colón opened in 1908 as an opera house built in French Renaissance style, and since that time has remained the focus of operatic activity in Argentina. In that capacity it is one of the most important musical centers in Latin America. Other areas of the country, then as now, are served by touring companies, except for La Plata, the capital of the province of Buenos Aires, which enjoys regular seasons at the Teatro Argentino. The architecture of the new theater was based on opera houses in Frankfurt am Main (1880), Munich (1825), Paris (1875), and Vienna (1869), and it remains one of the memorable and sumptuous heritages of the nineteenth century European tradition. Verdi's *Aida* opened the new house on May 25, 1908, with a good but not distinguished cast conducted by Luigi Mancinelli. Panizza's *Aurora* was commissioned by the Argentine government for the inaugural season, and its premiere took place on September 5 in the original Spanish version. This work attempted to fuse folkore with the prevailing Italian verismo style. The initial season counted seventy-seven performances of seventeen operas, including the incomparable Chaliapin as the protagonist in Boito's *Mefistofele*. The government granted a concession to operate the house for the first sixteen years, highlights of which saw Toscanini conducting fifteen productions in 1912, Tullio Serafin conducting in 1914, and Saint-Saëns conducting his own *Samson et Dalila* in 1916. Although European operas dominated the repertoire, fourteen works by Argentinean composers were mounted by the company. De Rogatis's *Huemac*, which premiered on July 22, 1916, abounds in Argentinean musical characteristics and, like *Yupanky*, is based on an Inca subject.

Following World War I, Weingartner arrived to conduct *Parsifal* and *The Ring* (with Lotte Lehmann) in 1922, and the following two seasons featured *Boris Godunov*, *Prince Igor*, and *The Queen of Spades*, all in Russian. The Colón had finally achieved international status. Beginning in 1925, all the resident organizations (ballet, chorus, opera, and two orchestras) achieved permanent status, with all responsibility transferred to an administrative commission of the city of Buenos Aires. Interest in native works continued with Boero's *El Matrero*, a dramatic legend based on gaucho folk traditions which was premiered on July 12, 1929. Filled with local dances and tunes, it ranks as one of the landmark early Argentinean operas. Along with this interest in developing native opera was an internal Argentinean movement with strong links to European traditions exemplified by such operas as *El Sueno del Alma* (1914) and *La Magdalena* (1939).

The 2,485-seat theater (with an additional 1,000 standing-room places) has been officially subsidized by the city since 1931, and all artistic personnel are appointed by and responsible to the municipal government. In 1935 the city took over the administration of the house, which resulted in a far more international repertoire. It also led to over half a century of economic and political influences affecting the theater. Between the two world wars, the Teatro Colón was one of the world's leading opera houses, featuring such works as a complete *Ring* cycle under Weingartner. During the time at which the Argentinean economy was growing, each season offered ten to twelve different productions with an average of six performances of each. One of the postwar highlights was Sir Thomas Beecham, appearing in his last opera season, conducting *Carmen, Fidelio, Otello, Samson et Dalila,* and *Die Zauberflöte* in 1958, the fiftieth anniversary of El Teatro Colón.

The organization has continued to strongly support indigenous opera, and after World War II it increased the production total to some forty-seven operas by twenty-eight native composers through 1973. All operas are currently performed in the original language. Beginning in 1990 the theater changed from a stagione system to a repertory system in recognition of both the cost and the availability of international artists. Since 1986 productions have been videotaped, but these are not currently available to the public. In contrast to many companies, the Colón rents out its halls to private institutions, thus encouraging guest appearances of the world's premiere musical organizations such as the New York Philharmonic and the Vienna Philharmonic.

BIBLIOGRAPHY: Roberto Caamaño, ed., *La Historia del Teatro Colón, 1908–1968,* 3 vols. (Buenos Aires, 1969). Alfredo Fiorda Kelly, *Cronología de las óperas, dramas liricos, oratorios . . . en Buenos Aires* (Buenos Aires, 1934). Ladislao Kurucz, *Vademecum Musical Argentino* (Buenos Aires, 1983). Malena Kuss, *Nativistic Strains in Argentine Operas Premiered at the Teatro Colón,* Ph.D. diss. (UCLA, 1976). Teatro Colón archives.

ACCESS: Cerrito no. 618, Buenos Aires 1309. (55 541) 35 5414; fax (55 541) 11 12 32. Lic. Sergio Renan, General Director.

[From materials supplied by the company]
TRANS. DELFINA SABOGAL-TORI

Australia

ADELAIDE (1,013,000)

The State Opera of South Australia

The State Opera of South Australia is unique in Australia as the nation's only statutory authority opera company. It was founded in 1976 by an act of State Parliament to "present, produce, manage and conduct theatrical and operatic performances of any kind as may in its opinion tend to promote the art of the opera and related theatrical arts." The State Opera has enjoyed strong support from the premiere, who, until 1989, retained the Arts Ministry portfolio for himself. In early 1988 the State Opera suffered a large deficit ($560,000) which resulted in a complete change of management, operations, and financing. In July 1988 William Gillespie was hired as general manager, and he has succeeded in restructuring the company over the last three years. The company has now paid off the 1988 deficit in full while still producing forty performances of seven operas, as well as concerts and school tours. It returned to a full season of four operas in 1991. The company's new management has attracted significant increases in subscribership (currently the company is within 4 percent of doubling the number of subscribers it had in 1988), corporate support, and national publicity, and still maintains the lowest priced opera tickets in the country. In 1989, Western Mining Corporation, which is headquartered in Melbourne, made its first-ever arts sponsorship commitment to this organization. Hugh Morgan, Western Mining's managing director, stated at the time that the sponsorship was "in part due to the new entrepreneurial management style of the State Opera. It is an attribute with which we identify strongly."

As part of the company's restructuring, the State Opera has relinquished control of the 967-seat Opera Theatre in Adelaide (presently Her Majesty's Theatre) and now uses the larger 1,827-seat Festival Theatre for productions. This reflects in part the company's strategy of sharing productions with international and interstate opera companies, the need to manage costs, the desire to reach a broader audience with large-scale productions of grand opera, and the desire to use the full resources of the Adelaide Symphony Orchestra and the Adelaide Dance Theatre when these are needed. The restructuring has not simply meant better management of the company. With 77 percent of the budget now being spent on production costs, a significant and consistently high level of artistic values has been maintained. Recent and future artistic highlights include a free production of *Tosca* as part of the 1990 Adelaide Festival of the Arts, attended by 20,000 people; the local premiere of *Aida*, starring Rita Hunter, in May 1990; a sold-out *Marriage of Figaro* in Her Majesty's Theatre in July 1990; *Samson et Dalila* in October 1990, featuring the San Francisco Opera/Lyric Opera of Chicago production; and, scheduled for August 1991, the Australian stage premiere of Richard Strauss's *Elektra* starring Marilyn Zschau and Yvonne Minton and directed by Bruce Beresford. The 1991 season also includes productions of *Rigoletto*, *Don Giovanni*, and *Madama Butterfly*.

The company currently employs over 500 artists and theater staff, and supports an active education and outreach program as well as regular season productions. In its Statement of Policy, the State Opera of South Australia describes its commitment to offer "a broad cross-section of the main operatic repertoire [and] a proportion of newer or otherwise less-familiar works; maximize employment opportunities for Australian musicians and other artists; offer opportunities to young singers and other artists of high promise to develop their talents; promote co-ordinated programming and casting with other Australian companies; [and] seek to encourage the acceptance of opera as a popular and accessible part of Australia's recreational and cultural life; [it regards] an educational programme as a vital and integral part of its policy." The audited final budget for 1988–1989 was $2.18 million. This generated a surplus of $390,000, enabling the company to pay back to the treasury its full accumulated debt. The current subscriber list numbers 2,975, which means that 40 percent of annual capacity is prebooked. The current budget is met from the following sectors: 57 percent, South Australia Government grant; 33 percent box office; and 10 percent private sector support.

ACCESS: 20 Rowlands Place, Adelaide 5000. (61 8)233 4866; fax (61 8) 231 7646. William Gillespie, General Manager. David Kram, Music Director.

[From materials supplied by the company]

MELBOURNE (2,964,800)

Victoria State Opera

The Victoria State Opera was inaugurated as a professional company on March 3, 1977, with Offenbach's *La Belle Hélène* in the Princess Theatre. It was preceded by the Mont Albert Choral Society in the 1940s, the Hawthorn Operatic Society, and the Victorian Light Opera Company (VLOC), which specialized in Gilbert and Sullivan operettas. As an interest in opera grew, the Savoy Opera Company continued the traditions of the VLOC, and a new company, the Victorian Opera Company (VOC), was formed to produce operas. By 1970 the VOC was ready to expand, and, in partnership with the Victorian Ballet Guild, it sought financial assistance from the Australian Council for the Arts. Strongly supporting the concept of state companies, the council backed an advisory committee administered by Peter Burch, which included the soprano Joan Hammond. This committee effectively became the VOC's board. Richard Divall was hired as music director in 1972, and for the next five years until the formation of the Victoria State Opera in 1977, he provided an exciting alternative to the traditional Australian Opera seasons with productions that included Donizetti's *Maria Stuarda*, Monteverdi's *L'Incoronazione di Poppea*, Poulenc's *Les Mamelles de Tirésias*, and Walton's *Façade*. The basis for the company's future growth was laid during these formative years: an enterprising repertoire which included new Australian operas, the establishment of a sound financial base, and the development of an outreach and educational program to build audiences.

Ken Mackenzie-Forbes was engaged as general manager in 1976, the same year the state government approved the company's official title. The National Theatre in St. Kilda was the principal house at this time, and it was not an ideal home for opera. Robin Lovejoy joined the company in 1977 as artistic advisor and brought a much-needed dramatic direction to his stagings of *Pelléas et Mélisande*, *Duke Bluebeard's Castle*, and Monteverdi's *L'Orfeo* during the VSO's first professional season in the Princess Theatre. Tailoring its productions around young up-and-coming talent, VSO gave early career opportunities to Jenny Drivala, Keith Lewis, Corneliu Murgu, and Louis Otey, among others. Prior to the move to the new Arts Centre in July 1984, the company mounted productions of Handel's *Alcina* (1978), *The Pearl Fishers* (1979), *Count Ory*, and *The Return of Ulysses* (1980), *Don Pasquale* (1981), *Iolanthe* (1982), and the world premiere of Brian Howard's *Metamorphosis*, which had been commissioned by the VSO (1983). Verdi's *Don Carlos* in July 1984 inaugurated the company's move to the State Theatre, which capped a remarkable and unexpected growth for the Victoria State Opera. Initial plans had anticipated the Australian Opera as the Victorian Arts Centre's principal tenant, but the rise of the VSO earned it the home ground. The first season in the State Theatre also included the world premiere of Barry Conyngham's *Fly*, a new production of Handel's *Julius Caesar*, and three concert performances of Berlioz's *The Trojans*.

Following its triumphal opening season in the Arts Centre, the VSO mounted August Everding's productions of *Lohengrin* in 1985 and *Madama Butterfly* for the inaugural Melbourne Spoleto Festival in 1986. Celebrating ten years of existence, Offenbach's *La Belle Hélène* returned to open the 1987 season. In its most recent planning document, *Towards the Second Decade*, the Victoria State Opera declared its intention to establish Melbourne as a major center of operatic activity by (1) doubling the season to eight operas, (2) mounting a Mozart Cycle to celebrate the composer's bicentenary, (3) encouraging new Australian works,

(4) engaging the world's leading artists, and (5) building a new administrative and rehearsal home for VSO [opening April 1991]. This amounts to a major reassessment of the company's original goals, and is in keeping with the growth of the organization artistically, educationally, and financially. With 1989 operating revenues in excess of $6.4 million, the company has become a major artistic institution in Melbourne. The 1991 subscription includes productions of *Aida*, *Iolanthe*, *The Italian Girl in Algiers*, *The Magic Flute*, and *The Marriage of Figaro*.

BIBLIOGRAPHY: Robert Gibbs, ed., *Victoria State Opera: Tenth Anniversary Season 1987* (Fitzroy, Victoria, 1987).

ACCESS: 77 Southbank Boulevard, South Melbourne 3205. (61 3) 686 1777; fax (61 3) 419 5071. Ken Mackenzie-Forbes, General Manager. Richard Divall, Music Director.

[From materials supplied by the company]

SYDNEY (3,531,000)

The Australian Opera

The Australian Opera, with a permanent artistic, technical, and administrative payroll of 215, is the national opera of the country. An ensemble company which performs in the larger metropolitan centers of Australia, its activities are supplemented by four smaller stagione-style companies that serve the separate states; the Victoria State Opera [see profile below], The State Opera of South Australia [see profile above], the Western Australian Opera Company, and the Lyric Opera of Queensland. In 1990 the Australian Opera (AO) appeared in Sydney, Melbourne (population 2,964,800), Adelaide (population 1,013,000; the 1,827-seat Festival Theatre opened in 1973), and Perth (population 1,083,400). The immensity of the task of touring opera in a country the size of Australia is best shown by the following analogy. When the AO traveled from its Sydney home to perform in Perth, the capital city of Western Australia, it covered a distance equivalent to a London company traveling to perform in Moscow.

In a typical year the Australian Opera performs for eleven months, during which it presents five or six new productions and between ten and twelve operas from repertoire, for a total of approximately 235 performances. It uses directors, designers, and conductors from every operatic center of the world as well as from Australia, while its performers are largely Australian. Normally only eight to ten non-Australian singers will be used out of a roster of almost one hundred principals and comprimarios, reflecting the ensemble basis of the company operations. Operas are almost always sung in the original language, and the Australian Opera was the second company in the world to introduce Surtitles to the opera stage.

The first recorded performance of opera in Australia was Henry Bishop's *Clari: The Maid of Milan* [premiered on May 8, 1823, in London] in 1834. The Anna Bishop Opera Company performed in New South Wales and Victoria between 1850 and 1860 followed by the [William Saurin] Lyster Grand Opera Company, which toured Australia until the early 1880s with numerous yearly performances. Montague Turner and George Musgrove were also active opera impresarios. The manager J. C. Williamson encouraged Nellie Melba to return in 1911 with a company that included Rosina Buckman, Eleanora de Cisneros, and John McCormack. The famous diva returned for a farewell tour in 1924 with Dino Borgioli and Toti dal Monte. Between the world wars, the Imperial Grand Opera Company mounted a number of excellent productions. In 1952 opera companies in Melbourne and Sydney attempted to form a national opera. With the establishment of the Elizabethan Trust in 1954, a national company seemed a possibility at last. Charged with the responsibility of developing the arts in Australia, the trust was in a position of great influence. About the same time, the New South Wales state government supported a competition for the design of an opera house to be built in Sydney. Joern Utzon won, and his design has been a continuing source of both controversy and acclaim. The Elizabethan Trust sponsored its first opera season in July 1956; the Australian Opera was born, and it presented four Mozart operas in a tour of all six capital cities which lasted eight months. The fledgling company traveled 8,370 miles in its first year, giving 169 performances. A key event in the growth of the AO came in 1965 when the great Australian soprano, Joan Sutherland, and her conductor husband, Richard Bonynge, returned to Australia to begin their long association with the company. The AO joined forces with J. C. Williamson Theatres to form the Sutherland/Williamson Grand Opera Company. These 1965 performances kindled the public's imagination and brought new and excited audiences into the theater, laying the groundwork for the continued development of the company.

In 1970 the Australian Opera was incorporated as a separate entity, outside the Elizabethan Theatre Trust. In 1973 the world-famous 1,500-seat Sydney Opera House opened with Prokofiev's *War and Peace*, and the company was provided with a permanent home. As an ensemble company, the AO employs a year-round body of performers, both chorus and principal artists. As well as fostering local talent in production, design, and performance, the AO has also featured guest artists from overseas, particularly Australian artists who have built important careers in Europe and America. Many artists who had earlier left the country to build careers elsewhere because of the lack of opportunity in their homeland have been able to return to work either as permanent company members or as guest artists, with both the AO and the smaller state companies.

In its early years the Australian Opera regularly toured outlying areas of its home state, New South Wales, as well as frequently visiting the country's capital cities. Touring is now, for the most part, confined to the major cities of Sydney and Melbourne, primarily due to the enormous cost. Fortunately, the company continues to reach a large audience through productions which are broadcast nationally over Australian Broadcasting Corporation Television. *Adriana Lecouvreur, Die Fledermaus, Lucia di Lammermoor, Dialogues of the Carmelites, The Daughter of the Regiment, Il Trovatore, The Magic Flute, The Mikado, La*

Traviata, Cenerentola, Voss, La Bohème, The Merry Widow, Die Meistersinger von Nürnberg, The Gondoliers, Otello, Un Ballo in Maschera, and, most recently, *The Gypsy Princess, Les Huguenots,* and *Così Fan Tutte* have all reached nationwide audiences through the medium of television. These operas have been screened along with gala concerts featuring Joan Sutherland and Luciano Pavarotti with Richard Bonynge conducting, and a special concert featuring Marilyn Horne with Joan Sutherland, also conducted by Bonynge. Almost half the homes in Australia viewed these events. The success of the broadcasts were demonstrated when the AO's production of *La Bohème* won the 1989 International Emmy Award for arts programs. As a marketing device, all opera videos are available both locally and internationally.

The company has long worked to help foster local composition, and 1986–87 was particularly notable in introducing to audiences in Adelaide, Sydney, and Melbourne a new major Australian opera, *Voss,* by composer Richard Meale, with libretto by David Malouf based on the novel by Patrick White. A recording of *Voss* has been released worldwide by Polygram/Phillips, and it is now available on videotape as well. There are several new works in progress for the company, and for the past six years AO has sponsored the National Opera Workshop, a program designed to give composers and librettists the practical experience of seeing their work produced. The Esso Young Artists program develops emerging singers through vocal and dramatic coaching. The Opera Action education program involves thousands of primary, secondary, and tertiary students each year through a combination of activities including special Youth Performances at the Sydney Opera House, access to dress rehearsals, and the circulation of comprehensive teaching kits aimed at supplementing school curriculum. Workshops are also held at the company's own Opera Centre.

The Australian Opera's revenue, more than $25 million, is derived primarily from the box office, which last season accounted for 60 percent of income. Corporate and individual donors gave another 10 percent, and public subsidies from the Australia Council and the governments of New South Wales and Western Australia accounted for the remaining 30 percent. The 1991 season includes new productions of *Don Giovanni, La Clemenza di Tito, Rigoletto, Der Rosenkavalier,* and the world premiere of *Mer de Glace* by Richard Male. The repertoire also features Gounod's *Romeo and Juliette, Così Fan Tutte, The Magic Flute, Lucrezia Borgia, Macbeth, Otello, Carmen, The Mikado, Turandot,* and Britten's *Turn of the Screw* and *Death in Venice.* In addition there will be a concert performance of Wagner's *Tristan and Isolde.* The company has scheduled some 215 performances in Sydney, Melbourne, and Perth, plus two productions in Adelaide in cooperation with the Adelaide Festival Centre Trust. Three operas will be simulcast nationally through ABC Television. Collaborating in the productions are the newly formed Australian Opera and Ballet Orchestra, the State Orchestra of Victoria, and the West Australian Symphony Orchestra.

BIBLIOGRAPHY: John Cargher, *Opera and Ballet in Australia* (Stanmore, 1977). Ava Hubble, *More than an Opera House* (Sydney, 1978). Harold Love, *The Golden Age of*

Australian Opera: W. S. Lyster and His Companies, 1861–1880 (Sydney, 1981). Barbara Mackenzie and Findlay Mackenzie, *Singers of Australia: From Melba to Sutherland* (Melbourne, 1967).

ACCESS: The Opera Centre, 480 Elizabeth Street, Surry Hills, N.S.W. 2010. (61 2) 699 1099; fax (61 2) 699 3184 Donald McDonald, General Manager. Moffatt Oxenbould, Artistic Director.

ANTHONY CLARKE

Austria

BREGENZ (24,561)

Bregenzer Festspiele

[One of the most successful postwar festivals, the Bregenzer Festspiele was founded in 1946 as an open-air summer festival on the shores of Lake Constance. Casting of international artists, especially members of the Vienna Staatsoper, is done in large-scale operas and operettas on the 4,800-seat Floating Stage (opened 1945 with Puccini's *Turandot*), the 1,753-seat Festival House (opened July 18, 1980, with Karl Böhm conducting Beethoven's Ninth Symphony), and the 692-seat Theater am Kornmarkt (opened June 21, 1955). The festival primarily cultivates operas that can be produced in a larger-than-life production on Europe's largest floating stage. The 1990 season included Catalani's *La Wally* and *Der fliegende Holländer*. The 1991 season featured productions of Bizet's *Carmen* on the floating stage and the Austrian premiere of Tchaikovsky's *Mazeppa* in the Festspielhaus (premiered in Moscow, February 15, 1884), both utilizing the Ballet Sofia.]

Artistic Director Alfred Wopmann has stated that festivals are the places where the special, the solitary, and the unique should be transformed into an event. Under his leadership, the festival has mirrored and championed a number of ideas which are mentioned in the following short summary. Like places of pilgrimage, festivals must represent the secrecy of the wonderful—the charisma of the magical. Beneath the massive mountain range of the Pfänder—the symbol of the city of Bregenz—on Lake Constance is Europe's largest and most unique floating stage. Sky and water—which mean freedom—determine the scenery of this theater, and not the confinement of closed rooms which have been used in towns since the Renaissance. The sunset at Lake Constance constitutes the overture of the play and changes (as in *Die Zauberflöte*) the whole stage into a sun. This particular union of nature, art, and landscape creates the mystery of the floating stage, transforming it into a magic place. In order to conform to this genius loci, the stage must take its measures from nature. The proportions of the stage and costumes and all movements, sound, and light have to be established in relation to this natural setting—therefore, they must be enlarged. Singers and actors must consequently be supported by an "involving" decoration that helps the audience to see and understand the play. The dramaturgic idea is to visualize the art in order to make it understood. Quite generally, open-air performances add a new dimension of excitement and originality. Compared to former centuries, our modern life has come a long way from nature. This loss is compensated for by the demand to go "back to nature," even at the theater. Senta's plunge into the lake from a thirty-meter-high lighthouse is much more convincing because it is real and vivid, than her jump in the background of the stage.

A great audience—almost 5,000 spectators per performance and more than 100,000 a season—expects a magnificent, unique, and spectacular show in front of a magnificent natural background. Since this new style has been created, people speak about the "Bregenz *Magic Flute*," the "Bregenz *Hoffman*," and the "Bregenz *Dutchman*"; about a new style of production that shows a well-known play in new dimensions and in a new light. This explains why so many new spectators were attracted by the performances on the floating stage in the last few years. The Bregenz Festival strives for a similar distinctive dramatic theory and stage aesthetics for the opera performances in the festival house, which opened in 1980. In contrast to the production of popular operas on the floating stage, opera rarities are performed here. A special interpretation makes them understandable for the audience. This experience was fully successful in 1988 with the production of *Samson et Dalila* by Camille Saint-Saëns; it had to be repeated in 1989. In 1990 this trend was continued with the opera *La Wally* by Alfredo Catalani, a contemporary of Puccini. All these considerations have a great deal in common: The interest of the public should be aroused by the particular place and style of the performance and the particular choice of plays. In harmony with the reaffirmation of nature, the summer festival intends to give a sign for a cultural revival that is open for the spiritual and artistic debate of the values of the past, present, and future.

ACCESS: Postfach 119, Festspiel- und Kongreßhaus, A-6901 Bregenz. (43 5574) 49 20 2 24; fax (43 5574) 49 20 2 42. Alfred Wopmann, Artistic Director.

ANGELIKA WORSEG

GRAZ (255,000)

Vereinigte Bühnen

As the second largest city in Austria, Graz has a long and distinguished musical history. Pietro Mingotti's Italian opera company introduced the genre to the city in 1736, and the works of Mozart dominated the repertoire by the end of the eighteenth century. A new opera house was opened on September 16, 1899, with Schiller's *Wilhelm Tell*. On May 16, 1906, Richard Strauss conducted the first Austrian performance of *Salome* here. Many singers launched their careers here, such as Tichatscheck (1835) and Materna (1865, at the Thalia-Theater in von Suppé's *Leichte Kavallerie*). Moreover, by the twentieth century, a number of well-known conductors—namely Karl Böhm, Clemens Krauss, and Karl Muck—had been associated with the house. The 1,276-seat Opernhaus was completely renovated and enlarged between 1983 and 1985. It reopened on January 12, 1985, with Johann Joseph Fux's *Angelica Vincitrice di Alcina* [originally premiered in Vienna on September 21, 1716].

BIBLIOGRAPHY: R. Baravelle, *50 Jahre Grazer Opernhaus, 1899–1949* (Graz, 1949). Rudolf List, *Oper und operetta in Graz* (Graz, 1966). Erich H. Müller, *Angelo und Pietro Mingotti: Ein Beitrag zur Geschichte der Oper im XVIII. Jahrhundert* (Dresden, 1917).

ACCESS: Kaiser Josef Platz 10, A-8010 Graz. (43 316) 82 64 51 55; fax (43 316) 82 64 51 2 20. Gerhard Brunner, Intendant. Gundula Janowitz, Operndirector.

[From materials supplied by the company]

LINZ (203,910)

Landestheater Linz

Linz, Austria's third largest city, is a very ancient settlement that spent most of its history as a small, sleepy provincial town. Only in the last two centuries has Linz grown into a modern industrial city. The last decade of the eighteenth century saw the first real flowering of opera. *Die Zauberflöte* was performed in 1793, followed the next year by *Die Entführung aus dem Serail*. *Don Giovanni* and *Le Nozze di Figaro* were produced in 1796. The modern history of theater in Linz began, however, with the building of the new 756-seat Landestheater (Großes Haus) in 1803, which was modeled on the Theater an der Wien. Unfortunately, the theater suffered from inadequate size and critical technical shortcomings, basic problems that remain to this day despite rebuilding, renovations, and many improvements over the years. A major renovation supervised by Clemens Holzmeister took place in 1958, and the theater reopened with Richard Strauss's *Arabella* on December 20 of that year. The repertoire depended initially on Viennese taste. Although the capital took precedence, an effort was always made to present new works in Linz as soon as possible. For example, Auber's *La Muette de Portici*, premiered in Paris in 1828, could be seen in Linz as early as 1829. Moreover, Donizetti's *L'Elisir d'amore* was produced in 1832, the same year it premiered in Milan [the Vienna premiere was April 9, 1835]. The singers in Linz adhered to a high standard, and some of them developed into major international artists—a situation that continues to this day.

In the early years after 1803, the opera directors could only employ five solo singers (bass, tenor, one female singer, and "two middle voices"), but from 1820 onward there were up to three dozen actors who also had to appear in operatic performances. At the turn of the century there were thirty soloists, and just before the First World War there were as many as forty-five. In the current season there are twenty-four soloists permanently engaged in addition to guest artists. The present chorus has forty-two members. The initial orchestra of some 15 musicians was supplied by the music director. In 1814 a permanent theater orchestra was organized with 26 instrumentalists. This number has steadily increased, and today the 106 members of the Bruckner Orchestra form a pool of musicians for all the musical productions at the Landestheater.

Programming was conservative until the 1950s, when a number of operas were given their Austrian premieres, including Egk's *Die Zaubergeige* (1952), Max Liebermann's *Leonore 40/45* (1953), and Hindemith's *Mathis der Maler* (1955). In the 1970s a series of world premieres of operas by Austrian composers included Eder's *George Dandin*, Balduin Sulzer's *In seinem Garten liebt Don Perimplin Belisa*, Heinrich Gattermeyer's *Kirbisch*, and Karl Kogler's *Kohlhaas*. Currently the Japanese composer Toshiro Mayuzumi is working on an opera for Linz. There is a simultaneous effort to bring to the public a series of important contemporary works from the international repertoire. Poulenc's *Dialogues des Carmélites*, Klebe's *Die Fastnachtsbeichte* and *Blood Wedding*, Sandor Szokolay's *Samson*, and Menotti's *The Consul* have been produced as a part of this series. Rounding out the repertoire are works that, although worthy, are unjustly neglected. The last few seasons have seen productions of Rossini's *Guglielmo Tell*, Boito's *Mefistofele*, Weber's *Oberon*, and Berlioz's *Benvenuto Cellini*.

ACCESS: Promenade 39, A-4020 Linz. (43 732) 27 76 51; fax (43 732) 27 76 51 308. Roman Zeilinger, Indendant. Manfred Mayrhofer, Music Director.

ULRICH SCHERZER

SALZBURG (139,426)

Salzburger Festspiele

The city of Salzburg grew up around the cathedral founded by St. Virgil in 774, and for hundreds of years it was the center of the diocese and the seat of the archbishop. Music flourished under the patronage of both the church and the Salzburg princes. With the abolition of the court in 1806, musical life stagnated, and the once famous city reverted to the status of a provincial town. Fortunately, the Dommusikverein und Mozarteum, founded in 1841, signaled a revitalization of cultural forces, and the organization sponsored its first music festival in 1842 honoring the unveiling of the Mozart Memorial. Several decades later, in 1870, Karl Freiherr von Sterneck founded the Internationale Mozart-Stiftung, a historically important event in the intensification of musical momentum. That organization began the first complete edition of Mozart's music in 1875, started promoting concerts and gatherings of musicians, and fostered both a library and an archive. Mozart festivals were held intermittently from 1877 to 1910, and the legendary Lilli Lehmann was associated with several of them both as a singer (*Don Giovanni* and *Figaro*) and as a stage director, beginning in 1901. The conductors Mahler, Mottl, Muck, Nikisch, Richter, Schalk, Strauss, and Weingartner all took part between 1879 and 1910, and there was talk of establishing a regular festival. The outbreak of World War I canceled what had been planned as its beginning, but the foundation had been laid for an annual summer festival that would rapidly become one of the premiere musical events in Europe.

The Salzburger Festspielhaus-Gemeinde was founded in Vienna by Heinrich Damisch and Friedrich Gehmacher after the war with the express purpose of establishing an annual festival in Salzburg for drama and music. As the composer's birthplace, special emphasis was to be accorded the works of Mozart. The artistic directors were Hofmannsthal (who had published a proposal for a permanent Salzburg Festival in 1919), Roller, Schalk, Strauss, and Reinhardt, whose production of Hofmannsthal's *Jedermann* opened the first festival on August 22, 1920. Opera first appeared in 1922 when *Le Nozze di Figaro* and *Die Entführung aus dem Serail*, conducted by Schalk, and *Don Giovanni* and *Così Fan Tutte*, conducted by Strauss, were mounted in the Salzburg Stadttheater. That same year the Internationale Gesellschaft für Neue Musik was founded with support from the Internationale Stiftung Mozarteum, and the first official International Society for Contemporary Music (ISCM) festival in 1923 replaced the Salzburg Festival music programs. Sufficient funding was not available to mount the 1924 festival, but the Winterreitschule was converted into a theater and renamed the Festspielhaus. Rebuilt in 1926 to increase the seating to 1,200, the theater hosted opera productions the next year. Over the next few seasons, Furtwängler, Knappertsbusch, Krauss, Toscanini, and Bruno Walter conducted memorable productions, but the Anschluss with Nazi Germany in 1938 seriously impacted the program. World War II put an end to festivities, and the festival, now called the Salzburger Theater- und Musik-Sommer, commenced in 1945.

Following the war the facilities were redesigned and rebuilt. There are now three festival halls available for performances. The Felsenreitschule, which had hosted open-air performances since 1926, was adapted by Clemens Holzmeister in 1968–1970 and now seats 1,549; the 2,177-seat Großes Festspielhaus, also designed by Holzmeister and built between 1955 and 1960 (it opened on July 26, 1960; with Herbert von Karajan conducting Strauss's *Der Rosenkavalier*) is the focus of large productions; and the 1,384-seat Kleines Festspielhaus (whose dimensions correspond to those of the Vienna State Opera) designed by Hütter and Holzmeister (built in 1925–1926, it opened with Beethoven's *Fidelio* conducted by Franz Schalk on August 13, 1927) and renovated by Hans Hoffmann and Erich Engels in 1963. In addition, the festival mounts performances in the Cathedral Square, which can seat 2,114 with standing room for an additional 400; the 700-seat University Church; the 724-seat Salzburger Landestheater, built in 1893, and the 807-seat Great Hall of the Mozarteum.

Supported by the traditional participation of the Vienna Philharmonic Orchestra, the festival has produced a total of 1,604 performances of opera through the 1987 summer season. Traditionally, emphasis has been placed on the works of Mozart, with 792 performances, followed by Richard Strauss, with 232 performances; Verdi, with 133 performances, and 81 performances of six different productions of Beethoven's *Fidelio*. The festival has also taken a leading role in the support of world premieres of new works: the new version of Strauss's *Die Ägyptische Helena* in 1933 and his *Liebe der Danae* in 1952; Gottfried von Einem's *Danton's Tod* in 1947 and *Prozess* in 1953; Rolf Liebermann's *Penelope* in 1954 followed by his *Schule der Frauen* in 1957; Carl Orff's *Antigonae* in 1949 and *Das Spiel vom Ende der Zeiten* in 1973; and Hans Werner Henze's *Bassariden* in 1966. More recently, audiences have been treated to Friedrich Cerha's *Baal* in 1981, Luciano Berio's *Un Re in ascolta* in 1984, Hans Werner Henze's reworking of Monteverdi's *Il Ritorno d'Ulisse in Patria* in 1985, and Krysztof Penderecki's *The Black Mask* in 1986.

Ideas for future Salzburg Festivals will be derived from six main guidelines articulated by Gerhard Wimberger, a member of the Festival Directorate: (1) Mozart as focus and point of departure; (2) Richard Strauss; (3) great European theater in opera, drama, and dance; (4) comedy in drama and opera, and in drama, especially great Austrian comedies; (5) baroque opera, and (6) contemporary works. To insure that the festival would not suffer from financial deficits, the Austrian Parliament passed a law on July 12, 1950, stating that any festival deficits would be covered partly by the federal government (40 percent) and 20 percent each by the province, the city, and the Tourism Promotion Fund. Gérard Mortier is the new artistic director effective 1991.

BIBLIOGRAPHY: F. Hadamowsky and G. Rech, eds., *Die Salzburger Festspiele, ihre Vorgeschichte und Entwicklung, 1842–1960* (Salzburg, 1960). Hugo von Hofmannsthal, *Festspiele in Salzburg* (Vienna, 1938, 3rd ed. 1952). J. Kaut, *Die Salzburger Festspiele* (Salzburg, 1982). J. Kaut, *Festspiele in Salzburg: Eine Dokumentation* (Salzburg, 1969). A. Kutscher, *Das Salzburger Barocktheater zu den Salzburger Festspielen* (Dusseldorf, 1939). Michael P. Steinberg, *The Meaning of the Salzburg-Festival: Austria as Theater and Ideology, 1890–1938* (Ithaca, N.Y, 1990). R. Tenschert, *Salzburg und seine Festspiel* (Vienna, 1947).

ACCESS: Postfach 140, A-5010 Salzburg. (43 662) 80 45 01; fax (43 662) 89 11 14. Gérard Mortier, Artistic Director.

[From materials supplied by the festival company]

VIENNA (metro 1,800,000; city 1,482,800)

Wiener Staatsoper

Although the origins of Vienna can be traced back to an ancient Celtic settlement on the banks of the Danube River, its importance as a city dates from 1273 when Rudolf I of Hapsburg was chosen King of the Germans. The Hapsburgs took control of the city in 1278 and steadily expanded it as the capital of their extensive Austro-Hungarian Empire. From the time of Frederick III in 1483 until 1806, when the title of holy Roman emperor was abolished by Napoleon, the Hapsburg archduke of Austria was almost always chosen holy Roman emperor with all the rights and privileges that title implied. Members of the family held numerous thrones in Europe from 1273 to the end of World War I in 1918. It was during the seventeenth century that opera was first performed in Vienna, and with the reign of Leopold I, opera became a recognized court event. In the 1700s and 1800s (the Theater am Kärntnerthor opened in 1708) Vienna became a world center of culture, especially music, and, although its fortunes have fluctuated since that time, it retains a prominent place, particularly in the operatic world. The city's operatic credentials are indeed impressive, but that history has always involved politics, intrigue, and public controversy, a fact of Viennese cultural life that continues unabated to this day. Gluck was associated with the Imperial Opera (and appointed court Kapellmeister in 1754) for a decade, and his *Orfeo ed Eurydice* premiered at the Burgtheater on October 5, 1762. The second of his reform operas, *Alceste*, with its remarkable preface, premiered in the same theater on December 26, 1767. When Gluck sought greener pastures in Paris, the Burgtheater was replaced gradually as Court Opera by the Theater am Kärtnerthor, and the challenge continued when Mozart's *Die Zauberflöte* received its first performance at Emanuel Schikaneder's Theater auf der Wieden on September 30, 1791, barely two months before the composer's *La Clemenza di Tito* was to receive its Vienna premiere. The impresario then moved as director of the new Theater an der Wien (the 1,073-seat house opened on June 13, 1801, with Franz Teyber's *Alexander*; it was renovated and reopened on May 28, 1962) where he produced the original version of Beethoven's *Fidelio* on November 20, 1805.

After the Napoleonic wars, no major opera was premiered in Vienna until Richard Strauss's *Die Frau ohne Schatten* on October 10, 1919. Emperor Franz Joseph decided in 1857 to replace the old fortifications that surrounded his palace with a new boulevard, the Ringstraße, to be dotted with buildings that would reflect the imperial city's stature. One of those structures would be the Oper am Ring. There was a competition to select the architect, and Eduard van der Nüll and August Siccard von Siccardsburg were selected from thirty-five submissions. They had designed a "French Renaissance" building which, to this day, remains one of the most attractive nineteenth-century European opera houses. The cornerstone was laid on May 20, 1863, and the emperor and empress both attended the opening presentation of *Don Giovanni* on May 25, 1869. The Hofoper under von Herbeck (1870–1875), Jauner (1875–1880), and Jaun (1880–1897) assembled a company that included some of the most distinguished singers and conductors of the time. When Gustav Mahler assumed the directorship (1897–1907), the Hofoper was to enjoy some of its most notable triumphs. In terms of repertoire Mahler was basically conservative, but he was totally committed to mounting integrated productions of established masterpieces. An uncompromising authoritarian figure with unconventional views, Mahler involved himself in the minutest of production details. With the brilliant Alfred Roller as his chief stage designer, he directed a series of memorable operas including *Tristan und Isolde* (1903), *Fidelio* (1904), *Don Giovanni* (1905), *Die Zauberflöte* (1906), and *Iphigénie en Aulide* (1907, the last season of his tenure). In the end, a campaign by all of the many people he had offended, including the critics, made Mahler's position untenable, and he resigned, fortunately with a contract with the Metropolitan Opera Association to conduct there in 1908. Mahler's singing actors, including Demuth, Gutheil-Schoder, Kittel, Kurz, Mayr, Bahr-Mildenburg, Schmedes, and Slezak, remained with the company under Weingartner (1907–1911) and Gregor (1911–1918). Perhaps the most memorable post-Mahler production at the Staatsoper was Strauss's *Der Rosenkavalier*, which had premiered at Dresden on January 26, 1911.

Austria became a republic after World War I, and the Hofoper became the Staatsoper. Times were hard, but the company, under the codirectorship of Richard Strauss and Franz Schalk (1919–1924), regained its former luster. In the years to follow, Elisabeth Schumann, Novotná, Ursuleac, the Konetzni sisters, Dermota, Tauber, Roswaenge, and Schorr joined the company, along with conductors Josef Krips, Clemens Krauss, and Bruno Walter. When the Nazis proclaimed the Anschluss in March 1938, the Staatsoper lost many of its leading artists. Kipnis, Lehmann, List, Piccaver, Schorr, Schumann, Tauber, and Walter were among those who left Austria. Appropriately, *Gotterdämmerung* conducted by Knappertsbusch, was the last performance in the old house, on June 30, 1944. Closed on the personal orders of Field Marshal Hermann Goering, the Staatsoper was destroyed by Allied bombs on March 12, 1945.

After the Second World War, the company performed at the Wiener Volksoper (which opened with *Le Nozze di Figaro* on May 1, 1945, with Krips conducting) and the Theater an der Wein (with Krips again conducting, this time *Fidelio* on October 6) for ten years until the rebuilt 2,200-seat opera house (1,642 seats and standing room for 567) could be reopened. Erich Boltenstern and Otto Prössinger were commissioned to replace the destroyed Vienna State Opera, and instead of the exact replica that had been envisioned, they completely rebuilt the auditorium, the stage, and the backstage areas. In 1954 Karl Böhm was again the director, and he conducted the opening night performance of *Fidelio* on November 5, 1955. Böhm, Krauss, and Krips built a formidable ensemble in the years after the war. Dermota, Gueden, Hotter, Jurinac, Kunz, Lipp, Patzak, Schoeffler, Schwarzkopf, Seefried, and Welitsch highlighted casts of international stature. When Herbert von Karajan succeeded Böhm in March 1956, another golden era, in conjunction with La Scala (Teatro alla Scala) in Milan, emerged. The most powerful figure since Mahler, Karajan's regime lasted until 1964 and merged the artists of La Scala with such rising stars as Christa Ludwig, Birgit Nilsson, and Leonie Rysanek. In 1969 director Heinrich Reif-Gintl oversaw the centennial of the theater with a repertoire of forty-seven operas and five ballets. The gala itself was celebrated on May 25, 1969, with Leonard Bernstein conducting Beethoven's *Missa Solemnis* followed by *Fidelio* conducted by Karl Böhm.

Reif-Gintl's successor, Rudolf Gamsjäger, continued Karajan's star system with some modifications, which included the highly successful local premiere of Janáček's *Katya Kabanova* and Nicolai Ghiaurov's portrayal of Boris Godunov. With the arrival of Egon Seefehlner for the first of his stints in 1976, a number of major twentieth-century works were introduced into the repertoire, including *Erwartung, Duke Bluebeard's Castle, Die Tote Stadt, Kabale und Liebe, Der junge Lord,* and *Karl V.* Lorin Maazel's short tenure (1982–1984) attempted to come to grips with the problem of maintaining a high production standard when too many operas were cast with too few artists who were not permanent members of the ensemble. His decision to offer several performances of the same opera over a short period of time to keep the production fresh and tight was unfortunately no more successful than previous efforts, and Seefehlner returned in 1984. The current director, Claus Helmut Drese, assumed the position in 1986 after a highly successful reign at the opera in Zürich, Switzerland. He assumed the leadership of a company that has always been intimately involved in the personality, culture, and aspirations of both Vienna and the Austrian people. Politics and intrigue have always played a major role in the company, as they have in Milan. In this sense, these two distinguished companies are unique, perhaps along with the Théâtre National de L'Opéra de Paris, in the opera world of today.

CHRONOLOGY OF DIRECTORS: Franz von Dingelstedt, 1869–1870. Johann von Herbeck, 1870–1875. Franz von Jauner, 1875–1880. Wilhelm Jann, 1881–1897. Gustav Mahler, 1897–1907. Felix Weingartner, 1908–1911. Hans Gregor, 1911–1918. Franz Schalk, 1918–1919. Richard Strauss/Franz Schalk, 1919–1924. Franz Schalk, 1924–1929. Clemens Krauss, 1929–1934. Felix Weingartner, 1935–1936. Erwin Kerber, 1936–1940. Heinrich Strohm, 1940–1941. Ernst Schneider, 1941–1943. Karl Böhm, 1943–1945. Franz Salmhofer, 1945–1954. Karl Böhm, 1954–1956. Herbert von Karajan, 1956–1964 (shared with Walter Erich Schäfer, 1962–1963, and Egon Hilbert, 1963–1964). Egon Hilbert, 1964–1968. Heinrich Reif-Gintl, 1968–1972. Rudolf Gamsjäger, 1972–1976. Egon Seefehlner, 1976–1982. Lorin Maazel, 1982–1984. Egon Seefehlner, 1984–1986. Claus Helmut Drese, 1986–present.

BIBLIOGRAPHY: Anton Bauer, *150 Jahre Theater an der Wien* (Wien, 1952). Anton Bauer, *Opern und Operetten in Wien* (Graz, 1955). Wilhelm Beetz, *Das Wiener Opernhaus, 1869 bis 1955* (Wien, 1955). Hans Christian and Harald Hoyer, *Wiener Staatsoper, 1945–1980* (Wien, 1981). Max Graf, *Die Wiener Oper* (Wien, 1955). Franz Hadamowsky, *Die Wiener Hoftheater (Staatstheater): 1776–1966; 1966–1975,* 2 vols. (Wien, 1966–75). Rudolf Klein, *Die Wiener Staatsoper* (Wien, 1967; repr., 1969). Heinrich Kralik, *Die Wiener Oper* (Wien, 1963). Emil Pirchan, Alexander Witeschnik, and Otto Fritz, *300 Jahre Wiener Opern-theater: Werk und Werden* (Wien, 1953). Marcel Prawy, *Die Wiener Oper* (Zürich, 1969). Anton Seebohm, ed., *The Vienna Opera* (Wien, 1985; New York, 1987). Alexander Witeschnik, *Wiener Opernkunst von den Anfängen bis zu Karajan* (Wien, 1959).

ACCESS: Opernring 2, 1010 Wien. (43 222) 5 14 44 01; fax (43 222) 5 14 44 23 30. Dr. Claus Helmut Drese, Direktor. Claudio Abbado, Musikdirektor.

[From materials supplied by the company]

Wiener Volksoper

The 1,472-seat house, originally known as the Kaiser-jubiläums Stadttheater, opened on December 15, 1898, in an unfashionable part of Vienna on Währinger Straße. Between then and May 20, 1903, the unbelievable total of 166 works were produced. When Rainer Simons, son of the famous Munich Hofoper baritone Carl Simons, was appointed director in 1903, the focus changed from legitimate theater to popular opera. As the Volksoper it opened with a production of *Der Freischütz* on September 15, 1904. The company would quickly gain renown through the breadth of its repertoire, which extended from popular opera to operetta to French vaudevilles. Simons remained with the company until 1917 and was responsible for the Vienna premieres of such works as *Manon Lescaut*, *Salome* (May 25, 1907, starring Clotilde Wenger), and *Tosca* (February 21, 1907, conducted by Alexander von Zemlinksy), and singers of the caliber of Lotte Schöne and Jeritza (November 23, 1911, in the premiere of *Der Kuhreigen*) made their debut with the company. The latter appeared in a memorable performance of *Lohengrin* on October 18, 1912, with Leo Slezak. Until the house was closed in 1928, a number of young artists were brought to the public's attention including Ursuleac (1924), Konetzni (1926), Emanuel List (1922 as Mephisto in Gounod's *Faust*), and Ludwig Weber (1912 as Fiorello in *Il Barbiere di Siviglia*). When the theater reopened in November 1929 it was renamed the Neues Wiener Schauspielhaus, and for the next decade only occasional operas and operettas were produced, with one of the highlights being Max Reinhardt's incredible production of Offenbach's *La Belle Hélène* in June 1932. It was during this period (1938) that Hilde Gueden made her debut as Hilda Gerin in Benatzky's operetta *Herzen im Schnee*. As of October 28, 1938, the theater was called the Städtische Wiener Volksoper; from 1941 until the curtain fell on July 13, 1944, it was called the Opernhaus der Stadt Wien. Both the auditorium and the stagehouse were modernized during this period, and the company specialized in a popular repertoire.

Alfred Jerger's improvised production of Mozart's *Le Nozze di Figaro* reopened the house on May 1, 1945, with artists from the Staatsoper and Josef Krips conducting members of the Vienna Philharmonic in the pit. Due to the widespread destruction, the company was forced to share the facility with the Staatsoper which also performed in the Theater an der Wien until 1955. Each house had its own character and supporters, and there remained logistical as well as financial problems to be resolved. The ballet had to support both houses; the Vienna Philharmonic, which acted as the house orchestra for the Wiener Staatsoper, remained at the Theater an der Wien; and the Volksoper built its own ensemble from the house orchestra. At this point in time the Volksoper was considered a part of the Austrian State Theater which was funded by the national government. The director, Egon Hilbert, was a strong supporter of opera, but, given the enormous cost of rebuilding the Staatsoper am Ring, he had to deal with the future artistic direction of both the Theater an der Wien and the Volksoper. Should the Volksoper pursue the production of operettas as artworks, broaden the repertoire, or cater to guest stars and guest ensembles? The company needed its own ballet, a point well made with Marcel Prawy's first European production of an American musical, *Kiss Me Kate*, on February 14, 1956. However, the question remained: Which company in Vienna should have priority to produce which works?

After von Karajan's 1960 *Die Fledermaus*, the Volksoper produced *Die Zauberflöte* that December. Salmhofer retired in 1963 and was replaced, after much speculation, with Albert Moser, who was then secretary-general of the Staatsoper. Karajan later brought Moser to the Salzburg Festival as president. Moser broadened the repertoire from Gluck and Haydn to Leonard Bernstein (with 199 performances of *West Side Story*) in productions that reflected the Viennese milieu. He also initiated the Opernstudio der Volksoper to train the younger generation of singer-actors. The well-known bass-baritone Karl Dönch took over from Moser in 1973. A favorite at the Staatsoper since 1947, Dönch even sang the role of Jupiter in Offenbach's *Orpheus in der Unterwelt* at the Volksoper on his seventieth birthday (January 8, 1985). He was also responsible for affecting day-to-day management controls to improve the efficiency of the company. Extensive alterations were done to the theater in 1973–1974 which increased capacity to 1,472 seats and 114 standing-room places. Eberhard Waechter, who made his debut at the Volksoper as Silvio in *Pagliacci* in 1955, took over from Dönch in 1988, continuing the house's tradition of singers as directors. As the continuing history of the Volksoper unfolds, it is important to keep in mind that the story of the musical arts in Vienna is inseparable from the political and economic realities of the Austrian capital which is characterized by multilevel confusion matched only, perhaps, by Paris.

CHRONOLOGY OF DIRECTORS: Rainer Simons, 1903–1917. Raoul Mader, 1917–1919. Felix Weingartner, 1919–1924. Fritz Stiedry, 1924–1925. Hugo Gruder-Guntram, 1925–1928. Hermann Fischler, 1929–1938. Anton Baumann, 1938–1941. Oskar Jölli, 1941–1944. Franz Salmhofer, 1945–1963. Albert Moser, 1963–1973. Karl Dönch, 1973–1988. Eberhard Wächter, 1988–present.

BIBLIOGRAPHY: See entries under Wiener Staatsoper.

ACCESS: Währinger Straße 78, A-1090 Wien. (43 222) 5 14 44 01; fax (43 222) 5 14 44 32 15. Ks. Eberhard Waechter, Direktor.

OTTO FRITZ

Belgium

BRUSSELS (2,221,818)

Théâtre Royal de la Monnaie

The modern nation of Belgium resulted from the defeat of Napoleon at Waterloo in June 1815. The Congress of Vienna, in its attempt to redraw the map of Europe, united Belgium and the kingdom of the Netherlands under William I. The customs, religion, and traditions of the two were not compatible, and the Belgians began agitating for independence on August 25, 1830. Independence was declared within a matter of weeks. Under the leadership of Charles Rogier, the first prime minister, a constitution was adopted in October and Prince Leopold of Saxe-Coburg was elected as its first king. A constitutional monarchy exists to this day. Brussels became the capital and cultural center of the country, and the Brussels Conservatoire Royal de Musique, under the enlightened direction of Francois-Joseph Fétis and François Auguste Gevaert, was one of the great nineteenth-century musical institutions. The country has two official languages, French and Flemish, and thus two parallel cultures. Peter Benoit founded the Flemish Opera in 1893, and there are important opera houses in Antwerp (Koninklijke Vlammse Opera), Brussels (Kroninklijke Muntschouwburg or Théâtre Royal de la Monnaie), Ghent, Liège, and Verviers.

For the past three centuries there has been a theater on the same spot where the La Monnaie theater stands today. It was at the end of the seventeenth century that the Italian Bombarda, treasurer to the governor Maximilien-Emmanuel, had a theater built in Brussels, which at that time was a city that had been devastated by shelling. The theater was erected in the place of the former Hôtel Ostrevent, where coins were minted. Hence its name, "La Monnaie" (The Mint). The building was opened in 1700 and its program included both music and theater. The five-tier auditorium, with, even at that time, 1,200 seats, did not yet have any heating. Some of the boxes boasted their own small stove. The fortunate few enjoyed this luxury, while the remainder had to shiver their way through to the interval when they could thaw out in the heated foyer.

Over a century later, a new theater was erected immediately behind the older building, which had now fallen into disrepair. On May 26, 1819, the new theater opened its doors. Then, on January 21, 1855, the auditorium and the stage, which were lit with oil lamps, went up in flames. Only the walls and the famous Peristyle by the architect Damense escaped intact. The architect Joseph Poelaert, later to become well known for the Colonne du Congrès and the Palais de Justice in Brussels, supervised the reconstruction. He redesigned the auditorium and, in particular, created the caryatids. The new theater was reopened with great ceremony on March 28, 1856. From that time onward the program was almost exclusively devoted to opera. The theater experienced a golden age in the 1870s and 1880s, which saw the world premieres of Massenet's *Hérodiade* on December 19, 1881, and Chabrier's *Gwendoline* on April 10, 1886. Nellie Melba made her operatic debut as Gilda in *Rigoletto* on October 13, 1887, and Emile Wauters did a portrait of her at that time which now hangs in the Musée Charlier in Brussels.

The fortunes of the theater declined prior to World War I, and during the war, German occupation forces organized several opera seasons which included Richard Strauss conducting *Der Rosenkavalier*. Fiscal restraints hampered the operation during the 1920s and 1930s, and in the aftermath of World War II the city of Brussels gave up the ownership of the theater to the national government. Up to 1980 its operatic history was not notable, although Elisabeth Schwarzkopf gave her final operatic performance as the Marschallin in *Der Rosenkavalier* in 1972 and returned to stage the same opera in 1981. It was increasingly clear that the times had changed and that a radical new direction in artistic management was indicated. It was also evident that the theater was in urgent need of renovation. The most basic safety regulations, as well as the demanding music and theater requirements facing the new management, led to the undertaking of major renovation work during the 1985–1986 season. The Ministry of Public Works was responsible for the work, and, when completed, the theater had undergone an impressive face-lift. The most important changes were to the stage itself. The stage area, with six levels above stage and three basement levels, was completely gutted and rebuilt within the existing walls. The old hoist-and-pulley system was replaced by fully mechanized and computer-controlled equipment. Behind the proscenium there was built a large lift for raising the sets from the three basement levels. The orchestra pit was enlarged and can even accommodate a Wagnerian-scale orchestra with 106 musicians. Moreover, it can be raised to the level of the audience or the stage.

The 1,140-seat house itself, which had been dubbed one of the most beautiful theaters in Europe, was totally refurbished. A magnificent new curtain can now be raised according to the Greek, German, or Italian systems. The roof was raised two levels to accommodate a new rehearsal room, a second foyer, and adequate office space. Designers from the United States, Italy, and France created new floors and ceilings throughout. On November 12, 1986, a glittering gala was held for the reopening of La Monnaie. As general director of La Monnaie since July 1981, Gérard Mortier has thoroughly reorganized the chorus and the orchestra, overseen the complete refurbishing of the opera house, and installed a production team dedicated to modernizing both the repertoire and production concepts. The Symphony Orchestra of La Monnaie, under the direction of Sylvain Cambreling, has expanded into a full-fledged 96-member symphony orchestra which provides musical accompaniment for all the opera productions and also performs as a symphony orchestra and in a wide variety of smaller formations. Assisted by Sir John Pritchard, a permanent guest conductor, Hans Zender, and Christoph von Dohnanyi, Cambreling has succeeded in raising the musical standards of the company to an international level. La Monnaie has no permanent company of singers, so casting is accomplished with roughly forty regular singers supplemented with guest artists such as Gwyneth Jones and José van Dam. Costumes, props, and sets are all created at the opera house by a large permanent team of technical staff. Recent seasons have averaged eight productions featuring a mixture of standard repertoire, revivals of neglected works, and several world premieres including *La Passion de Gilles* (1983) by Philippe Boesmans and *Das Schloss* (1986) by André Laporte. A highlight of the 1990–1991 season was the controversial world premiere of John Adam's opera *The Death of Klinghoffer* on March 19, 1991. Directed by Peter Sellars, who was also responsible for *Nixon in China* (1987), the work deals with the real story of the killing of an elderly Jewish tourist on the cruise ship *Achille Lauro* in 1985.

BIBLIOGRAPHY: A. de Gers, *Théâtre royal de la Monnaie, 1856–1926* (Brussels, 1926). Jacques Isnardon and Lionel Renieu, *Histoire des théâtres de Bruxelles depuis leur origine jusqu'à ce jour*, 2 vols. (Paris, 1928). Jules Salès, *Théâtre Royal de la Monnaie, 1856–1970* (Nivelles, 1971).

ACCESS: Rue Léopold, 4, 1000 Bruxelles. (32 2) 217 22 11; fax (32 2) 218 35 27. Gérard Mortier, Directeur. Sylvain Cambreling, Permanent Conductor.

[From materials supplied by the Belgian Institute for Information and Documentation]

Brazil

RIO DE JANEIRO (13,845,243)

Teatro Municipal

When Spain and Portugal signed the Treaty of Tordesillas in 1494, the Portuguese gained control of the eastern portion of South America. Pedro Álvares Cabral landed on what is now Brazil on April 22, 1500, and the Portuguese colonized the territory over the next one hundred years. Rio de Janeiro was declared the capital of Brazil in 1763. When France invaded Portugal in 1807, the Portuguese royal family fled to Brazil where they made Rio de Janeiro the capital of Portugal as well. King John VI returned to Portugal in 1821 but left his son Pedro as regent of Brazil. On September 2, 1821, Pedro declared Brazil independent and had himself proclaimed Emperor Pedro I. The country remained a monarchy under his son, whose "Golden Age of Pedro II," from 1840 to 1889, signaled modernization and stability. His action in freeing the slaves, however, led to widespread dissatisfaction and, with the support of the military, Brazil proclaimed itself a republic on November 15, 1889.

Although opera made its first appearance in 1767, it did not flourish until the presence of the royal family stimulated all the arts. In 1813 the Real Teatro de São João began producing operas, and, renamed the Imperial Teatro de São Pedro de Alcântara in 1824, it featured a repertoire of Rossini and, later, Bellini and Donizetti. Touring Italian opera companies visited frequently during the nineteenth century. Although Italian opera was officially cultivated, the Imperial Academy of Music and National Opera opened in 1847 with the patronage of Pedro II. This led to the first native operas by Álvares Lôbo, Alves de Mesquita, and Carlos Gomes, whose *Il Guarany* was premiered at La Scala (Teatro alla Scala) on March 19, 1870. The Teatro Provisório opened in 1852 with Verdi's *Macbeth*, and, renamed the Teatro Lírico Fluminense in 1854, was the center of operatic production until the end of the century. The Teatro Municipal opened on July 14, 1909 (the first major opera was *La Gioconda* on September 1, 1909). The next year featured an international season with Bellincioni, Schiavazzi, and Galeffi. Teatro Municipal remains to this day the city's primary opera house. The theater has its own chorus and orchestra, the Orquestra do Teatro Municipal. Seasons have featured international stars including Brazil's own Bidú Sayão, who retired from the stage in 1958 after farewell performances in Rio de Janeiro. Another highlight of that season was the world premier of Heitor Villa-Lobo's first opera *Izaht* (composed 1912–1914) at the Teatro Municipal on December 13, 1958. Artists who travel to South America often play the circuit of the Teatro Colón in Buenos Aires, the Teatro Municipal in Rio de Janeiro, and the Teatro Municipal (opened September 12, 1907) in São Paulo.

BIBLIOGRAPHY: Ayres de Andrade, *Francisco Manuel da Silva e seu tempo*, 2 vols. (Rio de Janeiro, 1967). L. H. C. de Azevedo, *Música e músicos do Brazil* (Rio de Janeiro, 1950). Edgard de Brito Chaves, Jr., *Memórias e glórias de um teatro: Sessenta Anos de História do Teatro Municipal de Rio de Janeiro* (Rio de Janeiro, 1971). P. de Oliveria Castro Cerquena, *Un século de Opera en São Paulo* (São Paulo, 1954). G. de Melo, *A música no Brazil desde os tempos coloniais até o primerio decénio da República* (Rio de Janeiro, 1908, 2nd ed., 1947). Luiz Heitor Corrêa de Azevedo, *Relaçao das óperas de autores brasileiros* (Rio de Janeiro, 1938). Paulo de Oliveira Castro Cerquera, *Um sécolo de ópera em São Paulo* (São Paulo, 1954).

ACCESS: Ave Rio Branco, Rio de Janeiro. (55 21) 224 2895. Mr. Dalah Archcar, General Director.

[From materials supplied by the company]

Bulgaria

SOFIA (metro 2,225,200; city 1,208,200)

Sofiyska Narodna Opera (Sofia National Opera)

The Russian liberation of Bulgaria from the Ottoman Empire and the Turks in 1878 opened the country to European musical influences. The Stolichnata Dramatichna Opera Trupa began staging excerpts from European classical operas as early as 1891 in the Slavyanska Beseda Hall. The famous Bulgarian tenor Konstantin Mikhaylov-Stoyan (1853–1914), who was a principal artist with the Bolshoi in Moscow from 1888 to 1899, returned to his native country in 1899 to give concerts. He returned again in 1907 with the bass Ivan Vulpe and his wife Bogdana Gyuzeleva-Vulpe, and their concerts were so successful that the Opera Druzhba was founded in 1907 as a society to encourage opera. Mikhaylov-Stoyan became the first Bulgarian opera producer, with performances in the Naroden Theater in 1908. A company including Vulpe, Prokopova, Raichev, and Stefan Makedonski (for whom the State Musical Theater "Stefan Makedonski" in Sofia is now named) offered the first full season of opera in 1910.

These efforts resulted in the founding of the Sofia National Opera in 1921, and, with support from the government, it became the National State Opera in 1922. Bulgaria has produced such distinguished artists as Boris Christoff (whose career was supported by a grant from King Boris of Bulgaria) and Nicolai Ghiauroff, who made his debut as Don Basilio in Rossini's *Il Barbiere di Seviglia* in Sofia in 1955. A new 1,300-seat opera house opened in Sofia in 1954, and the company specializes in works from the standard repertoire as well as contemporary operas by native composers. The company celebrated its fiftieth anniversary in 1958 with productions of *Boris Godunov*, *War and Peace*, *Die Zauberflöte*, *Otello*, and *Faust*, among a host of others. Among the outstanding artists of the company over the years have been Julia Wiener, Nadia Afejan, Assen Selimski, Dimiter Uzunov, and Ljubomir Bodurov. Of special pride to the company is the superlative opera chorus. In recent decades the company has maintained some thirty-five operas in repertoire and has generally mounted five to six new productions each season. However, the current economic and political instability has severely curtailed the schedules of all Bulgarian theaters.

BIBLIOGRAPHY: Zlata Bozhkova, *Sofiiska Narodna Opera memoari* (Sofia, 1975). V. Krastev, *Entsiklopediya na balgarskata muzikalna kultura* (Sofia, 1967). Konstantin Mikhaylov-Stoyan, *Po vaprosa za osnovavaneto na Balgarskata narodna opera* (Sofia, 1907). *Narodna Opera Sofiya, 1944–1969* (Sofia, 1970). Eugenie Pantscheff, *Die Entwicklung der Oper in Bulgarien von ihren Anfangen bis 1915* (Wien, 1962).

ACCESS: Dondukov Boulevard, 58, Sofia 1500. (359 2) 88 43 65. Svetozar Donev, Director.

[From materials supplied by the company]

State Musical Theater "Stefan Makedonski"

The musical theater has always played a major role in Bulgarian culture. Classical operettas, revues, vaudeville, children's plays, and modern musical comedies have provided entertainment for a broad public over the years, and especially since the end of World War II. In a deliberate move to bring professionals together to explore this genre, the government established the State Musical Theater in 1948, and four years later renamed it in honor of the famous actor Stefan Makedonski. As the most recent manifestation of a Bulgarian involvement with operetta, which goes back some seventy-five years, the State Musical Theater is the heir to a tradition that reached its high point during the 1930s. At that time private ensembles such as the Free Theater of the Renaissance, the Cooperative Theater, and the Odeon performed numerous works for enthusiastic audiences. An impressive standard was established which survived the chaos of the war and was reborn in 1948.

Structured like a grand opera company, the State Musical Theater employs fifty-seven soloists, a chorus of fifty-four members, fifty-eight dancers, and an orchestra of eighty-nine musicians. Young performers are engaged for a trial season, and, if they succeed, receive a three-year contract. That, in turn, may lead to permanent employment. The ensemble serves as an apprentice program for professional work mainly because there is no academy or conservatory that trains singers in all the skills that they will need in a working theater. The artists are supported by a professional staff which includes 14 writers, producers, and directors as well as 198 technicians for production and stage work. All these people are supervised by a management team of 15 people. The heads of each department serve together as an advisory committee for long-range planning as well as daily activities. As the only major musical theater in Bulgaria, the State Musical Theater attracts young talent from throughout the country. In light of the recent economic and political changes, considerable thought is being given to new artistic directions, new sources of income, and new marketing strategies.

The previous situation in which the budget was part of overall state planning under the direction of a central Cultural Bureau is no longer applicable.

A similar situation exists with regard to the selection of repertoire for the company. In the past, works were chosen by a committee on the basis of the political situation. Seasons were filled with classic operettas, especially those by Soviet composers. During the 1960s a new generation brought a fresh aesthetic and new sensitivity to the company, and for the first time musicals from the West were introduced, albeit to mixed reactions. Works such as *My Fair Lady* and *Kiss Me Kate* appealed more to the younger generation, while the more nationalistic Bulgarian works by Dimiter Vocheff and Jewel Levi appealed to traditional taste. A golden age arrived in the 1970s with such works as *The Man from La Mancha*, *West Side Story*, *Oklahoma*, and *Cabaret*. The company toured to Moscow with *The Man from La Mancha* in 1973 and scored a tremendous success. Both audiences and critics were enthusiastic about the artists and the production itself.

During the 1980s the repertoire expanded to include works long considered standard fare in European opera houses such as *Die Fledermaus*, *La Belle Hélène*, *Der Zigeunerbaron*, *Die Lustige Witwe*, and *Eine Nacht in Venedig*. For the younger set, *The Fantastics* and other contemporary works were offered. Once or twice a season, gala performances of old classics were mounted to highlight the strengths of the company. Tours were undertaken throughout Bulgaria to bring these works to a broader public. In recent years increasing numbers of operas have been introduced into the repertoire and an attempt has been made to support native composers. Unfortunately, these works are often not competitive with the standard repertoire, as Bulgarian audiences have been isolated from major artistic trends for a number of years. This is not only a problem with audiences. Young performers are also limited in their training and come to the State Musical Theater with either musical, theatrical, or ballet training. An academy that offers training in a variety of lyric theater skills is an urgent priority in Bulgaria. Thus, the "Stefan Makedonski" has become, by default, a training ground.

Given the current economic and political conditions in the country, there is strong support for the introduction of a star system in which a stagione concept would replace the ensemble repertoire system. Only time will tell what approaches to keeping the theater alive and healthy will prevail. The current director is the actor Vidin Daskaloff. Supported by a talented ensemble of performers and directors, he is attempting to meet the challenges posed by the new social order. A major decision has been made to separate the company into segments specializing in opera, operetta, and musicals. Major tours are planned for the 1991–1992 season to the Soviet Union, Egypt, and Yugoslavia. Negotiations have been opened with Germany and Israel in the anticipation of future engagements. Moreover, a major planning effort is underway to finance the much-needed renovation and restoration of the theater itself, including the technical and storage facilities. The key problem for both the administration and the artists is exactly how to meet the new audience expectations, and especially those of the younger generation.

ACCESS: 3 P. Volov Street, Sofia 1500. Vidin Daskaloff, Director.

ROUMYANA KARAKOSTOVA
TRANS. PETER KALEV

Canada

EDMONTON (metro 785,465; city 573,982)

Edmonton Opera

Founded as a fur trading post during the exploration of the Canadian West, Edmonton today is the thriving capital city of the Province of Alberta. A large metropolitan population supports a rich cultural, academic, and sports community. Edmonton has more theaters per capita than any other city in Canada, and the Edmonton Symphony Orchestra and a variety of smaller serious music groups are very well attended, as is the Alberta Ballet. Edmonton is home to world champions in ice hockey, figure skating, and football, and it is not uncommon for sports personalities to appear as supernumeraries in operas such as *Aida*. The University of Alberta is a major research and educational institute with a growing Fine Arts department which regularly assists Edmonton Opera's Production Division.

In 1963 the tenor Jean Létourneau founded the Edmonton Professional Opera Association, and he served as artistic director until 1966. The first production was *Madama Butterfly* featuring Ermanno Mauro. Edmonton Opera was structured as a not-for-profit association with a volunteer board of directors responsible for governing artistic and financial policies, fund-raising, and advocacy. The general director was the chief executive officer responsible for administrative and artistic direction. The artistic director participated in artistic planning, including casting, and occasionally directing. Irving Guttman, the first artistic director of the Vancouver Opera (1960–1974), took over from Létourneau and has served in that capacity until the present day. The company's name was changed to the Edmonton Opera Association in 1966. Guttman has cast such luminaries as Sutherland (*Lucrezia Borgia* in 1972), Quillico, Sills, Carreras, and Neblett (the last three in their first Canadian performances) as well as many others in a variety of operas. Under Guttman, Maureen Forrester made her operatic debut in *Un Ballo in Maschera* in 1971 and sang her first Herodias in Richard Strauss's *Salome*, a production that won the Canadian Music Council Award for the best opera broadcast in 1977. In 1978 the Canadian premiere of Verdi's *Attilla* was recorded by the Canadian Broadcasting Corporation and again won the award for the best opera broadcast of the year. Guttman's contribution to the arts in Canada was unique, and in 1988 he was awarded the Order of Canada. The current general director, Robert Hallam, has strengthened the fiscal stability of the company by building an expanded subscriber base and soliciting government, foundation, and private support.

Ticket sales account for one-third of Edmonton Opera's annual budget of $2.6 million, with the balance donated from various public and private sources. All productions are mounted in the 2,690-seat Jubilee Auditorium and main-stage productions are typically 85 percent sold out. Edmonton Opera has a repertoire of more than forty operas and operettas. As a regional company, Edmonton Opera produces western Canadian and Edmonton premieres of both new and traditional works and is committed to developing the careers of young Canadian artists.

BIBLIOGRAPHY: *Edmonton Opera 25 Years: Silver Celebration* (Edmonton, 1988). *Opera Canada*, 1960– .

ACCESS: No. 202 11456 Jasper Avenue, Edmonton, Alberta T5K 0M1. (403) 482 7030; fax (403) 482 0916. Robert Hallam, General Director. Irving Guttman, Artistic Director.

[From materials supplied by the company]

MONTRÉAL (metro 2,921,357; city 1,015,420)

L'Opéra de Montréal

[Founded in 1642 as a French missionary outpost, Montréal evolved into the capital of Canada's musical life and remains to this day the second largest French-speaking city outside Paris. Opera was provided by touring companies until 1910 when Albert Clerk-Jeannotte organized a local repertory company. Although the Montreal Opera Company produced some thirteen operas in its initial season, the effort failed after just three years and was followed for one more season by the National Opera Company of Canada. Touring companies again provided short seasons. Les Variés Lyriques was founded in 1936 by Lionel Daunais and Charles Goulet and entertained large audiences until 1955 with a repertoire consisting mainly of operettas. Pauline Donalda, the legendary Canadian soprano who was renowned as the rival of Melba, founded the Opera Guild of Montreal in 1942 and acted as its artistic director until 1969. Twenty-nine operas were produced during this time, primarily from the standard repertoire, and the emphasis was on local artists. A major effort was begun in 1964 by the Montréal Symphony Orchestra (MSO) under Zubin Mehta in cooperation with the Place des Arts (a complex of three halls completed in 1967), and opera became a part of the MSO season until 1971. Performing at the 2,885-seat Salle Wilfrid Pelletier, which had opened in 1963, first-class productions of *Otello*, *Salome*, and *Tristan und Isolde* were mounted. At this time the provincial government, which had been subsidizing opera at the Place des Arts, formed l'Opéra du Québec, which suffered from a double season in both Montréal and Québec City and ended its productions in 1975.]

The Opéra de Montréal was founded in 1980 and produced Puccini's *Tosca* as its initial offering. During its first eight years of existence the company accumulated a deficit in excess of $1.3 million, and a thorough overhaul of the organization was undertaken. Bernard Uzan was brought in from the Tulsa Opera in 1988 as general director. In a move to consolidate the financial and artistic leadership, he was named artistic director in 1989, the same year in which Roger D. Landry was elected chairman of the Board of Directors. The new administration moved quickly to reorganize the company's structure and improve the management. During the 1989–1990 season the deficit was erased, the total annual budget rose to $7.1 million, and four major productions were mounted. André Gagnon's opera *Nelligan* had its world premiere and was given the Felix Award as the best production for 1990. The work paid tribute to one of Québec's greatest poets, Émile Nelligan, and attained a total of thirty performances in Montréal, Québec, and Ottawa, attracting some 25,000 spectators.

The Montréal Opera Guild was founded in June 1989 to assist the company financially and to promote the Opéra de Montréal on an international level. The Atelier lyrique provides musical and dramatic training for young Canadian artists. This young ensemble undertakes tours and outreach programs throughout the city with the help of the Conseil des Arts de la Communauté Urbaine de Montréal. Plans have been announced for an expanded 1991–1992 season which will include productions of *Tosca*, *Rigoletto*, *Eugene Onegin*, *Nabucco*, *La Belle Hélène*, *Il Barbiere di Siviglia*, and *Hänsel und Gretel*. The last two operas will feature the young artists of the Atelier lyrique.

BIBLIOGRAPHY: Ruth C. Brotman, *Pauline Donalda: The Life and Career of a Canadian Prima Donna* (Montreal, 1975).

ACCESS: 260, Boulevard de Maisonneuve Ouest, Montréal Québec H2X 1Y9. (514) 985 2222; fax (514) 985 2219. Bernard Uzan, Directeur général et artistique.

[From materials supplied by the company]

OTTAWA (metro 820,000; city 300,763)

National Arts Centre/Centre national des arts

In 1842 Queen Victoria's advisors prudently relocated the Canadian Parliament to Bytown, a small lumbering community at the juncture of French and English Canada, which also lay safely distant from Canada's formidable neighbors. Ottawa, as Bytown became, is now the core of a National Capital region that encompasses adjacent municipalities on both the Ontario and Quebec sides of the Ottawa river. The combined population of 820,000 reflects Canada's dual French and English heritage, and many residents are fluently bilingual in the two official languages. The National Arts Centre, a crown corporation enacted by the Canadian Parliament in 1963, was established in Ottawa to "develop the performing arts in the National Capital region and to assist the Canada Council in the development of the performing arts elsewhere in Canada." An impressive building occupying a 6.5-acre site on the bank of Rideau Canal, the National Arts Centre was officially opened in 1969. Before long the centre had become a dynamic presence in the fields of music, theater, dance, and variety in Canada, both as a national showcase and through the mounting of its own productions. The operas produced each summer as part of Festival Canada (1971–1977) and Festival Ottawa (1978–1983), in particular, won international recognition. By 1983, despite the Centre's achievements in the field of opera, successive funding cuts resulted in a dramatic decision to suspend the operations of Festival Ottawa, arguably its most prestigious and successful program. During a subsequent hiatus of five years, operas were given, with some exceptions, in concert performance only. By 1988, although funding levels continued to necessitate a high proportion of earned revenues, opera production had resumed on a limited basis, and the subsequent period has been one of reevaluation and rebuilding.

The National Arts Centre, completed in 1969 at a cost of $46 million, is an ideal facility in which to present opera. This is largely due to the advice of a committee of eminent Canadian music specialists, appointed in the early 1960s, which established the criteria for a hall and a resident orchestra that were to be the core of a national arts festival focused on opera and music. Facilities and personnel were put into place with this goal in mind. The handsome, unpretentious Opera Hall, the largest of the centre's four auditoriums, has been praised by many for its aesthetic, acoustical and technical attributes. The Earl of Harewood, in his report on opera in Canada in 1971, described it as "a real jewel" and saw the centre as an "inspiration to quality." Configured for opera, the hall has 2,133 seats and an orchestra pit designed to accommodate 110 musicians. To breathe life into the bricks and mortar, the National Arts Centre Orchestra (NACO), a classical orchestra of forty-six musicians, was established as a resident ensemble that could move from the concert stage to the orchestra pit for opera and ballet performances. Behind the scenes, a production staff was assembled to fabricate scenery, properties, and costumes in the centre's workshops and a technical staff was recruited to operate the stage equipment. In charge of these resources were Director General G. Hamilton Southam, General Manager Bruce Corder, and Music Director and principal conductor Mario Bernardi. Maestro Bernardi returned to Canada in 1967 from the Sadler's Wells Opera to become the architect of both the orchestral seasons and the festival program.

In July 1971 the curtain rose on a new production of Mozart's *Le Nozze di Figaro*, and opera was born at the National Arts Centre. The initial production, conceived by Sir Tyrone Guthrie but realized by Michael Geliot, was an immediate success and became a cornerstone of a Mozart repertory. This was a natural development since the NACO under Bernardi was building a reputation as Mozart specialists. The festival, running through the month of July, soon expanded to fourteen performances including two new productions, one revival, and ten to fifteen chamber concerts, recitals, and orchestral events. In the first five seasons the repertoire grew to include Mozart's *Così fan tutte*, *Don Giovanni*, *The Abduction from the Seraglio*, and *Die Zauberflöte*; Rossini's *Le Comte Ory*; Offenbach's *La belle Hélène*; and Verdi's *La Traviata*, in which Josephine Barstow made her Canadian debut. By 1975, particularly under Anthony Besch and Peter Rice's dazzling *Die Zauberflöte* the reputation of the orchestra and the festival was such that the *Toronto Star* called it "the Salzburg of the north."

In 1976 a new *Figaro*, this time directed by Lofti Mansouri and designed by Toni Businger, was widely praised. However, it was Tchaikovsky's *The Queen of Spades* that attracted international attention that summer for the striking scenography of Josef Svoboda, the conducting of Franz Paul Decker, and landmark performances by Canadian tenor Jon Vickers and contralto Maureen Forrester. For the next festival Kaslik and Svoboda repeated their successes when they teamed up in Strauss's *Ariadne auf Naxos*. During the following seasons the festival continued to delight audiences and critics alike with productions such as Britten's *A Midsummer Night's Dream* and Massenet's *Cendrillon* with Frederica von Stade, Maureen Forrester, and Louis Quilico, in 1979. In the early 1980s, productions of Donizetti's *La Fille du Régiment* and Mozart's *Idomeneo* were added to the repertoire.

Despite looming financial worries, a major production of Handel's *Rinaldo* with Marilyn Horne, Samuel Ramey, and Benita Valente was created in 1982 and then presented as a gift to the Metropolitan Opera Association for its one hundredth anniversary season. Frank Corsaro and Mark Negin's impressive realization of Handel's masterpiece became the first baroque opera ever presented at the "Met" where, with Mario Bernardi conducting, it was a highlight of the 1983–1984 season. A revival of *The Abduction from the Seraglio* in 1982 marked the final opera conducted by Maestro Bernardi, who had been a vital part of music and opera at the centre since it opened in 1969. In addition to his duties as music director, he had conducted twenty-five of the thirty-two productions presented during the first eleven festivals and many of the summer concerts as well. His departure coincided with an administrative reorganization of the Festival Department into the Music Department, which added summer programming to its responsibilities for the orchestra's concerts, tours, and chamber music programs.

The following year, Franco Mannino assumed the posts of principal conductor and artistic advisor with the Music Department. For Festival Ottawa 1983 he conducted Rossini's *La Cenerentola* in a spirited revival of Jean-Pierre Ponnelle's San Francisco Opera production. Maestro Mannino would conduct no other fully staged operas during his tenure at the centre, and his plans for future opera seasons were never realized. Although this was not known at the time, the second offering of the 1983 festival, John Copley's staging of Tchaikovsky's *Eugene*

Onegin, was to be the last created by Festival Ottawa. At the close of the season the centre's financial situation was precarious. A series of funding cuts begun in 1978 meant that in real dollars the 1983–1984 parliamentary appropriation was 14 percent less than that granted for the initial 1969 season. As the centre's policy has always been to refrain from competing with other arts organizations for private and foundation monies, an impossible situation faced Director General Donald MacSween. In a move designed both to avert financial crisis and to draw attention to the centre's predicament, he suspended Festival Ottawa.

Although dormant at home, Festival Ottawa's productions continued to be seen elsewhere. *Eugene Onegin* was broadcast by the Canadian Broadcasting Corporation, and Paris; Washington, D.C.; New York; Miami; Detroit; Quebec City; Montréal; Toronto; and Vancouver have all been host to one or more of the productions. Over the next few years, one or two operas were performed in concert versions each season, and Lehar's *The Merry Widow* and Handel's *Saul* were given staged productions. In 1988, Gabriel Chmura, newly appointed music director and principal conductor, announced a cycle of Mozart operas, and in July a revival of *Le Nozze di Figaro* relaunched opera at the centre. The year 1989 saw a revival of *Don Giovanni*, and 1990 featured an elegant new production of *Così fan tutte*, complete with surtitles in both English and French.

In its thirteen seasons the festival had sought to fulfill the centre's regional and national mandates by striving to set a benchmark of quality that would stimulate the growth of opera in Canada. In large measure it succeeded and won the support of the Canadian opera community. Chmura's Mozart cycle demonstrated the capacity of the centre to stage first-rate opera. Future plans, as described in a policy paper entitled *The Third Decade and Beyond*, lie in working closely with other Canadian opera companies on joint projects that will showcase their work in the national capital. As these links are nurtured and grow, the National Arts Centre should return to the forefront of opera production in Canada.

CHRONOLOGY OF MUSIC DIRECTORS: Mario Bernardi, 1967–82. Franco Mannino, 1982–86. Gabriel Chmura, 1987–90.

BIBLIOGRAPHY: Louis Applebaum and Jacques Herbert, *Report of the Federal Cultural Policy Review Committee* (Ottawa, Nov. 1982). Arnold Edinborough, *The Festivals of Canada* (Toronto, 1981). National Arts Center, *Annual Reports* (Ottawa, 1967–90). *Opera Canada*, 1960–

ACCESS: National Arts Centre, Music Department, P.O. Box 1534, Stn. "B", Ottawa, Ontario K1P 5W1. (613) 996 5051. Jack Mills, Music Producer.

MARK KRISTMANSON

TORONTO (metro 3,427,168; city, 612,289)

Canadian Opera Company

A company from Rochester, New York, gave Toronto its first taste of opera in 1825. Jenny Lind appeared there in 1851, but the first grand opera was Bellini's

Norma, given at the Royal Lyceum Theatre by the touring Artists' Italian Opera in 1853. The Holman English Opera Troupe, which first appeared in Toronto in 1858, resided at the Lyceum between 1867 and 1873, thus becoming Canada's earliest attempt at a permanent opera company. The present company's roots go back to 1946, when the Royal Conservatory of Music set up its own Opera School under Arnold Walter, with Nicholas Goldschmidt as music director. Herman Geiger-Torel joined as stage director two years later. Goldschmidt and Geiger-Torel mounted the school's first Opera Festival in February 1950. Shortly after the productions of *La Bohème*, *Don Giovanni*, and *Rigoletto* at the 1,525-seat Royal Alexandra Theater (1907, restored 1963), the Opera Festival Association was incorporated, and in 1954 it began to mount its own productions as the Opera Festival Company of Toronto. Formal connections with the conservatory were broken in 1957, and the next year it operated unofficially as the Canadian Opera Company. The name was officially changed to the Canadian Opera Association in 1960, but the company is still popularly kown as the COC. The main company was based in Toronto, and a touring company performed throughout North America initially with piano but later (1968) with orchestra. Herman Geiger-Torel became artistic director in 1956 and was named general director in 1959. The Toronto Symphony was contracted as the pit orchestra (1968–1976), thus solidifying the seasons of both organizations. Geiger-Torel served until his retirement in 1976, when he was succeeded by Lofti Mansouri, who increased the operating budget from $2.68 million in 1977 to $14.4 million in 1988, when he moved to San Francisco. Geiger-Torel's philosophy was to encourage and employ Canadian singers, and most of Canada's leading opera singers have performed with COC. Mansouri introduced the stagione system of long runs of a single opera throughout the year, a decision that resulted in the termination of the affiliation with the Toronto Symphony and negotiations with a company orchestra.

Throughout its history the Canadian Opera Company has performed in a variety of theaters in Toronto, from the Eaton Auditorium and the Royal Alexandra Theatre to Maple Leaf Gardens. However, since the building of the multipurpose 3,167-seat O'Keefe Centre in 1960, most of the company's large-scale productions have been mounted there. The COC moved into the Joey and Toby Tanenbaum Opera Centre in 1985; the building had formerly been a gasworks, knitting mill, and cherry factory. The renovation of the entire building was completed in 1987 and marked the first time that the company had its own home. All productions are currently rehearsed in the Opera Centre, which also houses the Imperial Oil Opera Theatre, administrative offices, the prop shop, and wig and makeup facilities. Costumes are built at Malabar costume house, and sets are constructed and stored in two other facilities. For more than a decade the COC has been actively seeking to build an opera house under whose roof the entire operation could be centralized.

The COC is committed to making opera more accessible, understandable, and enjoyable. Touring productions are presented in different areas of Canada each year, and in 1987 the COC established its first composers-in-residence program to encourage the composition of new operas. Actually, COC began producing world premieres in 1967 with Harry Somers' *Louis Riel* in 1967, and R. Murray Schafer's *PATRIA 1: The Characteristics Man* in 1987 was the seventh in a series of distinguished first performances. In 1983 the company introduced surtitles in a production of *Elektra*. This is an innovative process whereby a capsulized translation of an opera's libretto is projected onto a screen on the proscenium during the performance. The process has since been implemented by opera companies throughout North America and Europe, including the Royal Opera House Covent Garden, the Glyndebourne Festival Opera, the San Francisco Opera, and New York City Opera. Regular performances in schools, community centers, libraries, and senior citizen homes are capped by the Summer Festival which features opera performances in a tent at Harbourfront. The mainstage O'Keefe Centre performances are broadcast nationwide each year through the Canadian Broadcasting Corporation stereo network, and Texaco Canada Petroleum Incorporated's *Great Opera Peformances* are syndicated on more than two hundred public stations in the United States.

Funded by a grant from Imperial Oil Limited, the Canadian Opera Company Ensemble began in 1980. The establishment of the ensemble was the COC's first step toward developing a permanent roster of singers. The company is currently in the process of developing a resident company of Canadian artists, many of whom are former members of the original COC Ensemble. Under recently appointed (January 1989) General Director Brian Dickie, one of the company's major goals is to prepare artistically, logistically, and financially to move into the new Ballet Opera House which will be shared with the National Ballet of Canada. After many years of lobbying by the Ballet Opera House Corporation (which is jointly run by the COC and the National Ballet), the Province of Ontario committed $65 million plus the land for the site in the summer of 1988. Based on this commitment, the municipality of Metropolitan Toronto authorized another $20 million in April 1990, and the government of Canada authorized $88 million in September 1990. More than $100 million needs to be raised from the private sector. However, a change in the provincial government in September 1990 resulted in a withdrawal of the $65 million commitment, although the site was reaffirmed. Despite this substantial loss, the Ballet Opera House Corporation is actively pursuing alternative ways to keep the new complex on track. Designed by architect Moshe Safdie, the house is now scheduled to open sometime in the mid-1990s.

The 1990–1991 season, the COC's fortieth anniversary year, is the largest season in the company's history. It includes nine main-stage operas, seven of which will be presented at the O'Keefe Centre and two of which will be mounted in Toronto's newly restored 1,500-seat Elgin Theatre. Three of these operas, Mozart's *Così fan tutte*, and *La Clemenza di Tito* (both in the Elgin), and *Le Nozze di Figaro*, will be staged in June 1991 to coincide with the citywide bicentennial of the composer's death as part of the "Glory of Mozart" celebration. At the company's smaller theater space, the Imperial Oil Opera Theatre at the Joey and Toby Tanenbaum Opera Theatre, the COC presented Monteverdi's *The Coronation of Poppea*, a production that subsequently toured to six Ontario cities. Also scheduled at the Imperial Oil Opera Theatre is the world premiere of John Oliver's new opera, *Guacamayo's Old Song and Dance*.

BIBLIOGRAPHY: Earl of Harewood, *Opera in Canada: A Report* (Toronto, 1971). Lofti Mansouri and Aviva Layton, *Lofti Mansouri: An Operatic Life*, (Toronto, 1982). *Opera Canada*, 1960– . Kenneth Peglar, *Opera and the University of Toronto, 1946–1971* (Toronto, 1971). *Remembered Moments of the Canadian Opera Company, 1950–1975* (Toronto, 1976). Toronto *Telegram*.

ACCESS: 227 Front Street East, Toronto, Ontario M5A 1E8. (416) 363 6671; fax (416) 363 5584. Brian Dickie, General Director.

[From information supplied by the company]

VANCOUVER (metro 1,380,729; city 431,147)

Vancouver Opera

From humble beginnings as the western terminus of the transcontinental line of the Canadian Pacific Railway (CPR), Vancouver has grown to become the third largest city in Canada and the country's most important Pacific port. Serious operatic endeavors date from the inauguration of the CPR's Vancouver Opera House, which opened on February 9, 1891, with the Emma Juch English Opera touring company presenting Wagner's *Lohengrin*. For a number of reasons, the art form failed to take root, and staged performances of a professional caliber were rare until the 1950s. Founded in October 1958, Vancouver Opera (VO) presented its first production, *Carmen*, with Merriman, Cassilly, and Quilico, in April 1960. The stage director, Irving Guttman, was engaged as artistic director, a post he held until 1974. During his tenure the season gradually expanded to three full productions of between four and six performances each. Highlights of those years included Richard Bonynge conducting *Faust* (1963), Joan Sutherland and Marilyn Horne in *Norma* (1963), Placido Domingo in *Tosca* (1968), and Sutherland as Lucrezia Borgia (1972).

In the fall of 1966, Richard Keyes of the Royal Opera House Covent Garden was invited to come to Vancouver to set up a training program for young singers. Although the program only lasted three years, it demonstrated VO's commitment to nurturing young artists. At the end of the 1973–1974 season, Guttman left to establish the opera school at the Courtenay Youth Music Centre and to pursue guest staging opportunities, and Richard Bonynge was engaged to replace him. The season was expanded to four productions, and the repertoire that was presented was more adventurous. A new Canadian Artists' Program was instituted, but again the effort was phased out, this time after only two years. During his tenure Bonynge pressed for the creation of an Opera Orchestra—previously the musicians had been obtained from the Vancouver Symphony—and it was established in the fall of 1977.

Brian Hanson, general manager of the VO since 1969, was replaced by Barry Thompson, who had served as manager of the Edmonton Opera Association. In April 1978 Barry Thompson resigned and Hamilton McClymont was appointed general manager. He remained in that position until his resignation in May 1982. During McClymont's tenure, Vancouver Opera had its first and only principal conductor, Maestro Anton Guadagno. Cathrine Miciak took over from McClymont as interim general manager, followed by Valerie Beale as general manager, and Beverly Trifonidis, who assumed the post in November 1984. Irving Guttman returned as artistic director for the 1982–1983 and 1983–1984 seasons. Brian McMaster, general administrator of the Welsh National Opera, served as artistic director from 1984 to June 1989, a tenure that included the Canadian premieres of Janáček's *The Cunning Little Vixen* and *From the House of the Dead*.

BIBLIOGRAPHY: *Opera Canada*, 1960–

ACCESS: 1132 Hamilton Street, Vancouver, BC V6B 2S2. (604) 682 2871; fax (604) 682 3981. Beverly Trifonidis, General Manager. Guus Mostart, Artistic Director.

JOAN DRIEDGER

Chile

SANTIAGO (4,858,342)

Opera del Teatro Municipal

Founded in 1541, Santiago is the capital and cultural center of Chile. The country won its independence from Spain in 1818, and the political changes led to a fascination with Italian opera. Rossini, Bellini, Donizetti (whose *Lucia di Lammermoor* was premiered in 1844), and Mercadante (whose *Il Giuramento* opened in 1847) dominated the repertoire. The Teatro de la Universidad began regular opera seasons in 1844, and in 1853 the opera was moved to the larger and more elegant Teatro de la República. Verdi's *Ernani*, which had premiered in Venice on March 9, 1844, reached Santiago in 1847. This same work opened the new Teatro Municipal in 1857, and various theatrical entertainments have alternated in the house since that time. The nineteenth-century fascination with Italian opera was followed by an interest in the development of a national musical idiom, but the only native opera produced in Chile before the twentieth century was Eleodoro Oritz de Zárate's *La florista de Lugano* in 1895.

Following World War II there was an increased interest in bringing all the arts to the people. Cultural organizations such as the National Ballet and the various professional orchestras gave an expanding priority to broad artistic goals. The Municipal Theater [Teatro Municipal, which is run by the Corporacion Cultural De La I. Muncipalidad De Santiago], as one of the most active cultural centers in Latin America, sought to define long-term goals based on increasing the number and quality of productions in such a way as to open its program to the entire community. The first five-year plan, which was inaugurated in 1981, improved the orchestra, ballet, choir, and technical support staff without increasing the municipal subsidy. In fact, the public subsidy has remained constant over the past ten years. At the same time, the artistic level of the international seasons was improved through diverse and novel ways of financing. The Municipal Theater's opera season is among the finest in Latin America. Scheduled between May and November, it alternates with the symphony and ballet and normally offers five operas in a total of thirty performances. Works are double-cast with both national and international singers. In the last decade some forty-seven operas have been produced with a total of 320 performances. Among the international stars who have appeared in Santiago are Fiorenza Cosotto, Renata Scotto, Sylvia Sass, Paolo Montarsolo, and Richard Cassilly.

The marked improvement in artistic standards can be seen in a number of areas. For example, the Houston Grand Opera leased the Municipal Theater's production of *Samson et Dalila*, and the Teatro Municipal of Rio de Janeiro is a partner on a coproduction of *Eugene Onegin*. Moreover, young Chilean singers are making their mark at the international level. Verónica Villaroel, Viviana Hernández, Graciela Araya, Carmen Luisa Leteller, Teresa Lagarde, Santiago Villablanca, and Patricia Brockman all perform widely outside of Chile. The public has responded to the improvements, and audiences are up some 300 percent over the last decade. The 1990 season consisted of *Salome*, *Madama Butterly*, *La Fille du Régiment*, *Cavalleria Rusticana*, *I Pagliacci*, and *Faust*.

BIBLIOGRAPHY: Mario Cànepa Guzmán, *La ópera en Chile, 1839–1930* (Santiago, 1976). Samuel Claro Valdés and Jorge Urrutia Blondel, *Historia de la música en Chile* (Santiago, 1973).

ACCESS: Castilla 3680, Santiago. (56 2) 332804; fax (56 2) 337214. Andres Rodriguez P., Director General.

[From materials supplied by the company]
TRANS. DELFINA SABOGAL-TORI

People's Republic of China

BEIJING (9,750,000)

Central Opera Theater

[Peking opera is by far the most famous type of regional theater in China. Two styles, *erh-haung* and *his-p'i* were introduced into Peking around 1790 and formed the core of what was to become a combination social and theatrical event. Eventually fostered and supported by the Imperial Court under the Empress Dowager Tz'u-hsi, the form flourished until the fall of the Manchu dynasty in 1911. Important citizens continued to support Peking opera during the republican period (1912–1949). With the establishment of the communist People's Republic of China, the more traditional opera has waxed and waned, and changes have been made in themes and texts to support the aims of the revolution. The Beijing Opera is the principal company and is located at Ho Fang Jiao. The company can be reached at (86 1) 338 149. As it celebrates its two hundredth birthday, the form is no longer popular with the majority of citizens, and its future is in question.]

The Central Opera Theater in China, founded in 1953, is New China's first state-run opera theater. Adopting techniques of European vocal music and orchestra, and using both the form and creative experience of European opera for reference, the Central Opera Theater creates and produces works with distinctive Chinese national features. For the purpose of enriching the cultural life of the Chinese people and promoting cultural exchanges with other countries, the Central Opera Theater not only performs Chinese operas but also introduces to the Chinese audience world-famous classical and contemporary operas from other countries.

The Central Opera Theater has the largest contingent of opera performers in China, including both older artists who have made major contributions to the cause of opera in the past decades and younger performers who have established themselves in recent years. Among them, a number have won awards in vocal music competitions at home and abroad. Supporting the singers is a professional orchestra as well as a team of costume and set designers and builders. With a professional organization of writers, composers, conductors, directors, designers, and performers, the Central Opera Theater has built a strong audience following. National works such as *Liu Hulan* (1954), *The Song of the Grassland* (1955), *Thunder in Spring* (1959), *Wangfu Cloud* (1962), *Ayguli* (1966), and *The Great Wall of South China Sea* (1966) formed the basis for a later birth of a European-type opera with distinctly Chinese characteristics. Complementing this repertoire are standard operatic fare such as *La Traviata* (1956), *Madama Butterfly* (1958), and *Eugene Onegin* (1962). The company was relatively inactive during the Cultural Revolution (1966–1975), but the Central Opera Theater was restored to its earlier status toward the end of the 1970s. New productions of *Carmen* (1982) and *Le Nozze di Figaro* (1984) played to enthusiastic audiences. In 1985 the company broke new ground with *The Fantasticks*, followed by *The Music Man* in 1987. Luciano Pavarotti conducted a very popular master class for young artists at the Central Opera Theater in 1986.

The company has premiered a number of new works in an attempt to broaden the repertoire. *Flower-Guardian* (1979), *Peng Dehuai Sits on the Sedan Chair* (1980), *The Hundredth Bride* (1981), *The Youth of Today* (1982), *The Wedding Sonata* (1983), and *The Homeland* (1984) are all examples of contemporary Chinese opera. Several of these works were honored with prizes from the Chinese Ministry of Culture. The company's production of *La Traviata* won the Outstanding Performing Prize in 1979 on the celebration of the thirtieth anniversary of National Day. Moreover, the live recording of the company's performance of *Carmen* won the Charles Cros Grand Prix Internationale Du Disque in France in 1983. The Central Opera Theater (COT) toured the Soviet Union in 1958 and Japan in 1987. The trip to Japan featured a production of *Nymph—Ono no komachi*, an opera based on an ancient Japanese legend. In 1988 the company brought *Madama Butterfly* and *Carmen* to Hong Kong, and that same year the Savonlinna Opera Festival in Finland featured both productions. The company continues to attempt to bring the best of European and Chinese opera to audiences in the People's Republic as well as to the rest of the world. The COT frequently sends small touring ensembles to the villages to bring programs to the widest possible audience in China. Currently there are 110 artists, a 76-member orchestra, 42 production personnel, and 23 directors and designers.

BIBLIOGRAPHY: R. Alley, *Peking Opera* (San Francisco, 1984). C. Mackerras, *The Chinese Theatre in Modern Times from 1840 to the Present Day* (London, 1975). C. Mackerras, *The Rise of the Peking Opera, 1770–1870: Social Aspects of the Theatre in Manchu China* (Oxford, 1972).

ACCESS: Dong Zhi Men Wai Zuo Jia Zhuang, Beijing. (86 1) Operator. Liu Lian-Chi, Director.

LIU LIAN-CHI

SHANGHAI (12,320,000)

Shanghai Opera House

Like Beijing, the capital of China, Shanghai is an independent municipality and not under the jurisdiction of the provincial government. Officially created by the municipal government in October 1956, the Shanghai Opera House is charged with fostering and producing the finest works of Chinese dance, drama, and opera. Its immediate predecessor was the Shanghai Experimental Opera House which was a loose configuration of four independent performance companies. Important Chinese operas in a repertoire of over sixty large works include *The Marriage of Xiao Er-hei*, *The White-Haired Girl*, *Jiang Sister*, *The Red Guards of Hong-hu Lake*, *The Story of West Chamber*, and *Yue Fei*. Beginning in the 1960s the company began to produce European operas, and *Madama Butterfly*, *La Bohème*, *Tosca*, and *Così fan tutte* were all premiered in Shanghai. *Turandot* is scheduled as the major production for 1990 in an opera season that generally includes the months of May and October. The rest of the year is filled with various entertainments of both Chinese and European origin. The production schedule normally includes some two hundred performances per year.

BIBLIOGRAPHY: R. Alley, *Peking Opera* (San Francisco, 1984). C. Mackerras, *The Chinese Theatre in Modern Times from 1840 to the Present Day* (London, 1975). C. Mackerras, *The Rise of the Peking Opera, 1770–1870: Social Aspects of the Theatre in Manchu China* (Oxford, 1972).

ACCESS: 10, Lane 100, Changshu Road, Shanghai 2000 40. (86 21) 335359. Shi Hong-E, Director.

SHI HONG-E

Czechoslovakia

BRATISLAVA (1,725,766)

Slovenské Národné Divadlo (Slovak National Theater)

[The capital of the kingdom of Hungary from 1563 to 1853, Bratislava has a long and illustrious history as the center of Slovak musical life. Until World War I, Bohemia, Moravia, and Slovakia were provinces of the Hapsburg Empire. After Austria-Hungary entered the war, Czech and Slovak nationalists met in the United States and signed the Pittsburgh Agreement which provided for equal representation in a provisional government. In 1918 Czechoslovakia declared itself an independent country (Bratislava was the capital of Slovakia), and this free republic lasted until Nazi Germany successfully pressed territorial claims in 1938. The resulting Munich Pact gave national territory to Germany, Hungary, and Poland, and in 1939 the republic ceased to exist as a political entity. Following World War II, Czechoslovakia became a socialist country allied to the Soviet Union, a relationship that is currently in flux. An opera house was first built on the site of the present theater in 1776, and there are records of regular Italian opera performances beginning in 1791. The current opera house opened in 1886, and performances in German, Italian, and Hungarian predominated until 1919, when on December 10, Smetana's *The Bartered Bride* opened, which was sung in Slovakian. Nineteen twenty saw the beginning of the Slovak National Opera Society with a performance of Smetana's *The Kiss* on March 1.]

The Slovak National Theater (SNT), founded in 1920, is a theater of a central European type supporting an opera, a ballet, and a drama company. Each of the ensembles is autonomous, with its own artistic director. Until 1955 all three companies performed in the former 611-seat Town Theater built by Hellmer and Fellner. When the drama company moved into its new house in 1955, the SNT was renamed the Opera House. A new theater complex with three stages is under construction and should be completed in 1995. The SNT Opera performs some

165 times between September and June, with a repertoire that includes baroque operas, standard repertoire, and contemporary Slovak works. The artistic orientation of the company was strongly influenced by Milan Zuna, Oskar Nedbal, and Karel Nedbal during the 1920s and 1930s. In 1924 the company toured to Barcelona and Madrid with Smetana's *The Bartered Bride* and Dvořák's *Rusalka*. In 1926 Oskar Nedbal staged the company's first Slovak opera, the neo-Romantic *Wieland the Smith* by Ján Levoslav Bella. By the 1930s the company had become a major force on the Central European operatic scene. Under the leadership of Karel Nedbal, productions embraced not only national and international classics but also numerous operas by Leoš Janáček and Richard Strauss. The company mounted the Czech premiere of Prokofiev's *The Love for Three Oranges* in 1931, and in 1935 staged the first production of Shostakovich's *Lady Macbeth* to be mounted outside the Soviet Union. During the decade, annual tours were made to Vienna in exchange for guest performances by the Wiener Volksoper in Bratislava. Between 1920 and 1938 a number of prominent artists appeared at the opera: Mascagni, Richard Strauss, and Lucon; the sopranos Destinnová, Novotná, Huni-Mihacsek, Németh, Sari, Pauly, and Kunc-Milanov; mezzos Anday and Olezevska; tenors Burian, Mařák, Smirnov, Slezák, Pataky, Graarud, Tauber, Fleta, and Dermota; baritones Baklanov, Jerger, and Svéd; and basses Ludikar and Shaliapin.

Since 1945 the opera has been closely connected with and influenced by the intense development of original Slovak operatic work. Eugen Suchoň's *The Whirlpool* premiered in Bratislava in 1949 prior to an extensive foreign tour. The world premieres of Suchoň's historical opera *Svätopluk* (1960) and five operas by Ján Cikker, *Juro Jánošik* (1954), *Beg Bajazid* (1957), *The Verdict* (1979), *The Siege of Bystrica* (1983), and *The Insect Play* (1987) all took place on the SNT stage. Among other important contemporary works produced by SNT are *The Emperor's New Clothes* (1969) by Juraj Beneš, *The Lady of the Dawn* (1976) and *The Teardance* (1979) by Bartolomej Urbanec, and the *Opera-Collage* (1986) by Tibor Frešo. Between 1971 and 1977, while Zdenek Košler was in charge, notable productions included Janáček's *The Macropulos Case*, Bartok's *Bluebeard's Castle*, and a new production of Cikker's masterpiece, *Resurrection*. Some of the artistic highlights of the past decade include the Slovak premiere of Berg's *Wozzeck*, an unconventional modern staging of Verdi's *Rigoletto*, and the production of Gounod's *Faust*, which appeared at the 1990 Edinburgh Festival.

Among current principal artists, Peter Dvorský and Sergej Kopčák appear in major opera houses all over the world, and Lucia Popp, Edita Grunberová, Gabriela Beňačková, and Magdaléna all started their professional careers on the Bratislava stage. In recent years the company has represented Slovak culture at festivals in Wiesbaden, Oviedo, and Edinburgh, and the ensemble has toured throughout Europe and the USSR. SNT has also hosted major operatic companies, including the Bolshoi, Sofia National Opera (Sofiyska Narodna Opera), State Opera and Komische Oper Berlin, Belgrade National Opera (Opera Narodnog Pozorista u Beograda), Wiener (Vienna) Volksoper, the Opera of the Stanislavski, and Nemirovich-Danchenko Theater, as well as companies from Leipzig, Lódž, Antwerp, Ljubljana, and Leningrad. The current repertoire includes twenty-three operas by fourteen composers. The supporting house orchestra, the Bratislava Symphony Orchestra, also presents symphony concerts.

BIBLIOGRAPHY: Štephan Hoza, *Opera na Slovensku*, 2 vols. (Bratislava, 1953). *Pamätnica Slovenského národného divaldá* (Bratislava, 1960).

ACCESS: Gorkého č. 4, 815 86 Bratislava. (42 7) 542 26. Miloš Pietor, Director, SNT. Juraj Hrubant, Artistic Director, SNT Opera.

JULIUS GYERMEK

BRNO (2,058,530)

Janáček's Opera Brno

Founded in the 800s, Brno was the original capital of Moravia. German influences prevailed, especially after the battle of White Mountain in 1620 diluted Czech cultural characteristics, but the creation of the Czechoslovakian Republic after World War I gave impetus to the establishment of indigenous organizations. The musical history of the city, and especially of opera, is dominated by the figure of Leoš Janáček, one of the musical titans of the country. German Singspiels probably mark the beginning of musical theater in Brno, but the presentations of Gluck's *Orfeo ed Euridice* in 1779, Beethoven's *Fidelio* in 1811, and Weber's *Der Freischütz* in 1822 clearly indicate an interest in serious musical drama. Given the German influences, it was inevitable that the first permanent opera house in the city would be the new 1,200-seat German theater that opened in 1882. Taking its lead from Vienna, both the technically up-to-date house and the repertoire followed German models. The Czechs countered with an unassuming theater two years later, and for the first decade, as the Provisional Theater, an attempt was made to produce works for the local taste. In 1894 the theater was renovated as the National Theater, and Janáček's *Jenufa* was premiered there on January 21, 1904, as *Jeff Pastorkyna*. This was the first of the composer's operas to be produced, and its premiere went almost unnoticed. The Prague premiere of *Jenufa* on May 26, 1916, attracted far more attention. Of the composer's nine operas, all but *Výlety páně Broučkovy* (*The Excursions of Mr. Brouček*) were premiered in Brno.

When Czechoslovakia achieved independence in 1918, the former German City Theater became the home of the Czech National Theater Company and the premieres of *Káťa Kabanová* (November 23, 1921), *Příhody lišky Bystruošky* (*The Cunning Little Vixen* on November 26, 1924), *Věc Makropulos* (December 18, 1926), and *Z mrtvého domu* (*From the House of the Dead* on April 12, 1930) were all premiered there. The new 1,400-seat Janáček Theater opened in 1945 as the largest and most technically advanced theater in the country at that time, and a fitting memorial to a native son.

BIBLIOGRAPHY: Gustav Bondi, *Geschichte des Brunner Deutschen Theaters, 1600–1924* (Brunn, 1924). I. Horsbrugh, *Leoš Janáček* (London, 1981). A Němcová and S. Přibáňová, *Příspěvek k dějinám opery Národniho divadla v Brně, 1884–1919* (Brno, 1963). A. Rille, *Die Geschichte des Brünner Stadttheaters, 1734–1884* (Brno, 1885) J. Vogel, *Leoš Janáček: His Life and Works* (London, 1962).

ACCESS: Dvorákova 11, 657 70 Brno. (42 5) 26311. František Preisler, Director.

[From materials supplied by the company]

PRAGUE (1,122,023)

Národní Divadlo Prague (National Theater Prague)

Once the new art form had been articulated in Florence, it did not take long for opera to appear at the court in Prague. With its excellent court orchestra, the city was a suitable home for Emperor Rudolf II, who was devoted to music. Touring Italian ensembles provided the initial performances, but by the beginning of the eighteenth century Prague had a public theater of its own. Three noblemen, Count Sporck, Count Thun, and Count Nostitz, all supported opera. The latter built a theater for plays and opera on Carolinplatz in which Mozart's *Le Nozze di Figaro* was produced only seven months after its Vienna premiere. This was the same theater in which *Don Giovanni* was premiered on October 29, 1787, followed by *La Clemenza di Tito* in honor of Emperor Leopold II on September 6, 1791. A number of outstanding artists have been associated with this theater, including Carl Maria von Weber, Richard Wagner, Gustav Mahler, Carl Muck, and Wilhelmine Schröder-Devrient. The first Czech opera, František Škroup's *Dráteník*, was premiered here on February 2, 1826. The completely renovated theater is still in active use.

Prague's earliest permanent theater was begun by the official 120-member Board for the Founding of the Czech National Theater which was established by the Bohemian Diet. The resulting building was designed by Josef Zítek, who had won the spirited competition, and the foundation stone was laid on May 16, 1868. Zítek had projected a magnificent building in neo-Renaissance style, in spite of the fact that the site was much too small, a problem that would only be remedied after World War II. A gala performance of Smetana's *Libuse* was given in honor of Crown Prince Rudolf on June 11, 1881, with the official opening scheduled for September 11. However, tragedy struck on August 12 when the inside of the almost completed theater was gutted by fire. The board quickly raised additional monies and, expanded and restored by Zítek's disciple, Josef Schulz, the new 1,129-seat Czech National Theater [Národní divadlo] opened on November 18, 1883, with another performance of *Libuse*. Czech opera was now free to develop its own ensemble with indigenous national characteristics to distinguish it from the dominant German culture. This was the period of the masterpieces of Bedrich Smetana, and eight of the composer's works, led by *The Bartered Bride* (1866), remain to this day in the forefront of the National

Theater repertoire. From the beginning, however, the National Theater fostered an international repertoire, as evidenced by the works of Gluck, Mozart, Weber, Wagner, Rossini, Bellini, and Thomas, which were produced as early as the second season.

The first director was František Adolf Šubert, who led the company for thirteen years and built an excellent ensemble of singers and actors. The opening of the National Theater marked the beginning of equality between the Czech and German cultures. In 1887 the German opera moved into a new 1,050-seat theater, currently named the Smetanovo Divadlo, which is now the second opera house of the National Theater. The National Theater was from the beginning a two- or three-branch theater, with opera the most important art form. Alongside the operas of Smetana, the works of Dvořák, Fibich, and Blodek, as well as the new Italian and French works such as *Aida* and *Carmen*, were produced. Russian operas and ballets were introduced, including the first performances of Tchaikovsky's *Eugene Onegin* (December 6, 1888, in Czech) outside Russia. Under the leadership of the conductor/composer Karel Kovařovic, the National Theater/ Opera embraced current operatic trends during the first decade of the twentieth century. Premieres of such works as Massenet's *Werther* (January 13, 1901), Charpentier's *Louise* (February 13, 1903), Puccini's *Tosca* (November 21, 1903), Strauss's *Elektra* (April 25, 1910), and *Der Rosenkavalier* (March 4, 1911, barely six weeks after the Dresden premiere) shared the stage with the works of Richard Wagner. This was also the time of world-renowned singers such as Otakar Marák, Karl and Emil Burian, and Ema Destinová [Emmy Destinn].

The founding of the Czechoslovakian Republic on October 28, 1918, brought the administration of the National Theater under the civil authorities. With the death of Kovařovic on December 6, 1920, the conductor/composer Otakar Ostrcil took the reins and led the opera company from 1921 to 1935, producing ten cycles of Czech operas as well as a Mozart cycle during his tenure. He revived the works of Leoš Janáček, and he produced Berg's *Wozzeck* as early as November 11, 1926—the first production outside Germany. His successor was the long-time head of the Czech Philharmonic, Václav Talich, who concentrated his efforts on bringing the important works of German composers to the stage—Beethoven, Mozart, and Strauss. During the hectic days of fall 1938, the anti-Nazi Neue Deutsche Theater in Prague closed its doors, thus ending the friendly rivalry of the two opera houses. The National Theater was able to continue until September 1, 1944. Shortly after the end of the war a second Czech ensemble performed in the Neue Deutsche Theater building, but in 1948 the National Theater annexed the house (now the Smetana Theater located at Vitezného února; telephone [42 2] 269746), thus creating the current configuration, namely; one large company of soloists, two orchestras, and two choirs performing repertoire in three locations simultaneously. The former Neue Deutsche Theater, which had opened in January 1888, also had a distinguished history. It was the home of such outstanding conductors as Leo Blech, Otto Klemperer, Arthur Bodansky, Erich Kleiber, Alexander Zemlinsky, William Steinberg, and George Szell, as well as the singers Leo Slezak, Alfred Piccaver, Friedrich Schorr, Hans Hotter, Kurt Baum, Risë Stevens, Harriet Henders, Rosa Pauly, and Hilde Konetzni.

The Smetana Theater was completely renovated and refurbished between June 1967 and March 1973, and additional space was built for rehearsal facilities and administration. Shortly thereafter, on April 2, 1977, the National Theater was closed for six years in order to refurbish the house in time for its one hundredth anniversary celebration. The historical building was carefully restored, and state-of-the-art technical equipment was installed. A 500-seat experimental theater was added next to the National Theater, and a new building with rehearsal rooms, offices, and public rooms was constructed. Every effort was made to retain the original look and feel of the buildings while at the same time bringing them up to modern theatrical standards.

Since the war, the emphasis has been on Slavic repertoire. For example, Zdenek Chalabala conducted a cycle of Prokofiev operas and ballets in 1963. The operas of Smetana, Dvořák, Janáček, and Martinů form the basis of the repertoire. The company has continued to appoint outstanding Czech composers and conductors to important positions: O. Jeremiás; J. Seidl, the present National Theater director; Jirí Pauer; J. Krombholc; Z. Kosler; F. Vajnar; and, since August 1987, Václav Riedlbauch. Effective September 1990, Ivo Žídek, for a number of years the leading tenor of the company, became intendant, and the bass Dalibor Jedlička was apppointed head of the opera. The present repertoire of the National Theater/Opera includes approximately thirty-five operas divided more or less equally between the international repertoire and works by Czech composers. The schedule includes representative standard operas and such novelties as Debussy's *Pelléas et Mélisande*, Strauss's *Die schweigsame Frau*, Prokofiev's *Die Verlobung*, and Stravinsky's *Oedipus Rex*. Each month thirty-five to forty operas and twelve to fourteen ballets are performed. Five or six operas and two or three ballets are offered in new productions each season, and the operas are cast with seventy-four permanent soloists.

The annals of the National Theater indicate that the company has during its history made sixty tours to twenty countries, including Japan, performing works from its normal repertoire. Most of the operas are performed in Czech, with Mozart's *Don Giovanni* and a few Italian operas being the exceptions. Occasional guest artists from all over the world are engaged for special productions, especially during the International Prague Spring Festival. The season lasts from the beginning of September to the end of June, with musical events alternating with plays. All types of entertainment are scheduled in the new 500-seat Ständetheater—the third theater in the expanded complex—which has become the permanent home of the Laterna magica. The recording firm of Supraphon has systematically released all eight operas of Smetana and most of the stage works of Dvořák as well as some of the works of Zdeněk Fibich, Vilém Blodek, Josef Bohuslav Foerster, and Vítězslav Novák utilizing artists of the National Theater. In addition to the works of Janáček and Martinů, a number of contemporary composers have been recorded.

CHRONOLOGY OF DIRECTORS: František Šubert, 1883–1900. Karel Kovařovik, 1900–1920. Otakar Ostrčil, 1921–1935. Vávlav Talich, 1936–1945. Jiři Panner, 1946–1952. Jiři Pauer, 1953–1955. Ivo Zídek, 1990–present.

BIBLIOGRAPHY: Pavel Eckstein, *A Brief Outline of Czechoslovak Opera* (Prague, 1964). Pavel Eckstein, *The Czechoslovak Contemporary Opera: Pictures and Information* (Prague, 1967). Jan Němecek, *Opera Národního Divdla v období Karla Kovařovice, 1900–1920*, 2 vols. (Praha, 1968). Otakar Novy, *Narodni Divadlo 1883–1983: A Short History of its construction* . . . (Prague, 1983). František Pala, *Opera Národního Divadla v období otakara ostrčila*, 4 vols. (Praha, 1962–70). Tomislav Volek, *Repertoire Nosticovského Divadla v Praze z let 1794, 1796–97* (Praha, 1961).

ACCESS: Pošt Přihrádka 865, 112 30 Praha 1. (42 2) 203128; fax (42 2) 232 12 06. Ivo Žídek, Director.

PAVEL ECKSTEIN
TRANS. MARC ÄNDERS

Denmark

COPENHAGEN (5,301,400)

Det Kongelige Teater og Kapel

As the capital and cultural center of Denmark, Copenhagen (derived from Købmandehavn or Merchant's Harbor) dates from the eleventh century, when it was a fishing village. Its natural harbor destined the area as a center for trade, and in 1416 it became the capital of the country. Music began to flourish in the fifteenth and sixteenth centuries, assuming an international character by the seventeenth century under Frederik III and Christian V. Ballet and opera in both the French and Italian styles were popular, and an opera house was built in Copenhagen in 1702. The broader public gained access to opera when a new theater later renamed the Royal Theater opened in 1748. Pietro Mingotti, among others, presented seasons of Italian opera there. A national Singspiel tradition was established during the second half of the century by J. E. Hartmann's *Balders død* (1779) and *Fiskerne* (1780). The introduction of Italian opera, particularly Rossini, during the 1820s influenced native composers, and from this time on Danish opera assumed a more European form. The founder of the modern Danish school, Carl Neilsen (1865–1931), was the leading figure in opera, with *Saul og David* (premiered November 28, 1902) and *Maskarade* (premiered November 11, 1906) one of the best Danish comic operas. The noted composer was appointed Kapelmester (music director) in 1908 and proved to be a strong supporter of the works of Richard Wagner during his appointment, which lasted until his resignation in 1914. The complete "Ring" tetralogy received its Danish premiere between April 30 and May 5, 1909, and was performed in Danish. Lauritz Melchior debuted as Silvio in *Pagliacci* during Neilsen's tenure, on April 2, 1913. Melchior's debut as a tenor was in the same house on October 8, 1918, as Tannhaüser. The country has been a constitutional monarchy since 1849, and the arts are strongly supported by both the populace and the royal family. The

Royal Opera gives performances on the Old Stage, which dates from 1874, and the New Stage, which opened in 1931 adjacent to the Old Stage.

BIBLIOGRAPHY: K. Altung, *Det Kongelige Teater, 1889–1939* (København, 1942). A Aumont and E. Collin, *Det danske Nationaltheater, 1748–1889* (København, 1896–1899). Georg Leicht and Marianne Hallar, *Det Kongelige Teaters repertoire, 1889–1975* (København, 1977). A. E. Müller, *Die Mingottischen Opern-Unternehmungen, 1732–1756* (Dresden, 1915). R. Neiiendam, *Det Kongeliges Teaters historie* (København, 1921–1970). Gerhard Schepelern, *Italierne paa hofteateret*, 2 vols. (København, 1976).

ACCESS: Postboks 2185, DK-1017 København K. (45 1) 322020; Gamle Scene (45 1) 141765; Nye Scene (45 1) 143285; fax (45 1) 144606. Poul Jørgensen, General Manager.

[From materials supplied by the company]

Estonia

TARTU (est. 110,000)

Teatre Vanemuine

[Modern Estonia dates from the Treaty of Nystad in 1721, when Sweden deeded the territory to Russia after the Great Northern War. Following the revolution, Estonia declared its independence in 1918 and in 1920 signed a treaty with the Soviet Union that confirmed the Estonian government. A year after Estonia was annexed as a republic of the Soviet Union on August 6, 1940, Nazi Germany invaded the country and occupied it until it was driven out in 1944. Tartu has been the cultural and religious center of the country for hundreds of years, and the first university in the Baltic states was founded there by the Swedes in 1632.] The theater of Vanemuine was founded in 1870, shortly after the first Estonian song festival formalized fifty years of native choral activity. That same year the Estonia Theater was founded in Tallinn, so we can date the beginning of Estonian theater from that time. From 1878 to 1903 the destiny of the theater was guided by August Wiera, under whose initiative the first musical theater piece was produced, P. A. Wolff's *Preciosa* with an overture and musical numbers modeled after the operas of Carl Maria von Weber. The first complete opera, Etienne Méhul's *Joseph*, premiered in 1899. The same opera had premiered in Stockholm in 1856 and would be performed in Estonian in Tallinn in 1919. In 1906 a new theater building was completed, and Karl Menning, who was a disciple of Max Reinhardt and Otto Brahm, took over as director of Vanemuine. Menning was responsible for its development as a professional theater. In 1908 the theater orchestra began to give regular symphony concerts, an activity that continues to the present day.

In 1915 Menning left and the theater reverted to producing mostly popular operettas. It was not until 1935 that the first Estonian opera was produced. *The Vikings* by Evald Aav signaled an artistic change with important national consequences. Eino Uuli was appointed opera producer and Eduard Tubin became the principal conductor. Their dedication to quality brought the artistic level of Vanemuine to new heights. Together with Ida Urbel, who headed the new ballet program, they molded the characteristic of Vanemuine seasons; for examples, ballet, drama, opera, and musical theater. In 1939, just prior to World War II, the theater was rebuilt and a new 500-seat hall was added. The complex was totally destroyed in 1944, and for the next twenty-three years Vanemuine performed in the former Germain Theater. In 1967 a new complex opened with a 682-seat theater and an 838-seat concert hall. Performances continued in the old Germain Theater, which now was known as the Small House.

The actor Kaarel Ird led the company from 1940 to 1986, staging everything except ballets, and his productions played regularly in both Leningrad and Moscow. One of his trademark productions was Tchaikovsky's *The Queen of Spades*. In 1950 *Flames of Vengeance* by Estonian composer Eugen Kapp inaugurated a series of open-air performances, and Gustav Ernesak's *Baptism of Fire* (1958) was notable as an example of the work of native composers. From 1986 Theater Vanemuine has been led by Ago-Endrik Kerge. His production of Rossini's *Il Barbiere di Siviglia* (1981) and Mozart's *Le Nozze di Figaro* (1983) earned high praise and remain in the repertoire. Vanemuine gives approximately 180 musical performances (opera, operetta, and ballet) each season and averages four premieres each year, which are attended by some seventy-six thousand spectators. In recent years ideological pressures have declined, and each theater is now free to develop its own repertoire so the offerings are more diverse. In addition, Vanemuine has explored cooperative efforts, including the exchange of artistic personnel with other theaters. Close working relations currently exist with Potsdam and Olomouc (Czechoslovakia), and contacts have been made with Tampere Theater in Finland and Uppsala Stadtstheater in Sweden. The latest partners are the theaters of Liberec (Czechoslovakia) and Lüneberg.

With the growth of independence, Vanemuine must cover an increasing percentage of its own costs; at present it must pay for some 35 percent. Tickets are quite inexpensive, but the audience is declining in real terms due to economic constraints. With a company of some five hundred, half of whom belong to the artistic staff, both production and touring costs are under great pressures. The orchestra of some sixty members has recently formed the Tartu Symphonics, a concert group that is supported by the city government. The significance of Vanemuine is not only confined to the cultural life of Tartu. As one of the two Estonian opera houses—the other is the Estonia Theater in Tallinn—it determines to a considerable extent the picture of opera and ballet in the entire country. Lavish productions not possible elsewhere in the country are a major attraction to citizens from the entire Baltic region.

ACCESS: RAT "Vanemuine," Vanemuise tn. 6, 202400 Estonia/Tartu. (7 97) 34 159; 33 885/324; fax (7 97) 01434 31466. Ago-Endrik Kerge, Artistic Director. Mart Raik, Managing Director.

KALLE HEIN

Finland

HELSINKI (metro 987,009; city 489,965)

Finnish National Opera

[Finland was under Swedish rule until the end of the war with Tsarist Russia when, under the 1809 Treaty of Hamina, it became a grand duchy in the Russian Empire. The capital was moved to Helsinki in 1812, and gradually the city began to assume cultural importance. Touring companies from Germany and Italy presented operas, but no native opera took root. When independence was achieved in 1917, Finnish musical life was freed to pursue its own identity.] The history of the Finnish National Opera dates back to a November night in 1873, when Donizetti's *Lucia di Lammermoor* was performed in a small provincial theater by the newly formed Singing Section of the Finnish Theater, predecessor of the present-day Finnish National Opera. Economic difficulties, however, forced a break of several years, and it was not until 1911 that the Domestic Opera was founded. The driving forces at the beginning were Edvard Frazer and Aïno Ackté. Ackté, who was the director for a single season (1938–1939), had debuted at the Metropolitan Opera Association during the 1903–1904 season as Marguerite in *Faust* on February 24, 1904. That same season at the Met saw the debuts of Caruso, Fremstad, and Edyth Walker—an impressive indication of the vocal strengths of that company. [Ackté was also the founder of the Savonlinna Opera Festival in 1911, which she directed until 1930.]

The Domestic Opera was made into a limited company in 1914 and its name was changed to the Finnish Opera. After Finland achieved its independence, the company—now the Finnish National Opera—moved into its new permanent house, the old Russian Aleksanterin Teatteri, a small, 500-seat theater built in 1879. Verdi's *Aida* opened the new home on January 19, 1919, and for the first time the company did not have to share seasons in the 1,100-seat National Theater, which had opened in 1902 with little expectation of operatic performances. The 1920s brought a rash of native operas, few of which have survived the test of time. Scheduled side by side with selections from the standard repertoire, they served the purpose of educating a larger public to appreciate an art form that had begun catering to a small educated elite. The Finnish Opera was expanded in 1921 with the foundation of a ballet company which had its first premiere in January 1922. On that date, *Swan Lake* by Tchaikovsky and Petipa-Ivanov was performed in its entirety for the first time.

The decades following World War II have brought a great change. Coupled with an explosion of talented native singers was an unprecedented growth in interest from a broader public. The foundation of the now famous Savonlinna Opera Festival where, for three or four weeks each summer, operas are mounted in the courtyard of a splendid medieval castle, marked a turning point in both national and international support. The result is that to the average citizen, opera has ceased to be seen as an elitist art. Support is such that plans for a new National Opera and Ballet have proceeded to the point where completion is only a few years away. Finland will finally get its first "real" 1,400-seat opera house in 1992 where, for the first time, full-size productions of Wagner's operas will be possible.

During the decade 1974–1984, the opera repertoire was replete with powerful Finnish musical dramas. New audiences were introduced to the intricacies of the form through works whose themes were closely connected with the history of Finland. Joonas Kokkonen's *Last Temptations* and Aulis Sallinen's *Red Line* struck sympathetic chords and have served as calling cards of the Finnish National Opera on tours abroad. *Last Temptations* premiered in Stockholm and Oslo (1976), London (1979), Wiesbaden and Zürich (1981), and East Berlin (1983), while *Red Line* premiered in London, Stockholm, Zürich, Moscow, and Lenningrad. Both operas were performed at the Metropolitan Opera in 1983. The successes of the 1980s also included Paavo Heininen's *Damask Drum*, which was based on ancient Japanese No drama. The newest production among native operas was *Vincent* by Einojuhani Rautavaara, which premiered in May 1990 in celebration of the centennial of van Gogh's death.

The Finnish National Opera's performing season extends from the beginning of August through the following May. The season features four or five operatic premieres as well as three to four ballet premieres. The repertoire typically encompasses a dozen operas and ten ballets. Some of the operas are presented in Finnish and some in the original language, in which case Finnish translations appear as surtitles. Twenty-five of the 380 employees are principal vocalists, and 75 are engaged by the orchestra. In the course of the 1989 season, the Finnish National Opera gave a total of 233 performances with audiences totaling over 114,000. The company played to 95 percent capacity, due, in part, to subsidized ticket prices. The National Opera is a foundation with a governing majority held by representatives of the Ministry of Education. The institution enjoys direct state aid and receives the greatest part of its budget from state funds.

BIBLIOGRAPHY: Aïno Ackté, *Taiteeni taipaleelta* (Helsinki, 1935) Seppo Heikinheimo, *Martti Talvela: Jättiläisen muotkuva* (Helsinki, 1978).

ACCESS: Bulevardi 23–27, PL 188, SF-00181 Helsinki. (358 0) 12921; fax (358 0) 1292 301. Ilkka Kuusisto, Director. Ulf Söderblom, Chief Conductor.

LEENA NIVANKA

SAVONLINNA

Savonlinna Opera Festival

The Savonlinna Opera Festival, one of Finland's oldest music festivals, has been held since 1912. The organizer of the festival at that time was the world-famous singer Aino Ackté, whose first period of festivals took place between 1912 and 1916, and whose last attempt was made on the brink of the depression in 1930. At this point the financial difficulties were overwhelming, so the festival had to be abandoned even though it already had a fine reputation abroad. The opera festival made its comeback in 1967, the ground having been prepared by the Savonlinna Music Days, which had begun in 1955 and to which an opera course was added a few years later. These and the gradual achievement of an increasingly higher artistic standard provided the springboard for the modern opera festival.

The teacher of the opera course, Peter Klein, had the grand idea of staging a performance of Beethoven's *Fidelio* in Olavinlinna Castle using the resources and personnel of the class. However, as the idea developed, it quickly expanded into an opera festival. *Fidelio* was performed with a cast that included both students and Finnish artists of international reputation. The premiere on July 16, 1967, was a resounding success; the opera festival had been brought back to life. Between 1967 and 1972 the town of Savonlinna was the organizer of the festival. In autumn 1972, with the municipal organization proving cumbersome, the festival was placed on a national footing with the formation of the Savonlinna Opera Festival Patron's Association. Martti Talvela agreed to chair the Artistic Board, consisting of Finland's leading musical experts. These changes decisively altered the festival's image both at home and abroad.

Martti Talvela was artistic director of the Savonlinna Opera Festival until 1980, when his place was taken by the opera singer Timo Mustakallio. During Mustakallio's administration the proportion of foreign artists increased following the decision to present works (with the exception of *The Magic Flute*) in their original languages. From 1984 to 1987, the post of artistic director was held by the pianist Ralf Gothóni. This period was one of dynamic expansion. Extending the festival by one week allowed more productions, and the founding of the Savonlinna Music Institute made it possible to train all the singers, with the Opera Festival Foundation, as well as the instrumentalists, with the Savonlinna Music Days, under one roof.

A series of visits by foreign opera companies, beginning with the Estonian Theatre in the summer of 1987, has made the SOF a showcase for Finnish music making and a stimulating forum for international arts. The Central Opera of

China appeared in 1988, the Royal Opera Stockholm (Kungliga Teatern) in 1989, and the Tokyo Nikikai Opera Theatre in 1990. The 1991 festival has scheduled productions of *The Bartered Bride* and *Aida*, as well as Prokofiev's ballet *Romeo and Juliet*, and the guest company will be the National Theatre of Prague (Národní Divadlo Prague), which will perform *Don Giovanni* and Dvořák's *Rusalka*. In another move to further internationalize the SOF, the Music Institute will begin cooperating with the Leningrad Conservatory in 1991. About 80,000 people attend the opera festival each year, with 15 percent of them being foreigners who are visiting Finland.

BIBLIOGRAPHY: Aïno Ackté, *Taiteeni taipaleelta* (Helsinki, 1935). Seppo Heikinheimo, *Martti Talvela: Jättiläisen muotokuva* (Helsinki, 1978).

ACCESS: Olavinkatu 35, SF-57130 Savonlinna. (358 57) 514 700; fax (358 57) 218 66. Risto Ruuth, Managing Director.

[From materials supplied by the company]

France

LYON (metro 1,220,844; city 418,476)

Opéra de Lyon

As the third largest city in France, Lyon has a distinguished history of opera dating back to 1688 when the first opera house, the Jeu de Paume, opened its doors. It was destroyed by fire on November 29 of that year, but performances continued in a makeshift replacement until the city government created an official academy for fine arts, including opera, in 1714. Throughout the first half of the eighteenth century various locations were used for opera. Finally, in 1756 a new theater, built by J.-G. Soufflot, opened under the direction of Michelle Poncet and Jean Lobreau. This 1,800-seat house was rebuilt and opened with François Boieldieu's *La Dame blanche* in 1831. Enlarged to its present 3,000-seat capacity in 1842, it was first called the Théâtre Impérial, then the Grand Théâtre, and currently the Opéra Grand Théâtre. The first French version of *Die Meistersinger von Nürnberg* was produced here on December 30, 1896. Regular seasons resumed after World War II, and the company mounts a number of contemporary works, both in the 3,200-seat Auditorium Maurice Ravel and in the 1,200-seat Opéra de Lyon.

BIBLIOGRAPHY: G.-M.-J. Vuillermoz, *Cent ans d'opéra à Lyon: Le centenaire du Grand-Théâtre de Lyon, 1831–1931* (Lyon, 1932).

ACCESS: 9 Quai Jean Moulin, B.P. 1219, F-69203 Lyon Cedex 01. (33 7) 260950; fax (33 7) 78278805. Jean-Pierre Brossmann, Directeur Général.

[From materials supplied by the company]

MARSEILLE (metro 1,110,511; city 878,689)

Opéra de Marseille

An ancient city, Marseille was founded by the Phoenicians some six hundred years before the birth of Christ and has been a major Mediterranean port for over two thousand years. Theatrical events played a major role in the culture of the area, and a theater to host such events was built as early as 146 B.C. Indeed, Marseille has a long and distinguished musical history and, beginning with the seventeenth century, has held a place second only to Paris in the musical life of France. The advent of opera dates from the founding of the Marseille Music Academy, where Pierre Gaultier de Marseille established a fine reputation for producing outstanding works. Gaultier received Lully's authorization to produce opera outside Paris, the first time such a privilege had been granted. The composer, who also wrote the libretto, opened his establishment with his own opera, *Le Triomphe de la Paix*, on January 28, 1685. During the next several seasons, Gaultier repaid his mentor with productions of *Armide*, *Phaëton*, *Le Triomphe de l'Amour*, *Atys*, and *Bellérophon*. After Gaultier left Marseille to run the opera in Lyon, his brother Jacques took over the company in 1693. Although there was no permanent company, opera performances took place on an irregular basis until the City of Bordeaux erected its 1,158-seat Grand Théâtre Municipal in 1780. Designed by the architect Victor Louis, this was one of the finest opera houses in Europe at the time and generated not a little envy in other provincial centers. Bordeaux was a competitive Atlantic Ocean port on the west coast of France, and public pressure to build an opera theater in Marseille after 1780 was constant. As an important port on the Mediterranean Sea, Marseille was visited by many famous individuals, including kings and popes, and, as the home of numerous wealthy merchants, there were funds available for the arts.

A group of prominent citizens formed the Compagne Rabaud to build a local theater to meet this public demand. Designed by the Parisian architect Charles-Joachim Benard, the largely wooden structure took one year to complete. The cornerstone was laid July 14, 1786, and on October 30, 1787, the Compagne Rabaud took possession of the building. The Grand Théâtre (or the Salle Beauvau as it was called, after Maréchel, Prince de Beauvau, who was governor of the province) was opened in 1787 with Stanislas Champein's opéra bouffe *La Mélomanie* [premiered in Paris on January 23, 1781], following two plays that were also part of the inauguration ceremonies. The first general director was André Beaussier, who was not the choice of the owners, and after two years he was succeeded by Laurent Garet. Monetary problems were to plague the theater from the beginning, and the Grand Théâtre would be closed periodically throughout its history. The first public subsidy came in 1813 from the Conseil Municipal for the following season, but it was never used. The structure was renovated in 1820, and in 1821 Rossini's *Il Barbiere di Siviglia* began its triumphant run. During the nineteenth century many of the contemporary French and Italian composers were represented in the repertoire, often shortly after their premiere performances. In 1836 benches were installed in the auditorium, enlarging the capacity to 1,800 patrons. Gas lighting was introduced in 1837. The operas of Verdi were first produced in 1849. The auditorium was enlarged in 1855 by elongating the first gallery, a decision that resulted in some bad sight lines. During this period a stagione system was inaugurated in the house, and singers such as Alboni and Miolan-Carvalho performed. On March 11, 1863, Gounod conducted a performance of his opera *Faust*. The 1864–1865 season was canceled, but by the next season things had stabilized so that approximately ninety performances were offered over eight months. This was the season in which Adelina Patti made her Marseille debut in Meyerbeer's *L'Africaine*, which had premiered earlier in Paris, on April 28, 1865.

After granting a large subsidy in 1881, the city of Marseille assumed control of the theater in 1882 from la Société Rabaud and it became a public theater. The first director under the new arrangement was Beroard, who cut ticket prices drastically to entice the audience to return. Massenet's operas were premiered in Marseille during this period and were conducted by the composer. By 1896 the benches that had been installed some sixty years earlier had been replaced with seats. Flaissières, the mayor of Marseille, took a personal interest in the opera, and for thirty years his policies would be important to the stability of the house, especially the financial administration that was implemented in 1901. Puccini assisted in the French premiere of *La Fanciulla del West* in Marseille on November 8, 1912 [premiered in New York on December 10, 1910]. Flaissière's fiscal management had proven so successful that the house turned a profit in 1916 without any public or private subsidy. Today only the colonade remains from the original structure, which was destroyed by fire on November 13, 1919, barely one month into the new season.

After the fire, there were no opera seasons until the new 2,028-seat theater opened in 1924 (it was inaugurated on December 4 with *Sigurd* by Ernst Reyer). This theater was the brainchild of a collective of architects that included Henri Ebrard, Gaston Castel, and Georges Raymond working with the indefatigable mayor. A superb example of art deco architecture, the new house was similar in concept to the famous Palacio de Bellas Artes in Mexico City. January and February 1928 saw the implementation of a new mini-festival of contemporary operas which included Georges Hüe's *Dans l'Ombre de la Cathédrale*. Titta Ruffo made his Marseille debut in 1931, and the next season Georges Thill made his debut in *Carmen*. The complete *Ring* cycle was produced in French in 1936, the same year the house was renamed the Opéra Municipal. Renaldo Hahn came to conduct *Le Nozze di Figaro* and *Die Entführung aus dem Serail* in December 1937, and Tito Schipa guested in *Lucia di Lammermoor* in 1938. Performances were sporadic during World War II, and the main workshop (sets and costumes) was destroyed on May 27, 1944. In July 31, 1945, the theater, which would soon become known as the Opéra de Marseille, passed under the control of the city. A colleague of the mayor, Jean Marny, was appointed the first artistic director, and he, along with Ernest Magne and Henry Vincent, made up the triumvirate that ran the theater.

The twenty-fifth anniversary of the new theater was celebrated with a gala production of Wagner's *Maître chanteurs de Nuremberg*. Mado Robin triumphed in a stunning *Lucia di Lammermoor* in 1950, followed the next year by Victoria de los Angeles, who debuted in *Madama Butterfly*. The highlight of the 1952 season was *Die Walküre* with Martha Mödl, Leonie Rysanek, Hans Hotter, and Max Lorenz. Darius Milhaud's *Le Pauvre Matelot* and Poulenc's *Dialogues des Carmélites* were featured in the 1960 season. The 1960s continued the policy of international guest artists with such stars as Gwyneth Jones and Elisabeth Schwarzkopf. Daniel Lesur's *Andrea del Sarto* was given its world premiere on January 24, 1969. Tito Gobbi's production of *Falstaff*, in which he also starred, was the outstanding production in 1971. Guests in the 1970s included Eva Marton and Pavarotti. The present house seats 1,786 as a result of interior renovations completed in 1972 to compensate for the bad sight lines. The orchestra pit was remodeled at the same time. In 1987 the city of Marseille celebrated the bicentenial of its opera, and the theater was completely restored again with capacity increased to 1,832. The bicentennial season opened with *Boris Godunov* and closed with Jacques Karpo's production of *Simon Boccanegra*. In the 201 seasons of the opera, some 613 works by 260 composers have been performed. To this day the Opéra de Marseille remains one of the larger lyric theaters in France and is noted for its excellent acoustics. The theater currently employs over 400 artists, administrators, and technicians.

BIBLIOGRAPHY: Jacques Cheilan-Cambolin, *Un aspect de la vie musicale à Marseille au XVIIIe siècle: Cinquante ans d'opéra* (Aix-en-Provence, 1972). Emile Spiteri, ed., *Marseille, notre Opera, Petite Histoire et Grands Evenements (1787–1919 et 1924–1987)* (Marseille, 1987).

ACCESS: 2, rue Molière, F-13001 Marseille. (33 91) 552142/10/11. Jacques Karpo, Directeur Artistique.

ALEX MATTALIA
TRANS. RENÉE SCHMUKI AND EVA BEAUDET

NANCY (metro 400,000)

Opéra de Nancy et de Lorraine

Opera of consequence began in the old duchy of Lorraine when the Grand Duke Leopold commissioned a new opera house in 1709. His new directeur de la musique, Henry Desmarets, had previously served in the court of King Philip V of Spain, and several years before his appointment in Nancy, his opera *Iphigénie en Tauride* had premiered at the Théâtre National de l'Opéra de Paris on May 6, 1704. He composed *Le Temple de l'Astrée* for Leopold I, which opened the new theater on November 9, 1709. This theater was replaced by the Municipal Theater, built near the Place Stanislas, which regularly produced operas and operettas by Favart, Gluck, Grétry, Pergolesi, Rameau, and Rousseau. After the Municipal Theater burned to the ground in 1906, construction was delayed for both political and economic reasons. Finally, after the end of World War I, the new 1,270-seat Grand Théâtre de Nancy was completed in 1919. It was inaugurated with a gala production of Ernst Reyer's *Sigurd*, which had received its premiere at the Théâtre Royal de la Monnaie in Brussels on January 7, 1884. As the commercial center of Meurtheet-Moselle, Nancy is a thriving community that supports an active ballet and opera company. The city assumed the management of the theater in 1959, and it achieved municipal status in April 1985, at which time the name of the theater was changed to l'Opéra de Nancy et de Lorraine. Drama productions were moved into the new Centre dramatique National when it was completed, and the old theater now presents opera and ballet. Notable productions of the past several seasons include Janáček's *La Maison des Mortes* (1988), Tippett's *King Priam* (1988), Shostakovich's *Lady Macbeth* (1989), *Pelléas et Mélisande* (1989), Strauss's *Le Chevalier à la Rose* (1989), and Jean Prochomides's *La Noche Triste* (1989).

CHRONOLOGY OF DIRECTORS (SINCE 1959): Michel Sanduz, 1959–1970. Jean-Claude Riber, 1970–1973. Louis Ducreux, 1973–1976. Elie Delfosse, 1976–1979. Jean-Albere Cartier, 1979–1982. Antoine Bourseiller, 1982–present.

ACCESS: 1, rue Sainte-Catherine, F-54000 Nancy. (33 8) 376501; fax (33 8) 32 90 96. Antoine Bourseiller, Directeur Général.

[From materials supplied by the company]
TRANS. RENÉE SCHMUKI

NICE (metro 449,496; city 338, 486)

Opéra de Nice

Opera in Nice is primarily a late nineteenth- and twentieth-century phenomenon. The city of Nice built an opera house in 1828 copied from the highly successful Real Teatro di San Carlo in Naples which had opened in 1817. Named the Théâtre Royal, it housed both French and Italian companies until 1860, when the name was changed to Théâtre Impérial; the name was again changed in 1871 to Théâtre Municipal. Wagner's *Lohengrin* received its French premiere there, albeit in Italian, on March 21, 1881; two days later, the theater burned to the ground. The Théâtre Municipal was replaced with a 1,230-seat opera house that opened in 1885. A number of important French premieres such as Verdi's *La Forza del Destino* (1873) and *Otello* (February 1891) have been mounted here. In addition, the house has hosted the world premieres of Massenet's *Marie-Magdeleine* (February 9, 1903) and Manuel da Falla's *La Vie Brève* (April 1, 1913). The Nice Philharmonic supports the opera season as well as presenting a season of symphony concerts.

ACCESS: 4, rue St. François de Paule, (33 93) 80 59 83; fax (33 93) 80 34 83. Directeur Général, Théâtre de l'Opéra de Nice.

[From materials supplied by the company]

PARIS (metro 8,706,963; city 2,188,918)

Théâtre National de L'Opéra de Paris

The importance of Paris as a cultural center dates back to the twelfth century, and theatrical entertainments that depended on music as a central element began to flourish some five hundred years later with the collaboration between Lully and Molière. Their joint achivement, the Comédie-ballet, unified play and ballet in a form that greatly expanded the orchestral and vocal forms. Although Italian operas had been widely performed in Paris prior to this time, the Italian style did not interest the French. When Lully was granted exclusive rights to the Académie Royale de Musique in 1672, he was singularly placed to impose his vision of opera on the French. His hastily built theater opened on September 15, 1672, with a pastorale for which Lully had written the music. The major event occurred on February 11, 1673, with the premiere of *Cadmus et Hermione*. A Tragédie-Lyrique of epic proportions, *Cadmus et Hermione* signals the birth of the national French opera which Pope Innocent X had once suggested that Louis XIV might initiate. For many, this also marks the beginning of the principal opera company of Paris, a company whose history extends to the present day. When Molière died on February 17, 1673, Lully convinced the king that the Salle du Palais-Royal was the only suitable theater for the Académie, and was permitted to move in immediately. *Alceste* in 1674 and *Thésée* in 1675 firmly established French opera, and, with the king's support, Lully now controlled all the theaters in Paris.

Opera remained in the original Salle du Palais-Royal until it was destroyed by fire on April 6, 1763. The decision to rebuild and enlarge the theater necessitated a temporary home for the company, and a move was made to the inadequate Salle des Tulleries. Necessary remodeling was completed and the company moved into the Salles Machines des Tulleries on January 24, 1764. Fortunately, the new [Deuxième] Salle du Palais-Royal opened on January 26, 1770, with a festive performance of a revised version of Rameau's *Zoroastre*; the original had premiered at the Académie Royal de Musique on December 5, 1749. The new 2,500-seat theater was three times the size of the original and was the first French theater built on an oval plan. As though fate had come knocking again, the new house was destroyed by fire barely a decade after its inaugural. Shortly after a performance of Gluck's *Orphée* on June 8, 1781, the house, including all the sets and costumes, burned to the ground. The company found temporary refuge in the tiny Salle-des-Menus-Plaisirs du Roy, a theater about the size of the opera house in the Château de Versailles. [This theater was also destroyed by fire, in April 1788.] Queen Marie-Antoinette immediately commissioned the architect Lenoir to design a new house for the company, the Salle de la Porte-Saint-Martin. The stage matched that of the Salle du Palais Royal, but the construction was so quickly done that the house needed extensive repairs and alterations in 1782 and was widely thought to be unsafe throughout its tenure. It too was destroyed by fire, in May 1871.

The revolution exploded with the storming of the Bastille in 1789. The city of Paris took control of the Académie, and the historic "Liberté des Théâtres" was proclaimed on January 13 and March 2, 1791. This proclamation allowed any citizen to build a theater and produce works, and it protected the works of living authors, measures that completely upset the status quo. The old Académie Royal de Musique became L'Opéra for a year, was changed to Académie de Musique for several months, and then reverted to the original title on September 17, 1792. The Théâtre de la Parte-Saint-Martin was condemned as unsafe, and the new Salle Montansier opened in 1794 opposite the Bibliothèque Nationale. Under the control of the Paris Commune, the company, now named the Théâtre des Arts, moved in and played for the first time to the general public. At this point, being perceived as somewhat superfluous to the aims of the revolutionary government, the opera company took a back seat to the rise of the Opéra-Comique. With its immediate popular appeal stressing entertainment and relaxation, the new genre was a marvelous and much needed antidote to the anxiety and deprivation of the times.

By 1802 Napoleon had taken effective control of the company, now named the Théâtre de l'Opéra, by giving his minister of the interior veto power over major decisions. He instituted major reforms in 1807 in an attempt to restore the Opéra to its former prestige as a national showcase. The decades until the company could move to its new sumptuous home, the Palais Garnier, which opened on January 5, 1875, were governed by a series of directors and conductors. Gavaudan, Viardot, Nourrit, Duprez, and Faure were among a stable of outstanding singers. Important premieres, including Spontini's *La Vestale* on December 16, 1807; Rossini's *Guillaume Tell* on August 3, 1829, featuring Cinti-Damoreau and Adolphe Nourrit; and Meyerbeer's *Robert-le-Diable* (1831), were among the many highlights in an era of Grand Opera. The failure of Berlioz's *Benvenuto Cellini*, which lasted only six performances after its premiere on September 10, 1838, was quickly forgotten with premieres of Donizetti's *La Favorite* (1840), Verdi's *Les Vêspres Siciliennes* (1855) and *Don Carlos* (1867), and Meyerbeer's posthumous *L'Africaine* (1865).

The old Opéra burned down (and history thus repeated itself) on October 29, 1873, and for two seasons the company was relegated to the Salle Ventadour, a theater that had earlier housed the Théâtre de l'Opéra-Comique. Charles Garnier's magnificent 2,156-seat theater had been planned during the previous decade—in fact, preliminary work began on August 1, 1861—but had been delayed first by construction difficulties and then by the Franco-Prussian War. The Second Empire of Napoleon III fell victim to the French defeat, and the Third Republic was established shortly after the end of the war. The newly elected president had the honor of opening the house, which had been a personal project of the now dead emperor; a project that eventually would cost in the neighborhood of 100 million gold francs. Once installed in the Palais Garnier (Gabrielle Krauss made her debut that night as Rachel in *La Juive*), the company seemed to lose the initiative that had characterized its seasons since Spontini's *La Vestale* and, except for the long overdue productions of Wagner's operas, settled into a repertoire of revivals and repeats. It was almost as if the grandeur of the house itself overshadowed the purposes for which it had been built. Prior to World War I, ballet and orchestral music led the way in Paris, and between the world wars the Opéra produced only one work of historical importance, Milhaud's *Maximilien* on January 4, 1932. The director, Jacques Rouché, produced some seventy-one operas and seventy-three ballets during his tenure (1915–1944), and, as the last independent head of the company, he knew (as did Rudolf Bing at the Metropolitan Opera Association) what repertoire would keep a major house in business.

Times had already changed due to the Réunion des Théâtres Lyriques Nationaux in 1939 which brought the Opéra and the Opéra-Comique together under state control. Government bureaucracy with all its regulations now intruded directly into the artistic process. The occupation of France during World War II reinforced the conservative programming, and after the war the company was adversely affected by internal strife resulting from the lack of adequate funding as well as a revolving artistic administration. The absence of enough first-rate French singers contributed to the stagnation, and, in comparison with Milan, New York, and Vienna, the Opéra was drab indeed. The 1963 *Don Carlos*, Pierre Boulez's *Wozzeck*, and Marguerite Walmann's 1966 production of *Turandot* were glittering exceptions. Production problems were compounded by the fact that the Palais Garnier was closed several times for reconstruction. Finally, with the appointment of Rolf Liebermann as administrative head and Georg Solti as artistic advisor in 1971, the Opéra had a team sufficiently talented to steer the company back into a leadership role in the opera world. The company was reorganized as an international house à la the "Met," and, with the closure of the Opéra-Comique in April 1972, a more varied repertoire became available. The historic Opéra-Comique, whose founding dates back to 1715 reopened in December 1976. [The address is Salle Favart, 5 rue Favart, F-75002 Paris; telephone (33 1) 47 42 53 71; fax (33 1) 42 86 85 78.] With an increased subsidy (at that time, the largest in the opera world), the company was able to mount a varied and exciting repertoire, and, until they were replaced in 1980, Liebermann and Solti followed a new and enlightened course.

Limited seating at the old opera house meant that over the years numerous patrons could not be served. During the 1980s pressures mounted for a new house, and over 750 architectural designs were submitted by July 1983. In September of that year the Canadian architect Carlos Ott's contemporary design was selected by the committee, and Gérard Mortier was named director in May 1985. Both political and economic issues continued to be raised, and in February

1986 Mortier resigned. Daniel Barenboim was named musical and artistic director of the company in July 1987 and signed a controversial five-year contract in May 1988 which included an unprecedented salary. The dream at that time was a repertory system of some 25 operas, including a significant number of new productions, in a season of some 250 performances. However, newly reelected French president Mitterand chose not to name a director of the new 2,716-seat Opéra Bastille. Instead, he appointed Pierre Bergé to run the Association of Opera Theaters of Paris which had overall responsibility for the Opéra, the Opéra Bastille, and the Opéra-Comique. One of Bergé's first actions was an attempt to renegotiate Barenboim's contract. There is still no mutually agreeable solution at this time, although Barenboim has been officially fired. The new house was to have been inaugurated on July 13, 1990.

CHRONOLOGY OF DIRECTORS: Halanzier-Dufresnoy, 1875–1879. Vaucorbeil, 1879–1884. Ritt and Pedro Gailhard, 1885–1892. Bertrand, 1892–1893. Bertrand and Pedro Gailhard, 1894–1898. Pedro Gailhard, 1899–1906. Pedro Gailhard and P. B. Gheusi, 1907. Broussand and André Messager, 1908–1914. Jacques Rouché, 1915–1940. Philippe Gaubert, 1940–1941. Marcel Samuel-Rousseau, 1942–1944. Reynaldo Hahn, 1945–1946. Henri Busser, 1946–1951. Emmanuel Bondeville, 1952–1959. A. M. Julien, 1959–1962. Georges Auric, 1962–1970. Rolf Liebermann, 1971–1980. Bernard Lefort, 1980–1982. Massimo Bogianckino, 1983–1986. Jean-Louis Martinoty, 1986–present.

BIBLIOGRAPHY: W. L. Crosten, *French Grand Opera: An Art and a Business* (New York, 1948; repr. 1972). Félix Crozet, *Revue de la musique dramatique en France...* (Grenoble, 1866). N. Demuth, *French Opera: Its Development to the Revolution* (Sussex, 1963). Charles Dupechez, *Histoire de l'Opéra de Paris un siècle au Palais Garnier, 1875–1960* (Paris, 1961). J. Gourret, *Histoire de l'Opéra de Paris* (Paris, 1978). B. Horowicz, *Le théâtre d'opéra* (Paris, 1946). Henri Legrave, *Le théâtre et le public à Paris de 1715 à 1750* (Paris, 1972). A. Lejeune and S. Wolff, *Les quinze salles de l'Opéra de Paris (1669–1955)* (Paris, 1955). *Petite encyclopédie illustrée de l'Opéra de Paris* (Paris, 1974). J. G. Prod'homme, *L'Opéra (1669–1925)* (Paris, 1925). Albert Soubies and Charles Malherbe, *Histoire de l'Opéra-Comique...* (Paris, 1892–93). Stéphane Wolff, *Un demi-siècle d'Opéra-Comique (1900–1950)* (Paris, 1953). Stéphane Wolff, *L'Opéra au Palais Garnier (1875–1961)* (Paris, 1962).

ACCESS: 8, rue Scribe, F-75009 Paris. (33 1) 42 66 50 22; fax (33 1) 42 66 50 10. Jean-Philippe Saint-Geours, General Director. Jean-Louis Martinoty, General Administrator.

Opéra Bastille, Place de La Bastille, Paris 75012. (33 1) 40 01 16 16; fax (33 1) 43 44 94 01. Myung Whun Chung, Music Director.

[From materials supplied by the company]
TRANS. EVA BEAUDET

ROUEN (metro 379,879; city 105,083)

Théâtre des Arts

This city northwest of Paris on the Seine River is perhaps most famous as the place where Joan of Arc was burned at the stake by the English on May 30,

1431. More recently it has become known as the home of the famous Dupré family of organists. Its operatic traditions date back to the opening of the Théâtre de Rouen in 1776. The house carried the name Théâtre de la Montagne for a brief year in 1793 (when François Boieldieu's first opera, *La Fille Coupable*, was premiered on November 2) before becoming the Théâtre des Arts in 1794. Destroyed by fire in April 1876, it was rebuilt (opening in September 1882 with Meyerbeer's *Les Huguenots*) and continued to hold regular seasons until its destruction by bombs in June 1940. Camille Saint-Saëns's famous opera, *Samson et Dalila*, received its French premiere in the Théâtre des Arts on March 3, 1890, some thirteen years after its first production in Weimar, and Ernst Reyer's last opera, *Salammbô*, also received its first French performance here on November 10, 1890. After World War II, operas were produced in the Théâtre Cirque until a new 1,500-seat Théâtre des Arts was finished in November 1962. A typical season lasts from October to May and encompasses approximately seventy-five opera and ballet performances. In contrast to prewar repertoire, the current offerings are more enterprising.

BIBLIOGRAPHY: Robert Eude, *Petite Histoire du Théâtre des Arts* (Rouen, 1963). Henri Geispitz, *Histoire du Théâtre des Arts de Rouen, 1882–1913* (Rouen, 1913). Henri Geispitz, *Histoire du Théâtre des Arts de Rouen, 1913–1940* (Rouen, 1951).

ACCESS: B.P. 1253, F-76177 Rouen Cedex. (35 71) 41 36 00. Directeur Général.

[From materials supplied by the company]

STRASBOURG (1,605,300)

Opéra du Rhin

Strasbourg was an important medieval city, and work on its Gothic cathedral was begun in the 1000s. There is a record of theatrical activity in Strasbourg as early as the sixteenth century. The city was free until 1681, when it became a part of France, and its cultural life was broadly based among diverse elements of the population. Guilds existed for various vocations including musicians. A makeshift opera house was opened in the Place Broglie ("Théâtre des Planches") in 1701 where only French operas were performed. A citizen corporation opened a second theater in 1733, the Petit Théâtre or Théâtre des Drapiers, where visiting German ensembles performed. The original house was destroyed by fire on May 29, 1799, and the now-resident French company transferred to the Petit Théâtre. It was, however, too small for opera, and in 1805 the company moved to temporary quarters in the converted Saint-Étienne church. A new house designed by Berigny and Boudhors was inaugurated on May 20, 1821, with André Grétry's *La Fausse Magie* [premiered February 1, 1775, in Paris]. This theater was subsidized in the German tradition by the city and was extremely active hosting such stars as Celestine Galli-Marié, who debuted there in 1859. The repertoire included most of the contemporary composers. In fact Richard Wagner's *Tann-*

häuser was premiered here on July 12, 1855, almost five years before the Paris premiere.

The house suffered substantial damage in the seige of Strasbourg during the Franco-Prussian War in 1870. After the war, Strasbourg was ceded to Germany, and artistic life once again flourished as Prussia lent strong support to the arts in its new western outpost on the Rhine River. The present 1,229-seat theater was the result of a major reconstruction of the original house, and it opened in 1873. Now known as the Théâtre Municipal, an epoch of outstanding conductors began: Otto Lhose (1897–1904), Hans Pfitzner (1908–1919), Wilhelm Furtwängler (1910–1911), Ernest Munch (1910–1914), Otto Klemperer (1914–1917), Max von Schillings (1915), and Georg Szell (1916–1919). The Treaty of Versailles returned Strasbourg to France after World War I, and Paul Bastide organized a permanent company at the opera, remaining as music director until 1938. As a conductor who was comfortable with both French and German operas, the works of Wagner and Richard Strauss were popular as well as operas from the standard repertoire. Strauss conducted his *Elektra* and *Ägyptische Helena* in 1932, and Josef Krips was on the podium for *Die Meistersinger von Nürnberg*. The theater was closed in 1939 and 1940, and the city was occupied in May–June 1940, remaining under German control until February 1945. Restored in 1944–1945, the theater opened after the liberation with Bizet's *Carmen*; then, in December 1945, there was a gala performance and French premiere of Berlioz's *Béatrice et Bénédict* conducted by Paul Bastide, who had returned to rebuild the company. Roger Lalande (1948–1953) succeeded Bastide, and was himself followed by Frederic Adam and Ernest Bour (1955–1960) and by Frederic Adam (1960–1972). During this period the company mounted the French premieres of Berg's *Wozzeck* (1959), Janáček's *Jenufa* (1962), and Orff's *Carmina Burana* (1963).

L'Opéra du Rhin is a postwar joint creation of the cities of Strasbourg, Colmar, and Mulhouse which is aimed at maximizing local cultural resources. In 1972 it was quite obvious that no one of the three cities could hope to support a variety of performance arts, especially ensembles of quality. Alain Lombard was appointed artistic director in 1972 and led the successful partnership until 1980. With the Opéra in Strasbourg, the Atelier lyrique in Colmar, and the Ballet du Rhin in Mulhouse, decentralization allowed each community to participate fully in the joint effort while assuring quality productions that were beyond the reach of any single partner. In addition, joint productions were undertaken with Karlsruhe and Lyon. Once the production costs are met, each theater that cooperates may stage the individual work with its own personnel, thus spreading the risk factor among several partners. Guest artists can be shared in the same production among several houses. As one of the main French regional operas, the Opéra du Rhin is dedicated to providing high-quality productions with both local talent and guest artists. During this period Jean-Pierre Ponnell was a major contributor to some twelve productions, including eight that he directed, starting in 1965. Young singers who appeared in these productions included Helena Döse, Donminic Cossa, Kostas Paskalis, Luis Lima, Christine Barbaux, Catherine Malfitano, Rachel Yakar, Leo Nucci, Nucci Condo, Robert Hale, Inga Nielsen, Ursula Schröder-Feinen, Stefka Estatieva, and Maria Dragoni, many of whom later became famous. Elisabeth Grümmer, Hans Hotter (who staged *Siegfried* and portrayed the Wanderer), and Birgit Nilsson (who sang in Rudolf Hartmann's French premiere of *Tannhäuser*) proudly represent an earlier generation. Among the French artists, Régine Crespin, Rita Gorr, and Yves Bisson are only a few of the many who performed in Strasbourg.

René Terrasson, formerly an opera singer and currently a stage director, has been the director of the Opéra du Rhin since 1980. He was hired from the Opera de Nantes where he had served in a similar capacity since 1973. As the first Occidental stage director to be invited by the People's Republic of China, he directed a production of Bizet's *Carmen* in Bejing in 1982. The company is unique in France in its ability to cater to two distinct cultures and two language audiences—French and German, and the repertoire exemplifies this diversity. What has resulted is a combination Stadttheater and international opera house that combines standard works with operettas, contemporary works for the stage, and a substantial number of first performances. The Opéra du Rhin today has over ten thousand subscribers from this diverse population and a yearly audience of some one hundred thousand. The 1989–1990 season included *Norma*, *Don Giovanni*, *Samson et Dalila*, *Hänsel und Gretel*, and *Boris Godunov*.

BIBLIOGRAPHY: Geneviève Levallet-Haug, *Histoire Architecturale du Théâtre de Strasbourg* (Strasbourg, 1935).

ACCESS: 19, Place Broglie, F-67008 Strasbourg Cedex. (33 88) 75 48 43; fax (33 88) 24 09 34. René Terrasson, Directeur Général. J. P. Wurtz, General Manager.

[From materials supplied by the company]
TRANS. RENÉE SCHMUKI

Germany

AUGSBURG (243,000)

Städtische Bühnen

Founded in 14 B.C. by Augustus, Augsburg has had a long and distinguished musical history. It enjoyed a leading position in Europe during the Renaissance, a flowering that unfortunately came to an abrupt end due to the Thirty Years War which lasted from 1618 to 1648. From that time until the middle of the nineteenth century, the city was outside the mainstream of music in Germany. The production of Carl Maria von Weber's second opera, *Peter Schmoll und Seine Nachbarn*, in March 1803, was an exception to a regular fare of visiting opera companies primarily from Italy. However, the formation of the Städtische Orchestra in 1865 and the opening of the 994-seat Stadttheater in 1867 signaled the return of a vigorous music life to Augsburg. Prior to a major renovation and expansion of the house in 1938–1939, the first German production of Verdi's *La Battaglia di Legnano* took place on January 27, 1932. The theater was destroyed by bombs on February 25, 1944. Rebuilt in 1954–1956, the 1,016-seat house reopened with Mozart's *Le Nozze di Figaro* on November 10, 1956.
ACCESS: Kasernstraße 4–6, 8900 Augsburg 11. (49 821) 3 24 49 01. Intendanz.

[From material supplied by the company]

BAYREUTH (60,000)

Bayreuther Festspiele

The German town of Bayreuth is famous for two opera houses. The first, the Markgräfliches Opernhaus, resulted from the marriage of Margrave Friedrich of Hohenzollern to Frederica Sophie Wilhelmine of Prussia, the sister of Frederick the Great. Wilhelmine, determined to bring the musical brilliance of the Prussian court to Bayreuth, commissioned the famous Giuseppe and Carlo Bibiena to construct a delightful baroque opera house. Many of the most renowned singers of the day appeared there, and musical activities flourished until Wilhelmine's death in 1758. The Bavarian State Opera still offers some productions in the theater. The second, the Richard-Wagner-Festspielhaus, is the tangible result of the composer's exile in Switzerland in 1849–1850. Along with the profound aesthetics and philosophy of opera that he was able to articulate at this time was the dream of a practical man of the theater. To achieve his vision he knew instinctively that a special festival in an as-yet-unrealized theater would have to be initiated. Unhappy with the opera of his day, Wagner believed not only that new works would have to be created but that both the space in which they were produced and the audiences that experienced these "art works of the future" would have to change. The theater itself, the Festspielhaus, resulted from a visit of the composer to Bayreuth in 1871. Seeking an appropriate site for the production of his music dramas, Wagner hoped that the Markgräfliches Opernhaus would serve his purposes; however, it was totally unsuitable. Fortunately, several leading citizens supported his idea, and he was given land by the town. The cornerstone was laid some months later on May 22, 1872, an occasion on which Wagner conducted Beethoven's Ninth Symphony. Difficulties in raising the necessary funds resulted in a theater that Wagner himself considered to be temporary. Drawing heavily on the classical Greek amphitheater, the 1,925-seat Festspielhaus incorporated the composer's own theatrical ideals, including a hood over the orchestra pit to throw the instrumental sound back over the stage.

The theater opened with *Das Rheingold* on August 13, 1876, with Hans Richter conducting. This marked the first performance of the entire *Der Ring des Nibelungen*, with *Die Walküre* (August 14), *Siegfried* (August 16), and *Götterdämmerung* (August 17) following in quick succession. The entire "Ring" was performed three times that first season, with the final performance taking place on August 30. As with any new venture there were artistic problems, and Wagner hoped to correct them the following year. However, the enormous deficit meant that the Festspielhaus would remain empty until *Parsifal* was premiered on July 26, 1882. Festivals were held sporadically until 1951, after which they occurred each summer.

Following the composer's death, his widow Cosima assumed control of the festival, and *Tristan und Isolde* in 1886 was her first production. She turned over control of the festival to her son Siegfried after the 1906 season, and he gradually initiated changes in the traditional production concepts. After Siegfried's death in 1930 (the same year Cosima died) the festival was run by his widow Winifred who, lacking background and experience in production, engaged Heinz Tietjen as artistic director. Tietjen, reigning intendant of the Deutsche Staatsoper Berlin, was one of the outstanding conductors and producers of his generation. He retained the traditional orientation of the festival and continued to engage some of the finest artists of the period until the Festspielhaus was closed due to wartime conditions in 1944. The association of Hitler with the festival marred, politically if not artistically, its reputation in the eyes of many. After the war, reopening was delayed until an arrangement could be worked out to allow Wagner's grandsons, Wieland and Wolfgang, to assume control. By the terms of Siegfried's will, Winifred was the sole owner of the Festspielhaus, but a denazification court had forbidden her to continue her work there. Wieland Wagner's production of *Parsifal* on July 30, 1951 (London, Windgassen, Uhde, and Mödl conducted by Hans Knappertsbusch) clearly suggested the new paths that the festival would follow in the years to come. Any return to the past was both politically and artistically unthinkable; new aesthetic and production concepts were necessary.

Wieland's revolutionary productions, which depended so much on symbolism and suggestion, ceased with his death in 1966, and his brother Wolfgang assumed control of the festival. Wolfgang Wagner, who had earlier concerned himself primarily with administrative matters, was now forced to involve himself in artistic areas, and he has managed to continue the postwar commitment to experimentation and new ideas. The festival continues to produce a select group of Wagner operas each summer to sold-out houses of enthusiasts from around the world. As in the past, the opera world's finest conductors, designers, directors, and singers are attracted to the festival because of its high standards and marvelous artistic reputation. The 1990 festival ran from July 25 to August 28 with performances of *Der Fliegende Holländer* in a new staging conducted by Giuseppe Sinopoli, *Lohengrin* conducted by Peter Schneider, *Der Ring des Nibelungen* conducted by Daniel Barenboim, and *Parsifal* conducted by James Levine.

BIBLIOGRAPHY: Robert Hartford, ed., *Bayreuth, The Early Years: An Account of the Early Decades of the Wagnerian Festival as seen by the Celebrated Visitors and Participants* (London, 1980). Michael Karbaum, *Studium zur Geschichte der Bayreuther Festspiele (1876–1976)*. Dietrich Mack, *Bayreuther Festspiele* (Bayreuth, 1969). Käte Neupert, *Die Besetzung der Bayreuther Festspiele, 1876–1960* (Bayreuth, 1961). Walter Erich Schäfer, *Wieland Wagner* (Tübingen, 1970). Geoffrey Skelton, *Wagner at Bayreuth* (London, 1971). Geoffrey Skelton, *Wieland Wagner, the Positive Skeptic* (London, 1971). Various Authors, *100 Jahre Bayreuther Festspiele*, 13 vols. (München and Regensberg, 1973–).

ACCESS: Richard-Wagner-Festspielhaus, Festspielhügel 1–2, 8580 Bayreuth. (49 921) 2 02 21. Wolfgang Wagner, Artistic Director.

[From materials supplied by the company]

BERLIN (3,409,737)

Deutsche Oper Berlin

Since the city was reunited on November 9, 1989, Berlin has three opera houses, two of which are located in the former Russian sector of the occupied city, a sector once designated the capital of the German Democratic Republic:

the Deutsche Staatsoper Berlin (Unter den Linden) which, as the successor to the Hofoper founded in 1742 by Friedrich II, has the longest tradition, and the Komische Oper, which the director Walter Felsenstein founded in 1947 in the restored Metropoltheaters on Behrenstraße. The only opera house in West Berlin—an entity created in 1949 with the merging of the American, British, and French sectors, which was affiliated with the Federal Republic of Germany—was the present-day Deutsche Oper Berlin. All three houses lie on the main east–west thoroughfare which goes through the Brandenburg Gate. The youngest of the three houses, the Deutsche Oper Berlin, was built in 1912 on the site of the old Deutsche Opernhaus on Bismarkstraße by the citizens of Charlottenburg. In 1925 the house was taken over by the city of Berlin and renamed the Städtische Oper. Ten years later it came under control of the German Reich and was again called the Deutsche Opernhaus. Four air raids between March 1943 and January 1944 reduced the theater to rubble.

After the defeat of Nazi Germany, the company performed for sixteen years in the relatively undamaged Theater des Westens on Kantstraße near the Zoological Garden. As the Städtische Oper Berlin it developed a reputation as an outpost for the contemporary music of the West in a city that was still divided only by borders and money exchange, and not yet by the Berlin Wall. In 1956 the Berlin Senate decided to rebuild the former Deutsche Opernhaus for the highly regarded company. The winning architect, Fritz Bornemann, was determined to preserve as much of the old building as possible and yet create a modern opera theater for some two thousand spectators. Following Ferenc Fricsay's suggestion, the Senate gave the theater the title Deutsche Oper Berlin, thus relating it directly to the tradition of the 1912 Deutsche Opernhaus in Charlottenburg while at the same time establishing an artistic counterweight to the Deutsche Staatsoper, the so-called Oper Unter den Linden, which had reopened in 1955 in East Berlin.

A few weeks prior to the gala opening on September 24, 1961, the physical division of Berlin by the wall was completed. A large part of the public from East Berlin as well as from the surrounding areas of the Deutsche Demokratische Republik (DDR) were now effectively excluded. At the same time, however, the Deutsche Oper Berlin became the only opera house in the western sectors of the city and had, even more than before, along with the Berlin Philharmonic and the Staatlichen Schauspielbühnen, an obligation to create an unmistakable profile of the Bundesland Berlin and to project that image worldwide. On November 12, 1989, three days after the wall had come down in Berlin and throughout Germany, the Deutsche Oper Berlin could at last fulfill its mission: that of the center of art and education for both East and West. [As a gesture to compatriots who were now allowed to travel,] an additional afternoon performance of Mozart's *Die Zauberflöte* was offered free to the citizens of East Berlin and the surrounding areas of the DDR, where currency was still not convertible.

Of all three theaters in Berlin, the Deutsche Oper Berlin has the most varied repertoire and offers the most performances; some 316 performances each season of forty to sixty works in repertoire plus as many ballets, among which are a large portion from the first half of the twentieth century. Each season five new opera productions and two ballet premieres provide for the ongoing reinvigoration of the repertoire. A permanent ensemble of some thirty-five singers is strengthened with twice as many international guests each season. Among the 1,000 employees of the house are the 141 members of the orchestra and a chorus of 112. The company measures itself against the international competition in regular television and radio broadcasts. In the new rivalry with the two other Berlin houses, the Deutsche Oper Berlin asserts and maintains its identity through the variety of its offerings and the persistent cultivation of the contemporary—specifically, works of the twentieth century as well as the development of new music theater forms.

The artistic profile of the various Charlottenburger Opera houses (this unofficial title includes all the various companies, names, and buildings mentioned previously) has always been dependent on the personality of its leader, who was usually a stage director/producer or a conductor. The experienced producer, director, and former singer Georg Hartmann was selected as the first general manager in 1911. Hartmann brought novelties such as the first German production of Puccini's *La Fanciulla del West* during his initial season and, during the second season, the first production of *Parsifal* after the original performance ban outside Bayreuth had been lifted. An entire series of premieres was produced, although most lasted for only a few performances and are forgotten today. He modified earlier works to fit the times, and in this he continued the tradition of Hans Gregor's Komische Oper (1905–1911) where *Hoffmanns Erzählungen* achieved worldwide success in a version that twenty years later would be mandatory. [Gregor's company opened on November 17, 1905, with Offenbach's masterpiece and closed six years later on February 14, 1911, with Franz Neumann's *Liebelei.*] *Hoffmanns Erzählungen* was followed by *Orpheus in der Unterwelt*, *Die Schöne Helena*, *Die Schwätzerin von Saragossa*, and *Die Prinzessin von Trapezunt*, all in new versions, thereby establishing a Berlin Offenbach tradition. Among the stars of these performances were Herta Stolzenberg (who had fascinated the composer at the first performance of *La Fanciulla del West*) and Meta Seinemeyer, who later went to Dresden and took part in the world premiere of Ferruccio Busoni's *Doktor Faust*.

The principal conductor, Ignaz Waghalter, was as comfortable with Wagner and Beethoven [the 2,098-seat house opened on November 7, 1912, with *Fidelio*] as he was with Offenbach and Puccini. Hartmann brought to his ensemble a number of singers who, like Waghalter, had been engaged at Gregor's Komische Oper and who had performed elsewhere for a year after their theater went bankrupt. The Deutsche Opernhaus opened during the unstable times of the First World War, and after the conflict it was constantly threatened by insolvency. The governing board decided in 1923 to replace Hartmann with Wilhelm Graf Holthoff von Faßmann and to hire a general music director (GMD) with sweeping authority. The latter post was given to Leo Blech, who had held a similar position at the Hofoper (later the Staatsoper) since 1911. The new team began with the long-awaited premiere of Emil Nikolaus von Reznicek's *Holofernes* with the legendary baritone Michael Bohnen, who would later direct the Städtische Oper Berlin, in the title role.

To ensure the future of the opera house on Bismarkstraße a fundamental reorganization was necessary: In 1925 the city of Berlin took over all the limited shares on favorable terms, and the theater became the Städtische Oper under the control of the Prussian Cultural Bureau. The conductor/director Heinz Tietjen became general manager and Bruno Walter was named GMD. With a fresh ensemble of talented young singers (Maria Ivogün and Carl Martin Oehmann, to name only two) they created an enormous artistic momentum. Bruno Walter conducted distinguished and highly regarded performances of both classics and modern works, including *Don Pasquale*, *Ariadne auf Naxos*, *Entführung aus dem Serail*, and *Turandot*. Fritz Zweig, who had just been engaged by the company, conducted an equally challenging repertoire that stretched from Mozart and operetta to the important premieres of Busoni's *Brautwahl* and Janáček's *Katja Kabanova*. Both conductors were involved in staging as well; however, the tone of the company's productions derived from the personality of stage director Karl Heinz Martin. Individual singers such as Lotte Lehmann and Lauritz Melchior soon appeared at the Staatsoper and in international engagements, but they always returned as guests. Among the conductors were personalities as diverse as Paul Dessau, Robert F. Denzler, Georg Sebastian, and Fritz Stiedry.

In the aftermath of the worldwide depression, one of Berlin's three opera houses had to be closed. The "Krolloper," which had been operating under Klemperer as the Staatsoper am Platz der Republic, was sacrificed. Even the Städische Oper was not spared from the crisis. After Bruno Walter left for the Gewandhaus in Leipzig in 1929, Tietjen also withdrew in order to concentrate on his obligations at the Staatsoper Unter den Linden. He handed over his official duties to his deputy, Kurt Singer, a doctor, director, and musician. During the Third Reich, Singer, as director of the "Kulturbundoper," evolved a sort of art ghetto before he was murdered in Theresienstadt. When Carl Ebert was named general manager of the Städtische Oper in 1931, the company enjoyed a short improvement. Emerging from Max Reinhardt's ensemble with a reputation as an actor and director, Ebert had since 1927 been general manager of the theater in Darmstadt, one of the most productive houses in the Weimer Republic. In less than two seasons Ebert assimilated the artistic traditions of the Krolloper (integrating that audience into his subscription system) and produced contemporary music theater. Premieres of Weill and Schreker were offered along with popular Verdi interpretations in the "Darmstadt Style." He engaged Jürgen Fehling, Gustav Gründgens, and Arthur Maria Rabenalt as stage directors. The director of his management team was Rudolf Bing, who was later involved in the building of the Glyndebourne Festival [Bing was general manager from 1936 to 1946] and who was the longtime general manager [1951–1972] of the Metropolitan Opera Association.

Shortly after the Nazis took over Germany, Carl Ebert and several of his key associates were banished from their positions and a dark chapter in the history of the Charlottenburger Opera House began. Although Max von Schillings, a conductor and composer of unquestioned musical ability, was engaged, he died shortly after assuming his duties. There followed a terrible interregnum during which the repertoire was cleansed. The company stood again at the edge of ruin, and only a complete takeover by the Third Reich ensured survival. The respected baritone Wilhelm Rode was appointed general manager, but he involved himself only in directing. His deputies were Irma Beilke and Günter Treptow. Initially as the Reichsoper and then again as the Deutsche Opernhaus, the theater was remodeled and a "Führerloge" was added. Under the special protection of Heinrich Goebbels, the Reichminister for Information and Propaganda, the theater flourished financially but stagnated artistically for twelve years. The only unquestionable contribution of Rode was the discovery of a long list of young singers. The production style was, on the one hand, dependent on an ideologically corrupt realism and, on the other hand, influenced by the typical colossal mania of a dictatorship. The theater, which was otherwise operated as one of the strictest in the sense of National Socialism, endured countless speeches from Goebbels. Wagner's operas were misused in an almost crude manner for propaganda purposes; for example, texts such as "Für deutsche Land das deutsche Schwert" [For German land the German sword] appeared prominently on the theater programs. [The original house was destroyed on November 23, 1943. After World War II the company played in the 1,529-seat Theater des Westens (former home of the Volksoper) on Kantstraße from 1949 until 1961.]

Under the direction of Michael Bohnen, who did not shy away from the exhausting task of clearing up the debris, a handful of artists was assembled who had endured in Berlin to the end or who had just returned. He received permission from the British commander to produce *Fidelio* for the occupation forces in the slightly damaged Volksoper. Shortly thereafter he obtained a concession for the operation of a regular opera house that again would be called the Städtische Oper. Bohnen, who had managed a meaningful film career along with his singing between 1933 and 1945, stumbled two years later over one of the many intrigues that were rampant in Berlin at the time. After a one-year vacuum, Heinz Tietjen again took over the company. Although he inherited a generally solid ensemble, there was still additional building to be done. He immediately engaged Dietrich Fischer-Dieskau and Josef Greindl, and brought Leo Blech back to Berlin. His most important appointment, however, was that of Ferenc Fricsay as general music director following Fricsay's sensational debut with *Don Carlos*. After a fifteen-year break with the international music scene which ended with Bohnen's production of *Peter Grimes*, the world premieres of Egk's *Circe* and Blacher's *Preussisches Märchen*, the German premieres of Menotti's *Der Konsul* and Liebermann's *Leonore 40/45*, and the long awaited return of *Cardillac* and *Oedipus Rex* signaled a new era.

Tired of the criticism of his tenure, Heinz Tietjen accepted an offer to be general manager of the Hamburgische Staatsoper in 1954. His successor was Carl Ebert, under whose leadership the Städtische Oper Berlin was to enjoy a golden age that has become legendary. The cultivation of contemporary works reached a highly controversial peak in the world premiere of Hans Werner Henze's *König Hirsch* as well as the first German performance of Schönberg's *Moses und Aron*, paralleled by the classics produced in the spirit of Glyndebourne. Among the many young artists started by Ebert on the road to world prominence was Pilar Lorengar, who remained faithful to the company for over three decades. The international acclaim that Carl Ebert brought to the Städtische Oper was the decisive factor when the Berlin Senate supported the reconstruction of the opera house on Bismarkstraße. Ebert would have enjoyed leading his ensemble into the new opera house, but he was already sixty-eight years old when he assumed his post in Berlin for the second time. It would be some time before the Deutsche Oper Berlin opened, but, despite his age, Ebert decided to remain at least until the new theater was ready for occupancy. Thus, a successor to Ebert had to be found to lead the company. A director and manager who, like Carl Ebert, had begun as an actor and who had drawn attention to himself as general manager in Darmstadt was chosen: Gustav Rudolf Sellner. Sellner had been in the theatrical limelight since directing the first German performance of *Moses und Aron* for Ebert.

It was planned that Ferenc Fricsay would serve as GMD, but he was already too ill to assume the responsibility and he only conducted the opening performance of *Don Giovanni* [September 24, 1961, staged by Ebert in the new 1,885-seat house] and several repeats. These were his last opera appearances. Sellner personally staged the second production in the new house, the world premiere of Giselher Klebe's *Alkmene* directed by Heinrich Hollreiser. Hollreiser, together with Karl Böhm, who conducted the third production [*Aida*], and Eugen Jochum, who was engaged the following season, determined the musical standards. The young choir director, Walter Hagen-Groll, developed a solid and sonorous opera chorus. An old colleague of Ebert from Darmstadt, Wilhelm Reinking, remained as head of scenery. Along with Wieland Wagner, who had designed and directed the *Aida* and, a little later, a legendary *Salome*, Reinking controlled the visual impact of the Deutsche Oper Berlin. The abstract floating temple that Reinking created for *Alkmene* was widely considered to be a model of what a modern set integrated with up-to-date stage equipment should accomplish. Next to the difficult task of providing the new and much bigger theater with a standard repertoire, Sellner also gave his attention to supporting contemporary music. Ephemera like Haubenstock-Ramatis's *Amerika* as well as works with a broad international success, such as Henze's *Der Junge Lord*, were represented in numerous premieres. [Other world premieres during this period included Milhaud's *Oreste* (1963), Sessions's *Montezuma* (1964), Dallapiccola's *Ulisse* (1968), Fortner's *Elizabeth Tudor* (1972), and Nabokov's *Love's Labour's Lost* (1973).]

Among the young singers engaged by Sellner, many on the good advice of his deputy Egon Seefehlner, were Evelyn Lear, Catherine Gayer, Barry McDaniel, William Dooley, and Donald Grobe. All were Americans, which perhaps best documents the relationship between Berlin and the Deutsche Oper and the United States. Next to the American colony, to which also belong Vera Little and George Fortune, is a strong Scandinavian group: the Finn Matti Talvela (after numerous performances of the title role in Mussorgsky's *Boris Godunov*, he died suddenly in the summer of 1989), Walton Grönroos (current director of the Finnish National Opera) and Matti Salminen belong to this group, as do the Swedes Bengt Rundgren and Ingvar Wixell. The Deutsche Oper Berlin again appointed a general music director in 1965. The young American Lorin Maazel assumed the post with youthful élan and managed to conduct Verdi with the same obsession as Wagner. He also conducted the first "lighter" opera to premiere in the house, Domenico Cimarosa's Spieloper *Die Heimliche Ehe*. Considerable attention was given to the 1967 Sellner/Maazel *Der Ring des Nibelungen*, not least due to the novel scenery of Fritz Wotruba. Under the aegis of Sellner, international tours carried the name of Berlin and the Deutsche Oper throughout the world, to Tokyo, Osaka, Athens, and Washington, D.C.

Gustav Rudolf Sellner turned the company over to Egon Seefehlner in 1972, a change that guaranteed continuity but with a different accent. Seefehlner brought what many opera fans had been missing: pure singers' operas. Thus, Ponchielli's *La Gioconda* was performed in the style of its premiere in a production by director/designer Filippo Sanjust. Among the singers who began their careers under Seefehlner are Agnes Baltsa and Caterina Ligendza. His choice of directors was courageous and has proven to be fruitful for the musical theater. He brought back Günter Rennert (who was working in Berlin for a short time at the end of the war); he entrusted Rudolf Noelte with *Don Giovanni*; Ernst Schröder was his discovery as an opera editor (in *Elektra* and *Ein Maskenball*). Lorin Maazel left the company in 1972, and Seefehlner hired Gerd Albrecht as first conductor and later promoted him to chief conductor. Jesus Lopez Cobos debuted in a performance of *La Bohème*, later conducting Rossini's *Der Türke in Italien* as his first new production.

Egon Seefehlner left in 1976 to head the Wiener Staatsoper, and the Berlin Senate appointed Siegfried Palm, director of the Kölner Musikhochschule and a prominent cellist of contemporary music, as his successor. Palm continued the direction that his predecessor had pursued, that of a universal and many-sided music theater, rather than the direction some had hoped and many others had feared: that of an about-face in the direction of the avant-garde. Daniel Barenboim, Giuseppe Sinopoli, and Götz Friedrich are all artists who debuted at the Deutsche Oper Berlin under Palm and who, after Palm's departure, brought a great deal of credit to the profile of the company. Barenboim made his house debut with *Die Hochzeit des Figaro*, followed by *Tristan und Isolde*, and *Aida*, all three productions directed by Götz Friedrich. Sinopoli debuted with *Macbeth* and followed with new productions of *La Fanciulla del West*, *Madama Butterfly*, *Arabella*, and *Salome*. Götz Friedrich, who was well known to Berliners through numerous productions at the Komische Oper as the assistant of Walter Felsenstein (*Salome*, *Jenufa*, *Der Troubadour*, and *Porgy and Bess* were among the most important), debuted in 1977 with Verdi's *Falstaff*. Later, in 1981, when the Berlin Senate decided not to renew Palm's contract, Friedrich was chosen as his successor.

Nine years after the departure of Gustav Rudolf Sellner, the company again had a director as general manager. [The Theater des Westens on Kantstraße is also directed by Götz Friedrich. The 1,401-seat house, which originally opened on October 1, 1896, was completely rebuilt and renovated, and reopened on December 30, 1978, with *Cabaret*. Additional work was deemed necessary, and the theater was closed in April 1984. A production of *Guys and Dolls* reopened the house on December 14, 1984.] Friedrich's intention was to make a connection with the "progressive Berlin music tradition," and he began his tenure with an opera that had been forbidden in Berlin for fifty years, Janáček's *Aus einem Totenhaus*. Fritz Zweig had mounted the Berlin premiere as the final production of Klemperer's Krolloper in 1931. This time, Vaclav Neumann conducted the staging of the new general manager. *Die Tote Stadt* by Erich Wolfgang Korngold was also a risk. Even longer out of the repertoire in Berlin [the opera premiered on December 4, 1920, simultaneously in Hamburg and Cologne, and received its first Berlin performance on April 12, 1924], *Die Tote Stadt* had been largely forgotten since 1945. Friedrich staged the work during his second season with Hollreiser on the podium; the latter's vehement and insightful conducting articulated the sensuality of the music and made the visual interpretation effective. Another opera which, after a half century of silence would receive a sensational rediscovery, was Meyerbeer's *Hugenotten*. The 1987 revival was directed by John Dew and conducted by Jesus Lopez Cobos who, as general music director since 1981, was in charge of two new productions each season.

Hans Neuenfels, who in his seventies established the model for a contemporary interpretation of Verdi with *Troubadour* in Nürnberg and *Aida* in Frankfurt, continued his work with *Macht des Schicksals*. Lopez Cobos again conducted, and the excellent ensemble was led by Julia Varady, who was becoming a representative of the company. A reworking of the Slavic repertoire began with Janáček's *Auf einem Totenhaus* followed by *Katja Kabanowa*. Both operas were staged by Günter Krämer and conducted by Jiri Kout with sets by Andreas Reinhardt, who had also provided sets for *Die Tote Stadt* and Friedrich's staging of the three-act *Lulu*. The same team produced two additional Slavic operas: the original version of Shostakovitch's *Lady Macbeth von Mzensk* and Janáček's *Die Sache Makropulos*. However, the central project for the 1980s was the new interpretation of Richard Wagner's *Der Ring des Nibelungen* conducted by Lopez Cobos. The "Time Tunnel" (inspired by the Washington, D.C., Metro) designed by Peter Sykora for Götz Friedrich's production has meanwhile, as a synonym for the "Berlin Ring," literally gone around the world: on tour in Tokyo, Yokohama, and Washington, D.C. A new revised production was seen in London 1989–1991.

General manager Friedrich considers the building of a young ensemble among the critical challenges for the future that will carry the company into the third millennium. Both the Foundation of the Deutsche Oper Berlin and the American-Berlin Opera Foundation, Inc., offer twelve-month scholarships that underwrite practical training for up to four young singers. Each receives extensive coaching and is also cast in smaller roles from the beginning. Many of these students will be accepted into the ensemble after their training, and some have achieved international careers. This is, however, not the only source of talent for the Deutsche Oper Berlin; a substantial list of young singers who made their debuts on other stages have been "discovered" here. Beside Germans such as Peter Seiffert, who advanced from Tamino and Don Ottavio to Lohengrin, stands an important group of Americans including Gwendolyn Bradley and Lenus Carlson. The Scandinavian tradition is represented by singers such as Bengt-Ola Morgny, who came to Berlin directly from the Göteborg Musikhochschule, and Eva Johansson, who was cast as Elsa in the new Lopez Cobos/Friedrich production of *Lohengrin* in June 1990. Given the situation of a newly united country, the Deutsche Oper Berlin, with all its assets and the artistic contributions of its thirty-year history, challenges itself to continue to win the support of the public.

CHRONOLOGY OF DIRECTORS: Georg Hartmann, 1912–1924. Heinz Tietjen, 1925–1930. Carl Ebert, 1931–1933. Wilhelm Rode, 1934–1944. Michael Bohnen, 1945–1947. Heinz Tietjen, 1948–1954. Carl Ebert, 1955–1960. Gustav Sellner, 1961–1971. Egon Seefehlner, 1972–1975. Siegfried Palm, 1976–1980. Götz Friedrich, 1981–present.

BIBLIOGRAPHY: *Beiträge zum Musiktheater (Jahrbücher der Deutschen Oper Berlin)* (Berlin, 1982–). Werner Bollert, *50 Jahre Deutsche Oper Berlin* (Berlin, 1961). Horst Georges, *Deutsche Oper Berlin* (Berlin, 1964). Gisela Huwe, ed., *Die Deutsche Oper Berlin* (Berlin, 1984). *Das Opernorchester in Charlottenburg, 75 Jahre. Vom Deutschen Opernhaus zur Deutschen Oper Berlin* (Berlin, 1987). *25 Jahre Deutsche Oper Berlin: Eine Dokumentation der Premieren von 1961 bis 1986* (Berlin, 1986).

ACCESS: Richard-Wagner-Straße 10, 1000 Berlin 10. (49 30) 34 38 1; fax (49 30) 34 38 2 32. Prof. Götz Friedrich, Generalintendant. Jesus Lopez Cobos, Generalmusikdirector.

CURT A. ROESLER
TRANS. JONATHAN MUIR

Deutsche Staatsoper Berlin (Unter den Linden)

The Deutsche Staatsoper Berlin is not only one of the oldest but also one of the most beautiful and productive opera houses in Europe. The opening of the Königlichen Hofoper Unter den Linden on December 7, 1742, with the premiere of Carl Heinrich Graun's *Cleopatra e Cesare*, was, without doubt, a European-wide celebration of both theater construction and music culture. Georg Wenzeslaus von Knobelsdorff, chief architect of the Prussian King Friedrich II, was commissioned to build the opera house in 1740. He took his artistic inspiration from the Italian Andrea Palladio, whose Renaissance Villa Capra, the so-called Rotonda in Vicenza, was finished in 1567. Knobelsdorff designed a clearly articulated long building with six column vestibules and entrances on three sides. The three lobbies inside (the Apollo-Saal, the Opernsaal, and the Korinthischen Saal) serve the stage and can also be joined with the Opernsaal to form an enormous ballroom. In its exterior classical clarity, its festive interior atmosphere, and its functionality the opera house had no equal in Europe at that time. The Lindenoper created at the same time the most precise model of Friedrich's desire that cultural buildings in Berlin suggest a "German Athens." A first-class ensemble of excellent Italian singers, French and Italian dancers, and German and Bohemian instrumentalists under the direction of Hofkapellmeister Carl Heinrich Graun achieved performances of aristocratic elegance. During his tenure, over two dozen of the composer-conductor's own operas were performed along with those of his contemporaries, usually in the Italian style.

The theater was, above all, exclusively at the disposal of the Prussian Court as well as for opera performances in Italian during Carnival and for masked balls. Nevertheless, those travelers who were invited to the performances enthusiastically spread the reputation of Berlin as the new opera metropolis far beyond the borders of Prussia. This first golden age of the Berlin Opera only lasted until the Seven Years War. Because of the war, the house remained closed between 1756 and 1764, the highly acclaimed ensemble fell apart, and Carl Heinrich Graun died. A revival of Graun's last opera, *Merope*, reopened the theater on December 20, 1764, but the gala event was overshadowed by the financial crisis in Prussia that was brought about by the devastating war. It was not until the 1770s that the artistic situation stabilized with the engagements of the first German prima donna, Elisabeth Schmeling-Mara, and a talented Hofkapellmeister, Johann Friedrich Reichardt. The first public concerts of the Hofkapelle again enriched the musical life of Berlin. In 1787, one year after the death of Friedrich II, Carl Gotthard Langhans, who had created the Brandenburg Gate, completely rebuilt the interior of the Lindenoper. The stage opening was widened, the parquet was reduced and fitted with seats, and the partitions between the boxes were set back to provide better sight lines. The house reopened on January 2, 1788, with the premiere of Reichardt's *Andromeda*.

Although the Nationaltheater am Gendarmenmarkt had been producing German Singspiels (including Mozart) since the 1780s under Carl Theophil Döbbelin, German-language works first appeared in the repertoire of the Hofoper in the 1790s. [Reichardt's *Brenno*, which premiered at the Hofoper in the original Italian on October 16, 1789 (the same year Reichardt's *Claudine von Villa Bella* with Goethe's text had received its first public performance on August 3), was given in a concert version in German on January 24, 1798, as the first German-language performance in the house.] Ordinary citizen were allowed to buy tickets in 1789 (Karl Ditters von Dittersdorf's oratorio *Hiob* initiated the new policy) for noncourt entertainments following the end of the official court opera season. The repertoire of the Hofoper was based on the operas of Neumann, as well as those of Hofkapellmeister Reichardt, Alessandri, Righini, and Himmel. Only

Gluck's *Alceste* represented the international repertoire on the stage of the Lindenoper. [According to Lowenberg's *Annals of Opera*, the work was first produced in German on October 15, 1817.] The house was closed once again when Napoleon's troops occupied Berlin in 1806. The Hofoper and the Nationaltheater were united as the Königliche Schauspiele under a single director in 1811, and the actor-director-writer August Wilhelm Iffland administered the theaters until 1814. Iffland, and especially his successor (and a good friend of Goethe) Karl von Brühl, who remained as Generalintendant from 1814 to 1828, struggled against the prevailing wind to regain European glory for the Lindenoper.

Brühl began his era with the Berlin premiere of Beethoven's *Fidelio* [October 11, 1815]. Moreover, he engaged as set designer the well-known architect Karl-Friedrich Schinkel, whose famous *Zauberflöte* sets of 1816 were among his many contributions to Unter den Linden's theater history. It is true that Brühl's attempt to bring Carl Maria von Weber to Berlin as Hofkapellmeister was thwarted by the court, but he was responsible for the beginning of German national opera with the world premiere of Weber's *Der Freischütz* on June 18, 1821, performed in the new Schauspielhaus am Gendarmenmarkt and conducted by the composer. The engagement in 1820 (until 1840) of the Italian composer and former Hofkapellmeister of Napoleon, Gasparo Spontini, as the first Prussian Generalmusikdirector was clearly a compromise with the conservative taste of the court. It secured at the same time an artistic personality who would raise the musical standard of the soloists, the instrumentalists, and the chorus substantially higher. Fortunately, Brühl's successor, Wilhelm von Redern successfully argued for more German operas in the repertoire. After the Hofoper had presented the works of Gluck, Mozart, and Meyerbeer along with the contemporary French and Italian operas, the company discovered a Berlin composer—Albert Lortzing—and performed his works with persistent success. Both *Die beiden Schützen* and *Czaar und Zimmermann* were performed in Berlin in 1839.

Giacomo Meyerbeer, a musical personality of European renown, was appointed the new Generalmusikdirektor on January 1, 1843. He not only secured social status for his musicians, he also increased their financial benefits, initiated authors' licenses, and performed three works of living German composers each year. The young Richard Wagner found Meyerbeer to be an unselfish advocate. The new director's first season was tainted by the great fire that completely destroyed the opera house on August 18, 1843, and the company was forced to perform in the Schauspielhaus. Following Carl Ferdinand Langhan's complete restoration, the opera house reopened on December 7, 1844, with the world premiere of Meyerbeer's *Ein Feldlager in Schlesien*. [Jenny Lind had been invited to Berlin that year by Meyerbeer, and she made her sensational debut in the premiere, following that with *Norma* on December 15.] Unfortunately, Meyerbeer was forced to relinquish his position on November 26, 1848, and was available only to conduct concerts and guest in the pit. It was hoped that the engagement of Otto Nicolai as Hofkapellmeister in 1848 would ensure artistic continuity, but the composer died on May 11, only a few weeks after the triumphant world premiere of his *Lustigen Weiber von Windsor* on March 9, 1849, in Berlin.

The period between 1851 and 1886 was characterized by the conservative Generalintendant Botho von Hülsen who, despite engaging a number of international opera stars [Désirée Artôt, Lilli Lehmann, and Adelina Patti, among others], was unable to maintain the artistic level of Spontini and Meyerbeer. The works of Wagner, Mozart, Meyerbeer, and Verdi appeared in Berlin infrequently, and were replaced instead by ballets such as *Flick und Flock* and *Aladin oder die Wunderlampe*. In general, Hülsen supported appearances rather than innovation, a tendency that his successor Bolko von Hochberg (appointed in 1886) continued. Hochberg did, however, improve the musical direction of the Lindenoper. With the engagements of Joseph Sucher (1888), Felix von Weingartner (1891), and Karl Muck (1892), the company returned to the top level of European opera houses. The twenty-year involvement of Richard Strauss (1898–1918), first as Hofkapellmeister and later as the Generalmusikdirector, extended and intensified the new standards. From Mascagni in the 1890s to Thomas and Bizet at the turn of the century, Mozart rose again to the top under the advocacy of Strauss. Moreover, when one counts the yearly performances at both the Lindenoper and the Kroll-Oper since the 1890s, Richard Wagner also regained his popularity during the period before World War I.

With the end of the war and the November Revolution of 1918, the days of the "Königlichen Schauspiele" and the pompous representational style of the Lindenoper were over. [In November 1919 the new Ministry of Culture assumed control and the Lindenoper was renamed the Staatsoper.] Democracy reigned in the former Hofoper, and monthly people's performances attracted new audiences to the house. A widely representative personnel council selected the conductor-composer Max von Schillings (1919) as the new Intendant. The dominance of Richard Wagner's works remained, followed by the operas of Puccini, Verdi, and Richard Strauss. The most popular work of the 1920s was Puccini's *Madama Butterfly*, which retained this position until 1955. As Max von Schillings (1919–1925), Leo Blech (1918–1923; 1926–1937), and Erich Kleiber (1923–1934) secured the highest musical standards in performance, the director Franz Ludwig Hörth and designers Panos Aravantinos and Emil Pirchan sought to reform the productions. Among the important artistic directions during the 1920s, however, was the fact that contemporary composers found themselves a home in Berlin. The company produced world premieres or first performances of the works of Křenek (*Zwingburg*, on October 21, 1924), Pfitzner (*Das Herz*, on November 12, 1931), Schreker (*Der singende Teufel*, on March 2, 1927), Busoni, Janáček, Stravinsky [*Renard* and *Mavra*, on June 7, 1925], Weill (*Royal Palace*, on March 2, 1927), and Milhaud (*Christoph Columbus*, on May 5, 1930). A high point was the world premiere of Alban Berg's *Wozzeck* on December 14, 1925. With the opening of the Kroll-Oper in 1924 under the direction of Otto Klemperer, stage directors Ernst Legal, Gustaf Gründgens, and Jürgen Fehling, and designers Caspar Neher, Teo Otto, and Oskar Schlemmer filled a second house with dramatic and scenic experiments. [While the stagehouse of the Lindenoper was being rebuilt, the ensemble performed at the Kroll-Oper, alternating with the resident company until the refurbished Staatsoper reopened in November 1927.] In 1931 a majority of the Prussian Landtag voted to close the Kroll-Oper, thus ending this progressive operatic development.

At the beginning of the fascist era a number of important artists, including Erich Kleiber, Otto Klemperer, and, later, Leo Blech left the Staatsoper for political and racial reasons and emigrated. In spite of these losses, Heinz Tietjen, Intendant of the Berlin Staatsoper since 1927, was able to retain and enlarge his solid ensemble of singers although he was unable to withdraw completely from the patronization of the self-proclaimed Prussian Minister-President Hermann Goering. Twice he stood up against the official cultural politics: with the world premieres of Werner Egk's *Peer Gynt* (November 24, 1938) and Rudolf Wagner-Regeny's *Die Bürger von Calais* (January 28, 1939). The musical story lay in the hands of Robert Heger, Johannes Schüler, Werner Egk, and occasionally Wilhelm Furtwängler and Herbert von Karajan. Giuseppe Verdi was the most popular composer, followed by Wagner, Puccini, Strauss, and Mozart. The theater was heavily damaged by bombs on April 9, 1941. As a prestigious symbol of fascist cultural politics, the Lindenoper was quickly rebuilt (but unfortunately, without concern for its historical architecture). On December 7, 1942, it reopened with Furtwängler conducting *Die Meistersinger von Nürnberg* in celebration of the two hundredth anniversary of the Lindenoper, only to sink once again in debris and ashes on February 3, 1945. The ensemble had already been released for required work in the armaments factories with the beginning of "Total War." A few soloists in union with the Staatskapelle gave concerts in the Schauspielhaus on Gendarmenmarkt.

Immediately following the end of the war, the ensemble was reconstituted under the direction of Ernst Legal with the support of the Soviet occupation forces. The company used the lightly damaged Admiralspalast on Friedrichstraße as an interim performance site. The theater hosted opera concerts beginning on August 23, and on September 8, 1945, the Admiralspalast officially opened with Gluck's *Orpheus und Eurydike*. Despite the most difficult conditions, material deprivations, and economic and political tensions, which were only intensified with the partitioning of Berlin in 1948, Ernst Legal, Heinrich Allmeroth, and Max Burghardt were able to build a broad operatic repertoire that included the works of Verdi, Puccini, Mozart, Tchaikovsky, Wagner, and Richard Strauss. An important artistic event during this period, the often discussed world premiere of the antiwar opera *Die Verurteilung des Lukullus* by Bertold Brecht and Paul Dessau, occurred on March 14, 1951. [Brecht and Dessau began their long artistic collaboration in the United States when they were both in exile due to the war. The new version, *Das Verhör des Lukullus*, was presented on October 12, 1951.] As early as 1948 Ernst Legal had initiated contact with Erich Kleiber, who had returned to Europe from exile in Argentina; he had been conducting at the Teatro Colón in Buenos Aires since 1937. In 1951 the former Generalmusikdirektor returned to Berlin, where he encouraged the reconstruction of the Lindenoper; construction began in 1952, and the 1,396-seat opera house opened again on September 4, 1955.

A team of architects led by Richard Paulick was determined to retain Knobelsdorff's artistic spirit and the unique harmony of the building while at the same time ensuring the functional requirements of a modern opera house. The attempt to secure the musical direction of the Lindenoper for Erich Kleiber floundered on the conductor's apprehension about the interference of politics in art. Shortly before the opening, Franz Konwitchny took over as Generalmusikdirektor and conducted the first premiere in the new-old house, Richard Wagner's *Die Meistersinger von Nürnberg*. In the years that followed, the company developed an ambitious repertoire with three emphases: the German opera from Handel and Gluck through Mozart, Beethoven, Weber, and Wagner, to Richard Strauss; the international repertoire with the principal works of the Italian, Russian, and French opera; and a continuing commitment to contemporary works (nine world premieres were mounted between 1957 and 1989, four of them by Paul Dessau). The building of the Berlin Wall in 1961 meant a drastic break in the development of the Lindenoper as over two hundred employees who lived in West Berlin were dismissed. Young artists representing many ensembles, both domestic and foreign, helped to secure the company's performance capability; consequently, in spite of the loss of international singers, the Deutsche Staatsoper quickly stabilized. Under Hans Pischner (1963–1984), the commissioning of new operas and ballets significantly increased. In addition, the company increased its tours, visiting practically every European country plus making ten visits to Japan, thus demonstrating the high artistic standards of the Staatsoper.

Since 1961 the musical history of the Lindenoper has been determined by the capable talents of Otmar Suitner, Heinz Fricke, Heinz Rögner, and Siegfried Kurz. The chief regisseur from 1965 to 1990 was Erhard Fischer, ably assisted by Horst Donnet, Ruth Berghaus, and Christian Pöppelreiter, who explored a many-colored spectrum of scenic interpretation including the realistic music theater of Walter Felsenstein and the epic theater of Bertold Brecht, which were both assimilated and further developed. Günter Rimkus succeeded Hans Pischner as Intendant during the comprehensive reconstruction of the theater, which lasted from 1983 to 1988. This massive project combined a painstaking curator's restoration of the building itself with numerous technical improvements of the stage machinery. Most of the work was completed during the regular rehearsal and performance schedule but finally it became imperative to close the house for ten months in 1986. The opening of the Berlin Wall on November 9, 1989, followed by the unification of the two Germanies on October 3, 1990, resulted in political pressures that the Deutsche Staatsoper Berlin be brought again into a position as a leading German, as well as a first-rate European, opera house. During the 1990–1991 season there will be approximately 280 performances including some 40 concerts and 60 ballet evenings. The current opera repertoire includes 42 operas with new productions of *Il Trovatore*, *Pelléas et Mélisande*, *Madama Butterfly*, *Falstaff*, and Meyerbeer's *Die Afrikanerin*. Current plans project a commitment to the operas of Mozart, Strauss, and Wagner until 1992, which is the 250th anniversary of the founding of the Lindenoper. Udo Zimmermann is composing a "Don Quichotte" opera to a libretto by Christoph Hien for the anniversary season. Also scheduled is a new production of Richard Wagner's *Der Ring der Nibelungen* under the artistic direction of Daniel Barenboim and Harry Kupfer.

CHRONOLOGY OF DIRECTORS: [Königliche Hofoper] Baron von Sweerts, 1742–1757. Baron von Pöllnitz, 1763–1771. Graf Zierotin-Lilgenau, 1771–1775. Baron von Arnim, 1775–1786. Freiherr von der Reck, 1787–1795. August Wilhelm von Iffland, 1796–1814. Karl von Brühl, 1815–1828. Wilhelm von Redern, 1830–1842. Theodore von Küstern, 1842–1851. Botho von Hülsen, 1851–1886. Bolko von Hochberg, 1886–1902. Georg von Hülsen-Haeseler, 1903–1918. [Berliner Staatsoper] Max von Schillings, 1919–1925. Heinz Tietjen, 1927–1945. [Deutsche Staatsoper Berlin] Ernst Legal, 1945–1952. Dr. Heinrich Allmeroth, 1952–1954. Prof. Max Burghardt, 1954–1962. Prof. Hans Pischner, 1963–1984. Prof. Günter Rimkus, 1984–present.

BIBLIOGRAPHY: Hans Curjel, *Experiment Krolloper, 1927–1931*, ed. Eigel Kruttge (München, 1975). *Deutsche Staatsoper Berlin* (Berlin, 1980). Hugo Fetting, *Die Geschichte der Deutschen Staatsoper* (Berlin, 1955). Christian Friedrich, *Staatsoper Berlin* (Berlin, 1953). Ruth Freydank, *Theater in Berlin von den Anfängen bis 1945* (Berlin, 1988). Manfred Haedler, *Deutsche Staatsoper Berlin: Geschichte und Gegenwart* (Berlin, 1990). Julius Kapp, *Geschichte der Staatsoper Berlin* (Berlin, 1942). Werner Otto, *Die Lindenoper* (Berlin, 1980). Werner Otto and Walter Rösler, eds., *Deutsche Staatsoper Berlin* (Berlin, 1972). Werner Otto and Günter Rimkus, *Deutsche Staatsoper Berlin, 1945–1965* (Berlin, n.d.). Alexander Ringer, ed., *The Early Romantic Era. Between Revolutions: 1789–1848* (London, 1990). Frank Volker, *Die Deutsche Staatsoper zu Berlin* (Leipzig, 1972).

ACCESS: Unter den Linden 7, D–1080 Berlin. (37 2) 20 35 40; fax (37 2) 20 82 671. Prof. Günter Rimkus, Intendant. Siegfried Kurz, Generalmusikdirektor.

MANFRED HAEDLER
TRANS. MARC ÄNDERS

Komische Oper

As the first newly founded opera in Germany after the Second World War, the Komische Oper opened in December 1947. The former German capital city lay in ruins, and the major opera houses, including the Deutsche Staatsoper Berlin (Unter den Linden) and the Städtische Oper were destroyed. Within days after the end of the war, well-known singers made their way back to their old haunts so that the former opera companies could begin to perform in temporary sites. The need of the people for culture, and above all for theater, was very compelling; this need was not only for entertainment to distract from the pain and suffering but also for the search for answers to existential problems. The director Walter Felsenstein was the founder and first artistic director of the Komische Oper. His goal was to reform traditional opera into music theater in which the dramatic plot would be clarified using both musical and theatrical means. For him each music statement on the opera stage was the expression of a humanistic answer to a human conflict. Felsenstein turned to a new audience that did not cater to beautiful singing and refined technique but rather could critically follow and evaluate the musical action on the stage through an understanding of inherent human functions and conflicts. Similar to Bertold Brecht, who was building his Berliner Ensemble at the same time, Walter Felsenstein wanted the separation of stage and audience to overcome the separation of artistic product and artistic enjoyment. The truth of his music theater was to be verifiable at any time. Felsenstein observed that "raising music making and singing on stage to a compelling, truthful and indispensable human statement was and is the basic question if one is to speak about music theater. Music theater is when a musical plot is brought to theatrical reality and unconditional believability through singing actors. . . . A basic requirement for a pure and meaningful theatrical experience is the incorporation of the audience into the drama and poetry of a stage process through the understandable, believable and unquestionable truth of a creative performance art."

Felsenstein fits directly in the long tradition of major artists who have attempted to realize similar goals—in Germany, Handel, Mozart, Weber, Wagner, Schönberg, and Berg, for example. Berlin even had an opera house with similar ideas. The director Hans Gregor had founded the first "Komische Oper" in 1905, and its music theater orientation was in direct contrast to the strong vocal orientation of the Hofoper during the former's six short years of existence. Felsenstein also had a spiritual connection with the Krolloper which, from its founding in 1843 until it was destroyed in World War II, served as a theater for the common people. During its most influential period, under the direction of Otto Klemperer from 1927 to 1931, it was the most progressive company in Berlin. The name Komische Oper derives from the tradition of the opéra comique. It referred not to a repertoire of lighter works but rather to a unified performance style represented by the French popular theater as opposed to the grand opera of the nineteenth century.

Performances on the site of the present theater date back to 1764, when traveling actors entertained the public. Later premieres of the works of Lessing and Schiller alternated with German Singspiels and French opéra comique. Designed by Ferdinand Fellner and Hermann Heller, the 1,338-seat "Theater unter den Linden" on Behrenstraße was built between 1890 and 1892 as a home for musical revues. It was renamed the Metropoltheater in 1898, and the revues it presented stamped the character of the evolving capital of Germany. In the 1920s the Metropol became an operetta house featuring the works of Leo Fall, Emmerich Kálmán, and Franz Lehár. Severely damaged by bombs in March 1945, the house was rebuilt and opened as the Komische Oper on December 23, 1947. The 1,028-seat theater underwent reconstruction in 1965–1966 primarily to enlarge the stage. Johann Strauß's *Die Fledermaus* in Felsenstein's staging opened the house, and his productions (*Carmen, Die Zauberflöte,* Janáček's *Das schlaue*

Füchslein, *Hoffmanns Erzählungen*, *Othello*, *La Traviata*, Offenbach's *Ritter Blaubart*, and *Der Fiddler auf dem Dach* quickly made the company into a popular and internationally acclaimed music theater. With its best productions the company was able to fuse music and theater in an understandable and contemporary style that captured and moved the audience. The artistic orientation and working methods enabled the ensemble to go beyond the notes to the spirit of the score. A number of operas were freed from their traditional inaccurate routines in this way. Through comprehensive preparation and a rehearsal period that often lasts a number of months, an unmistakable realization of the work appears that carries the stamp of the theater. Without tampering with the substance of the work, contemporary theater dealing with current issues is thus created.

The special characteristic of the Komische Oper is the ensemble work. Preparation for a production is a team effort of the director, conductor, dramatic advisor, designers, and performers. This attracts talented artists to the company and allows younger performers to develop an artistic personality. Conductors who have worked with Felsenstein include Gert Bahner, Robert Hanell, Rudolf Kempe, Dimitri Kitajenko, Otto Klemperer, Hans Löwlein, Kurt Masur, Vaclav Neumann, Geza Oberfrank, Leo Spieß, Karl-Fritz Voigtmann, Hans-Joachim Willert, and Meinhard von Zallinger. Wolfgang Hammerschmidt, Horst Seeger, Götz Friedrich, and Stephan Stompor have served as dramatic advisors. Götz Friedrich, Joachim Herz, and Carl Riha began as assistants to Felsenstein and are now all prominent directors in their own right. The designers Rudolf Heinrich, Eleonore Kleiber, Heinz Pfeiffenberg, Caspar Neher, Wilfried Werz, and Reinhard Zimmermann were creative partners in many productions.

Each performer in the company brings a unique personality and talent to the team's production concept. The casting and musical direction normally remain unchanged through the production run, and only after an exhaustive series of rehearsals are any changes made. Casting is based on vocal compatibility, acting talent, and individual suitability for the role. Under Felsenstein's guidance the Komische Oper has developed a type of singer-actor who is able to communicate the truth of the character and the relationship to other people. The soprano Irmgard Arnold, the tenor Hanns Nocker, the buffo-tenor Werner Enders, and the bass Rudolf Asmus were and are, among others, faithful members of a stable ensemble in which they played leads as well as character roles. Until Felsenstein's death the artists worked almost exclusively in his ensemble; guest roles in other theaters were very seldom undertaken. Glory and prestige resulted from performances of the company as well as from international tours.

Following Walter Felsenstein's death in 1975, Joachim Herz assumed the artistic direction of the Komische Oper. Among his many productions, the two settings of *Lulu*, *Aufstieg und Fall der Stadt Mahagonny*, and *Peter Grimes* stand out. A new team was appointed in 1981, with Werner Rackwitz as Intendant, Harry Kupfer as stage director, Rolf Reuter as conductor, and Hans-Jochen Genzel as dramatic advisor. Together with Tom Schilling, Reinhart Zimmermann, and Eleonore Kleiber, they led the company with a fresh perception and artistic style. In recent seasons a Mozart cycle (*Idomeneo*, *Die Entführung aus dem Serail*, *Die Hochzeit des Figaro*, *Don Giovanni*, *Così fan tutte*, and *Die Zauberflöte*), *Die Meistersinger von Nürnberg*, Mussorgsky's original version of *Boris Godunov*, *Die verkauften Braut*, Gluck's *Orpheus*, Aribert Reimann's *Lear*, and Siegfried Matthus's *Judith* have provided the public with unique and fascinating examples of the art of the Komische Oper. The company performs fifteen operas and five ballets in repertoire each season, of which four or five works are new productions. The repertoire is kept deliberately small to ensure time to rework productions after the premiere, should that prove necessary. Currently, the company schedules some 270 performances a year, of which 70 percent are operas, 25 percent are ballets, and the remainder are concerts. The repertoire ranges from the early baroque to premieres of contemporary works, such as Siegfried Matthus's *Der letzte Schuß* (1967), *Judith* (1985), and Georg Katzer's *Das Land Bumbum* (1978). All performances are in German in order to ensure the maximum understanding of each audience member. It is not unusual for the company to perform a work 200 to 400 times (*Ritter Blaubart* has been given 350 times since 1963.)

BIBLIOGRAPHY: Hans Curjel, *Experiment Krolloper, 1927–1931* (München, 1975). *Jahrbuch der Komischen Oper Berlin*, 12 vols. (Berlin, 1961–1973). Peter Paul Fuchs, ed., *The Music Theater of Walter Felsenstein* (New York, 1975). Hans-Jochen Irmer and Wolfgang Stein, *Joachim Herz: Regisseur im Musiktheater* (Berlin, 1977). Fritz Jacobsohn, *Hans Gregors Komische Oper, 1905–1911* (Berlin, n.d.). Clemens Kohl and Ernst Krause, *Felsenstein auf der Probe* (Berlin, 1971). Werner Otto and Götz Friedrich, eds., *Die Komische Oper Berlin, 1947–1954* (Berlin, 1954). Horst Seeger, ed., *Musikbühne: Probleme und Informationen*, 4 vols. (Berlin, 1974–77). Horst Seeger and Mathias Rank, eds., *Oper heute: Ein Alamanch der Musikbühne* (Berlin, 1978–   ). Stephan Stompor, ed., *Walter Felsenstein Schriften zum Musiktheater* (Berlin, 1976). *10 Jahre Komische Oper* (Berlin, 1958). *20 Jahre Komische Oper* (Berlin, 1967). *Die Komische Oper in drei Jahrzehnten* (Berlin, 1978). *Vorstellungen vom Musiktheater: Ein Almanac auf das 40. Jahr der Komischen Oper* (Berlin, 1987).

ACCESS: Behrenstraße 55–57, O–1086 Berlin. (37 2) 2 20 27 61. Prof. Dr. sc. Werner Rackwitz, Intendant.

HANS-JOCHEN GENZEL
TRANS. MARC ÄNDERS

DARMSTADT (134,200)

Staatstheater

Theatrical traditions in Darmstadt date back to the seventeenth century when Landgraf Ludwig IV promoted Singspiels in his renovated equestrian hall in 1683. As early as 1711 the building was rebuilt into an opera house. The composer Christoph Graupner, who had written several operas for Hamburg, was appointed Kapellmeister in 1709 by Landgraf Ernst Ludwig, who was himself a composer and lover of opera. Three of Graupner's operas, *Lucio Vero e*

Berenice (1710), *Telemach* (1711), and *La costanza vince l'inganno* (1719), were premiered in Darmstadt. Großherzog Ludwig I (1790–1830) commissioned the architect Georg Moller to construct a Ducal Theater, and the original 1,370-seat Großes Haus opened with a performance of the revised version of Spontini's *Fernand Cortez* on November 7, 1819. Theater activity was severely restricted during the revolutions of 1830 and 1848, but shortly thereafter the company produced the first German performances of Verdi's *Les Vêpres Siciliennes* (March 14, 1857) and *Don Carlos* (March 29, 1868). Gounod's *Faust* also received its first German performance here, on February 10, 1861. The house was partially destroyed by fire in 1871, and the new theater opened [restored 1904–1905] with Richard Wagner's *Lohengrin* in 1879.

With the ascension of the last grand duke, Ernest Ludwig (1892–1918), the city rapidly established a wide reputation as a center of the arts, especially contemporary works, which interested the new ruler. Well-known conductors, including Friedrich Rehbock, Bruno Kittle, Ernst Lert, Paul Ottenheimer, and Erich Kleiber were engaged, and the opera presented spring festivals with famous guest artists. Felix Weingartner worked at the theater during World War I (1915–1919) and measurably improved the orchestra. In 1918, at the conclusion of the war, Darmstadt became the regional capital (until 1945) and the theater came under the control of the state of Hesse. A new administration under Gustav Hartung not only continued the opera house but also produced events in the older theater. The program was especially noted for its cultivation of contemporary works and attracted artists of the first rank to perform in Darmstadt. Michael Balling, appointed Generalmusikdirektor (GMD) in 1919, was a significant Wagner and Bruckner conductor, while Joseph Rosenstock (GMD, 1925–1927) specialized in Stravinsky and the new Vienna composers. Karl Böhm (GMD, 1927–1931) started his career in Darmstadt; Hans Schnidt-Isserstedt and Carl Maria Zwissler (GMD, 1933–1936) both conducted before the war. At this same time the productions were exploring new paths. Under the Intendant Carl Ebert (1927–1931), the stage settings of Wilhelm Reinking made an important contribution to the modern music theater.

During the Third Reich, new music was prohibited, but under conductors such as Heinrich Hollreiser (1938–1939) the opera continued to produce an interesting repertoire. In 1944 the theater was destroyed by bombs. The Orangerie and then the Stadthalle temporarily housed operas and plays from 1945 to 1972, while a twenty-seven-year search process explored optional sites for a permanent house. During this interim period, especially under the Intendant Gustav Rudolf Sellner (1951–1961) and designer Franz Mertz, a typical Darmstadt performance style evolved. A memorable German premiere of Prokofiev's *The Gambler* was produced in 1956 which highlighted this style. After Sellner, Gerhard Hering (1961–1972) managed the theater, and he engaged the conductor Hans Drewanz as GMD, a position Drewanz still retains. The new 956-seat Großes Haus on Marienplatz was opened on October 6, 1972 with Beethoven's *Fidelio* under the Intendant Günther Beelitz. He was succeeded by Kurt Horres (1976–1984), and a number of productions of contemporary opera, such as Klebe's *Die Fastnachtsbeichte* in 1983, were mounted in keeping with the theater's traditions. His successor was Peter Brenner who served from 1984 to 1990, and, as of 1991, Peter Girth will be the Intendant.

BIBLIOGRAPHY: Hermann Kaiser, *Das Grossherzogliche Hoftheater zu Darmstadt: 1810–1910*. (Darmstadt, 1964). Hermann Kaiser, *Modernes Theater in Darmstadt* (Darmstadt, 1955). Hermann Kaiser, *300 Jahre Darmstädter Theater in Berichte von Augenzeugen* (Darmstadt, 1972). Hermann Kaiser, *Vom Zeittheater zur Sellner-Bühne* (Darmstadt, 1961). *275 Jahre Theater in Darmstadt* (Darmstadt, 1980).

ACCESS: Auf dem Marienplatz, 6100 Darmstadt. (49 6151) 28 11 01. Dr. Peter Girth, Intendant. Hans Drewanz, Generalmusikdirektor.

[From materials supplied by the company]
TRANS. JONATHAN MUIR

DORTMUND (587,731)

Städtische Bühnen

As an industrial city in the heart of the Ruhr district, Dortmund has a long cultural tradition. The first municipal opera house was designed by the architect Martin Dülfer and opened on September 17, 1904, with a gala performance of Wagner's *Tannhäuser*. The project was financed by a combination of public funds and voluntary contributions from the community. The motto carved over the entrance defines the effort: "An aspiring city cannot do without the arts. Generous hearts built this house or the muses." Until the theater was destroyed in 1944, opera, operetta, and ballet had their comfortable home here along with the drama. The predecessors of this theater were various private undertakings which performed in hotels and other available locations. A professional theater was formed in 1800 which offered operas and plays. In 1807 Mozart's *Die Zauberflöte* was performed in the Gildenhaus, which also hosted Weber's *Der Freischütz* in 1826. Regular opera performances were given in the Kühnschen Saal after 1837, a theater that remained active under a number of directors until 1903. When it was destroyed by fire, an operatic era came to an end, for the house had supported the larger works of Verdi and Wagner as well as the standard repertoire.

The first official Stadttheater opened in Brügmannschen Zirkus in 1871 featuring the works of Mozart, Lortzing, and the popular operettas and Lustspiels. A spirited competition with the Kühnschen Saal led to the bankruptcy of the Brügmannschen Zirkus, and the Stadttheater moved into the Künschen Saal in 1875 and remained there for the next twenty-eight years. Regular support for the opera after 1904 lay in the capable hands of the administration. The first director of the new theater was Hans Gelling who pursued a collaboration with Essen until 1907. During the early years, Wagner's entire "Ring" tetralogy as well as Richard Strauss's *Salome* and *Rosenkavalier* were produced. Under the musical direction of Georg Hüttner, who had taken over the Dortmunder Orchesterverein in 1887 and had built it into an acceptable symphony, this orchestra became the house ensemble for the seven-month season of operas and operettas. In spite of difficult circumstances during World War I, Hüttner was able to refine the orchestra until his death in 1919.

Hüttner's successor was Wilhelm Sieben, who carried the title of Städtischer Musikdirektor. Together with Johannes Maurach, the first director to carry the title of Intendant of Dortmund, Sieben began to improve the quality of the productions. In collaboration with a series of Intendants, he created a high-quality golden age of music theater in Dortmund until World War II. Along with the standard repertoire, the company produced the contemporary works of Hindemith, Wellesz, Krenek, and Weill. Included in the ensemble were outstanding singers such as Helene Wildbrunn, Margarete Teschemacher, and Karl Schmitt-Walter. The orchestra reached a maximum of 103 musicians, and, in 1937, when the auditorium was completely refurbished, Peter Hoenselaars was given the title of Generalintendant. Theater life in the city remained generally intact during the early years of the war. Once the theater was destroyed by bombs in 1943, however, the company had to search for temporary quarters. Goebbels's declaration of total war in 1944 resulted in the closing of all German theaters.

After the war a new beginning was attempted in suburban halls under very difficult circumstances. With Mozart's *Zauberflöte* on September 17, 1947, the company took up residence in the Pädagogischen Akademie. Some thirteen years later a small theater next to the ruins of the old Stadttheater was ready, and it was opened with Beethoven's *Fidelio*. In spite of technical and artistic problems, the company remained in that theater for sixteen years. There were some memorable moments, including the productions of Busoni's *Doktor Faust* (1952–1953), Krenek's *Leben des Orest* (1953–1954), and Wagner's *Das Liebesverbot* (1956–1957). Three world premieres were also produced during this time: Manfred Gurlitt's *Nana* (1957–1958), Erik Riedes's *YÜ-NU* (1957–1958), and Gerhard von Westermann's *Prometheische Fantasie* (1959–1960). Under the leadership of Wilhelm Schüchter as both Intendant and Generalmusikdirektor, residence in the small theater ended in triumph with Verdi's *Othello* and Gottfried von Einem's *Der Prozeß* and the move to the new Großes Haus was accomplished. A modern theater with the latest technical equipment to serve a range of theatrical needs had been designed by Heinrich Rokotten and Edgar Tritthart. The new 1,160-seat theater opened on March 3, 1966, with Richard Strauss's *Der Rosenkavalier* starring Elisabeth Grümmer and Kurt Böhme. The initial season also featured the world premiere of Walter Steffens's *Eli* and new productions of *Die Zauberflöte*, *Der Troubadour*, and Hindemith's *Mathis der Mahler*.

A growing financial crisis reached a head at the beginning of the 1970s. Expenses that exceeded the public subsidy for the theater generated a great deal of criticism. A project to collaborate with the cities of Bochum and Gelsenkirchen fell through, and by 1972, the cultural minister, Alfons Spielhoff, recommended closing the music theater and reducing the Philharmonic Orchestra to a general-purpose ensemble. As a result of the broad public outcry, funding remained at current levels. Wilhelm Schüchter died shortly after *Die Walküre* was premiered on February 5, 1974. This was to have been the first production of a planned "Ring Cycle," and, fortunately, Schüchter's successor, Marek Janowski, completed the enormous undertaking. In addition, with Paul Hager, he produced *Die Meistersinger von Nürnberg* in 1977 and *Parsifal* in 1979. The 1980s continued the Wagner and Strauss tradition of the company, and, with the appointments of Horst Fechner (1983) and Klaus Weise (1985), the repertoire has been enlarged to include rarities by Rossini and Weill as well as the world premiere of Günter Wiesemann's *Brot und Spiele* (1988–1989).

CHRONOLOGY OF DIRECTORS: Hans Gelling, 1904–1907. Alois Hofmann, 1907–1913. Hans Bollmann, 1913–1919. Johannes Maurach, 1919–1922. Karl Schäffer, 1922–1927. Richard Gsell, 1927–1933. Georg Hartmann, 1933–1937. Peter Hoenselaars, 1937–1944. Willem Hoenselaars, 1945–1947. Herbert Junkers, 1947–1950. Paul Walter Jacob, 1950–1962. Hermann Schaffner, 1962–1965. Wilhelm Schüchter, 1965–1974. Dieter Geske (provisional), 1974–1975. Paul Hager and Karl-Heinz Engels, 1974–1983. Dieter Geske (provisional), 1983–1985. Horst Fechner, 1985–present.

CHRONOLOGY OF MUSIC DIRECTORS: Georg Hüttner, 1904–1919. Wilhelm Sieben, 1920–1951. Rolf Agop, 1952–1962. Wilhelm Schüchter, 1962–1974. Marek Janowski, 1975–1979. Hans Wallat, 1979–1985. Klaus Weise, 1985–1990.

BIBLIOGRAPHY: Arno Bosselt, *Die Entstehung und Entwicklung der Städtischen Bühnen Dortmund* (Dortmund, n.d.). Arthur Mäpel, *Das Dortmunder Theater von seinen Anfängen bis zur Gegenwart* (Dortmund, 1948). *100 Jahre Philharmonisches Orchester der Stadt Dortmund, 1887–1987*, (Dortmund, 1987).

ACCESS: Großes Haus, Hansastraße, 4600 Dortmund. (49 231) 5 42 2 55 47; fax (49 231) 5 42 2 24 61. Horst Fechner, Generalintendant.

SONJA MÜLLER-EISOLD
TRANS. JONATHAN MUIR

DRESDEN (metro 1,757,400; city 518,057)

Staatsoper Dresden (Semperoper)

The first German music theater work produced in Dresden was Heinrich Schütz's *Orpheus und Euridice*, which premiered on November 19, 1638. During the early part of the eighteenth century, Italian operas from Venice and Rome were produced in the large (1,500–2,000 seat) opera house on the Zwinger which was designed by Pöppelmann. The city was well known throughout Europe for the musical and visual excellence of its opera productions, and, with the advent of outstanding singers such as Maddalena Allegranti, Francesco Ceccarelli, and Giuseppe Tibaldi, the opera seasons were competitive with those produced in other major cities. Italian opera, always the favorite of the broader public, triumphed throughout the 1700s, and it was not until the kingdom of Saxony was established by the Vienna Congress in 1815 that German opera finally emerged. Count Heinrich Vitzthum directed the first court theater in 1817, which quickly caused the demise of the Italian opera company under the leadership of the Italian impresario Francesco Morlacchi in 1832. Carl Maria von Weber who composed *Der Freischütz*, *Euryanthe*, and much of *Oberon* in Dresden, became the Royal Saxon Kapellmeister on January 17, 1817, and he studiously avoided the Italian repertoire. The success of the court theater led to a heightened interest in a permanent house, and between 1838 and 1841 Gottfried Semper designed and built his first opera house in Dresden, the Royal Saxon Opera House.

With the ongoing struggle between German and Italian opera, it is interesting to note that both Verdi (*Nabucodonosor*, March 9, at the Teatro alla Scala) and Wagner (*Cola Rienzi, der Letzte der Tribunen*, October 20, at the Royal Saxon Opera House) experienced their first great successes in 1842. Wagner's first conducting assignment in his magnificent new home was von Weber's *Euryanthe* on January 10, 1843, and he would conduct both the opera and the orchestra until 1849 when his involvement in the political events of May made it imperative for him to leave the city. Following *Rienzi*, his next opera, *Der fliegende Holländer*, premiered in the house on January 2, 1843, followed by a very successful premiere of *Tannhäuser* on October 19, 1845. The opera house was destroyed by fire on September 21, 1869, and Semper was again commissioned to design a replacement. This new 1,323-seat opera house opened February 2, 1878, with a performance of Goethe's *Iphigenie auf Tauris*, beginning a golden era for theater in Dresden.

Franz Wüllner, who had served as Hofkapellmeister from 1877, was replaced by Ernst von Schuch in 1889, and Schuch would remain as director of the court opera until his death in 1914. Schuch was a fervent supporter of Wagner's works and produced them cast with some of the outstanding singers of the era, including Gudehus, Malten, Perron, and Karl Scheidemantel. He also nurtured the young Richard Strauss, whose *Feversnot* (with Annie Krull and Karl Scheidemantel) premiered on November 21, 1901; followed by *Salome* (with Marie Wittich and Carl Burian) on December 9, 1905; *Elektra* (with Annie Krull, Schumann-Heink, Margarethe Siems, and Carl Perron) on January 25, 1909; and *Der Rosenkavalier* (with Siems, Minnie Nast, Eva von der Osten, Scheidemantel, Fritz Soot, and Perron) on January 26, 1911. Schuch held thirty-three full orchestra rehearsals to perfect Strauss's magnificent new score, and the result was a major triumph. Fritz Busch took over as director in 1922 and continued the tradition of supporting contemporary opera. Under his leadership the company mounted the premieres of such works as Busoni's *Doktor Faust* (May 21, 1925) and Hindemith's *Cardillac* (November 9, 1926). Richard Strauss returned with premieres of *Intermezzo* (November 4, 1924, with Lotte Lehmann and Joseph Correck) and *Die ägyptische Helena* (June 6, 1928, with Elisabeth Rethberg and conducted by Fritz Busch; Strauss himself conducted the Vienna premiere five days later on his birthday, with Jeritza as Helen). On March 7, 1933, Hitler's National Socialist party was voted into power, and a boycott of all Jews was ordered. Both Alfred

Reucker, the Intendant, and Busch were forced out by the Nazis, and Strauss attempted to withdraw *Arabella*. Despite the composer's reservations, the contract was firm, and it was premiered on July 1, 1933. Conducted by Clemens Krauss, the initial production featured Viorica Ursuleac, Alfred Jerger, Margit Bokor, Friedrich Plaschke, and Kurt Böhme.

Karl Böhm assumed control of the house in 1934 and would remain at the helm until 1942, when he was replaced by Karl Elmendorf (1942–1945). The premiere of Strauss's next opera, *Die schwiegsame Frau*, took place on June 24, 1935, conducted by Böhm with Maria Cebotari in the leading role. Neither Hitler nor Goebbels attended, an obvious reference to the librettist, Stefan Zweig, who was Jewish. After four performances the work was officially banned. The composer's next work to be premiered in Dresden was *Daphne* on October 15, 1938, again with Böhm conducting. As the clouds of war covered Europe, opera performances took on an almost surrealist character. Weber's *Der Freischütz*, on August 31, 1944, was the last performance in the theater before it was destroyed by incendiary bombs on February 14, 1945. Following the war the opera company performed in several locations, including the old 1,103-seat Schauspielhaus. Plans were announced for a new Semper theater in June 1976, and it was constructed by Wolfgang Hänsch between 1977 and 1985. A gala production of Carl Maria von Weber's *Der Freischütz* marked the reopening of this historic house on February 13, 1985.

BIBLIOGRAPHY: Otto Funke, *Festschrift zur Jahrhundertfeier der Dresdner Oper, 1834–1934* (Dresden, 1934). W. Höntsch and U. Püschel, eds., *300 Jahre Dresdner Staatstheater* (Berlin, 1967). Friedrich Kummer, *Dresden und seine Theaterwelt* (Dresden, 1938). Alexander Ringer, ed., *The Early Romantic Era, Between Revolutions: 1789–1848* (London, 1990). H. Schnorr, *400 Jahre Deutsche Musik-kultur: Geschichte der Dresdner Hofkapelle* (Dresden, 1948). F. von Schuch, *Richard Strauss, Ernst von Schuch und Dresdens Oper* (Dresden, 1951).

ACCESS: Theaterplatz 2, D–8010 Dresden. (37 51) 4 84 20. Mr. Christoph Alberecht, Intendant.

[From materials supplied by the company]
TRANS. JONATHAN MUIR

DÜSSELDORF-DUISBURG (metro 675,437; city 573,500)

Deutsche Oper am Rhein

The Deutsche Oper am Rhein was established in 1956 as a partnership between the industrial cities of Düsseldorf and Duisburg with the objective of building a solvent and efficient ballet and opera using the Opernhaus in Düsseldorf and the Theater der Stadt Duisburg. The two cities shared a viable, though fragile, theatrical performance history. The original opera house in Düsseldorf was built in 1875 and completely restored in 1906. Partially destroyed during the war in 1943, it reopened in 1944 after repairs. The theater was closed in 1954–1955 for complete restoration, and the 1,342-seat house reopened again on April 22, 1956, with Beethoven's *Fidelio*. The original 1,118-seat Stadttheater in Duisburg was built in 1912 and renovated in 1950. In reviewing artistic expectations and realities after the war, it seemed clear to both municipalities that a cooperative venture would result in a company much stronger than either could or would support alone.

The early seasons were administered by Intendant Hermann Juch (1956–1964) who mounted the premiere of Klebe's *Die Räuber* in 1957 as well as the German premiere of Shostakovitch's *Die Nase* in 1963. Juch was succeeded by Grischa Barfuss (1965–1985), under whose leadership Krzysztof Penderecki's *Passio et mors Domini Nostri Jesu Christi secundum Lucam* was given its stage premiere in 1969. This specially commissioned work was premiered in the cathedral in Münster, West Germany, on March 30, 1966, and made a deep impression. Barfuss, in turn, was succeeded by Kurt Horres in 1986. The present company presents roughly 430 performances of both ballet and music theater pieces each season, with a permanent company that includes ninety soloists, seventy dancers, and an eighty-member chorus. These are supported by two symphony orchestras totaling 224 members and technical and administrative personnel. The company offers five new opera productions and two new ballet evenings each year, and in the 1989–1990 season, some thirty-eight operas and eight ballets were in the repertoire. Along with the standard repertoire, the company is dedicated to reviving unknown and forgotten works, producing complete cycles of the works of a few outstanding composers, supporting contemporary music, and exploring new and avant-garde theater aesthetics.

The Deutsche Oper am Rhein's tour to Moscow in 1987 demonstrated clearly the artistic progress and quality of the company. Four productions, including Wolfgang Fortner's *Bluthochzeit* (premiere 1957), shared German culture with the citizens of the Soviet Union. The company's production of Franz Schrecker's *Die Gezeichneten* (conducted by Generalmusikdirektor Wallat, directed by Günter Krämer, and with sets by Xenia Hausner) received notable acclaim when it was performed at the Théâtre Royal de la Monnaie in Brussels in 1988 and also when it toured in Vienna in 1989. One of Schrecker's most popular works, *Die Gezeichneten*, premiered in Frankfurt am Main on April 25, 1918, and established the composer in the front rank of the avant-garde of his time. The Deutsche Staatsoper Berlin (Unter den Linden) hosted the company during the Berliner Festwochen in October 1989 in productions of Giselher Klebe's *Der Jüngste Tag* and Erich Wolfgang Korngold's *Die tote Stadt* (premiere December 4, 1920). The highlight of the 1989–1990 season, however, was the beginning of a new "Ring" cycle in cooperation with the Cologne Opera conducted by Hans Wallat and directed by Kurt Horres with sets by Andreas Reinhardt. The 1989–1990 season included *Aida*, Mussorgsky's *Krovanchina*, Penderecki's *Die Teufel von Loudun*, *Das Rheingold*, *Die Walküre*, Britten's *The Rape of Lucretia*, *Fidelio*, Rossini's *La Donna del Lago*, *La Traviata*, *Der Freischütz*, *La Cenerentola*, and *Die fliegende Holländer*. The 1990–1991 season includes *My Fair Lady*, *La*

Donna del Lago, *Iphigenie in Aulis*, *The Rape of Lucretia*, *Siegfried*, *Götterdämmerung* (completing the "Ring" cycle), *Lulu*, Henze's *Die Bassariden*, Schumann's *Genoveva*, and *Die lustigen Weiber von Windsor*. In addition, thirty-two operas are kept in repertoire.

ACCESS: Düsseldorf Opernhaus, Heinrich-Heine-Allee 16a, 4000 Düsseldorf. (49 211) 89 08 01; fax (49 211) 32 90 51. Kurt Horres, Generalintendant. Hans Wallat, Generalmusikdirektor. Theater der Stadt Duisburg, König-Heinrich-Platz, 4100 Duisburg. (49 203) 33 09 01. Kurt Horres, Generalintendant.

[From materials supplied by the company]
TRANS. JONATHAN MUIR

ESSEN (623,000)

Theater und Philharmonie Essen

The original 786-seat opera house, which opened on September 16, 1892, with Lessing's *Minna von Barnhelm*, was destroyed on March 26, 1944; it was rebuilt in 1950. First German performances of such operas as Ernst Krenek's *Karl V* (1950), which was originally composed for the Wiener Staatsoper in the early 1930s, Alban Berg's *Lulu* (1953), Luigi Dallapiccola's *Il Prigioniero* (1954), and Bohuslav Martinů's *Mirandolina* (1960) continued the tradition of contemporary works initiated by Schulz-Dornburg in the late 1920s. The new 1,125-seat Aalto-Theater, which was designed by Alvar Aalto, opened on September 25, 1988, with a festive performance of Wagner's *Die Meistersinger von Nürnberg*. The 1989–1990 season included Gounod's *Mireille* (premiered March 19, 1864, in Paris), Verdi's *Aida*, Nicolai's *Die lustigen Weiber von Windsor*, Klebe's *Die Fastnachts-beichte* (premiered 1983 in Darmstadt), Tchaikovsky's *Pique Dame*, Siegfried Matthus's *Graf Mirabeau* (premiered at the Deutsche Staatsoper Berlin, on July 14, 1989), Wagner's *Die Meistersinger von Nürnberg*, Verdi's *Don Carlos*, Offenbach's *Orpheus in der Unterwelt*, *Die Fledermaus*, and Bernstein's *West Side Story*. The company also hosted the Finnish National Opera performing *Eugene Onegin* and Aarre Merikanto's *Juha*.

BIBLIOGRAPHY: F. Feldens, *75 Jahre Städtische Bühnen Essen, 1892–1967* (Essen, 1967).

ACCESS: Aalto-Theater, Theaterplatz 11, 4300 Essen 1. (49 201) 81 22 01; fax (49 201) 81 22 1 05. Prof. Manfred Schnabel, Intendant. Guido Ajmone-Marsan, Generalmusikdirecktor.

[From materials supplied by the company]

FRANKFURT AM MAIN (629,553)

Städtische Bühnen

The original Opernhaus opened on October 20, 1880, with Mozart's *Don Giovanni*. With Otto Dessoff as music director, the theater quickly established a reputation as a progressive and innovative organization. Ludwig Rottenberg replaced Dessoff in 1889, and under his leadership (until 1923) the company mounted a number of historic productions. Debussy's *Pelléas et Mélisande* received its German premiere on April 19, 1907 (in German), and Franz Schreker's first opera, *Der ferne Klang*, was premiered on August 18, 1912. The German premiere of Bartok's *Duke Blue-Beard's Castle* took place on May 13, 1922. Clemens Krauss was music director between 1924 and 1929, when he was replaced by William Steinberg, who was removed by the Nazis in 1933. Conducted by Steinberg and staged by Herbert Graf, Schoenberg's *Von Heute auf Morgen* received its world premiere on February 1, 1930. Conducted by music director Bertil Wetzelsberger, Werner Egk's *Zaubergeige* was premiered on May 22, 1935. Other important premieres of the period include Carl Orff's *Carmina Burana* (1937) and *Die Kluge* (1943).

The stagehouse was rebuilt and modernized 1935–1938; destroyed by bombs on March 22, 1944. The company performed in several temporary accommodations after the war until moving into the rebuilt 1,387-seat Schauspielhaus, now renamed the Großes Haus, which opened on December 23, 1951, with Wagner's *Die Meistersinger von Nürnberg*. This theater was incorporated into a huge, multitheater complex, which was destroyed by fire on November 12, 1987. It is currently being rebuilt with a projected opening in April 1991.

CHRONOLOGY OF MUSIC DIRECTORS: Otto Dessoff, 1880–1888. Ludwig Rottenberg, 1889–1923. Clemens Krauss, 1924–1929. William Steinberg, 1930–1933. Bertil Wetzelberger, 1934–1936. Franz Konwitschny, 1937–1944. Bruno Vondenhoff, 1945–1951. Georg Solti, 1952–1961. Lovro von Matacic, 1962–1966. Christoph von Dohnányi, 1968–1976. Michael Gielen, 1977–1987. Gary Bertini, 1988–present.

BIBLIOGRAPHY: Heinrich Heym, *Frankfurt und sein Theater* (Frankfurt, 1963). Albert Richard Mohr, *Die Frankfurter Oper, 1924–44* (Frankfurt am Main, 1971). Albert Richard Mohr, *Frankfurter Opernhaus, 1880–1980* (Frankfurt am Main, 1980). Horst Reber and Heinrich Heym, *Das Frankfurter Opernhaus: 1880–1944* (Frankfurt am Main, 1971).

ACCESS: Untermainanlage 11, 6000 Frankfurt am Main. (49 69) 2 12 02; fax (49 69) 2 12 37 5 18. Intendanz.

[From materials supplied by the company]

HAMBURG (metro 2,300,000; city 1,593,600)

Hamburgische Staatsoper

Both civic pride and mercantile skill are reflected in the over three hundred year history of the Hamburg Opera House. The Opern-Theatrum opened on January 2, 1678, with Johann Theile's Singspiel *Adam und Eva oder Der Erschaffene, Gefallene und Aufgerichtete Mensch*. Resembling a barn, the wooden structure designed by the Italian architect Sartorio was the first public opera house in Germany. Up to this time operas were only performed at the various courts for a select and invited audience. Cultivated citizens, among whom were the Councillor Gerhard Scott (who directed the opera from 1678 to 1693), the lawyer Peter Lütjens, and the organist Johann Adam Reinken, were responsible for the founding of the theater, which was to be run as a private business. These individuals also formed the initial managing board. Although strongly opposed by the clergy, who resented the clear competition to their previously dominant church music, the Hamburg Opera quickly evolved into one of the leading musical organizations of the baroque period. Performances of the works of Reinhard Keiser, Thomas Selles, Johann Mattheson, and Georg Friedrich Händel brought acclaim to the city. Some seventy-two of Kaiser's musical theater works were premiered in Hamburg between 1694 and 1734. Händel was engaged in 1703 as violinist and cembalist, and his first opera, *Almira*, was premiered in 1705. Constant attacks from bigoted theologians, who decried the carnal nature of opera, coupled with financial mismanagement and modest public interest, forced closure of the theater in 1738. From then until the building was finally demolished in 1763 it served as a home for touring theater ensembles, and Italian opera dominated the stage. For example, the thirty-two-year-old Christoph Willibald Gluck visited the city in 1748 with the opera company of Antonio Mingotti, which presented a number of Italian operas.

On July 31, 1765, Konrad Ernst Ackermann opened his Comödienhaus on the same location, in which pure opera was replaced with a mixture of music theater and drama. Through Lessing's influence the building was renamed the Deutsches Nationaltheater in 1767. This writer and critic was the resident dramaturg of the opera until 1770, when he went to Wolfenbüttel as librarian, and his famous *Hamburgische Dramaturgie* appeared during this period. Friedrich Ludwig Schröder, who was the principal director from 1771 to 1812, strongly supported the drama. Under his leadership, brilliant productions of the works of Lessing, Schiller, and Goethe, as well as the German premieres of the great Shakespeare plays, dominated the stage, along with the Singspiels of Christian Weiß and Johann Adam Hiller. *Die Entführung aus dem Serail* in 1781 was the first Mozart opera to be produced, followed by *Don Giovanni* in 1789 (in which Mozart's sister-in-law, Aloysia Lange appeared), *Die Hochzeit des Figaro* in 1791, and *Die Zauberflöte* in 1793. The house was renamed the Hamburgisches Stadt-Theater in 1810, and, until it outlived its usefulness in 1827, productions of Beethoven's *Fidelio* (1816), Rossini's *Barbier von Sevilla* (1821), and Weber's *Der Freischütz* (1822) were among the highlights.

Designed by the architect Carl Friedrich Schinkel, the new Stadt-Theater (Theater am Dammtor) opened on May 3, 1827, with Goethe's *Egmont* featuring the music of Ludwig van Beethoven. This was the first theater on the location of the present Staatsoper on Dammtorstraße. Memorable performances of the following decades included Wilhelmine Schröder-Devrient's guest appearance as Leonore in Beethoven's *Fidelio* (1832), the performance of *Vestalin* with Gasparo Spontini conducting (1834), the world premiere of Friedrich von Flotow's *Alessandro Stradella* (1844), and *Rienzi*, staged and conducted by Richard Wagner (1844). That same year *Nabucco* was produced, marking the first performance of a Verdi opera in Germany. Despite artistic success, the company was constantly threatened by financial problems, and it was only with the appointment of Bernhard Pollini as director in 1873 that a new golden age began. Pollini not only explored the possibility of public subsidy, he also began a tradition of producing the operas of Verdi and Wagner, starting with *Aida* in 1876 and *Der Ring des Nibelungen* in 1878. He was responsible for the German premieres of *Othello* in 1888 and Tchaikovsky's *Eugen Onegin* in 1892. His choice of music directors was brilliant. Following the tenure of Hans von Bülow (1887–1890), Gustav Mahler served for six seasons (1891–1897). Mahler's thirteen new productions during the 1896–1897 season raised the company to new heights.

During the first third of the twentieth century, the Stadt-Theater was a haven for the works of Richard Strauss and Wagner. Contemporary operas, for example Hindemith's *Sancta Susanna*, Stravinsky's *Geschichte vom Soldaten*, and Janáček's *Jenufa*, were produced. Moreover, artists of the caliber of Enrico Caruso, Arthur Nikisch, and Eugen d'Albert were frequent guests. Lotte Lehmann, Elisabeth Schumann, Florence Easton, and Paul Schwarz all contributed to magnificent productions. The outstanding conductors Klemperer (1910–1913), Egon Pollack (1917–1932), and Karl Böhm (1931–1934) maintained musical standards at the highest level. The stagehouse was completely rebuilt in 1925–1929 and fitted with the latest stage machinery to accommodate the expanded production goals. Heinrich K. Strohm, who had become director in 1933, initiated the change of title to Hamburgische Staatsoper the following year. During the war the auditorium was completely destroyed; only the stagehouse survived the bombings of 1943. Three years later, on January 9, 1946, the company presented Mozart's *Die Hochzeit des Figaro* in an interim theater. Larger works had to be produced in the Schauspielhaus. Demolition of the ruined opera house began in February 1953, and the new auditorium opened on October 15, 1955, with Mozart's *Die Zauberflöte* (staged by Günther Rennert) as a completely rebuilt 1,675-seat complex designed by Gerhard Weber. Rennert had been the opera producer in Hamburg since 1946, and he served as the new Intendant as well. Due primarily to his leadership, contemporary works were given a central place in the postwar repertoire of the Hamburg Opera. Between 1953 and 1978 the company mounted twenty-nine world premieres, including works by Hense, Krenek, Klebe, von Einem, Blacher, Schuller, Searle, Menotti, and Penderecki. Leopold Ludwig was the general music director between 1951 and 1970, and during his tenure he conducted a total of 1,266 performances.

Rennert was succeeded by Heinz Tietjen (1956–1959) who, in turn, was followed by Rolf Liebermann (1959–1973). Liebermann influenced not only Hamburg but also the international opera world through his commissions of composers beginning with Hans Werner Henze's *Prinz von Homburg* during the 1959–1960 season and ending with Mauricio Kagel's *Staatstheater* (1971–1972) and Walter Steffen's *Unter dem Milchwald* (1972–1973). During the "Woche des zeitgenössischen Musiktheaters" (Week of Contemporary Music Theater) in February 1961 there were nine performances of contemporary music theater works within the space of eight days, including Britten's *Sommernachtstraum*, Blomdahl's *Aniara*, Berg's *Wozzeck* and *Lulu*, and Liebermann's *Schule der Frauen*. The tenor Placido Domingo began his world career in Hamburg under Liebermann's aegis. Horst Stein, whose forte was Wagnerian opera, succeeded Ludwig as general music director in 1972, remaining in that post until 1977. August Everding (1973–1977) succeeded Liebermann; it was during his tenure that most of the sets, costumes, and props were lost in a catastrophic fire on November 1, 1975. Artistically, Everding made his mark with the company tour to Israel with Schoenberg's *Moses und Aron* in 1974–1975; the creation of "Opera stabile," an experimental program for contemporary ballet and music theater, in 1975; his appointment of Götz Friedrich as stage director; and the engagement of world-class singers such as Edith Mathis, Peter Schreier, Hermann Prey, Birgit Nilsson, and Leonie Rysanek.

Christoph von Dohnányi took over as Intendant and principal conductor in 1977. He enlarged the repertoire with less frequently performed operas, and he engaged legitimate theater directors to try their hand at opera. Most of the productions at this time were performed more frequently by the same cast over a shorter period of time. The Opera in Hamburg celebrated its tricentennial on January 2, 1978, with a gala performance hosted by the German president. Kurt Horres served as Intendant in 1984 until the "dream director" Rolf Liebermann could be brought back to Hamburg the following year. During Liebermann's brief tenure the company made its precedent-setting tour to Japan. Peter Ruzicka was appointed Intendant for the 1988–1989 season, assisted by Gerd Alberecht. Their production of Franz Schreker's *Schatzgräber* was a major critical success. As one of the world's leading opera houses, the Hamburgische Staatsoper continues to produce the standard repertoire along with demonstrating a commitment to the cutting edge of the contemporary music theater. The 1990–1991 season included new productions of *Elektra* with Gwyneth Jones, *Le Nozze di Figaro*, *Werther*, *Parsifal*, Dieter Schnebel's *Vergänglichkeit* (replacing Stockhausen's *Montag aus Licht*), and Bellini's *I Capuleti i Montecchi*. Out of a permanent repertoire of forty-seven operas, the company scheduled *Fidelio*, *Der Liebestrank*, *Hänsel und Gretel*, *Zar und Zimmermann*, *Idomeneo*, *Die Zauberflöte*, *Tosca*, *Madama Butterfly* with Catherine Malfitano, *Lady Macbech von Mzensk*, *Eugene Onegin*, *Der Troubador*, *Don Carlos*, *Der fliegende Holländer*, *Tannhäuser*, and *Lohengrin*.

CHRONOLOGY OF DIRECTORS (SINCE 1921): Leopold Sachse, 1921–1931. Albert Ruch, 1931–1933. Heinrich K. Strohm, 1933–1940. Alfred Noller, 1940–1945. Albert Ruch, 1946. Günther Rennert, 1946–1956. Heinz Tietjen, 1956–1959. Rolf Liebermann, 1959–1973. August Everding, 1973–1977. Christoph von Dohnányi, 1977–1984. Kurt Horres, 1984. Rolf Liebermann, 1985–1988. Peter Ruzicka and Gerd Alberecht, 1988–present.

BIBLIOGRAPHY: Max W. Busch and Peter Dannenberg, eds., *Die Hamburgische Staatsoper, 1678–1945*. (Zürich, 1988). Max W. Busch and Peter Dannenberg, eds., *Die*

Hamburgische Staatsoper, 1945–1988 (Zürich, 1989). Joachim Henzel, *Geschichte der Hamburger Oper, 1678–1978* (Hamburg, 1978). Rolf Liebermann, *Opernjahre: Erlebnisse und Erfahrungen* (Bern, 1977). Hans-Dieter Loose et al., *Dreihundert Jahre Oper in Hamburg: 1687–1977* (Hamburg, 1977). Walter Erich Schäfer, *Günther Rennert—Regisseur in dieser Zeit* (Bremen, 1962). Irmgard Scharberth, *Musiktheater mit Rolf Liebermann: Der Komponist als Intendant* (Hamburg, 1975). *300 Jahre Oper in Hamburg*. Hamburg, 1977. Joachim E. Wenzel, *Geschichte der Hamburger Oper, 1678–1984*, 3 vols. (unpublished).

ACCESS: Große Theaterstraße 34, 2000 Hamburg 36. (49 40) 35 68 01; fax (49 40) 3 56 84 56. Prof. Dr. Peter Ruzicke, Staatsoperintendant.

SUSANNE LITZEL
TRANS. JONATHAN MUIR

HANNOVER (495,300)

Niedersächsische Staatstheater

The city's first opera performance, Cesti's *L'Orontea* [premiered in Venice, January 20, 1649] took place in 1678 in the Komödientheater, the small theater in the castle of the duke of Welfen in Hannover. The duke had attended opera in Venice the previous year. As these pleasure trips cost an enormous amount of money, the duke Ernst August was eager to build an opera house in Hannover. The Große Theater in the castle was built between 1687 and 1689. There developed a footrace between Hannover and Braunschweig, where the branch of the Welfens from whom Heinrich the Lion originated were in residence. Hannover barely won—the theater in the castle was completed less than a year before the one in Braunschweig. Moreover, the Hannover Welfen Duke made a piquant decision, by inaugurating the theater with an opera about Heinrich. The composer was Agostino Steffani, whom the duke had summoned from Munich to Hannover as his Hofkapellmeister. The 1,300-seat Große Schloßtheater, which was one of the most magnificent of its time, opened on January 30, 1689, with *Henrico Leone*. This was the first of many operas that Steffani composed for Hannover [also including *La Superbia d'Alessandro* (1690), *Orlando generoso* (1691), *Le Rivali concordi* (1692), *La Libertà contenta* (1693), and *I Trionfi del Fato* (1695), and *Briseide* (1696)] which were then translated into German and performed in Hamburg, among other cities. The days of glory were short-lived, however, for Duke Ernst August died in 1698 and his son Georg Ludwig became King George I of England in 1714; the opera house was closed shortly thereafter.

Georg Friedrich Händel came to Hannover as Hofkapellmeister on June 16, 1710, and attempted to resurrect the opera, but after a few short months he too went to London. Only after a seventy-year hiatus did music theater return to the city, and this time it was in the form of the German Singspiel. Initially only touring companies visited Hannover, but later the Hamburg theater manager F. L. Schröder and his successors (particularly G.F.W. Grossmann) put together a permanent ensemble. Opera in Hannover gained new impetus in 1831 with the engagement of the composer Heinrich Marschner, whose *Der Vampyr* [the premiere was on March 29, 1828, in Leipzig] was a notable public success that year. A few successful seasons, however, did little to solve the undeniable problems presented by the Große Schloßtheater itself. It was not possible to heat the auditorium, and the balconies were so badly designed that, should a fire occur, the audience would have to search through the entire castle for exits. Moreover, the dependence of Hannover at that time on the English royal house made a solution very complicated. It was not until 1815, when the city became the kingdom of Hannover under Ernst August, that a remedy became possible. The first permanent opera house opened in 1818 and catered to the French and Italian tastes of Ernst August. Rebuilt and renamed the Hofoper in 1837, the theater was not able to support a high standard of artistic activity. Ernst August then decided to build another theater in the center of the city, and he commissioned his architect Laves to proceed. Construction of the new opera house began in 1845; was completed under Ernst August's successor, George V, in 1852; and opened on September 1, 1852, with Goethe's *Tasso*. This began a golden age for Hannover during which such artists as the tenor Albert Niemann, the concertmaster Joseph Joachim (whose quartet gave regular recitals), and the conductor Hans von Bülow worked in the city.

In 1866 the kingdom of Hannover became another province of Prussia, and the theater was placed under the control of the administration in Berlin which determined all the repertoire. Hannover was unable to implement its own decisions, which was particularly regrettable because the ensemble was really excellent at the time. Richard Wagner even commented on the situation in a letter, as he had promised his "Ring" to Hannover rather than Berlin. This dependence on Berlin lasted, with a short break, for almost fifty years. The Intendants Hans Bronsart von Schellendorf, Bruno von Lepel-Gnitz, Ludwig Barney, and Paul Gerhard Freiherr von Puttkamer sought, in spite of the situation, to present the contemporary works of Wagner, Verdi, Puccini and Strauss as quickly as possible after their premieres. [Interestingly enough the Irish composer Charles Villiers Stanford's first opera, *Der verschlierte Profet*, premiered in Hannover on February 6, 1881.] The relationship with Berlin ended in 1921, at which time the Königlische Hoftheater became the Städtisches Opernhaus. [That same year, Egon Wellesz's first opera, *Die Prinzessin Girnara*, premiered in Hannover on May 15.] Artistic administration again became a local prerogative. The engagement of the cellist and conductor Rudolf Krasselt as Generalmusikdirektor (GMD) in 1924 brought new initiatives and a new profile to the company, and Krasselt was later appointed Intendant of the Städtische Oper. He built an ensemble with a national reputation and secured singers including Tiana Lemnitz and Peter Anders with multiyear contracts. Lemnitz sang in Hannover from 1929 to 1934 in a broad range of roles. Krasselt was especially interested in the work of the German-Italian composer Ermanno Wolf-Ferrari, producing nine of his thirteen operas, including the premiere of *Kuskuk von Theben*. Due to the fact that Krasselt was not comfortable with the Nazi party, he was relieved of his position at the end of the 1942–1943 season. On July 26, 1943, the theater was destroyed by Allied bombs, and burned completely down to the foundation.

Fortunately, the Galeriegebäude in Herrenhausen [a suburb of Hannover which boasts the oldest surviving garden theater in Germany, which was built between 1689 and 1691] was untouched, and, within weeks, a temporary theater was constructed, hosting its first opera performance of the war on August 13, 1943. After the end of the war Herrenhausen also hosted some of the first opera performances in Germany with *Cavalleria rusticana* and *Der Bajazzo* on July 11, 1945. The city of Hannover made an official commitment to rebuild the Laves opera house in November 1949, and after an eleven-month construction period, the 1,207-seat opera house on Georgstraße reopened with a festive performance of *Der Rosenkavalier* on November 30, 1950. During this period the company mounted a number of German premieres including Britten's *Owen Wingrave* [world premiere on May 16, 1971], von Einem's *Jesu Hochzeit*, and the world premiere of Henze's *Boulevard Solitude* (1952) in Jean-Pierre Ponnelle's production. The Intendant Kurt Ehrhardt and his successor Reinhard Lehmann built an ensemble theater with such artists as Helen Donath, Bernd Weikl, Christa Ludwig, Franz Crass, Deborah Polaski and Waltrude Meier, who all began their careers in Hannover.

In January 1970 the Landestheater Hannover became the Niedersächische Staatstheater, incorporating the Staatsoper Hannover and the Staatsschauspiel, which performs in the historic Ballhof. The opera is a repertoire company offering some thirty-five different works each season. Within that repertoire are six premieres, two repeats, and two ballet premieres. The 1,207-seat theater was completely renovated both inside and out, in 1984–1985. The current company of 830 includes an orchestra of 111, 43 dancers, a 63-member chorus, and 40 soloists. The remainder are technical and administrative support personnel.

CHRONOLOGY OF RECENT MUSIC DIRECTORS: Rudolf Krasselt, 1923–1943. Franz Konwitschny, 1945–1949. Johannes Schüler, 1949–1959. Günther Wich, 1961–1965. George Alexander Albrecht, 1965–present.

BIBLIOGRAPHY: Kurt Bauer, *75 Jahre Opernhaus Hannover (1852–1927)* (Hannover, 1927). R. Rosendahl, *Geschichte der Hoftheater in Hannover und Braunschweig* (Hannover, 1927). K. H. Streibung, ed., *100 Jahre Opernhaus, 1852–1952* (Hannover, 1952).

ACCESS: Opernhaus, Opernplatz 1, 3000 Hannover 1. (49 511) 1 68 61 61; fax (49 511) 3 68 17 68. Hans-Peter Lehmann, Opern-Intendant. Georg Alexander Albrecht, Generalmusikdirektor.

SABINE HAMMER
TRANS. JONATHAN MUIR

KARLSRUHE (273,572)

Badisches Staatstheater

Significant operatic activities in Karlsruhe date from 1806, when the city was designated the capital of the Grand Duchy of Baden. Some four years later the

Grand Ducal Theater, designed by Friedrich Weinbrenner, opened on November 9 with a gala performance of Ferdinando Paer's *Achille* [which had its premiere on June 6, 1801, in Vienna at the Kärntnertor-Theater]. The theater burned to the ground on February 28, 1847, with the loss of sixty-three lives, but not before a strong operatic tradition had been established. The new Großherzoglich-Badisches Hoftheater, which was built by Heinrich Hübsch as a replacement, opened in 1851 under the direction of Eduard Devrient. Devrient, one of the leading theatrical figures of his generation, remained as director from 1851 to 1869. This was the beginning of an era that was to mark the theater as the "Little Bayreuth" due to the strong Wagner tradition that was fostered there. The first production of the complete *Die Eroberung Trojas* [Les Troyens] of Berlioz was given in Karlsruhe on December 6, 1890, conducted by Felix Mottl, who was music director from 1880 to 1904. Hermann Levi (1864–1872; Levi conducted Wagner's *Meistersinger von Nürnberg* only months after the Munich premiere), Josef Krips (1926–1933), and Joseph Keilberth (1933–1940) also served as music directors of the theater.

Following World War I, the Großherzogliche Hoftheater was renamed the Badisches Landestheater. Both Hans Pfitzner and Richard Strauss conducted in the house during the 1920s. After Josef Krips left Karlsruhe for the Wiener Staatsoper in 1933 he was succeeded by Joseph Keilberth. The last performance in the theater was Mozart's *Die Hochzeit des Figaro* on July 9, 1944. Due to wartime conditions, all theaters were closed on September 1, and the house was destroyed by bombs on September 26 and 27. The concert hall was reconstructed as the new Großes Haus am Festplatz and opened with Mozart's *Die Zauberflöte* on October 14, 1953. The company was invited to the Teatro la Fenice di Venezia (Venice), where it presented the Italian premiere of Carl Orff's *Die Kluge* on February 19–22, 1959. The international competition for a new Theater am Schloßplatz came to naught as there was no appropriate site. During this frustrating period the company entered into joint productions with the Théâtre Municipal in Nancy, France (1963) and the Opéra du Rhin in Strasbourg (1971). A new 1,002-seat house, designed by Helmut Bätzner, was built between 1970 and 1975. The end of an era of temporary accommodations ended with the last performance in the opera house, Mozart's *Così fan tutte* on June 29, 1975. The new house opened with Mozart's *Die Zauberflöte* on August 29, 1975. Historically, the house has served as an important stepping stone in the careers of younger artists such as Hermann Jadlowker, Erika Köth, Barry McDaniel, and Jess Thomas.

The 1990–1991 season included *Nabucco, Der Zigeunerbaron, Pique Dame, Zar und Zimmermann*, the German premiere of Penderecki's *Die schwarze Maske*, Handel's *Arianna in Creta* (the German premiere in Italian), *Julius Caesar, Pelléas et Mélisande, Capriccio, Tannhäuser, Ariadne auf Naxos*, and the world premiere of Helge Jörns's *Zufall der Liebe*. In addition, thirteen operas are kept in repertoire.

BIBLIOGRAPHY: G. Haass, *Geschichte des ehemaligen Grossherzoglich-Badischen Hoftheaters Karlsruhe, 1806–52* (Karlsruhe, 1932).

Germany

ACCESS: Großes Haus, am Ettlinger Tor, 7500 Karlsruhe 1. (49 721) 1 52 2 13 2 14; fax (49 721) 37 32 23. Günter Könemann, Generalintendant.

[From materials supplied by the company]
TRANS. MARC ÄNDERS

KASSEL (city 200,500)

Staatstheater

Theatrical history in Kassel dates from the reign of Landgrave Moritz der Gelehrte, under whose leadership the first theater in Germany, the Ottoneum, was built between 1604 and 1606. The next notable event was the opening of the new opera house in the palace of Prince Maximilian in 1764 with a gala premiere of Ignazo Fiorillo's *Diana e Endimione*. Opera flourished in Kassel under the direction of Louis Spohr, who was associated with the house from 1822 to 1857. His *Jessonda* (July 28, 1823), *Der Berggeist* (March 24, 1825), *Pietro von Abano* (October 13, 1827), *Der Alchymist* (July 28, 1830), and *Die Kreuzfahrer* (January 1, 1845) all received their premieres in Kassel. Moreover, the composer/conductor/violinist took the lead in promoting Richard Wagner, producing *Der fliegende Holländer* in his theater only five months after the Dresden premiere. Under Spohr the orchestra in Kassel was one of the finest in all Europe. The new 953-seat Opernhaus designed by Paul Bode and Ernst Brundig opened on September 12, 1959, with the premiere of Rudolf Wagner-Régney's *Prometheus*, directed by Paul Schmitz.

During the 1980s a number of operas were given world premieres, including Peter Michael Hamel's *Ein Menschentraum* (June 27, 1891), Walter Haupt's *Marat* (June 9, 1984), Wilhelm Dieter Siebert's *Liebe, Tod und Tango* (October 12, 1986), Walter Haupt's *Pier Paolo* (May 23, 1987), Josef Tal's *Der Turum* (September 19, 1987, during the thirty-seventh Berlin Festwochen in celebration of the 750th anniversary of the founding of Berlin), and Hans Werner Henze's collective project *Der heiße Ofen* (March 18, 1989). The 1989–1990 season included Mozart's *Don Giovanni* and *Titus*, Lortzing's *Der Waffenschmied*, *Lohengrin*, the world premiere of Wolfgang von Schweinitz's *Patmos* (which premiered at the Munich Biennial on April 28, 1990), the European premiere of Dominick Argento's *Asperns Papiere*, Paul Lincke's *Frau Luna*, and George Gershwin's *Lady Be Good*.

BIBLIOGRAPHY: *Theater in Kassel: Aus der Geschichte des Staatstheaters Kassel*... (Kassel, 1959).

ACCESS: Opernhaus, Friedrichsplatz 15, 3500 Kassel. (49 561) 10 94 01; fax (49 561) 10 94 2 04. Dr. Manfred Beilharz, Intendant.

[From materials supplied by the company]

KÖLN (1,030,000)

Opera der Stadt Köln

The new 1,380-seat opera house on Offenbachplatz opened May 18, 1957, with Carl Maria von Weber's *Oberon*. Highlighting this gala occasion was the Teatro alla Scala from Milan with Bellini's *La Sonnambula* and Verdi's *La forza del destino* starring Maria Callas, Leyla Gencer, and Giuseppe di Stefano. The resident company offered contemporary productions of Wolfgang Fortner's *Bluthochzeit* [presenting the world premiere on June 8] and Francis Poulenc's *Gespräche der Karmeliterinnen*. The general manager Herbert Maisch, who had directed the theaters in Cologne since 1947, was able to make a connection in this way with the traditions of the first real local opera house which had been built in 1902 on the Habsburger Ring. Opera had, of course, been performed in Cologne much earlier. At the end of the sixteenth century, before opera as we know it had evolved, some form of musical theater performances had taken place in the city. These were very simple works that appealed to the general public through the inclusion of couplets and dances. In the case of English players whose German was minimal, it was especially important to include devices that would catch the attention of the public. These "Singets Spil in Thon" were so successful that the transplanted performers were welcomed officially in Cologne. Without a permit from the city council, theatrical performances were forbidden, and such permission was often not given so the English troupe was clearly popular.

The Jesuit students also performed plays which included songs, dance, music. They would often insert arias from "real" Italian operas into their productions. This music had crossed the Alps, and a number of minor German princes engaged Italian opera ensembles at their courts. Due to the immense cost, the great Opera Seria were reserved for the nobility and their entourage; they were unknown to the common people. Cities such as Cologne that lacked a court had to make do with less. Touring ensembles performed works with music, but, as the actors were responsible for the songs as well as the dances, the scope of musical theater was limited. Occasionally, however, Italians journeyed to the Rhine Valley performing Italian opera buffas. The first professional ensemble appeared in Cologne in 1757 under the direction of the renowned impresario Angelo Mingotti. The repertoire consisted primarily of works by Nicolò Jomelli and Johann Adolf Hasse. About this same time the German troupes who performed in the area began to present small Italian works in German translations. They quickly discovered German Singspiels, which could be performed without trained singers. In the meantime the French had evolved the opéra comique, and it was not long before the Germans mastered this form as well. These were similar to the Singspiel in that spoken dialogue had replaced the Italian recitative, which itself was soon removed in favor of spoken German text.

Initially, these ensembles performed from their own wooden carts. The first permanent theater in Cologne was built in 1768 on Neumarkt by Joseph von Kurtz. It was a simple four-story wooden building that was drafty in winter and stifling in summer. For a fee one could bring one's own chair. Business was not good, and Kurtz left shortly; his theater, however, remained and was the only theater for a number of years. There were numerous ensembles, each performing for a few days, until Johann Heinrich Böhm offered the first performances of Gluck's *Alkeste* and Mozart's *Entführung*. Between 1781 and 1785 his company performed some thirty operas of Grétry, Benda, Salieri, Piccini, and Paisiello, among others. When Kurtz's theater had outlived its usefulness, Caspar Rodius erected a stone masonry theater which held 800 people. Böhm returned in 1791 to offer Mozart's *Don Giovanni*, Grétry's *Richard Löwenherz*, Haydn's *Ritter Roland*, and Mozart's *Zauberflöte* in the new officially licensed hall. A French ensemble arrived in Cologne in October 1794, and shortly thereafter the theater was placed under French control. For a brief period only French ensembles were allowed to perform. Long after the departure of the French, a much-needed consolidation of the theater took place in 1822 when the city commissioned Friedrich Sebald Ringelhardt to build a permanent theater. As the first theater director of Cologne, Ringelhardt assumed the responsibility at his own risk and remained as director for ten years. The first performances of Weber's *Freischütz*, Rossini's *Barbier von Sevilla*, Beethoven's *Fidelio*, and Mozart's *Così fan tutte* took place during his tenure. The Lortzing family were all members of the ensemble at this time.

The house was demolished in the summer of 1828 due to structural problems, but within nine months a new theater was finished on the same site, this one holding more than 1,500 people. For the first time there was a distinction made between actors and singers. This was necessary because of the increasing interpretive demands of the opera. After Ringelhardt's departure in March 1832, the next major change occurred in 1840 when Friedrich Spielberger was appointed director. He engaged Konrad Kreutzer, an outstanding conductor who had founded and directed a private orchestra and who now would represent a voice for the musical sector. Spielberger was also one of the first to welcome guest artists, among whom Jenny Lind, Joseph Tichatschek, and Josef Staudigl were the most prominent. Meyerbeer's *Robert der Teufel* and *Die Hugenotten* were added to the repertoire as drawing cards, and Donizetti's *Regimentstochter* became a box office hit and had to be repeated again and again. One year after Everhardt Theodore L'Arronge became director (in 1858), the theater on Komödienstraße burned to the ground and was not rebuilt until 1862; thus, most of his tenure was spent in temporary halls. L'Arronge was succeeded by Moritz Ernst, who introduced Wagner to Cologne with productions of *Der fliegende Holländer* and *Rienzi*. When he returned in 1875 he produced *Das Rheingold* and *Die Walküre*.

At the beginning of Kaiser Wilhelm's reign in September 1872, a new theater in Glockengasse was opened. This house quickly became a popular social center, and it typified the times. In 1881 Julius Hoffmann was appointed director, and his tenure was among the most successful in the history of the Cologne Opera. His ensemble included singers such as Ottilie Ottiker, Carl Zobel, Anton Udvary, and Carl Mayer. The star was the tenor Emil Goetze, whom Hoffmann paid the astonishing salary of sixty thousand Reichmarks per season. To complement these artists Hoffmann engaged international stars, including Nellie Melba, Gemma Bellincioni, Francesco Tamagno, and Francisco d'Andrade, who at the time performed in the original language (or in Italian) while the house ensemble sang in German. Hoffmann mounted all the new and attractive works, and Cologne experienced an opera boom. A new and even bigger 1,800-seat house was built on the Habsburger Ring and opened on October 6, 1902. Initially, both theaters presented both operas and plays, but the new house quickly became the opera house. Attendance was lower than expected, however, and after twenty-two years of successful management, Julius Hoffmann resigned. Max Martersteig took over as director in 1905. That year the Cologne Festival Society inaugurated a summer festival which produced *Fidelio*, *Figaros Hochzeit*, *Die Meistersinger*, *Tristan und Isolde*, *Feuersnot*, and Peter Cornelius's *Der Barbier von Bagdad* with Anna Mildenberg, Carl Jörn, Paul Knüpfer, Johanna Gadski, Leopold Demuth, Erik Schmedes, and Hermine Kittel, among others. This venture lasted with a few interruptions until World War I. During Martersteig's tenure, with Otto Lohse in charge of the opera, countless works were premiered, including seventeen world premieres, and famous composers and conductors as well as singers appeared as guests of the house.

The former heldentenor Fritz Rémond succeeded Martersteig and introduced a number of new works, including Schreker's *Irrelohe* and *Die Gezeichneten*, Korngold's *Die tote Stadt*, Braunfel's *Die Vögel*, Zemlinsky's *Der Zwerg*, and Strauss's *Die Frau ohne Schatten*. The young Margarete Teschemacher, Hildegard Ranczak, Else Ruzicka, Helge Roswaenge, Matthieu Ahlersmeyer, and Gerhard Hüsch were all members of the ensemble. Rémond retired in 1928 to be succeeded by Max Hofmüller. Eugen Szankar who succeeded Otto Klemperer as GMD in 1924 strongly favored contemporary operas. Such works as Kodály's *Háry János*, Wolf-Ferrari's *Die schalkhafte Witwe*, Braunfel's *Galatea*, and Prokofief's *Liebe zu den drei Orangen* appeared in the repertoire. The young Walter Felsenstein worked for two seasons under Hofmüller before he went to Frankfurt. Influences of the Thousand Year Reich were manifested not so much in Nazi-influenced operas as in the domination of the repertoire by the works of Wagner, Pfitzner, and other "pure" Germans. The works of Jewish composers were not performed, nor were Jewish artists engaged. The closing of all German theaters in the fall of 1944 put an end to this page of history after both the opera house and the theater were reduced to ashes by bombs during April and May of that year.

The production of *Madama Butterfly* in the great hall of the university in September 1945 marked a new beginning. That same season, seven other operas were produced. Herbert Maisch was engaged as the new director, and he brought special prominence to the opera. The Kammerspiele am Ubierring also served as a temporary performance site and hosted numerous performances of important operas by Liebermann, Karl Amadeus Hartmann, Hermann Reutter, and Hans Werner Henze. Miasch was particularly concerned with producing those works ignored during the Nazi period: Milhaud, Hindemith, Schoenberg, Braunfels, Britten, Bernstein, Menotti, von Einem, and Kurt Weill were all once again scheduled. Musical affairs were in the capable hand of Günter Wand and Richard Kraus, and Trude Eipperle, Rita Bartos, Anny Schlemm, Walburga Wegner, and Karl Liebl were mainstays of the ensemble. It was not until 1957 that the new opera house on Offenbachplatz opened. In 1959 Oscar Fritz Schuh succeeded Herbert Maisch and initiated a new system of double-casting. Outstanding guest artists would be engaged for the opening performances of new productions, followed by a repertoire scheduling of the same works with company singers. In retrospect this system marked the beginning of a broadened international respect for the house. Together with his music director, Wolfgang Sawallisch, Schuh mounted a series of contemporary operas: Luigi Nono's *Intolleranza*, Wolfgang Fortner's *In seinem Garten liebt Don Perlimplin Belisa*, Prokofiev's *Der feurige Engel*, and the world premiere of Nicolai Nabakov's *Der Tod des Grigori Rasputin*. Among the highlights of this era was Wagner's "Ring" cycle, which was begun in 1961. This marked Wieland Wagner's first interpretation of the "Tetralogy" and was a forerunner of his pioneering Bayreuth style. The cycle remained in the repertoire of the Cologne Opera for more than a dozen years.

Many felt that Schuh's contributions had earned Cologne the honor of being the cultural center of West Germany, but that distinction did not materialize, causing the director to resign his post. Arno Assmann and István Kertesz replaced Schuh and Sawallisch, substituting ensemble for star theater. A repertoire of popular works was interspersed with little-known operas such as Mussorgsky's *Chowanschtschina* and Rimsky-Korsakof's *Legende von der unsichtbaren Stadt Kitesch*. Contemporary works included Britten's *Billy Budd*, Henze's *Der junge Lord*, and Richard Rodney Bennett's *Ballade im Moor*. The artistic highpoint of Assmann's tenure was the world premiere of Bernd Alois Zimmermann's *Soldaten* [February 15, 1965] directed by Hans Neugebauer and conducted by Michael Gielen. Claus Helmut Drese replaced Assmann in 1968, and under his leadership, István Kertesz emerged as a major Mozart interpreter. Together with Jean-Pierre Ponnelle, four operas of a projected Mozart cycle were produced prior to his early death during a vacation in Israel. Drese's regime mounted important productions of Mussorgsky's *Boris Godunow* in the original version, Berg's *Lulu*, Hindemith's *Cardillac*, and Fortner's *Elisabeth Tudor*, as well as Verdi's *Stiffelius* and Debussy's *Pelléas et Mélisande* directed by Hans Neugebauer with the sensational sets of Achim Freyer. Drese left Cologne in 1975 for Zürich, where he remained until his appointment as director of the Wiener Staatsoper in 1986.

Following Drese's departure, the administration of the Cologne theaters was restructured. Opera and theater were completely separated, and for the last fifteen years Michael Hampe has impressed his personal stamp on the opera. The previous repertoire system, which assumed a stable casting for each production, was replaced by a modified stagione system. The new approach sought an ideal casting for a series of performances within a limited time frame. When that series was completed, the production was taken out of the repertoire, to be rescheduled only if another series was planned. The initial production of Hampe's administration clearly indicated what this meant. Hans Neugebauer directed *Wozzeck* (with sets by Achim Freyer) with Walter Berry, Gerhard Stolze, and Hermann Winkler. One of the strengths of the Cologne Opera was immediately apparent—contemporary music theater became alive on the stage. The first series of works exploited this strength: These included Mauricio Kagel's *Musiktheater*, Stravinsky's *Oedipus Rex* paired with Bartok's *Herzogs Blaubarts Burg*, Penderecki's *Die Teufel von Loudon*, Schoenberg's *Moses und Aron*, Britten's *The Turn of the Screw*, Stravinksy's *The Rake's Progress*, and, above all, Hans Werner Henze's *Wir erreichen den Fluß* in the definitive staging of Michael Hampe conducted by Wolfgang Rennert.

In the German repertoire, great attention was given to the works of Richard Strauss. New productions of six of his operas have appeared since 1975, including *Salome* and *Elektra* starring Gwyneth Jones. Wagner's *Die Meistersinger von Nürnberg* received broad acclaim, while productions of *Lohengrin*, *Parsifal*, and *Tristan und Isolde* met with less success. In cooperation with the Deutsche Oper am Rhein, a new production of Wagner's "Tetralogy" directed by Kurt Horres and conducted by Hans Wallat opened with *Das Rheingold* and *Die Walküre*, receiving mixed reviews. Since the middle of the 1970s the trend has been to perform most works in their original language—not only Italian and French, but also English. An exception has been the Slavic works, which are still performed in German. Among the most spectacular productions was Tchaikowsky's *Pique Dame*, conducted by Gerd Albrecht and directed by Rudolf Noelte, with Heannine Altmeyer, Martha Mödl, René Kollo, and Claudio Nicolai. A Janáček cycle opened with *Aus einem Totenhaus* and will include *Jenufa*, *Katja Kabanova*, and *Schlauen Füchslein*. The Italian repertoire has met with a mixed reaction. On the positive side, Jean-Pierre Ponnelle's production of *Madama Butterfly* was outstanding. Less successful were *Turandot*, *Tosca*, *Manon Lescaut*, *Un ballo in maschera* (with Anna Tomowa-Sintow, Giacomo Aragall, and Leo Nucci), *Simon Boccanegra*, *Andrea Chenier*, and *Lucia di Lammermoor* (with Lucia Aliberti). At the far extreme, a very unconventional staging of *Aida* by Virginio Puecher was judged completely unsatisfactory. Michael Hampe's productions of *Il matrimonio segreto* and *Il Barbiere di Siviglia* were runaway successes which included appearances by foreign guests. Furthermore, *Falstaff*, with Tito Gobbi in the title role, was very well received.

In the meantime, Cologne evolved as a real center for promoting the works of Gioacchino Rossini. After the *Barbiere*, popular stagings of *La gazza ladra* (with Elena Cotrubas), *L'Italiana in Algeri*, *La cambiale di matrimonio*, and *Il Signor Bruschino* were mounted. The repertoire of the Cologne

Opera has, for many seasons, featured a cycle of the seven most important Mozart operas. A significant production was offered each year until 1989. Inaugurated in 1969 under the leadership of Claus Helmut Drese, *La clemenza di Tito* was produced by the team of István Kertesz and Jean-Pierre Ponnelle. After *Don Giovanni*, *Così fan tutte*, *Die Zauberflöte*, *Die Entführung aus dem Serail*, and *Idomeneo*, *Le Nozze di Figaro* was scheduled in May 1975. The company has demonstrated a winning hand with French operas. Massenet's *Werther* with Kathleen Kuhlmann and Ponnelle's staging of *Carmen* (again with Kuhlmann, Barbara Daniels and Luis Lima) appealed to audiences. One of the most impressive productions of the last decade was an opera by Cologne's own Jacques Offenbach. The production of *Les Contes d'Hoffmann* honored the one hundredth anniversary of the composer's death and created a sensation far beyond the confines of the city. Conducted by John Pritchard, Cologne's principal conductor from 1977 to 1989, the production featured Placido Domingo in the title role, Edda Moser singing the female leads, and Tom Krause portraying the villains.

Pritchard was succeeded by James Conlon, who made his Cologne debut with Shostakovich's *Lady Macbeth von Mzensk* early in 1990, a production that was also featured in the Dresden Festival. Cologne strives to be an international opera house not only due to the conductors, directors, designers, and singers who are featured in its productions. It also collaborates on the international scene with other major houses such as the Théâtre National de L'Opéra de Paris, Royal Opera House Covent Garden in London, and the National Theater in Munich. An association with the major festivals, including Schwetzingen, Edinborough, and Salzburg (where, for example, Henze's version of Monteverdi's *Il ritorno di Ulisse*, which had originally been prepared for Cologne, met with great success) has been a part of the schedule for years. It is no surprise that the company is often approached for tours abroad. A wonderful example of this was the trip to Tel Aviv in 1982 to perform *Così fan tutte* and *Wozzeck*. The appearances were an overwhelming artistic success, due in no small part to the collaboration of the Israel Philharmonic Orchestra; even more important was the positive impact on German-Jewish relations in light of the bitter past. Due to the massive inflation of costs over the last two decades, it had been difficult to maintain the high quality of the operation. The budget has peaked, which, in effect, means diminished resources. Fortunately, the administration has achieved a large degree of autonomy, and receipts are 29 percent of the budget as opposed to a national average of some 15 percent. This indicates the high level of community support for the opera. Indeed, with average ticket sales of 92.4 percent, the Cologne Opera is, for all practical purposes, sold out.

CHRONOLOGY OF DIRECTORS: Friedrich Sebald Ringelhardt, 1822–1832. Julius Mühling, 1832–1837. Gustav Köckert, 1837–1840. Friedrich Spielberger, 1840–1846. Carl Beurer, 1846–1847. Eduard Gerlach, 1847–1850. Wilhelm Löwe, 1850–1851. Friedrich Spielberger, 1852–1853. Ferdinand Roeder, 1853–1855. Friedrich Kahle, 1855–

1858. Everhard Theodor L'Arronge, 1858–1863. Moritz Ernst, 1863–1869. Franz Kullach, 1869–1872. Heinrich Behr, 1872–1875. Mortiz Ernst, 1875–1881. Julius Hofmann, 1881–1903. Otto Purschian, 1903–1904. Otto Lohse, 1904–1905. Max Martersteig, 1905–1911. Fritz Rémond, 1911–1921.

CHRONOLOGY OF OPERA DIRECTORS: Fritz Rémond, 1921–1928. Max Hofmüller, 1928–1933. Alexander Spring, 1933–1945. Günter Wand and Erich Bormann, 1945–1947. Herbert Maisch, 1947–1959. Oscar Fritz Schuh, 1959–1963. Karl Zieseniß, Gerhard Hirsch, and Siegfried Köhler, 1963–1964. Arno Assmann, 1964–1968. Claus Helmut Drese, 1968–1975. Michael Hempe, 1975–present.

BIBLIOGRAPHY: Carl H. Hiller, *Vom Quartermarkt zum Offenbachplatz: Ein Streifzug durch vier Jahrhunderte musiktheatralischer Darbietungen in Köln* (Köln, n.d.).

ACCESS: Bühnen der Stadt Köln, Offenbachplatz, 5000 Köln. (49 221) 2 21 82 01; fax (49 221) 2 21 82 10. Michael Hampe, Intendant.

CARL H. HILLER
TRANS. CHARLENE CHADWICK

LEIPZIG (metro 1,360,900; city 550,000)

Opernhaus

As a major European music center since before the time of Bach, Leipzig has a long and illustrious operatic history. The premiere of Nikolaus Adam Strungk's *Alceste* on May 18, 1693, not only marked the opening of the city's first opera house but also ushered in a golden era of German opera. It was continued by Georg Philipp Telemann, who composed numerous operas for the theater, whose management he had assumed after Strungk's death. Around the middle of the eighteenth century, touring Italian opera companies were popular. The new Schauspielhaus opened in 1766 and hosted regular performances of opera produced by touring companies. For example, Pasquale Bondini, director of the Italian Opera in Prague, was the first to bring Mozart's *Don Giovanni* (June 15, 1788) as well as *Le Nozze di Figaro* (May 26, 1793) to Leipzig. The theater was rebuilt in 1817 to house a permanent company and was renamed the Stadttheater. As such it hosted seven premieres of Albert Lortzing's operas: *Die beiden Schützen* (February 20, 1837), *Czaar und Zimmermann* (December 22, 1837), *Hans Sachs* (June 23, 1840), *Casanova* (December 31, 1841), *Der Wildschütz* (December 31, 1842), *Zum Grossadmiral* (December 31, 1847), and *Rolands Knappen* (May 25, 1849). The very next year Robert Schumann conducted the premiere of his four-act *Genoveva* on June 25. The 1,900-seat Neues Stadttheater designed by C. F. Langhans opened on Augustusplatz in 1867. During the second half of the nineteenth century, Anton Seidl, Arthur Nikisch, and Gustav Mahler all conducted at the theater which attracted the finest vocal talent available at the time.

Prior to World War I, Felix von Weingartner's *Orestes* (February 15, 1902) and Ethel Smyth's *Strandrecht* (November 11, 1906) were premiered. Under the leadership of Gustav Brecher (1923–1933) after the war, the Leipzig Opera was a strong supporter of contemporary works and mounted the premieres of Ernst Krenek's *Jonny spielt auf* (February 10, 1927) and *Leben des Orest* (January 19, 1930) as well as Kurt Weill's *Aufstieg und Fall der Stadt Mahagony* (March 9, 1930). In a major tour de force just prior to World War II, the company produced two complete cycles of Richard Wagner's operas in chronological order. Destroyed by bombs in 1943, it took seventeen years before a new structure could be finished on the same site. The new 1,606-seat Opernhaus, designed by Kunz Nierade, opened on October 7, 1960, with a festive performance of Wagner's *Die Meistersinger von Nürnberg* conducted by Helmut Seydelmann. The world famous Gewandhaus Orchestra, which was formally associated with the opera since 1840, continues to serve in an artistic collaboration similar to that in Vienna.

BIBLIOGRAPHY: *Festschrift zur Eröffnung des neuen Leipziger Opernhauses* (Leipzig, 1960). *Leipziger Bühnen: Tradition und neues Werden* (Berlin, 1956). Alexander Ringer, ed., *The Early Romantic Era. Between Revolutions: 1789–1848* (London, 1990).

ACCESS: Augustusplatz 12, O–7010 Leipzig. (37 41) 7 16 80; fax: (37 41) 29 36 33. Udo Zimmermann, Intendant.

[From materials supplied by the company]
TRANS. MARC ÄNDERS

MANNHEIM (314,000)

Nationaltheater

Opera first flourished in Mannheim after an opera house was built in the sumptuous palace of Carl Philipp, the Elector Palatine, by Alessandro Galli-Bibiena in 1742. The theater, housed in the most impressive baroque building complex in all Germany, was inaugurated with Karl Gura's *Meride* on January 17, 1742. The cast was illustrious and, until its destruction in 1795, the theater hosted many brilliant productions. When the elector died at the end of that year his successor, Carl Theodore, initiated one of the golden ages of music and the arts. Supporting what history has termed the Mannheim School, the new elector funded music and musicians of the highest order. The rococo theater built in his summer palace in Schwetzingen in 1752 allowed him to enjoy theatrical productions year round, and it now houses the annual Schwetzinger Festspiele. Ignaz Holzbauer was both Kapellmeister and Hofkomponist from 1753 to 1778, and more than a dozen of his operas were premiered either at Mannheim or at Schwetzingen. J. C. Bach's *Lucio Silla* was premiered on November 4, 1774, in honor of the elector's name day. In addition to several outstanding castrati, the tenor Anton Raaff was a member of the company. Mozart was known to have visited Mannheim on four occasions, the last for a performance of *Le Nozze di Figaro* at the Nationaltheater in 1790.

The historic Nationaltheater, designed by Lorenzo Quaglio, was built between

1775 and 1777. Opera only became a staple of the repertoire, however, some fifty years later under Carl von Luxburg who was the director from 1821 to 1836. Vincenz Lachner was appointed first Kapellmeister in 1836 and proceeded to enlarge the opera repertoire until, at the time of his replacement in 1872, it was the equal of any theater in Germany. [The authoritative English-language reference work *Grove 6* states that the Nationaltheater celebrated its centennial in 1879 with a complete performance of Wagner's "Ring." Although not listed in other reference works, this would be one of the first, if not the first, productions of the complete cycle following the premiere at Bayreuth on August 13–17, 1876.] Hugo Wolf's *Der Corregidor* was premiered on June 7, 1896. The theater continued its tradition of quality innovation under Carl Hagemann, who was director just before and after World War I. Artur Bodansky (1909–1915), Wilhelm Furtwängler (1915–1920), Erich Kleiber (1921–1922), and Karl Elmendorff (1936–1943) kept the music standards at the highest levels. Egon Wellesz's *Alkestis* premiered on March 20, 1924, and during the 1930s the operas of Verdi, Wagner, and Richard Strauss dominated the repertoire.

The building was destroyed by bombs in 1943 during the war, and the new 1,200-seat Nationaltheater, designed by Gerhard Weber, opened on January 13, 1957, with a festive performance of *Der Freischütz*. Since that time the company has demonstrated a strong commitment to contemporary operas. The premiere of Paul Hindemith's *Das lange Weinachtsmahl* in 1961 was followed by Günther Bialas's *Hero und Leander* and *Der jüngste Tag* by Giselher Klebe. Most recently, Wolfgang Rihm's *Hamletmaschine* in the 1986–1987 season received international attention. Detlev Müller-Siemens's *Die Menschen* was commissioned by the Nationaltheater and received its world premiere during the 1990–1991 season. With fifty operas in the permanent house repertoire, the Nationaltheater maintains one of the largest active opera programs in Germany. The thirty-six house soloists are enhanced by international stars who appear in Festlichen Opernabended (special operatic galas) throughout the season.

CHRONOLOGY OF IMPORTANT DIRECTORS: Wolfgang Heribert von Dalberg, 1778–1802. Graf Carl von Luxburg. 1821–1836. Philipp Jacob Düringer, 1843–1853. August Bassermann, 1895–1904. Carl Hagemann, 1906–1910, 1915–1920. Ferdinand Gregori, 1910–1912. Francesco Sioli, 1924–1930. Herbert Maisch, 1930–1933. Friedrich Brandenburg, 1933–1945. Carl Onno Eisenbart, 1945–1946. Erich Kronen, 1946–1947. Richard Dornseiff, 1947–1949. Richard Payer, 1949–1950. Hans Schüler, 1951–1963. Ernst Dietz, 1963–1972. Michael Hampe, 1972–1975. Arnold Petersen, 1975–present.

BIBLIOGRAPHY: *Das Nationaltheater Mannheim, 1779–1970* (Mannheim, 1970). E. L. Stahl, *Des europäische Mannheim: Die Wege zum deutschen Nationaltheater, die klassische Zeit des Mannheimer Theaters* (Mannheim, 1940). E. L. Stahl, *Das Mannheimer Nationaltheater: Ein Jahrhundert deutscher Theaterkultur im Reich*, 2nd ed. (Berlin, 1940).

ACCESS: Am Goetheplatz, 6800 Mannheim 1. (49 621) 16 80–01; fax (49 621) 16 80 3 85. Arnold Petersen, Generalintendant.

[From materials provided by the company]
TRANS. JONATHAN MUIR

MÜNCHEN (1,293,999)

Bayerische Staatsoper

In the middle of the seventeenth century, a granary at the Salvatorplatz converted by the Elector Maximilian into a baroque theater became one of the first freestanding opera houses in Germany. Maximilian and his son Ferdinand Maria were both strong supporters of the arts. During the latter's tenure, the first recorded *Festa musicale* in Munich, the premiere of Giovanni Battista Maccioni's *L'arpa festante*, took place in August 1653. The composer's *Dramma musicale Ardelia* premiered in 1660. It was at these performances that the forerunner of the current Bayerische Staatsorchester first became involved in opera, and the orchestra remains to this day the one Munich orchestra that supports both concerts and operas. Prior to his engagement in Hannover, Agostino Steffani had his first six operas premiered in Munich: *Marco Aurelio* (1681), *Il Solone* (1685), *Audacia e rispetto* (1685), *Servio Tullio* (1686), *Alarico il Baltha, Re dei Goti* (1687), and *Niobe regina di Tebe* (1688). At this time Munich was one of the centers of court opera in all Europe.

Upon the return of the Elector Maximilian II Emmanuel from the Netherlands in 1715, French operas similar to those of Lully were the fashion. His successor, Karl Alberecht, preferred Italian opera, and the works of Pietro Torri [sixteen operas premiered in Munich between 1719 and 1736, including *Griselda*, on October 12, 1723, starring Faustina Bordoni in the title role] were especially popular. These performances of Italian operas put into sharp perspective the need for another opera house. One hundred years after the theater at the Salvatorplatz was opened, the Elector Maximilian Joseph III commissioned François Cuvilliés the Elder to build a rococo theater in the electoral palace—the Residenztheater or Cuvilliéstheater. The 525-seat (462 seats for opera) Altes Residenztheater (Cuvilliéstheater) opened on October 12, 1753, with Giovanni Ferrandini's *Cattone in Udica*. [Destroyed by bombs in 1943, it was rebuilt and reopened on June 12, 1958, with Mozart's *Die Hochzeit des Figaro* in celebration of the eight hundredth anniversary of the city of Munich.] The elector preferred Neapolitan operas as well as opera buffa, and during his reign, Mozart's *La finta Giardiniera* was commissioned and premiered on January 13, 1775. This fad reached its peak with the premiere of Mozart's *Idomeneo* in the theater on January 29, 1781, after which time German Singspiels and vernacular translations of French and Italian works dominated the repertoire.

The ancient Salvatorplatz theater was demolished in 1802, and in 1805 the ban on Italian opera instituted by Carl Theodore in 1787 was lifted, thus almost guaranteeing seasons filled with foreign works. In 1811 King Maximilian I laid the foundation stone of a Royal Court (Hof-) and National Theater designed by Karl von Fischer which was opened on October 12, 1818, with Ferdinand Fränzl's *Die Weihe*. The elaborate opera house was rebuilt by Karl von Klenze after a disastrous fire on January 14, 1823, and it reopened in 1825. [It was destroyed by bombs in 1943. Completely restored by Gerhard Graubner between 1959 and 1963, the 2,098-seat house opened with *Frau ohne Schatten* on November 21, 1963, and with Wagner's *Die Meistersinger von Nürnberg* on November 23, 1963.] Thanks to the donations of the Munich population, the theater was reconstructed according to the original plans. The Theater am Isartor, which opened in 1812 [the same year that Meyerbeer's first opera, *Jepthas Gelübde*, premiered at the Residenztheater on December 23] specialized in lighter entertainment under the direction of Peter von Lindpaintner. Lindpaintner was so successful that Ludwig I ordered the house closed in 1825 so that more serious cultural events could come to the fore.

The closure of the Theater am Isartor led to an open field for the National Theater, and when Franz Lachner, who was at Mannheim, was appointed general music director in 1836, the rise of the National Theater began. The reign of King Ludwig II is closely tied to the name of Richard Wagner, the composer he invited to Munich in 1864 to discuss a festival theater and a possible Musikschule. Despite Wagner's explosive ego and self-centered life-style, Ludwig served as his principal patron, supporting his many artistic visions. Court conductor Hans von Bülow conducted the brilliant world premieres of *Tristan und Isolde* on June 10, 1865, and *Die Meistersinger von Nürnberg* on June 21, 1868. On September 22, 1869, and June 26, 1870, the premieres of *Das Rheingold* and *Die Walküre* followed under the baton of Franz Wüllner, a choice that did not have the composer's blessing. With such activity the Hof- und National Theater was again in the center of the European musical world. At the same time, Carl von Perfall organized the first Munich summer festival of the works of Mozart and Wagner in 1875, a full year before the founding of the Bayreuth Festival. He managed to realize the earlier plan of Wagner with the building of the Bayreuth-inspired Prinzregententheater. [The 1,122-seat theater built by Heilmann and Littmann opened on August 21, 1901, with *Die Meistersinger von Nürnberg*. Following extensive renovation it reopened on January 9, 1988, with 873 seats.] Except for breaks during the two world wars, the festival has been mounted yearly since 1901. In 1905 the Sommerfestspiele occupied the Residenztheater (Cuvilliéstheater), the Hof- und Nationaltheater, and the Prinzregententheater. From 1910 to 1914 it was known as the Richard Wagner- und Mozart-Festspiele; from 1919 it was called the Münchner Festspiele, at which time the works of other composers were introduced. Richard Strauss's *Ariadne auf Naxos* was produced in 1921, and the composer's complete works were presented in 1988, the first time the festival had been devoted to the work of a single composer.

After a successful stint in Karlsruhe, the conductor Hermann Levi served as Hofkapellmeister in Munich from 1872 to 1900. One of Wagner's favorites, he conducted the premiere of *Parsifal* in Bayreuth on July 26, 1882. Not only did he promote the music dramas of Wagner, he also introduced the young conductors Richard Strauss and Wilhelm Kienzl to the basic principles of a performing style that did justice to Mozart and that had been neglected for decades. Under the leadership of these men, Munich evolved into a key player in the Mozart renaissance. Hermann Zumpe, who had assisted Wagner in the preparation of the first "Ring" cycle at Bayreuth in 1873–1876, conducted the first Wagner performances at the new Prinzregententheater in 1901–1903. Zumpe's successor Felix Mottl (1903–1911) prepared the ground for Richard Strauss in his hometown. From 1912 to 1922, Bruno Walter was responsible for the musical development of the Munich opera, and he was to be the last royal Generalmusikdirektor. With the works of Franz Schrecker, Erich Korngold, and others, he introduced the audience to the new aesthetic of contemporary opera. A memorable production was the world premiere of Hans Pfitzner's *Palestrina* on June 12, 1917, with Erb, Bender, Feinhals, Ivogün, and Krüger. From 1922 until 1936, Hans Knappertsbusch was in charge of the opera in Munich, and it was a glorious golden age. In addition to the Wagner performances, Knappertsbusch's extraordinary renderings of the Strauss operas were among the artistic highlights of the postwar period.

After Knappertsbusch was forced by the Nazis to leave Germany in 1934, Clemens Krauss succeeded him as music director in 1936. In spite of the difficult times, in cooperation with the designers Emil Preetorius and Ludwig Sievert and the producer Rudolf Hartmann, he created a fully integrated conception of musical drama. Highlights were the world premieres of *Der Mond* by Carl Orff on February 5, 1939, and two Strauss operas: *Friedenstag* on July 24, 1938, with Ursuleac, Patzak, and Hotter; and *Capriccio*, on October 28, 1942, with Ursuleac and Hotter. During the night of October 3, 1943, the National Theater was destroyed in an Allied bombing raid.

In 1945 Georg Hartmann and the music director Georg Solti authored a new beginning in the Prinzregententheater. Günther Rennert's staging of Beethoven's *Fidelio* conducted by Bertil Wetzelsberger marked the rebirth of the Bayerische Staatsoper on November 15 in the hastily repaired but functional Prinzregententheater. As the momentum increased, the first postwar Opera Festival was held in 1950. From 1952 to 1967, Rudolf Hartmann was general director with Ferenc Fricsay as his GMD for the first two years. The series of famous conductors continued with Joseph Keilberth from 1959 to 1968. In 1958 the Cuvilliéstheater, which had been destroyed in the war, was reopened. On November 21, 1963, the Bavarian State Opera moved back into the National Theater, which had been reconstructed according to the old plans. In 1967 Günther Rennert succeeded Hartmann as director of the National Theater. During the eleven years of his directorship—since 1971 with Wolfgang Sawallisch as GMD—opera and production theater continued the house tradition of integrated theater. Rennert's own productions set standards that, to a great extent, are still valid today. In 1974 the Bavarian State Opera toured Japan for the first time. Before August Everding became opera director in 1977, Wolfgang Sawallisch was in charge of the theater for an interim season. The highlight of Everding's five-year directorship was the world premiere of Aribert Reimann's *Lear* on July 9, 1978. During those years many standards of the traditional repertoire were mounted in new productions with prominent casts—extraordinary works were presented in extraordinary productions. Since 1982 Wolfgang Sawallisch has been director and GMD. Wagner's complete works were performed in a cycle of the one hundredth anniversary of the composer's death. In 1984 the Bavarian State Opera was the first Western opera house to tour the People's Republic of China. A milestone of more recent times was the new production of Wagner's *Der Ring des Nibelungen* in March 1987. In the Opera Festival of 1988 the complete works of Richard Strauss were performed. The German, Italian, and French operatic repertory is systematically renewed and continues to grow with the addition of the works of contemporary composers (Aribert Reimann's *Troades* was premiered in the 1986 festival). Reimann's opera marked the fifty-fourth operatic world premiere mounted by the company since Ermanno Wolf-Ferrari's *Die neugierigen Frauen* on November 27, 1903—a record equaled by few, if indeed any, other opera companies.

Typical of recent statistics, the 1988–1989 season included 307 performances in the Nationaltheater (with an audience of 592,097); 27 performances in the Altes Residenztheater (Cuvilliéstheater) (with an audience of 10,708); and 25 performances at other sites (with an audience of 3,667). The Staatsoper employed 44 soloists, 42 dancers, 96 choristers, 141 members of the orchestra, and 583 technical and administrative support personnel. The 1990–1991 season includes a repertoire of fifty-one operas, of which five are new productions, including the world premiere of Krzysztof Penderecki's *Ubu Rex* which is scheduled on July 6, 1991, as a part of the Münchner Opern-Festspiele 1991.

CHRONOLOGY OF RECENT DIRECTORS: Freiherr Johann Nepomik, 1824–1833. Freiherr von Poißl, 1833–1848. Hofrot von Küstner, 1848–1851. Franz von Dingelstedt, 1851–1858. Freiherr von Perfall, 1868–1892. Ernst Possart, 1893–1905. Freiherr von Speidel, 1905–1914. Clemens von Frankenstein, 1914–1918. Karl Zeiss, 1919–1924. Clemens von Frankenstein, 1924–1934. Hans Knappertsbusch, 1934–1935. Walleck, 1935–1938. [Staatsoper] Clemens Krauss, 1938–1944. Georg Hartmann, 1945–1952. Rudolf Hartmann, 1952–1967. Günther Rennert, 1967–1977. August Everding, 1977– present (Wolfgang Sawallisch, 1982–present as Operndirektor).

BIBLIOGRAPHY: *Festschrift der Bayerischen Staatsoper zur Eröffnung des wiederaufgebauten Hauses* (München, 1963). Heinrich Friess, *300 Jahre Münchner Oper* (München, 1953). Rudolf Hartmann, *Rudolf Hartmann: Das geliebte Haus* (München, 1979). Alfons Ott, *Kleine Geschichte der Münchner Oper* (München, n.d.). Günther Rennert, *Opernarbeit: Inszenierungen, 1963–1973* (München, 1974). Paul Schallweg, ed., *Festliche Oper: Geschichte und Wiederaufbau des Nationaltheaters in München*

(München, 1964). *25 Jahre Nationaltheater nach den Wiederaufbau* (München, 1989). Hans Wagner, *200 Jahre Münchener Theaterchronik 1750–1950*, supplement, 1951–60 (München, 1951, repr. 1961). Max Zenger, *Geschichte der Münchener Oper* (München, 1923).

ACCESS: Nationaltheater, Max-Joseph-Platz 2, 8000 München 1. (49 89) 2 18 51; fax (49 89) 2 18 53 04. August Everding, Generalintendant. Wolfgang Sawallisch, Staatsoperndirektor und Generalmusikdirektor.

[From materials supplied by the company]
TRANS. JONATHAN MUIR

NÜRNBERG (492,163)

Städtische Bühnen

Sigmund Staden's *Seelewig*, recognized as the first extant German opera, is thought to have been performed privately in Nürnberg in 1644. The city is perhaps most famous in operatic circles as the location for Richard Wagner's *Die Meistersinger von Nürnberg*. In comparison with its sister cities in Germany, Nürnberg has had an unpretentious theatrical history. The cornerstone for the first Stadttheater was laid on April 30, 1832, and the 1,000-seat theater opened on October 1, 1833. As the population expanded, the Altes Stadttheater became inadequate, and in 1887 the city fathers decided to build a new house. The contract was signed on June 28, 1898, and the 1,400-seat Stadttheater am Ring, designed by Heinrich Seeling, was built between 1901 and 1905. It opened on September 1, 1905, with a program that included excerpts from Wagner's *Die Meistersinger*. Several months before, on May 10, the old theater was closed and would remain empty until it was refurbished and opened as a drama theater on September 21, 1924.

In 1930, the Neue Stadttheater am Ring became the Opernhaus and the Alte Stadttheater was named the Schauspielhaus. When the Nazis came to power in 1933, Hitler designated Nürnberg as the site of the yearly convention of the National Socialist party, and both theaters were heavily used for propaganda purposes and events. The opera house was substantially rebuilt and redecorated in 1935 to include Hitler's "Führer-Loge." On September 10, with Hitler, Winifred Wagner, and members of the diplomatic corps in attendance, Wilhelm Furtwängler conducted Wagner's *Die Meistersinger von Nürnberg*. Both theaters were completely destroyed during an air raid on January 2, 1945. The Opernhaus was rebuilt in 1945 as a 1,061-seat opera house. The 1990–1991 season includes *Tannhäuser*, *Così fan tutte*, *Il Trovatore*, *Orpheus in der Unterwelt*, *Die Italienerin in Algier*, Hans Zender's *Stephen Climax* (premiered 1986 in Frankfurt am Main), and Paul Burkhard's *Feuerwerk*. An additional twenty-two operas and operettas remain in the repertoire.

BIBLIOGRAPHY: Peter Kertz and Ingeborg Strößenreuther, *Bibliographie zur Theatergeschichte Nürnbergs* (Nürnberg, 1964). Robert Plank, ed., *Festschrift anläßlich der*

Wiedereröffnung des Nürnberg Opernhauses, September 1935 (Nürnberg, 1935). *Schauspielhaus am Richard-Wagner-Platz. Städtische Bühnen Nürnberg-Fürth* (Nürnberg, 1961). Jürgen Söllner. *Nürnberger Theater: Das Opernhaus* (Nürnberg, 1986). Hermann Weninger, *Das Stadttheater in Nürnberg, 1833–1905* (Würzburg, 1932).

ACCESS: Opernhaus, Richard-Wagner-Platz 2–10, 8500 Nürnberg 70. (49 911) 16 35 23. Burkhard Mauer, Generalintendant. Christian Thielemann, Generalmusikdirektor.

[From materials supplied by the company]
TRANS. JONATHAN MUIR

STUTTGART (561,278)

Staatstheater Stuttgart

Two significant events led to the development of Stuttgart as an internationally acclaimed opera center in the eighteenth century. The first was the accession of Duke Carl Eugene as duke of Württemberg in 1744. Brought up in the court of Friedrich the Great in Potsdam, Carl Eugene was widely traveled, knew of the finest musical achievements in France and Italy as well as Germany, and was committed to building a ballet, an orchestra, and an opera of the very highest quality. The second event was the engagement of Nicoló Jommelli by the duke to compose an opera for his birthday celebration. At least two of Jommelli's operas had already been produced in the new opera house, which had opened in 1750; *Merope* on February 11, 1751, and *Didone abbandonata* that same season, and the Italian composer was very popular. The resulting birthday commission was *Fetonte*, which premiered on February 11, 1753. A bargain was struck, and Jommelli moved to Stuttgart in time for the premiere of *La clemenza di Tito* on August 30. His official appointment began on January 1, 1754, and he was given complete control of all opera productions. A concern for the total production prompted Jommelli to build the orchestra from twenty-four to forty-seven players and to integrate the ballet, chorus, and ensemble numbers into a unified whole. To accommodate some of his ideas, the theater was renovated in 1758–1759. By the time he left in 1768, some sixteen of his operas had been produced in Stuttgart alone, and twelve others were performed at the court residence at Ludwigsburg.

Ludwig became duke after Carl Eugene's death and discovered that the previous expenditures on music and the arts had left the treasury in disarray. The composer Franz Danzi tried to maintain the standards between 1807 and 1812, followed by Conradin Kreutzer (1812–1816) and Johann Nepomuk Hummel (1816–1819), but the golden age of Carl Eugene and Jommelli seemed lost. With the appointment of Peter Joseph von Lindpaintner, who came from the Isartor Theater in Munich in 1819, the house was again in strong artistic hands. Lindpaintner remained Hofkapellmeister in Stuttgart until his death in 1856 and was largely responsible for the heightened esteem in which the company was held in Germany and beyond. The next important operatic chapter in Stuttgart came when Max von Schillings was appointed Generalmusikdirektor in 1908, a position he would fill with honor until 1918. The old court theater had burned down in 1902, to be replaced by the Großes und Kleines Haus, which opened in 1912. The 1,400-seat Großes Haus designed by Max Littmann opened on September 15, 1912, with Mozart's *Die Hochzeit des Figaro*. That same year Richard Strauss conducted the world premiere of *Ariadne auf Naxos* (October 25 in the original version, with the one-act opera following Molière's *Le Bourgeois Gentilhomme*). The initial plan called for Max Reinhardt's Berlin acting company and an opera cast featuring Emmy Destinn, Karl Erb, and Frieda Hempel. The final casting was almost as interesting: Maria Jeritza, Hermann Jadlowker, and Margarethe Siems. Schillings's own *Mona Lisa* was premiered in the house on September 26, 1915, and remains one of the most popular German operas of the early twentieth century. In his final season as director, Schillings produced Siegfried Wagner's *An allem ist Hütschen schuld* (December 6, 1917).

In June 1918 the twenty-eight-year-old Fritz Busch came to Stuttgart from Aachen and introduced four seasons of exciting opera before he left to assume Fritz Reiner's position in Dresden in 1922. Under Busch the house celebrated the premieres of Ture Rangströms's *Die Kronbraut* on October 21, 1919, and Hindemith's *Mörder, Hoffnung der Frauen* and *Das Nusch-Nuschi* on June 4, 1921. The next general music director (1922–1937), Carl Leonhardt, managed to produce the complete operas of Richard Wagner in honor of the fiftieth anniversary of the composer's death. Fortunately the theater was damaged very little by the war, and in 1946 Hindemith's *Mathis der Mahler* received its long-overdue German premiere in Stuttgart. Another turning point for the company came in 1947 with the appointment of the conductor Ferdinand Leitner as opera director; he would become general music director in 1950. Leitner remained at the helm until 1969, and his reign was marked by artistic innovation, aesthetic daring, and high standards. He initiated an artistic collaboration with Wieland Wagner in a 1954 production of Beethoven's *Fidelio*, a collaboration that would result in some stunning operatic realizations. Leitner was succeeded by Václav Neumann (1969–1972), who conducted the premiere of Ján Cikker's *Das Spiel von Liebe und Tod* (1969). Silvio Varviso took up the reins in 1972, and when he was appointed music director of the Théâtre National de L'Opéra de Paris, Dennis Russell Davies succeeded him in 1980. In 1983–1984 some previously planned renovations were finally realized and the 1,396-seat Großes Haus opened again on November 1, 1984.

BIBLIOGRAPHY: *Festschrift der Württembergischen Staatstheater* (Stuttgart, 1962). Kurt Honolka, *Dreitausend Mal Musik: Stars und Premieren in Stuttgart und anderswo* (Stuttgart, 1978). R. Krauss, *Das Stuttgarter Hoftheater* (Stuttgart, 1908). Günther Rennert, *Opernarbeit: Inszenierungen, 1963–1973* (München, 1974).

ACCESS: Großes Haus, Oberer Schloßgarten 6, 7000 Stuttgart 10. (49 711) 20 32 2 01; fax (49 711) 20 32 3 89. Wolfgang Gönnenwein, Generalintendant.

[From materials supplied by the company]
TRANS. MARC ÄNDERS

Greece

ATHENS (9,990,000)

National Opera of Greece

Ruled by the Ottoman Empire since the fourteenth century, the Greeks finally won their independence in 1829. In the London Protocol of 1830 France, Great Britain and Russia agreed to protect the new state. The first known opera performance in Greece was Rossini's *Il Barbiere di Siviglia* on July 4, 1837, shortly after modern Greece achieved its independence. During the following decades a number of operas and operettas were produced, apparently for the large colony of foreigners living in the country as neither entertainment was a native genre. The Athens Conservatory, founded in 1871, instituted an opera school and presented European works. It was not until 1939 that the Ethniki Lyriki Skini (The National Opera) was founded in Athens. The company uses the Athens State Orchestra for its limited performances. Founded in 1955 by the National Tourist Organization, the Athens Festival imports major artists and ensembles and has no formal links with the National Opera.

ACCESS: Olympia Theater, 59, Academias Street, 10679 Athens. (30 1) 323 0049/322 5904. Nikos Synodinos, General Director.

[From materials supplied by the company]

Hungary

BUDAPEST (2,115,000)

Magyar Állami Operaház (Royal Hungarian Opera House)

The 1,310-seat Royal Hungarian Opera House, designed by Miklós Ybl, opened in 1884, but its more than one-hundred-year history is not the complete history of opera in Hungary. As everywhere in Europe, operas were performed in the private theaters of aristocratic families and in the Buda castle as early as 1786. There were approximately fifty such theaters, with the most important opera houses belonging to the Eszterházy princes. Joseph Haydn's extensive involvement as both composer and conductor was linked with theaters at Kismarton (Eisenstadt) and Eszterháza. Public performances started in Hungary at about the same time. German traveling companies performed in the theaters of Pest and Buda starting in 1786. The 3,000-seat Városi Színház (Town Theater) in Pest opened in 1812, and the program included two Beethoven overtures. Until the theater burned down in 1847, popular contemporary operas attracted a considerable public. Following the German example, the first Hungarian opera began in 1793 with József Chudy's *Pikkó Hertzeg és Jutka Perzsi*. However, the competition with the visiting German troupes, particularly the one that moved into the town theater in 1812, relegated native companies to the provinces.

Hungarian opera returned to the capital in 1833, and a company conducted by Ferenc Erkel moved into the new National Theater (Nemzeti Színház) in 1837. Rossini's *Il Barbiere di Siviglia* was the first staged opera. Erkel, who was to conduct the orchestra for forty-seven years (as well as inaugurating symphony concerts in 1853 with members of the theater orchestra), gradually developed a repertoire that included Auber, Bellini, Cherubini, Donizetti, Meyerbeer, Mozart, Rossini, Weber, and especially Verdi. However, his greatest merit was giving birth to Hungarian opera. As a composer, his own *Hunyadi Lászlo*, *Bánk bán*, and *Brankovics György*, all with historical plots, have remained in the repertoire to the present day. His aversion to Wagner, however, delayed *Lohengrin* until 1866, *Tannhäuser* until 1871, and *Die Meistersinger von Nürnberg* until 1883. Under Erkel (1838–1874), Hans Richter (1871–1875), and Sándor Erkel (1874–1900) the company established itself as the leading Hungarian ensemble. When Prussia defeated Austria in 1866, Austrian power in Hungary was severely weakened. The Hungarians forced the Hapsburg ruler to sign the Compromise of 1867 which created a dual monarchy of Austria–Hungary, uniting the Austrian Empire and the Hungarian Kingdom. This union remained intact some forty years until Serbian nationalists killed the crown prince of Austria–Hungary, Archduke Francis Ferdinand, precipitating World War I.

It became more important than ever to cater to the aspirations of the Hungarian people as Budapest, the capital of Hungary, experienced enormous growth. Emperor Franz Joseph I of Austria was crowned king of Hungary, and his new government decided to establish an independent state opera house. The most outstanding architect of the age, Miklós Ybl, began the construction in 1875. Erkel's company became the resident ensemble when the new Magyar Királyi Operaház (Royal Hungarian Opera House) opened in 1884. The opera house is one of the most important nineteenth-century monuments of Budapest. The neo-Renaissance building unites baroque and Renaissance stylistic elements, architecture and sculpture, and wood and metal work in harmonic unity. The representative function of the building is emphasized by rich ornament throughout. With state-of-the-art stage mechanisms, a modern automatic sprinkler system, an iron curtain, and a hydraulic cyclorama, it was the most modern theater of its age. A festive opening was celebrated on September 27, 1884, in the presence of Emperor Franz Joseph I. This gala, however, nearly ended in disaster when the curious crowd burst through the police lines to look at the magnificent new structure. The project had cost an enormous amount of money, and, in addition, the operation of the house demanded a sizable roster of singers, musicians, and staff. Training of vocalists in Hungary at the time was just beginning, and leading roles were assumed mostly by foreign artists. During those early decades, artists of the caliber of Sembrich, Lilli Lehmann, D'Andrade, and Caruso (his Radames on October 2, 1907, was not well received) were cast in major productions. There were no funds for new productions, so sets and costumes were all in the historic or Meinigen style. Despite these shortcomings, a rich repertoire of thirty-seven operas and seven ballets were performed during the inaugural season.

The first golden age of the Budapest Opera dates from the directorship of Gustav Mahler (1888–1891). Mahler raised the artistic level of the house significantly, and his ensemble included famous singers such as Bianca Bianchi, Laura Hilgermann, Italia Vasquez, David Ney, Lehel Odry, Richard Pauli, Henri Prévost, and Mihály Takáts. His successor was the no less famous Arthur Nikisch, and the legacy left by those two giants of music formed the basis for a tradition of excellence. A number of famous composers appeared in Budapest during this time. Massenet and Delibes conducted their own work, and on October 30, 1895, Mascagni directed *Cavalleria rusticana*. Leoncavallo, Kienzl, Goldmark, Humperdinck, and d'Albert all assisted in the performances of their operas. Puccini, who first visited Budapest in 1894 for performances of *Manon Lescaut*, returned later for the local premieres of *Madama Butterfly* and *La Fanciulla del West*.

The economic, political, and social impact of World War I brought the opera house to a standstill. Nevertheless, one of the greatest geniuses of Hungarian music, Béla Bartók, oversaw the premiere of *Duke Blue-Beard's Castle* on May 24, 1918 sung in German. This same work was presented in Hungarian on May 5, 1938, at the Maggio Musicale Fiorentino, to the delight of the Italian audience. Some eight years later another monument in the history of Hungarian opera, *Háry János* by Zoltán Kodály, was premiered on October 17, 1926. The period between the two world wars was one of economic and political instability in Hungary. In spite of this, the Opera House enjoyed another golden age, due in large part to two outstanding managers: the composer/professor Miklós Radnai and the writer/director/designer László Márkus. Each headed the house for ten years, demonstrating great expertise and unsurpassed artistic sense. They created an outstanding ensemble with a roster of excellent conductors, directors, and designers such as Sergio Failoni, Gusztáv Oláh, Kálmán Nádasdy, Zoltán Fülöp, and Tivadar Márk. The Szeged Open Air festivals and the Open Air Theater on Margaret Island were inaugurated with the participation of the Opera House. In addition, the Hungarian Opera toured to Nürnberg in 1929 and to Florence in 1938, performing in the latter city exclusively with works of Hungarian composers such as Liszt, Hubay, Dohnánye, Bartók, and Kodály. In 1940 the company performed at La Scala, and their repertoire included Respighi's *La Fiamma*. Gina Cigna, Maria Jeritza, Nanny Larsen-Todsen, Ebe Stignani, Beniamino Gigli, Marcel Journet, Jan Kiepura, Alexander Kipnis, Giacomo Lauri-Volpi, Aureliano Pertile, Helge Roswaenge, Richard Tauber, and Franz Völker all performed at the Budapest Opera. Visiting conductors included Thomas Beecham, Issay Dobroven, Wilhelm Furtwängler, Erich Kleiber, Hans Knappertsbusch, Fritz Reiner, Felix Weingartner, and Richard Strauss.

The outbreak of World War II and the German occupation raised serious difficulties in continuing the work of the Budapest Opera. The eventual siege of the city paralyzed all activity, and the last performance was held on December 23, 1944. Fortunately, the building was not seriously damaged and, after the liberation of Budapest, the technical staff rebuilt the theater and, on March 15, 1945, the Magyar Állami Operaház was opened again. In 1946 Aladár Tóth was appointed director, and he invited Otto Klemperer to join the company as principal conductor, a post Klemperer retained until 1950. Klemperer's Mozart cycles were artistic high points of the postwar era. Due to impacted scheduling in the opera house, the 2,220-seat Town Theater was united with the opera in 1951 and renamed the Erkel Theater in honor of Ferenc Erkel. Both houses featured numerous excellent guest artists: Theo Adam, Giacomo Aragall, Hildegard Behrens, Bergonzi, Caballé, Piero Cappucilli, José Carreras, Maria Chiara, Christoff, Domingo, Gedda, Ghiaurov, Gobbi, Moffo, del Monaco, Ievgeni

Nesterenko, Karl Ridderbusch, Rysanek, Scotto, Siepi, Simionato, Talvela, Windgassen, and many others; and conductors Gianandrea Gavazzeni, Georges Sebastian, Iuri Simonov, Lamberto Gardelli, and Giuseppe Patané. The Deutsche Staatsoper Berlin, Teatro Comunale di Bologna, the Sofiskya Narodna Opera (National Opera of Sofia), the Bolshoi of Moscow, the Komische Oper of Berlin, and the Opera Company of Cologne have all visited Budapest.

Since the 1960s the board of directors has worked to enlarge the repertoire to include revivals of early masterpieces such as Monteverdi's *Il Ritorno d'Ulisse* and *L'Incoronatione di Poppea* as well as productions of the finest twentieth century operas such as *Pelléas et Mélisande*, *Porgy and Bess*, *Katerina Ismailova*, *Wozzeck*, *Lulu*, *Aufstieg und Fall der Stadt Mahagonny*, *Die Kluge*, *The Telephone*, *Albert Herring*, *Peter Grimes*, and *The Rake's Progress*. It has become a tradition during the last decade that a new Hungarian opera be included in every season. Works by Sándor Szokolay (*Blood Wedding*, *Hamlet*, and *Samson*), András Milhály (*Together and Alone*), György Ránki (*Tragedy of Man*), Emil Petrovics (*C'est la guerre*, *Crime and Punishment*, and *Lysistrata*), Zsotl Durkó (*Moses*), and Sándor Balassa (*The Man Outside*) have all been premiered by the Budapest State Opera. The outstanding production staff has numbered Gusztáv Oláh, Zoltán Fülöp, Tivadar Márk, and Gábor Forray among its distinguished members. Moreover, a number of famous singers (Rosette Anday, Maria Németh, Eszter Réthy, Robert Ilosfalvy, Endre Koréh, Kálmán Pataky, Sándor Svéd, Mihály Székely, and Éva Marton) and conductors (Ferenc Fricsay, Anton Doráti, George Solti, and István Kertész) began their careers in Budapest. With an average of four hundred opera performances each season in the two theaters (and another one hundred or more performances of ballet), the current staff of 1,250 is more than adequate to support the program.

CHRONOLOGY OF ARTISTIC DIRECTORS: Sándor Erkel, 1884–1886. Gustav Mahler, 1888–1891. Arthur Nikisch, 1893–1895. Gyula Káldy, 1895–1900. Imre Mészáros, 1900–1901. Rezsó Máder, 1901–1907. Imre Mészáro, 1907–1913. Aurél Kern, 1913–1917. Dezsó Zádor, 1918–1919. Emil Ábrányi, Jr., 1919–1920. István Kerner, 1920–1921. Rezsó Máder, 1921–1925. Miklós Radnai, 1925–1935. László Márkus, 1935–1944. Miklós Lukács, July-October 1944. Zoltán Sámy, October-December 1944. Mihály Székely, Kálmán Nádasdy, and Pál Komáromy, February-April 1945. Pál Komáromy, 1945–1946. Aladár Tóth, 1946–1956. Imre Palló, 1957–1958. Tibor Faith, 1958–1959. Kálmán Nádasdy, 1959–1966. Miklós Lukás, 1966–1978. András Mihály, 1978–1986. Emil Petrovics, 1986–1990.

CHRONOLOGY OF DIRECTORS: Frigyes Podmaniczky, 1875–1886. István Keglevich, 1886–1888. Ferenc Beniczky, 1888–1891. Géza Zichy, 1891–1894. Elek Nopcsa, 1894–1897. Kálmán Huszár, 1897–1898. István Keglevich, 1898–1902. Miklós Bánffy, 1912–1917.

CHRONOLOGY OF MUSIC DIRECTORS: Ferenc Erkel, 1884–1893. Sándor Erkel, 1886–1900. Egisto Tango, 1913–1917. István Kerner, 1917–1923. Bernát Tittel, 1923–1928. János Ferencsik, 1957–1973; 1978–1984.

BIBLIOGRAPHY: Imré Balassa, *A hetvenötéves Magyar Állami Operaház, 1884–1959*

(Seventy-five years of the National Theater) (Budapest, 1959). Miklós Borsa and Pál Tolnay, *Az ismeretlen Operaház* (Budapest, 1984). Janos Kádár, *A Nemzeti szinház száz éves története* (100 years of the National Theater) (Budapest, 1940). Iván Kertész, *A Magyar Állami Operaház* (Budapest, 1975). Lajos Koch, *A Budapesti Operaház müsora [repertoire], 1884–1959* (Budapest, 1959). Laurisin Lajos, *A Magyar Királyi Operaház* (Budapest, 1940). *A Magyar Királyi Operaház, 1884–1909* (Budapest, 1909). *A Magyar Királyi Operaház, Jubileumi album, 1884–1934* (Budapest, 1934). Géza Staud, ed., *A Budapesti Operaház 100 éve* (Budapest, 1984). Ervin Ybl, *Az Operaház* (Budapest, 1962).

ACCESS: Andrássy ut 22, 1061 Budapest. (36 1) 312 550.

NÓRA WELLMANN

Republic of Ireland

WEXFORD (102,552)

Wexford Festival Opera

The Government of Ireland Act passed by the British Parliament in 1920 divided Ireland into two separate entities. The twenty-three southern counties fought for independence, and in 1921 the area became a dominion of Great Britain called the Irish Free State. Between 1932 and 1937 most of the ties with Great Britain were severed, and in 1937 a new constitution was adopted proclaiming a sovereign, independent, democratic state. Ireland cut all ties with Great Britain on April 18, 1949, and declared itself a fully independent state. The history of the Wexford Festival, one of Ireland's premiere cultural events, is both unlikely and extraordinary. Based in the attractive port at the mouth of the River Slaney at the southeast corner of the Republic of Ireland, the city dates its history back to a Viking settlement. The festival itself was precipitated by a visit from Scottish novelist and founder of *Gramophone* magazine, Sir Compton Mackenzie, in 1950 when he addressed the inaugural meeting of the local gramophone society and suggested that the production of an actual opera would be a better pursuit than listening to recordings. The following years, a group led by local physicians Tom Walsh and Des Ffrench and hotelier Eugene McCarthy took up the challenge. The Wexford Festival of Music and the Arts launched its first season from October 21 to November 4, 1951, with four performances of Balfe's *The Rose of Castille*. The final performances took place in the tiny Theater Royal, one of only two remaining Georgian theatres in the republic outside Dublin.

For its second season, Walsh, functioning as an artistic director, looked to Italy, which was then emerging from the chaos of the war. Singers were grateful for opportunities to travel, and over the next decade the festival was host to a string of new and established voices. Walsh and his team displayed an aptitude for spotting talent and for choosing operas that had been neglected. Thus, such names as Nicola Monti, Christiano Dallamangas, Afro Poli, Graziella Sciutti, Fiorenza Cossotto, and Plinio Clabassi found themselves in the modest theater singing the works of Donizetti, Bellini, and Rossini. They were joined by young artists from Ireland and the United Kingdom, including Heather Harper, Janet Baker, and Geraint Evans. Conductors included Bryan Balkwill, Charles Mackerras, and John Pritchard, while Peter Ebert and Anthony Besch frequently acted as producers. In this way the festival rapidly built a reputation in an era that was starved of good-quality opera productions in Europe. In 1952 the season was extended to two operas per year and a parallel program of recitals and concerts brought in distinguished musicians and orchestras. A lively concert and recital program has remained an integral part of the festival to this day.

The venerable Theater Royal began to show its age, and in 1960 the festival was closed for a year to allow for major renovation work which was supported by the Gulbenkian Foundation. The first half of the 1960s continued the successful formula of mainly Italian operas plus a scattering of German and French works. Two well-known operas were attempted (*Lucia di Lammermoor* and *La Traviata*), but it was generally agreed that the competition from the big-budget international houses made for unwelcome comparisons, and the policy of reviving neglected or unusual works has been maintained ever since. In 1965 the festival had an important "first" with Massenet's *Don Quichotte* starring Miroslav Cangalovic. Massenet had been largely ignored outside France, and the Wexford Festival was to play a leading role in restoring his image in subsequent years; to date, six of his operas have been produced for the festival. Originally, the Radio Eireann Light Orchestra played in the pit, but it was replaced in 1961 by the Royal Liverpool Philharmonic and in the following year by the Radio Eireann Symphony, which is now the National Symphony of Ireland. Each year Radio Telefis Eireann (R.T.E.) broadcasts the operas with the British Broadcasting Corporation (BBC) linking in to at least one of the productions. In 1988 R.T.E. videotaped Dvořák's *The Devil and Kate* and a double bill (Gazaniga's *Don Giovanni* and Busoni's *Turandot*) in association with the National Video Corporation in London.

In the mid-1960s Walsh resigned and a successor was sought. Brian Dickie, the twenty-six-year-old administrator of the newly formed Glyndebourne Opera Touring Company, became the first professional artistic director. He served for seven seasons and created a highly acclaimed, fresh style for the festival. French opera played an increasingly important role, and Dickie introduced modern works into the repertory, including operas by Britten, Janáček, and Prokofiev. He also added a third production to the season, stretching it out over two weeks. Unfortunately, his increasing commitment to the Glyndebourne Festival Opera, where he became opera manager in 1971 and later general administrator, led to his resignation in 1973. His successor, Thomson Smillie, served for five years and continued to widen the range of rare opera produced at the festival. He brought former associates in from the Scottish Opera in Glasgow, continuing the trend toward more eclecticism in both productions and performers. Smillie left in 1978 to join Sarah Caldwell in Boston and, more recently, to head up the Kentucky Opera. He was replaced by Adrian Slack, who maintained the new thrust of the festival for three more seasons.

In 1982 the festival's first woman at the helm emerged. Elaine Padmore was the BBC Radio producer in charge of opera, and thus had considerable experience both with the Wexford Festival and with the choice of works for broadcast in the United Kingdom. As a former professional singer, she brought along firsthand knowledge of the creative and interpretive side as well. As artistic director she has been involved in many significant changes at Wexford over the last decade in cooperation with the festival chairpersons. A much more vigorous program of associated events has been developed, in particular the morning-time Opera Scenes, which allows chorus members and young Irish singers the opportunity to appear before international audiences, critics, and representatives of other opera companies. In 1988 the festival appointed its first full-time managing director, Jerome Hynes, and in 1989 it increased its season by adding one extra performance of each opera plus three nights of recitals. Currently the festival runs for eighteen days, providing five performances of each opera in rotation plus three nights of celebrity concerts.

The sustained success of the festival for nearly forty years represents a major commitment from a considerable number of people. A development committee was formed in the late 1970s, and the acceptance of its recommendations has greatly strengthened the operation. The Theater Royal has been rebuilt (and expanded to 550 seats), and the backstage and technical facilities have been modernized, resulting in the current configuration. The basic organization of the festival has remained the same over the years. A voluntary council of some thirty people, representing local interests, major sponsors, and representatives of national and international music organizations, guides policy. Its requirements are administered by a small full-time secretariat which is assisted by a voluntary team during the festival. The artistic director selects all professional employees on an ad hoc, yearly basis, following a budget and guidelines provided by the council. In 1990 the total festival budget was about $850,000 funded by over 40 percent from box receipts, 25 percent in public funding, and the remainder from Friends of the Festival and business sponsors, most notably the Guiness Company, which has been involved for twenty-five years. Overall, the Wexford Festival Opera has proven to be a most robust event which has built up an unequaled reputation for staging rare or neglected operas in the charming intimacy of the Theater Royal and for providing young singers with the opportunity to appear in outstanding productions before a discerning international audience.

BIBLIOGRAPHY: Bernard Levin, *Conducted Tour* (London 1981). Kevin Lewis, *Memories of Wexford Festival Opera* (Wexford, 1984). John O'Hagen, *The Economic and Social Contribution of the Wexford Festival* (Wexford, 1989). Gus Smith, *Ring Up the Curtain* (Dublin, 1976).

ACCESS: Theater Royal, High Street, Wexford. (353 53) 053 22240; fax (353 53) 053 24289. Elaine Padmore, Artistic Director. Jerome Hynes, Managing Director.

IAN FOX

Israel

TEL AVIV (1,029,700)

The New Israeli Opera

The 1917 Balfour Declaration created a place for the Jewish people in Palestine. The history of opera in what was to become the independent state of Israel in 1948 began in 1923 through the efforts of the conductor Mordechai Golinkin. Golinkin produced a number of works in an open-air setting, but his inability to secure a permanent opera house led ultimately to the failure of his venture. The turning point occurred in 1947 when the Israel National Opera was established by the soprano Edis De-Philippe. On November 27, 1947, the same day on which the United Nations approved the partitioning of Palestine, she presented an opera gala of various excerpts in which she herself took a prominent role. Shortly after she starred in a full production of Massenet's *Thaïs*, the company began to expand. During the first ten years the company performed in the Habima National Theater; later it moved to a hall that had served as the temporary home of the Israeli Parliament. Between 1962 and 1965 the young Placido Domingo appeared in over three hundred performances of 12 productions primarily given in Hebrew. By the twenty-fifth anniversary of the company in 1972, De-Philippe had produced some 43 different operas, most from the standard repertoire and most sung in Hebrew. Upon her death in 1978 her husband and codirector, Simha Evan-Zohar, assumed control. The company produced operas until 1982, when it closed because the state could not provide funds for a permanent opera house. During the thirty-five years during which the company existed, some five thousand performances were presented from a repertoire of more than 140 operas, operettas, musicals, and ballets.

The New Israeli Opera was established in 1985 by the Ministry of Education and Culture and the municipality of Tel Aviv-Jaffa. Purcell's *Dido and Aeneas*, directed by Hanan Snir and conducted by Yoav Taimi, inaugurated the new company in June and was produced in cooperation with the Cameri Theater and the Israeli Chamber Orchestra. The following June, Mozart's *Le Nozze di Figaro* achieved critical acclaim, and subsequent seasons saw productions of *The Rise and Fall of the City of Mahagonny*, *La Traviata*, *La Bohème*, *The Turn of the Screw*, *The Barber of Seville*, *L'Elisir d'Amore*, *The Tales of Hoffmann*, *Hansel and Gretel*, and *Così fan tutte*. A number of sites were used for these productions, including the Cameri Theater, the Mann Auditorium, the Dohl Auditorium, and the amphitheater in Caesarea. In March 1989 the newly refurbished Noga Theater opened, and the company finally had a home with proper acoustics, an adequate orchestra pit, and lighting facilities suitable for the four to five years that were expected to pass before the completion of the new Golda Meir Performing Arts Centre, which will become its permanent home.

From the 1989–1990 season onward, the New Israeli Opera will present five or six productions each season. The repertoire for 1989–1990 included three new productions (*Hansel and Gretel*, *Così fan tutte*, and *Faust*) and two revivals (*La Bohème* and *The Turn of the Screw*). During the 1990–1991 season the Frankfurt Opera is presenting Verdi's *Macbeth* and Britten's *Midsummer Night's Dream*, and the company will produce *Faust*, *The Bartered Bride*, *Cenerentola*, *Die Entführung aus dem Serail*, *The Medium*, and *The Tales of Hoffmann*. Altogether, the season encompasses one hundred performances. To encourage and train the new generation of Israeli singers, the company instituted a summer opera workshop in 1988. Furthermore, the Association of Opera Lovers was founded to develop private support for the opera in order to supplement public funding from the Municipality of Tel Aviv-Jaffa.

ACCESS: 1, King David Avenue, Tel Aviv 64953. (972 3) 262256 9; fax (972 3) 265701. Uri Ofer, Managing Director. Gary Bertini, Artistic Director.

[From materials supplied by the company]

Italy

BOLOGNA (422,204)

Teatro Comunale di Bologna

Bologna has a long and distinguished theatrical history. Although the Teatro del Pubblico had hosted theatrical entertainments beginning around the middle of the sixteenth century, the first known opera produced in the city was local composer Girolamo Giacobbi's *L'Andromeda*, which premiered in 1610. There is some speculation that the same work was produced in Salzburg on February 15, 1618, which would make Giacobbi's work the first opera produced outside Italy. The success of the new genre over the next 150 years was supported by the aristocracy, with notable productions appearing in the Teatro Malvezzi which opened on March 27, 1653. After that building's destruction by fire in 1745, leading citizens supported by the papal government successfully lobbied for a new theater. Designed by Galli-Bibiena, the new 1,350-seat Teatro Comunale opened on May 14, 1763, with the premiere of Gluck's *Il Trionfo di Clelia* (with a libretto by Metastasio), an opera that does not seem to have been mounted anywhere else. The house has undergone several renovations (1818, 1853, 1859, and 1935 following a fire that destroyed the stagehouse), and it currently operates as an autonomous organization that employs artists and supports both a chorus and an orchestra that presents concerts. Verdi's *Don Carlos*, which premiered in Paris on March 11, 1867, received its first Italian performance (in translation) in Bologna on October 27 of the same year starring Antonio Cotogni and Teresina Stolz. On October 4, 1875, the Teatro Comunale revived Boito's *Mefistofele* in an altered version to great acclaim, completely reversing the failure of the premiere at the Teatro alla Scala some seven years earlier. Giuseppe Martucci conducted the first Italian performance of Wagner's *Tristan und Isolde* in a translation by Boito on June 2, 1888. During the second half of the twentieth century, the house has eschewed a permanent resident company in favor of engaging artists and a complete production team for each opera.

BIBLIOGRAPHY: Renzo Giacomelli, *Il Teatro comunale di Bologna (1763–1963)* (Bologna, 1965). Lamberto Trezzini, ed., *Due secoli di vita musicale: Storia del Teatro Comunale di Bologna*, 2 vols. (Bologna, 1966).

ACCESS: Piazza del Teatro, Via Zamboni 28–30, I-40100 Bologna. (39 51) 529999; fax (39 51) 529905. Giovanni Tangucci, Direttore artistico. Carlo Fontana, Sovrintendente.

[From materials supplied by the company]

FLORENCE (417,487)

Teatro Comunale di Firenze

The city of Florence can rightly claim to be the birthplace of opera, a genre that has played a central role in the evolution of European music. Arising out of the theatrical entertainments of the grand-ducal court, the early works of Caccini, Cavalieri, Corsi, and Peri paved the way for the first masterpiece of the new genre, Monteverdi's *La Favola d'Orfeo*, which was staged in Florence shortly after its premiere in Mantau. Supported by the enlightened aristocracy, opera remained for the next one hundred years a limited entertainment for a select audience. Although a number of operas were produced in Florence during the eighteenth century, the city was not known as one of the centers of the art form in Italy. The lack of a permanent orchestra and the conservative tastes of the aristocracy served to discourage the more successful international composers. However, when Alessandro Lanari assumed the operation of the Teatro della Pergola in 1830, a number of important premieres and first performances were scheduled. The premiere of Verdi's *Macbeth* on March 14, 1847, shortly after that of Ricci's *Li Birraio di Preston*, marked the high point of Florentine opera during the first half of the nineteenth century. Almost one hundred years later, the Teatro della Pergola would regain its performance luster as a performance site for the Maggio Musicale Fiorentino.

The idea of a new and spacious theater was first proposed by Vittorio Emanuele II, and on May 25, 1861, a constitution was adopted by the Societá Anonima del Regio Politeama Fiorentino "Vittorio Emanuele II." This society proposed the construction of an amphitheater that would seat up to 6,000 people for theatrical and operatic presentations. An open-air theater designed by Telemaco Bonajuti was built in a single year and was inaugurated on May 17, 1862, with Donizetti's *Lucia di Lammermoor*. In spite of a fire in 1864, which damaged the building, the Politeama quickly became the center of cultural life in Florence. In 1882 the enormous amphitheater was covered in order to better serve a variety of theatrical as well as equestrian events, and the theater was inaugurated with Verdi's *Nabucco*. Taken over by the Società Italiana Anonima Teatrale in 1910, the Politeama has been devoted mainly to opera and concerts and is now a major component of the Teatro Comunale di Firenzi.

The story of the Maggio Musicale Fiorentino in the cultural life of twentieth-century Florence dates from the historic event on December 9, 1928, when the newly formed Orchestrale Fiorentina under the directorship of Vittorio Gui gave its first public concert in the Politeama Fiorentino. This great theater had long been known for its equestrian spectacles and other events rather than for its contributions of the musical life of the city. In fact, before 1928 the cultural life of Florence was rather deficient in musical character, although the city was a center of the literary and visual arts. The Florentines dutifully followed the standard operatic fare which was given in the Teatro della Pergola and the Teatro Verdi. Accustomed to soloists rather than symphony orchestras, the public knew little of the orchestral literature of their own or previous centuries. An earlier performance of Schoenberg's *Pierrot Lunaire* on April 1, 1923, conducted by the composer with the participation of Alfredo Cassella, almost passed as an April Fool's joke. In fact, a Florentine critic described the music as the record of a meeting of the founder of the second Viennese School with Giacomo Puccini.

After December 9, 1928, the musical life of the city gradually changed as the result of the work of Vittorio Gui. Although a native of Rome, Gui loved Florence, and the Maggio Musicale Fiorentino would not have been born without him. The presence of a large Anglo-American colony in Florence contributed to his success. The Maggio Musicale Fiorentino, which was still a dream, would quickly become nationally and internationally important once Maestro Gui was able to fuse the necessary financial and artistic resources. A major boost to his efforts resulted from the acquisition of the Politeama by the Comune di Firenze in 1929. Partially subsidized by the city, the Stabile Orchestrale Fiorentina could now move into the Politeama, which was renamed the Teatro Comunale in 1930. Gui's original Orchestrale Fiorentina, later named the Orchestra del Maggio Musicale Fiorentino, was, by 1931–1932, being conducted by world-class musicians including Victor De Sabata, Willem Mengelberg, Stravinsky, and Richard Strauss; a true symphonic organization had been created. Prior to the first Maggio Musicale Fiorentino, the architect Giuntoli was commissioned to improve the theater. Both the auditorium and the stagehouse were renovated, with the latter being equipped with up-to-date stage machinery.

The 5,200-seat house reopened on April 22, 1933, with Verdi's *Nabucco*, which marked the historic inaugural performance of the now internationally famous Maggio Musicale Fiorentino. This was also the beginning of a new era in taste, as the older audiences were used to traditional operas in traditional productions. Under the leadership of Guido M. Gatti and Vittorio Gui, the opera now not only searched for excellent casts but also created a new style of production utilizing foreign directors and designers and unifying these elements with the orchestra, thus forging a new contemporary lyric theater. *Nabucco* was conducted by Gui and staged by Carl Ebert with sets by Pietro Aschieri. The soloists were a group of legendary artists: Carlo Galeffi, Alessandro Dolci,

Tancredi Pasero, Gina Cigna, Ebe Stignani, and Gabriella Gatti. That season continued with *Lucrezia Borgia* of Donizetti directed by Gino Marinuzzi, with sets by the great designer Mario Sironi. Gui then directed Spontini's *La Vestale* with a cast that included Rosa Ponselle and Ebe Stignani and sets designed by Felice Casorati. The renowned artist Giorgio De Chirico produced the sets for the production of *I Puritani*, which was conducted by Tullio Serafin. Ezio Pinza, Lauri-Volpe, and Mercedes Capsir sang the leading roles. Along with these operas, the program featured such avant-garde works as string quartets by Bartok and Schoenberg and the Max Reinhart production of Shakespeare's *Midsummer Night's Dream*, which also introduced the audiences to contemporary artistic thinking.

That same year the old Politeama became the Ente Autonomo del Teatro Comunale, housing what would become the oldest and most prestigious Italian musical festival and the only collaboration of a symphony and an opera company. The stated goals of the Maggio were to (1) rediscover forgotten masterpieces of the musical theater and produce them in musically authentic versions, (2) engage the finest performing and production theatrical artists from around the world, and (3) produce contemporary works, including unpublished scores. The Maggio orchestra quickly became a leading international orchestra apart from its festival collaborations. The festival was initially scheduled every three years, then biannually, and by 1937, every year. Under the direction of Vittorio Gui, Mario Rossi, Igor Markevitch, Bruno Bartoletti, and, recently, Riccardo Muti and Zubin Meta, it has attracted many prominent guest conductors, including Bruno Walter, Furtwängler, Mitropoulos, Scherchen, Giulini, Gavazzeni, Abbado, Prêtre, Solti, Sawallisch, Maazel, and Kleiber. The superintendents have included Mario Labroca, Pariso Votto, Remigio Paone, and Massimo Bogianckino, and the artistic directors have included Francesco Siciliani, Roman Vlad, and Luciano Alrettori.

In 1936 Mario Labroca succeeded Vittorio Gui and remained through 1944. The premiere of Luigi Dallapiccola's *Volo di Notte* took place on May 18, 1940. It was conducted by Previtali and demonstrates the continuing support for emerging composers. Perhaps best known for its opera productions, the Maggio Musicale Fiorentino has mounted world premieres of such works as Dallapiccola's *Volo di Notte* (1940) and Italian premieres of Busoni's *Doktor Faust* (1940) and Prokofiev's *War and Peace* (1953) as well as major revivals such as Lully's *Armide* (1950), Handel's *Orlando* (1959), Cavalli's *Didone* (1952), and Meyerbeer's *Robert le Diable* (1968). The Teatro Comunale was heavily damaged by bombs on May 1, 1944, and it did not reopen for regular performances until 1947. In the meantime, operas were performed in temporary quarters in the Teatro della Pergola and the Sallone dei Cinquecento di Palazzo Vecchio. Completely rebuilt and modernized in 1957–1958 by architects A. Giuntoli and C. Bartolini, the Teatro Comunale reopened with its capacity increased from 2,100 seats to 2,500. After the flood of November 4, 1966, it was restored again (and reduced to its present 2,006 seats) and the Teatrino del Comunale was built with intimate seating for some 600 people (the Piccolo Teatro was restored and renovated in 1984 with seating expanded to 650). The Maggio did not perform through 1947, and in 1948 Francesco Siciliani was named artistic director. Siciliani, who remained until 1957, engaged Maria Callas early on in her career. Her initial appearance was in *Norma* on November 30, 1948, and she returned in 1951 for *La Traviata*, *I Vespri Siciliana*, and *Orfeo ed Euridice* (also produced in 1952 and 1953), all prior to her successful debut at the Teatro alla Scala. The premiere of Dallapiccola's *Il Prigioniero* was in Florence on May 20, 1950, and was conducted by Scherchen.

The L'Ente Autonomo lirico del Teatro Comunale di Firenze operates a continuous season from September to July which includes ballets, operas, recitals, and symphony orchestra concerts. The Maggio Musicale Fiorentino, which takes place in May and June, itself includes opera performances as well as chamber and symphony concerts. It was designed to show off the city of Florence through a variety of artistic productions, conferences, contests, and so forth. The present orchestra includes 131 musicians, there is a chorus of 119, and the ballet has 58 dancers. Maestro Zubin Meta is the musical director, and the principal conductor is Myung-Whun Chung. The official archive of the theater has collected all documentation since 1933. Operas scheduled for 1990 included Henze's *El Cimarron*, *Katia Kabanova*, *Mefistofele*, *Rigoletto*, *Don Chisciotte*, Vladimir Belskij's *La Leggenda della Cittá Invisibile di Kitež*, *Don Giovanni*, *Mahagony*, *Il Trovatore*, and Valentino Bucchi's *Il Giuoco del Barone Giovanni Sebastiano*.

BIBLIOGRAPHY: Leonardo Pinzauti, *Il Maggio Musicale Fiorentino* (Florence, 1967). Robert Lamar Weaver and Norma Wright Weaver, *A Chronology of Music in the Florentine Theater* (Detroit, MI, 1978).

ACCESS: Via Solferino 15, I–50123 Florence. (39 55) 2779236; fax (39 55) 296954. Bruno Bartoletti, Direttore artistico. Massimo Bogianckino, Sovrintendente.

[From information supplied by the company]
TRANS. EVA BEAUDET

GENOA (714,641)

Teatro Carlo Felice

The Teatro Carlo Felice (designed by Carlo Barabino and supported by King Charles Felix) opened on April 7, 1828, with Bellini's *Bianca e Gernando*, which had premiered in Naples in 1826. Toscanini enjoyed great success in Genoa between 1891 and 1894. The theater was headed by Celestina Lanfranco between 1945 and 1970. Lanfranco was the first woman to serve as a general manager in Italy since the soprano Emma Carelli had managed the Teatro dell'Opera in Rome between 1912 and 1926. The Teatro Carlo Felice was demolished during World War II in September 1944 and was reopened on August 1, 1948, with Verdi's *Aida* conducted by Tulio Serafin. Due to a number of economic and political reasons, the house was only partially rebuilt following the war. Reconstructed for the 1979–1980 season as a 1,600-seat opera house, the Teatro Carlo Felice shares performances with the Teatro Margherita.

BIBLIOGRAPHY: Edilio Frassoni, *Due secoli di lirica a Genova (1772–1900); (1901–1960)*, 2 vols. (Genova, 1980). Edilio Frassoni, *Teatro Comunale dell'Opera di Genova* (Genova, 1973). Giovanni Monleone, *I 100 anni del Carlo Felice (1828–1928)* (Genova, 1928). Giovanni Monleone, *Storia di un Teatro: Il Carlo Felice* (Genova, 1979). G. B. Vallebona, *Il Teatro Carlo Felice: Cronistoria di un secolo, 1828–1928* (Genova, 1928).

ACCESS: Via XX Settembre 33/7, I–16100 Genoa. (39 10) 542792. Luciano Alberti, Direttore artistico. Franco Ragazi, Sovrintendente.

[From materials supplied by the company]

MILAN (1,464,127)

Teatro alla Scala

The history of opera in Milan dates back to 1644 when Francesco Manelli brought his *L'Andromeda* to Milan from Venice, where it had opened the first public opera house to be built anywhere, the Teatro Tron di San Cassiano, in the spring of 1637. For the next thirty years the Milanese depended on the Venetian repertoire for their operas. A measure of independence was finally achieved in 1686 when the Teatrino della Commedia was rebuilt to house opera, and a variety of works from other cities were produced. Control of the city passed from the austere Spanish to the more relaxed Austrians in 1708, and times were ripe for the growth of opera. The city of Milan has a history in which social and political affairs are somehow always involved with opera. The major house in the mid-eighteenth century was the Teatro Regio Ducal (opened December 26, 1717, with Gasparini's *Costantino*) which burned to the ground under mysterious circumstances on February 26, 1776. This house specialized in opera seria during the carnival season and opera buffa during the spring social season. Mozart directed the premiere of his *Mitridate, rè di Ponto*, which had been written for the Teatro Regio Ducal, on December 26, 1770, and returned for the premiere of *Ascanio in Alba* on October 17, 1771, as well as that of *Lucio Silla* on December 26, 1772. Those were rich musical times indeed. The destruction of the house did nothing to stop operatic momentum. The Empress Maria Theresa, duchess of Milan, moved quickly to alleviate the situation, and in July approved a design for a new opera house by Giuseppe Piermarini. Built on the site of a former church, the Santa Maria alla Scala, the opera house was named in honor of Regina alla Scala, the wife of Duke Barnabò Visconti of Milan, who had built the church in 1381. The theater, Il Nuovo Regio Ducal Teatro di Milano, opened on August 3, 1778, with Antonio Salieri's *Europa riconosciuta*. Thus, the La Scala we know was born.

From that day on, the Teatro alla Scala has played a major role in the development of Italian opera. As the premier opera house and company in Italy, it is also one of the most important opera organizations of the world. The opera composers who have written for La Scala (Rossini, Bellini, Donizetti, Verdi, and Puccini) read like a "Who's Who" of Italian opera theater. Moreover, when operas and ballets were not on the boards, gala political festivities celebrated events such as the coronations of Emperor Joseph II and Napoleon as king of Italy. When Napoleon was defeated at Waterloo in 1815, the region of Lombardy and its capital, Milan, reverted again to Austrian control. It was at about this same time that the city became recognized as the center of Italian opera. Of Rossini's prodigious output, *Aureliano in Palmira* (1813), *Il Turco in Italia* (1814), *La Gazza ladra* (1817), and *Bianca e Falliero* (1819) all had their premieres at La Scala. Important works of Meyerbeer and Mercadante, as well as Donizetti's *Lucrezia Borgia*, which premiered on December 26, 1833, with Henriette Méric-Lalande, Marietta Brambilla, and Luciano Mariani, all created a great sensation. Moreover, Vincenzo Bellini accorded the house his *Il Pirata* (October 27, 1827, starring Méric-Lalande, Giovanni Rubini, and Antonio Tamburini), *La Straniera* (February 14, 1829, with Méric-Lalande, Caroline Ungher, and Tamburini), and *Norma* (December 26, 1831, with Giuditta Pasta, Giulia Grisi, and Domenico Donzelli).

By the 1830s La Scala had become one of the leading European opera houses, and it was only one of some nine major opera houses in Milan that were responsible for historic performances. For example, the Teatro della Cannobiana mounted the premiere of Donizetti's *L'Elisir d'Amore* on May 12, 1832. Renamed the Teatro Lirico, it was the site of Enrico Caruso's Milan debut on November 27, 1897, in the premiere of Cilea's *L'Arlesiana*. Giuseppe Carcano's theater, which opened in 1803, mounted the premieres of Donizetti's *Anna Bolena* (December 26, 1830, with Giuditta Pasta and Giovanni Rubini) and Bellini's *La Sonnambula* (March 6, 1831, again with Pasta and Rubini singing the leads). Moreover, Count Francesco Dal Verme personally built the Teatro Dal Verme in 1872, where Puccini's first opera, *Le Villi*, premiered on May 31, 1884, followed by Leoncavallo's *Pagliacci* on May 21, 1892. By the time Verdi's first opera, *Oberto, Conte di San Bonifacio*, premiered on November 17, 1839, only the city of Paris could rival Milan as a center of contemporary opera. Bartolomeo Merelli, the general director, was astute enough to commission three more operas from the young Verdi, and two of them, *Nabucco* (March 9, 1842, with Giuseppina Strepponi and Giorgio Ronconi) and *I Lombardi alla Prima Crociata* (February 1, 1843, featuring Erminia Frezzolini-Poggi) were enormous successes. For a variety of artistic, financial, and political reasons, Verdi did not allow another premiere of his work until the famous *Otello* in 1887, which starred Francesco Tamagno as Otello, Victor Maurel as Iago, and Romilda Pantaleoni as Desdemona. This triumph was followed by *Falstaff* (1893), with Maurel as Falstaff and Antonio Pini-Corsi as Ford. However, the repertoire of La Scala also featured premieres of the work of Boito (*Mefistofele* on March 5, 1868), Ponchielli (perhaps best known for *Gioconda* on April 8, 1876), Catalani (whose last and best opera is *La Wally*, on January 20, 1892), and many other native composers. Ever since that time, aficionados have treasured memorable productions and performances, especially the Toscanini years (1898–1903, 1906–1908, and 1921–1929), De Sabata's reign (1931–1954), and Claudio Abbado's tenure (1972–1979).

The opera house itself benefited from a number of interior and exterior improvements over the years. The stage was substantially enlarged in 1807, and a total restoration was undertaken in 1838. Adjacent buildings that shielded the theater's facade were removed in 1857. Newly refined electric lighting was installed in 1883 just in time for *Otello* and *Falstaff*. During this same era the difficulties of subsidizing La Scala in the style in which it had been maintained were becoming more and more apparent. Public monies became increasingly unreliable, and on July 1, 1897, the city of Milan withdrew its support. For the first time in its distinguished history, La Scala would be closed for a season. The box holders (some notable families which had originally supported the opera in 1778 and which retain boxes to this day) and patrons rallied behind Duke Guido Visconti di Modrone, who appointed Giulio Gatti-Casazza as managing director. One of Gatti-Casazza's major decisions was to appoint the young Arturo Toscanini as the chief conductor of La Scala in 1898. A golden era had begun. Franchetti's *Germania* premiered on March 11, 1902, the same season during which Cilea's *Adriana Lecouvreur* opened at the Teatro Lirico. Giordano's *Siberia* was mounted in December 1903, and Puccini's legendary *Madama Butterfly* (with Storchio, Zenatello, and De Luca) premiered on February 17, 1904. Italian first performances of Richard Strauss's *Salome* (1906), *Elektra* (1909), and *Der Rosenkavalier* (1911) closely followed the Dresden premieres. Until the outbreak of World War I, the house was both an innovator and a preserver of tradition.

After the war La Scala became a self-governing organization with Toscanini as artistic director. The "great Toscanini period" (1921–1929) saw the expansion and improvement of the orchestra, the formation of a large professional chorus, and a general raising of artistic standards. It was to end with disagreements with the new political party of Mussolini. Between the world wars, a roster of vocal stars graced the productions at La Scala. Gigli, Lauri Vopli, Galeffi, Toti dal Monte, Cigna, Favero, Carosio, Stabile, Elmo, and Schipa are only the most notable among singers who are now historical legends. Besides Toscanini, Gui, De Sabata, Capuana, and Marinuzzi conducted regularly until World War II. The house was destroyed by bombs on August 16, 1943; Serafin conducted a performance of *Nabucco* with Barbieri, Bechi, and Siepi in the restored auditorium on December 26, 1946, and the completely restored opera house reopened on May 11, 1948, with Toscanini conducting the orchestra in a concert of Italian music. A new generation of singers had appeared to replace the stars of the 1920s and 1930s. Callas, Gobbi, Di Stefano, Del Monaco, Simionato, Bastianini, Corelli, Cossotto, Raimondi, Tagliavini, Bergonzi, Siepi, Albanesi, Barbieri, Tebaldi, and Tucci continued the illustrious vocal traditions of the past. In their own way they added to the vocal luster that had always been a hallmark of the house since its opening in 1778. De Sabata, Giulini, and Karajan all conducted regularly after the war, both inheriting and bequeathing operatic history.

Unfortunately, the last twenty years have seen a return to political infighting, inadequate budgets, and reliance on traditional repertoire, with occasional masterful productions by Visconti and Zeffirelli to carry otherwise undistinguished seasons. Vienna and New York both moved to the forefront of grand opera, and several houses in Germany took the honors for contemporary directions. With the appointment of Claudio Abbado as conductor in 1968 (direttore musicale in 1972; direttore artistico in 1977–1979), matters took a decided turn for the better. Moreover, a new generation of singers promises to continue the glittering vocal traditions of La Scala.

CHRONOLOGY OF ARTISTIC DIRECTORS: Arturo Toscanini, 1898–1903, 1906–1908, 1921–1929. Erardo Trentinaglia, 1931–1934. Jenner Mataloni, 1935–1940. Carlo Gatti, 1941–1943. Gino Marinuzzi, 1944–1947. Antonio Ghiringhelli, 1948–1952. Victor De Sabata, 1953–1956. Francesco Siciliani, 1957–1971. Massimo Bogianckino, 1972–1982. Carlo Maria Badini, 1983–present.

BIBLIOGRAPHY: F. Armani, ed., *La Scala, 1946–66* (Milano, 1967). F. Armani and G. Bascapé, *La Scala: Breve biografia, 1778–1950* (Milano, 1951). L. Arruga, *La Scala* (Milano, 1975). Pompeo Cambiasi, *La Scala e la Canobbiani, 1778–1906*, 5th ed. (Milano, 1906). Giulio Mario Ciampelli and B. Gutierrez, *La Scala nel 1830 e nel 1930* (Milano, 1930). Carlo Gatti, *Il Teatro alla Scala nella storia e nell'arte (1778–1963)*, 2 vols. (Milano, 1964). G. Gatti-Casazza, *Memories of Opera* (New York, 1941). Domenico Manzella and Emilio Pozzi, *I Teatri di Milano* (Milano, 1971). Luigi Lorenzo Secchi, *(1778–1978): Il Teatro alla Scala* (Milano, 1977). Giampiero Tintori, *Duecento anni di Teatro alla Scala (opere, balletti, concerti, 1778–1977)* (Gorle, 1979). Franco Zeffirelli, *An Autobiography* (New York, 1986).

ACCESS: Via Filodrammatici 2, 20121 Milan. (39 2) 807041; fax (39 2) 8879388. Carlo Maria Badini, Sovrintendente. Cesare Perucci, Direttore artistico.

[From materials supplied by the company]
TRANS. EVA BEAUDET

NAPLES (1,202,582)

Real Teatro di San Carlo

Formal opera in Naples dates from the premiere of Francesco Cirillo's *L'Orontea Regina di Egitto* in 1654 [sources indicate April 3 at the Teatro di San Bartolemeo], and by the end of the century the city had become the center of opera in Italy. The addition of two more major theaters, the Teatro dei Fiorentini and the Teatro Nuovo, catered to an expanded public interest. The Teatro di San Bartolemeo was demolished in 1737, and King Charles III commissioned Giovanni Medrano to build a new royal theater, the Real Teatro di San Carlo. The new house was inaugurated on November 4, 1737, with Domenico Sarro's *Achille in Sciro*, and is today the oldest and one of the most distinguished of Italy's autonomous opera houses. Completely redecorated in 1768 shortly before Mozart attended the premiere of Niccolò Jommelli's *Armida abbandonata* on May 30, 1770, boxes were added to the four tiers just in front of the stage. A second royal theater, the Teatro del Fondo, was opened in 1779 primarily to house Neapolitan opera buffa. The famous impresario Domenico Barbaia assumed direction of the royal theaters in 1810 and gave immediate notice of his vision with the first Italian performance of Spontini's *La Vestale* on September 8, 1811. This was followed by Gluck's *Iphigénie en Aulide* on August 15, 1812, another Italian premiere. Recognizing Rossini's great talent, Barbaia brought the composer to Naples to compose two operas per year, one each for the San Carlo and the Teatro del Fondo. Barbaia was eventually responsible for the productions of eight of the composer's operas at the Real Teatro di San Carlo: *Elisabetta regina d'Inghilterra* (October 4, 1815, with Colbran, Nozzari, and Manuel Garcia); *Armida di Borgogna* (November 11, 1817, with Colbran and Nozzari); *Mosè in Egitto* (March 5, 1818, with Colbran and Nozzari); *Ricciardo e Zoraide* (December 3, 1818, with Colbran and Nozzari); *Ermione* (March 27, 1819, with Colbran, Pisaroni, and Nozzari); *La Donna del lago* (September 24, 1819, with Colbran, Pisaroni, and Nozzari); *Maometto II* (December 3, 1820, with Colbran and Nozzari); and *Zelmira* (February 16, 1822, with Colbran and Nozzari).

Shortly after Rossini had been commissioned by Barbaia, the opera house burned down, on February 13, 1816. It was quickly rebuilt and reopened on January 12, 1817, some months before the composer's next premiere. Antonio Niccolini enlarged both the stagehouse and the auditorium, and the present theater reflects the refurbishing done at that time. Major operas of Bellini and Donizetti, including the latter's *Lucia di Lammermoor* (September 26, 1835, with Tacchinardi-Persiani and Duprez) as well as Verdi's *Alzira* (August 12, 1845) and *Luisa Miller* (December 8, 1849, with Gazzaniga) were given world premieres in the newly redecorated house. When Verdi was invited by the Italian government to suggest major operatic reforms, he recommended that three theaters (the Teatro alla Scala, the Teatro dell'Opera in Rome, and Naples) be designated as major national centers. Unfortunately, none of his plans came to fruition. In 1901 Caruso made his only operatic appearances in his native city in *L'Elisir d'Amore* and Massenet's *Manon*. Moreover, by way of a second historical footnote, Toscanini never conducted opera at the San Carlo.

Prior to World War I, practically every notable Italian singer and conductor appeared at San Carlo. Between the wars, although almost seventy local premieres were staged, the house suffered from the same economic and political constraints that affected all artistic organizations in Italy. During the war years, performances were scheduled during the daylight hours and the repertoire was very conservative. The foyer but not the house itself was badly damaged by bombs on August 4, 1943. The British occupation forces requisitioned the 1,530-seat opera house and opened it again on November 18. Singers of the caliber of Caniglia, Gigli, Schipa, Stignani, and Tagliavini were available for an impressive number of performances. The foyer was restored through the efforts of Allied forces beginning in May 1944 and completed in May 1946. It is currently the only regularly active opera theater in Naples.

BIBLIOGRAPHY: *Cento anni di vita del Teatro di San Carlo, 1848–1948* (Napoli, 1948). *Cronache del Teatro di S. Carlo, 1948–1968* (Milano, 1969). Felice De Filipis and R. Arnese, *Cronache del Teatro di S. Carlo (1737–1960)*, 2 vols. (Napoli, 1961, 1963).

ACCESS: Via Vittorio Emanuele, I-80100 Naples, (39 81) 7972412; fax (39 81) 7972306.

[From materials supplied by the company]
TRANS. EVA BEAUDET

PALERMO (731,481)

Teatro Massimo

Palermo, the capital of Sicily, was initially influenced by the operas being produced in Venice and Naples. With the birth of native son Alessandro Scarlatti in 1660, the city could boast its own major composer, and the local history of opera began with a production of his *Il Pompeo* in 1690. Several theaters were built to produce opera, including the Teatro della Misericordia and the Teatro della Corte del Pretore. The latter was opened in 1726 and was refurbished and enlarged in 1809 as the Real Teatro Carolino. The Carolino was directed during the 1825–1826 season by Gaetano Donizetti, whose *Alahor di Granata* premiered on January 7, 1826, with Antonio Tamburini in the title role. Bellini's association with the city dates from the same period. The Sicilian Parliament renamed the theater the Real Teatro Bellini in May 1848, but over the years, fewer operas were performed there. After World War I it was turned into a movie house, and it was destroyed by fire in 1964. In the meantime, as Palermo had expanded to the north, the need for a new theater to anchor the shifting center of population was increasingly apparent. There was a public outcry for a theater to replace the Sala Bellini which was too narrow and unsuitable for contemporary performances. In 1864 an international competition was announced for the design of the proposed opera house. There were thirty-five designs submitted, and the first prize went to Giovan Battista Filippo Basile. Construction began on January 12, 1875, and when it had been completed, the Teatro Massimo ranked in size only after the Théâtre National de l'Opéra de Paris (and now the rebuilt Wiener Staatsoper). The local government financed and built the 3,200-seat house, and it opened on May 16, 1897, with a gala performance of Verdi's *Falstaff* conducted by Leopoldo Mugnone. Enrico Caruso's career was launched that same season in Amilcare Ponchielli's *La Gioconda*.

In general the repertoire was very unadventuresome, although Leoncavallo's *La Bohème* was produced there in the revised version as *Mimi Pinson* in 1913. This was the seventh premiere since the Massimo opened, but none of the composers (Marinuzzi, Costantino, Donaudy, Storti, Giordano, and Mulè) with the exception of Giordano (whose *Andrea Chénier* premiered at the Teatro alla Scala) have remained in the repertoire. In 1936 the Teatro Massimo became an "Ente Autonomo" (self-governing institution) under Cardenio Botti as general director. The house was closed from 1941 to 1944 due to World War II. Over the years many famous artists have performed in the theater, including Tamagno, Pertile, Stabile, dal Monte, Gigli, Tagliavini, Cagnilia, Mazzoleni, Olivero, Gobbi, Bechi, Callas (in a 1949 performance of Brünhilde in Wagner's *Die Walkühre*), Tebaldi (in 1953 in Boito's *Mefistofele*), Di Stefano (in 1952 in *Rigoletto*), Simionato, Gencer, de los Angeles, Barbieri, Corelli, Del Monaco, Raimondi, Bastianini, Pavarotti (in *Madama Butterfly* in 1964 and 1968 with La Stella), Freni, Scotto, and Siepi. In 1960 Joan Sutherland made a triumphant appearance in *Lucia de Lammermoor*, followed the next season with *I Puritani*. The conductors Mugnone, Serafin, Gui, Capuana, Sanzogno, von Matacic, and Shippers (debuted in 1957 conducting Offenbach's *I Racconti di Hoffmann*) have all conducted at the Massimo. In 1957 the company also expanded its performances to include the summer months. The Teatro di Verdura in the Villa Castelnuovo, which was built during the last decade of the eighteenth century and sits among beautiful gardens and statuary, provided a perfect setting for this new program. One of the most beautiful outdoor sites for opera in Europe, it attracts audiences from throughout the world. Performances began with Verdi's *Otello* with Mario Del Monaco in 1957 under the direction of Leopoldo De Simone. Concerts, recitals, and ballets presented by companies from around the world, as well as operas, musicals, and operettas are programmed. Operating two theaters (three when the restoration of the Teatro Massimo is finished), the company currently employs a 113-member orchestra, a 94-member chorus, a 37-member ballet, and 345 technical and administrative support staff.

The elegant sets and costumes of the theater are among the finest in the operatic world. Zeffirelli's productions of *Falstaff*, *Lucia di Lammermoor* (1968), *I Puritani*, and *La figlia del regimento*, Colasanti and Moore's productions of *Otello*, *Turandot*, and *La Bohème*; Benois's *Boris Godunov*, Marchi's *Il Barbiere di Siviglia*; and Morici's *Cavalleria rusticana* are all representative of the outstanding work done at the Teatro Massimo. The theater has a tradition of mounting both obscure and forgotten works, such as Giordano's *Mese Mariano*, Rota's *Il cappella di paglia di Firenze*, Mannino's *Il diavolo in giardino* and *Luisella*, Malipiero's *Merlino Mastro d'organi* and revivals such as *I Capuleti e i Montecchi* (1954), *Beatrice di Tenda* (1959), *La Straniera* (1968), *Elisabetta, regina d'Inghilterra* of Rossini (1971), and Auber's *La Muta di Portici* (1972). Between 1958 and 1972 the company undertook numerous tours throughout Italy and Europe: in 1958, *Tosca* and *Turandot* for the Puccini celebration in Torre del Lago, returning in 1962 with *La Fanciulla del West* and *La Bohème*; in 1960, *Turandot* and *Falstaff* for the Wiesbaden Festival in Germany; in 1961, *I Puritani* and *La Bohème* in Stoccarda, followed in 1962 by *Otello* and *Don Pasquale*; in Paris also in 1962, *Turandot*, *Otello*, and *Don Pasquale*. In 1963, at Busseto for the Verdi celebration *Otello* and *Il Trovatore* were produced; in 1963 at the Schwetzingen Festival *Don Pasquale* was followed by *Il matrimonio segreto* in

1965; in 1969 at Dubrovnick, Yugoslavia, productions of *Don Pasquale*, *Il Barbiere di Siviglia*, and *Simon Boccanegra* were mounted; and finally, in 1972 at the Edinburgh Festival, Verdi's *Attila*, Bellini's *La Straniera*, and *Elisabetta regina d'Inghilterra* of Rossini were presented. Following a performance of Verdi's *Nabucco* in January 1974, the Teatro Massimo was declared unusable, and future performances were shifted to the Politeama Garibaldi, where the company still performs. The restoration and renovation of the Teatro Massimo began on September 28, 1988, and is still in progress.

Giuseppe Damiani Almejda was the designer for the Politeama Garibaldi which opened in 1874. Toscanni was there in 1892–1893 conducting Catalani's *Lorley* and Wagner's *Die fliegende Holländer*, among a number of other operas. On April 24, 1896, Puccini's *La Bohème* met with its first public success after the failure of its premiere in Torino on February 1, 1896. The 1,296-seat Politeama Garibaldi, built between 1867 and 1874, was never intended to be an opera house but rather a flexible site to host a variety of musical and nonmusical events including equestrian events. It was inaugurated with *I Capuleti e i Montecchi* by Bellini in 1874. Among the artists who performed in this theater were Melba, La Arkel, Tamagno, Maurel, Vignas, and Battistini. When the Teatro Massimo first opened, the Politeama ceased to be used for opera. It was indeed fortunate that the site was available when the Massimo was closed for restoration in 1974.

The administration of Girolamo Arrigo and Ubaldo Mirabelli took charge of the company in 1977, and new life was breathed into the organization. The repertoire has been among the most interesting in Italy since that time. Public subscriptions increased so that eight to fourteen performances of each production were now possible. A renewed commitment was made to the revival of forgotten operatic masterpieces, particularly of the eighteenth and nineteenth century. For example, Rossini's *Il Turco in Italia*, *Otello*, and *Le Comte Ory*; Mozart's *La Clemenza di Tito* and *Idomeneo*, Handel's *Alcina*; Offenbach's *La Belle Hélène*; and Wolf Ferrari's *Le donne curiose* were all revived. At the same time contemporary works were also produced, including Britten's *Il sacrificio di Lucrezia*, Prokofiev's *Guerra e Pace*, Janáček's *Jenufa*, Gershwin's *Porgy and Bess*, Poulenc's *Les Mamelles de Tyresias*, and Menotti's *Counsul*. Of considerable interest was the 1987 production of Strauss's *Die schweigsame Frau* which had not been performed in Italy since its premiere in Milan on March 11, 1936, as well as performances of Krenek's *Jonny spielt auf*. Complementing these German works were Malipiero's *La favola del figlio cambiato* (1980), Casella's *La donna serpente* (1982), Respighi's *Semirama* (1987), Pizzetti's *Fedra* (1988), Montemezzi's *L'amore dei tre re* (1989), and Alfano's *Risurrezione* (1990). In recent years young artists including Luciano Chailly, Alexander Rahbari, Pinchas Steinberg, Roberto Abbado, Carlo Rizzi, Alessandro Siciliani, Karl Mártin, Leo Nucci, Luciana Serra, Mariella Devia, Elisabeth Connell, and Nicola Martinucci have begun their careers here. In 1980 the company expanded its performances to Castellammare del Golfo (Trapani) and the Castello di San Nicola a Trabia (Palermo) during July and August, featuring masterpieces of eighteenth-century music by Mozart (*Bastinao e Bastiana*), Scarlatti (*Lesbina ed Adolfo*), Salieri (*Prima la musica poi le parole*), Pergolesi (*La contadina astuta*), Galuppi (*l'Amante di tutte*), Fioravanti (*Le cantatrici villane*), Cimarosa (*Le astuzie femminili*), and Paisiello (*l'Idolo cinese*). Since 1987 Graziella Sciutti has been the producer/director of this part of the program.

BIBLIOGRAPHY: Ignazio Ciotti, *La Vita Artistica del Teatro Massimo di Palermo (1897–1937)* (Palermo, 1938). Corrado Martinez, *Il Teatro Massimo: 40 anni di attività artistica dalla costituzione dell'Ente Autonomo (1936–1975)* (Palermo, 1980). Ottavio Tiby, *Il Real Teatro Carolino e l'800 musicale palermitano* (Firenze, 1962). Ottavio Tiby and Ignazio Ciotti, *I cinquant'anni del Teatro Massimo (1897–1947)* (Palermo, 1947).

ACCESS: Piazza G. Verdi, I-90138 Palermo. (39 91) 583600. Ubaldo Mirabeli, Sovrintendente. Girolamo Arrigo, Direttore artistico.

UBALDO MIRABELLI
TRANS. EVA BEAUDET

PARMA (174,827)

Teatro Regio

The first recorded theater in Parma (accommodating some 3,000 spectators) was the Il Farnese in the Palazzo della Pilotta built in 1618–1619 for Duke Ranuccio I by the architect Giovan Battista Aleotti d'Argenta. Loath to copy the existing models as represented by the l'Olimpico in Vicenza, Aleotti was able to create a new design that, nevertheless, was not used as a theater until 1628. It was inaugurated on December 21 with Claudio Achillini's spectacle *Mercurio e Marte* with music by Claudio Monteverdi. This gala event was part of the celebration of the wedding of Odoardo Farnese to Margherita de'Medici, and it set a precedent as all nine theatrical events that took place here from 1628 until 1732 were celebrations of weddings and other important court events. Closed in October 1732 with a performance to honor the Infante of Spain, the theater was severely damaged during World War II. Although it was restored in the 1950s as one of the oldest surviving theaters in Italy, it is rarely used today. Another active theater of the time was the Teatro della Rachetta, which was in use from 1688 to 1832. The Teatrino della Corte, commissioned by Ranuccio II and realized by the architect Lolli, was finished in 1689 in the ducal palace. It was inaugurated with Giuseppe Felice Tosi's *L'idea di tutte le perfezioni* in celebration of the duke's marriage to Dorothea of Neuberg. This small theater was torn down by Marie-Louise in 1827 to make room for a museum. One must remember that at this time in Italy many of the noble families had private theaters in their homes; for example, Santa Caterina, il Bergonzi, and San Giovanni. A theater at the Collegio de'Nobili called the Teatro Collegio was built in 1600 by Ranuccio I and rebuilt many times over the years.

This theater was destroyed in 1831 and replaced by a Collegio Marie-Louise. Minor events took place in the Teatro Bergonzi which housed the private Società Filodrammatici.

The most important theater was, of course, the Teatro Ducale, which was built in 1688–1689 by the reigning Duke Ranuccio II. The new theater was designed by Stefano Lolli and was made entirely of wood, as was the custom of the time. It was inaugurated with Antonio Gianettini's *Teseo in Atene*, and it was open to both nobility and commoners who could pay the price of admission. Restored and enlarged a number of times, it eventually could accommodate 1,200 spectators. The domination of the Farnese lineage ceased with the second treaty of Aix-la-Chapelle in 1748 which ended the War of the Austrian Succession. One of the results of this treaty was the assignment of the duchy of Parma to the Infante Philip Bourbon, second son of Elizabeth Farnese. During the resulting Bourbon ascendancy, the arts and letters flourished, earning for Parma the accolade as the "Athens of Italy." Guillaume du Tillot, minister and overseer of the royal household, was responsible for much of this artistic activity. He brought famous artists to the court, including the poet Carlo Innocenzo Frugoni and the composer Tommaso Traetta. This triumvirate attempted a reform of opera in the sense of interfacing Neapolitan operatic excess with the refined French taste of the time. One of the highlights was a production of Gluck's *Le feste d'Apollo*, a three-part extravaganza which included *Bauci e Filemone*, *Aristeo*, and *Orfeo* on August 24, 1769. In 1816 Napoleon's second wife, Marie-Louise of Austria, arrived in Parma as the new duchess. [After divorcing his first wife Josephine de Beauharnais, for lack of an heir, Napoleon married Archduchess Marie-Louise, who was the daughter of Emperor Francis I. She received the Italian duchies of Parma, Piacenza, and Gustalla in 1816 and ruled them until her death in 1847.] Her strong support of the arts resulted in a new golden age in Parma. Well aware of the facilities for performance available to the other courts in Europe, she immediately saw the need for a new theater.

Commissioned by the duchess, work was begun in 1821 on a new theater designed by Nicola Bettóli. The new Teatro Ducale (Teatro Regio after 1849) took eight years to complete. The original Teatro Ducale had served the city from its opening in 1688, but was thought to be too small and unimposing by Marie-Louise, and it was torn down in 1832. The interior of the new house was modelled by Bettóli on that of the Teatro alla Scala, although the 1,400-seat auditorium is considerably smaller. It was inaugurated after several delays with Bellini's *Zaira* on May 16, 1829, with a cast that included Luigi Lablache. Bellini's score was late in arriving and showed clear signs of haste, and he was operating under the disadvantage of being the second choice. On opening night the attention of the audience was directed to the magnificent curtain designed with its mural depicting "un Trionfo della Sapienza" which was a clear allegory of the duchess's government through its central figure of Minerva. Insulted that

Rossini had refused to accept the original commission, which had been under negotiation for many months, the audience greeted the performance with silence. [Rossini was at the time in Paris under contract to compose *Le Comte Ory*. In any case, the management of the new Teatro Ducale was controlled by Stefano Sanvitale, who wanted an opera by the young Bellini.] The audience reaction was perhaps prophetic, as *Zaira* was only revived once, at the Teatro della Pergola in Florence in 1836. The season, however, was a triumph with the great success of Rossini's *Mosè e Egitto* and *Semiramide*. The new Teatro Ducale quickly became the center of culture and musical life in Parma; indeed, the golden years of opera in Parma were to last for almost half a century. After this near disaster, Bellini's first success in Parma was the local premiere of *Norma* in 1834. For many years the repertoire of the theater was centered on the works of Rossini, Bellini, and Donizetti. The Teatro Ducale was renamed the Teatro Regio in 1849. Verdi's *Les Vêpres Siciliennes* had its heavily censored Italian premiere in Parma as *Giovanna de Guzman* on December 26, 1855, some six months after it opened in Paris to something less than rave reviews. It would not, however, take too many seasons before Verdi replaced Rossini as the dominant name in the repertoire.

During the second half of the nineteenth century, composers such as Bizet, Meyerbeer, Gounod, Halévy, Flotow, Massenet, Thomas, and Wagner appeared in the repertoire. Verdi's *Don Carlo* (1869) and *Aida* (1872) were both well received. At the same time, two other theaters were active in the area, the Teatro Campanini and the Teatro Reinach. The twentieth century began with the centenary honoring Verdi in 1913. The celebration was organized by Cleofonte Campanini who produced seven of the composer's works, including the *Requiem Mass*. Moreover, Toscanini's renowned production of *Falstaff* was of special historical note. During this period, very little Bellini, Donizetti, or Rosinni was produced, although Wagner's *Lohengrin* and *Tristan* were occasionally presented. Gradually Puccini and other younger composers were included in the schedule. The Second World War did not interrupt activities at the theater, and not even the economic hardships that followed the war managed to disrupt productions. Today, the 1,400-seat Teatro Regio remains one of the most important traditional Italian opera theaters. The audiences in Parma have retained their historical reputation of being very difficult to please. Particularly singers, but also conductors and composers, are routinely subjected to highly partisan comments and behavior. A major earthquake centered in Parma in 1983 caused extensive damage to the theater. Restoration began almost immediately and continues to this day.

BIBLIOGRAPHY: C. Alcari, *Il Teatro regio di Parma nella sua storia del 1883 al 1929* (Parma, 1929). Ivo Allodi, *I teatri di Parma dal "Farnesi al Regio"* (Milano, 1969). Valerio Cervetti and Claudio Del Monte, *Cronologia degli spettacoli lirici: (1879–19290; (1929–1979)*, 2 vols. (Parma, 1979, 1980). Maurizio Corradi Cervi, *Cronologia del Teatro regio di Parma (1928–1948)* (Parma, 1955).

ACCESS: Via Garibaldi 16, I-43100 Parma. (39 521) 795682/795690; fax (39 521) 284283. Angela Spocci, Direttore artistico. Dr. Francesco Quintavalla, Sovrintendente.
VINCENZO RAFFAELE SEGRETO
TRANS. EVA BEAUDET

ROME (2,816,474)

Teatro dell'Opera

The first opera to be performed in Rome was Agostino Agazzari's *Eumelio* in 1606 at the Seminario Romano. Pope Clement IX authorized Count Giacomo d'Albert to build the first public opera house in the city in 1669, and the Teatro Tordinono (Torre di Nona) was inaugurated in 1671. Among notable early theaters was the Teatro Valle, which hosted the premiere of Rossini's *La Cenerentola* on January 25, 1817, with Righetti-Giorgi, as well as three of Donizetti's works including *Il Furioso all'isola di San Domingo* (January 2, 1833), and *Torquato Tasso* (September 9, 1833). The Teatro Argentina, which opened with Domenico Sarro's *Bernice* on January 13, 1732, also premiered Rossini's *Il Barbiere di Siviglia* (February 20, 1816, with Righetti-Giorgi and Manual Garcia) and Verdi's *I due Foscari* (November 3, 1844) and *La Battaglia di Legnano* (January 27, 1849). It was perhaps Rome's leading opera house until the Teatro Costanzi opened in 1888. The Teatro Apollo, which was originally opened in 1671, survived several destructions and reincarnations and emerged as the Apollo, first featuring Paganini conducting the premiere of Rossini's *Matilde Shabran* (February 24, 1821). Among its distinctions, the Apollo premiered Verdi's *Il Trovatore* (January 19, 1853) and *Un ballo in maschera* (February 17, 1859). The Teatro Costanzi, designed by Achille Sfondrini and built by Domenico Costanzi, was a 2,293-seat opera house which opened on November 27, 1880, with a performance of Rossini's *Semiramide*. The music publisher Edoardo Sonzogno became general manager in 1888, and his series of competitions for significant operas was rewarded with the premiere of Mascagni's *Cavalleria rusticana* on May 17, 1890. Puccini's *Tosca*, the only opera that the composer wrote for the capital city, premiered on January 14, 1900, with Hariclea Darclée in the title role.

Of some historical interest is the fact that the soprano Emma Carelli became the first woman to direct an Italian opera house when she took over the Teatro Costanzi in 1911. She remained in this position until 1925, and the next season, the city of Rome assumed control. After a complete renovation which included the construction of a new facade, the house reopened as the Teatro Real dell'Opera on February 28, 1928, with a production of Boito's *Nerone*. Mussolini planned to make the Rome opera the leading Italian opera house, and he arranged to bring many of the finest Italian singers there. Tullio Serafin became the chief conductor and artistic director, and for several years the house produced memorable operas. The postwar seasons have varied from pedestrian to outstanding in direct relationship to the caliber of the singers, conductors, and directors. In a rare gesture to contemporary music theater, Philip Glass's *The Civil Wars: A Tree Is Best Measured When It Is Down* was premiered on March 22, 1984.

BIBLIOGRAPHY: Emma Carelli. *XXXanni di vita lirica* (Roma, 1932). Vittorio Frajese, *Dal Costanzi all'Opera. Cronache, documenti, recensioni*, 4 vols. (Roma, 1978). Matteo Incagliati, *Il teatro Costanzi (1880–1907)* (Rome, 1907). Mario Rinaldi, *Due secoli di musica al Teatro Argentina*, 3 vols. (Firenze, 1978). Iole Tognelli, ed., *Cinquant'anni del teatro dell'Opera* (Rome, 1979).

ACCESS: Piazza Beniamino Gigli, I-00100 Rome. (39 06) 463641; fax (39 06) 461253. Alberto Antignani, Sovrintendente.

[From materials supplied by the company]
TRANS. EVA BEAUDET

TRIESTE (235,014)

Teatro Giuseppe Verdi

The fact that the city has been ruled at various times by the Austrians, the French, and the Italians has ensured a public with a wide range of operatic tastes. The repertoire of the several important opera houses has always included a liberal measure of French and German, especially Wagner and Richard Strauss, operas not typically performed in other Italian houses. The first important opera house, the 800-seat Cesareo Regio Teatro di S. Pietro, featured the works of Cimarosa, Paisiello, and Salieri. The modern history of opera in Trieste begins with the opening of the larger Teatro Nuovo with Johann Simon Mayr's *Ginevra di Scozia* on April 21, 1801. Gianantonio Selva, the celebrated architect of Teatro la Fenice di Venezia, was commissioned to design a larger replacement for the Teatro San Pietro which had closed the year before. The 1,200-seat house was renamed the Teatro Grande in 1821, the Teatro Comunale in 1861, and, finally, the Teatro Comunale Giuseppe Verdi in 1901. In 1848 Verdi's *Il corsaro* was premiered (October 25), and two years later, on November 16, *Stiffelio* opened with Marietta Gazzaniga. The 3,000-seat Teatro Politeama Rossetti, which opened with Verdi's *Un ballo in maschera* in 1878, produced the complete "Ring" cycle on May 18–21, 1883, with Anton Seidl conducting.

The Teatro Giuseppe Verdi was pronounced an "Ente Autonomo" (self-governing institution) in 1936. Since obtaining a permanent house orchestra (la Filarmonia Triestina) in 1944, the theater has been able to mount an even larger variety of standard and new works.

BIBLIOGRAPHY: Guido Botteri and Vito Levi, *Il Politeama Rossetti (1878–1978)* (Trieste, 1978). Vito Levi, *La Vita Musicale a Trieste, Cronache di un cinquantennio: 1918–1968* (Milano, 1968). Vito Levi, Guido Botteri, and Ireneo Bremini, *Il Comunale di Trieste* (Udine, 1962). Giuseppe Stefani, *Il Teatro Verdi di Trieste: 1801–1951* (Trieste, 1951).

ACCESS: Riva 3 Novembre 1, I-34121 Trieste. (39 40) 62931. Raffaello de Banfield, Direttore artistico.

[From materials supplied by the company]

TURIN (1,012,180)

Teatro Regio di Torino

Although opera performances in Turin can be traced back to the early 1600s, the new Teatro Regio which opened on December 26, 1740, with Francesco Feo's last opera, *Arsace*, marks the beginning of Turin's rise to the top of the Italian operatic world. The architect who designed the new house, Benedetto Alfieri, was also responsible for the 1,000-seat Teatro Carignano which opened its doors thirteen years later in 1753. This theater was almost completely destroyed by fire in 1786, but was rebuilt the next year and is still in use today. A number of famous composers, including Gluck, Scarlatti, Cherubini, and Meyerbeer, wrote operas for the Teatro Regio, and for years it rivaled the best houses in Italy. The fortunes of the house waxed and waned during the nineteenth century, but the last decade of the century saw a number of historical events. Puccini's *Manon Lescaut* premiered on February 1, 1893, with Cesira Ferrani in the title role, and it was an overwhelming triumph. This was followed by the composer's *La Bohème* on February 1, 1896, again with Ferrani and with Pini-Corsi in the role of Schaunard. Arturo Toscanini was the conductor, and he opened the season with the very first Italian production of Wagner's *Götterdämmerung* (December 22, 1895). Toscanini remained as the music director until 1898 and returned for the 1905–1906 season.

The house was closed for extensive remodeling from 1901 to 1905. Richard Strauss conducted the Italian premiere of his *Salome* on December 22, 1906, a little over a year after its Dresden opening. These were, however, highlights that could not be sustained. The growing importance of both the Teatro alla Scala in Milan and the Teatro dell'Opera in Rome forced the city to retrench. Moreover on February 9, 1936, the Teatro Regio burned to the ground, leaving only the facade. The company continued to offer performances in a variety of theaters (including the Teatro Vittorio Emmanuelle and the Teatro della Moda), but it was not until 1963 that an official commitment was made to build a new opera house. In the meantime, all the support components that make up a great opera company (chorus, technicians, designers, orchestra, etc.) had been dispersed. Finally, over thirty years after the fire, Turin again had a major opera house. Designed by Carlo Mollino and Marcello Rossi, the new Teatro Regio opened on April 10, 1973, with Verdi's *I vespre siciliani* in a production directed by Maria Callas and Giuseppe Di Stefano.

BIBLIOGRAPHY: Alberto Basso, *Il Teatro della città dal 1788 al 1936* (Torino, 1976). Marie Thérèse Bouquet, *Il Teatro di Corte dalle origini al 1788* (Torino, 1976). Marie-Thérèse Bouquet and Alberto Basso, *Storia del Teatro Regio di Torino*, 2 vols. (Torino, 1976). L. Carluccio, Murat Cavallari, Ferro Viale, and V. Mazzonis, *Il Teatro Regio di Torino* (Torino, 1970). Mercedes Viale Ferrero, *La scenografia dalle origini al 1936*, 4 vols. (Torino, 1980–90). Luciano Tamburini, *I Teatri di Torino* (Torino, 1966).

ACCESS: Piazza Castello 215, I-10124 Turin. (39 11) 549126/548000; fax (39 11) 8815214. Piero Rattalino, Direttore artistico. Ezio Zefferi, Sovrintendente.

[From materials supplied by the company]
TRANS. EVA BEAUDET

VENICE (324,294)

Teatro La Fenice di Venezia

Opera first arrived in Venice in 1630 in the form of Monteverdi's *Proserpina rapita*, which was produced as part of the celebration of the marriage of Giustiniana Mocenigo. More important was the opening of the first public opera house in the world, the Teatro Tron di San Cassiano, which was inaugurated with Francesco Manelli's *L'Andromeda* in 1637. This had been a private theater of the Tron family, but when it was destroyed by fire in 1629 the decision was made to reopen it to the public. It was the site of the premiere of Monteverdi's *Il Ritorno d'Ulisse in Patria* in 1641. Venice was unique for a number of years as the only city that supported regular opera seasons every Carnival season. So popular was the new genre that no fewer than ten opera houses were opened in Venice during the seventeenth century alone. The Teatro SS. Giovanni e Paolo, which opened in 1639, featured Monteverdi's first opera for a public theater, *L'Adone*, during its first season and then premiered Monteverdi's *L'Incoronazione di Poppea* in 1642. The Teatro S. Moisè opened with the composer's *Arianna* in 1640, and the house continued to present operas until 1818.

The city's most famous opera house, the Teatro la Fenice, opened on May 16, 1792, with Giovanni Paisiello's *I Giuochi d'Agrigento*. Before it burned down in December 1836, it hosted the premieres of Rossini's *Tancredi* (February 6, 1818—an exciting season in Venice as the composer's *Il Signor Bruschino* had received its premiere at the Teatro San Moisè in January and the Teatro S. Benedetto, which had opened in 1755, had presented the world premiere of *L'Italiana in Algeri* on May 22); *Semiramide*, which opened on February 3, 1823, starring Isabella Colbran; Bellini's *I Capuleti e i Montecchi* on March 11, 1830 with Giuditta Grisi, and *Beatrice di Tenda* on March 16, 1833, starring Giuditta Pasta; and Donizetti's *Belisario* (February 4, 1836, with Caroline Ungher). The management elected to rebuild essentially the same house, and the new La Fenice opened on December 26, 1837. Its illustrious history continued with the premieres of no less than five of Verdi's operas: *Ernani* (March 9, 1844), *Attila* (March 17, 1846), *Rigoletto* (March 11, 1851, with Teresa Brambilla), *La Traviata* (March 6, 1853), and *Simon Boccanegra* (March 12, 1857) in the first and unsuccessful version.

The unification of Italy fostered the concentration of resources for opera in the cities of Rome and Milan. As a result, Venice found it increasingly difficult to compete on an international level. La Fenice was declared an Ente Autonomo (self-governing institution) in 1938, when the 1,500-seat house was last refurbished. Verdi's *Don Carlos* opened the house on April 21, and the enlarged orchestra pit was judged a success. The theater was forced to curtail operations during the war, but it had the distinction of being the first opera house in northern Italy to formally open after the liberation (May 8, 1945). In the 1950s the company produced operas as a part of the Festival of Contemporary Music, including the premieres of Stravinsky's *The Rake's Progress* (1951), Britten's *The Turn of the Screw* (September 1954, with Joan Cross and Peter Pears), and Luigi Nono's *Intolleranza* (1961). Unfortunately, the festival was discontinued in 1973. La Fenice continues to mount opera seasons, but with its rather small public subsidy and limited audience base, the times when it was an international center have become relegated to history.

BIBLIOGRAPHY: *La Fenice* (Milano, 1972). Nicola Mangini, *I Teatri di Venezia* (Milano, 1974). Mario Nani Mocenigo, *Il teatro La Fenice: Notizie storiche e artistiche* (Venezia, 1926).

ACCESS: Campo San Fantin 2549, I-30100 Venice. (39 41) 709344/786537; fax (39 41) 786562. Gianni Tangucci, Direttore artistico. Giuseppe La Monaca, Sovrintendente.

[From materials supplied by the company]

TRANS. EVA BEAUDET

VERONA (258,724)

Arena di Verona

Verona is the site of the largest and oldest Roman theater in Northern Italy. The Arena, which was built in the first century A.D., has a capacity in excess of 20,000 spectators. The Italian tenor Giovanni Zenatello instigated a series of opera performances there in 1913, beginning with Verdi's *Aida*, before a distinguished audience that included Mascagni, Pizzetti, and Puccini. The tenor had just married the well-known Spanish mezzo Maria Gay, who performed the role of Amneris. Except for the war years (1915–1918 and 1940–1945), the Arena di Verona has hosted summer seasons of opera concentrating primarily on works that lean toward the spectacular grand opera approach. As the stage of this ancient arena can easily accommodate several thousand performers, grandiose operatic productions are the order of the day.

BIBLIOGRAPHY: *Arena di Verona dal 1913 al 1977 tra musica e cronaca* (Verona, 1977). *1913–1963. Cinquant'anni di melodrama all'Arena di Verona* (Verona, 1964).

ACCESS: Piazza Bra 28, I-37121 Verona. (39 45) 22265/590966; fax (39 45) 590201. Carlo Perucci, Direttore artistico. Francesco Ernani, Sovrintendente.

[From materials supplied by the company]

Japan

TOKYO (8,156,000)

Nihon Opera Shinkokai (The Japan Opera Foundation)

Nihon Opera Shinkokai was established in 1981 to strengthen the management of the Fujiwara Opera and the Nihon Opera Kyokai. The former company primarily performs Italian operas in the original language, and the latter produces original Japanese operas. The tenor Yoshie Fujiwara (1898–1976), who had studied opera in Italy and debuted there in 1921, returned to Japan in 1923 where he was most successful in performing opera excerpts in concert. In 1934, he produced Puccini's *La Bohème* (June 6 and 7) in the Hibiya Public Hall, marking the birth of the Fujiwara Opera, Japan's first opera company. Since that time the company has mounted more than sixty works, primarily Italian operas. Fujiwara not only sang leading roles in the performances, he also acted as general manager for thirty-eight years. In 1952 and again in 1956 the company toured the United States with great success. Keisuke Shimoyakawa became general manager in 1972, Yosuke Shimoyakawa took charge in 1978, and in 1984 the current general director, Kiyoshi Igarashi, assumed his position. Each has continued the company's established traditions. Among the more adventuresome productions were Tchaikovsky's *Eugene Onegin* (1949), Dallapiccola's *Volo di Notte*, Stravinski's *Oedipus Rex* (1966), Mozart's *Idomeneo* (1978), Bellini's *I Capuleti e i Montecchi* (1981), Donizetti's *Maria Stuarda* (1984), and Verdi's *Macbeth* (1988). The company utilizes Japanese singers with some invited guests. Performances take place in the 1,350-seat Nissei Theater, which opened in 1964. The theater is located at 1–1–1 Yuraku-cho, Chiyoda-ku, Tokyo. Telephone (81 3) 503 3111; fax (81 3) 501 6816. The magnificent Tokyo Bunka Kaikan (Tokyo Metropolitan Festival Hall) has occasionally hosted opera productions. The high level of interest in Western opera is evidenced by the visits of major companies such as the Deutsche Oper Berlin, the Moscow Bolshoi, and London's Royal Opera House Covent Garden.

Nihon Opera Kyokai (The Japan Opera Society) was founded in April 1958 to foster and support operas by Japanese composers. The society originated the Japanese Opera Series in 1965, and, with a national subsidy, has staged some forty works to date. In April 1981 the society merged with the Fujiwara Opera, and together they created the Japan Opera Foundation as a management and fund-raising umbrella organization. The current general director of the society is Hiroshi Ohga.

ACCESS: Akasaka Noa Bldg., 7FL., 3–2–12, Akasaka, Minato-ku, Tokyo 107. (81 3) 224 9633; fax (81 3) 224 9810. Seiya Matsumoto, General Administrator.

[From materials supplied by the foundation]

Lithuania

VILNIUS (city 582,000)

Lietuvos Operos ir Baleto teatras

The Opera and Ballet Theater in Vilnius is the oldest and largest Lithuanian national art institution. The birth of the national theater in Lithuania was rather late in comparison with some neighboring countries. The first opera was staged in Lithuania on September 4, 1636, at the court theater of the Vilnius Lower Castle of the Grand Dukes of Lithuania and performed by the Polish King Ladislas Vasa's Court theater. It was a dramma musicale, *Il ratto di Helena*, by Virgilio Puccitelli. [Composed by Marco Scacchi, the opera was premiered in Warsaw in 1634, followed by the Gdansk premiere in 1636. Quite probably the same troupe performed the work in all three cities.] Up to the death of the grand duke in 1648, two more works by the same authors had been produced in Vilnius. Unfortunately only the opening night librettos published by the Vilnius University printing house have been preserved. Several theaters founded by various nobles began functioning at the beginning of the eighteenth century and were producing operas (mainly Italian) and ballets by the middle of the century. After 1750 a number of dramas called ballets were staged in the university theater. In 1785 several impresarios opened public theaters in both Vilnius and Klaipeda, and during the course of the nineteenth century and the beginning of the twentieth, the standard operatic repertoire was produced in those theaters.

Operas were performed in Italian, German, and Polish, and later in Russian. At the end of the eighteenth century and the beginning of the nineteenth, national theaters emerged in neighboring countries. The Lithuanian Grand Principality, however, lost its sovereignty in 1795. Lithuania itself was absorbed into the Russian Empire, and its Baltic coastline, together with Klaipeda, which had been conquered centuries before by the crusaders, now belonged to the Prussian Kingdom. After the 1831–1832 uprising against the czar, Vilnius University (which had fostered both music and theater) was closed. Following the 1863–1864 uprising, both public use of the Lithuanian language and the Lithuanian press were banned. [The ban remained in effect until the summer of 1904, when the Russians were at war with Japan. The 1905 revolution in Russia, which forced Nicholas II to allow an elected parliament, kept political energies focused inward.]

The idea of a national opera, which had been nurtured in secret, had an opportunity to evolve only after the native language and an open press were allowed. On November 6, 1906, the first Lithuanian opera, *Birute* by Mikas Petrauskas, was premiered in Vilnius sponsored by the "Vilniaus kankles" society. Fortunately a generation of gifted soloists was available to support native opera. Liuda Sipavičiūte, Juozas Babravičius, and Kipras Petrauskas, all performed nationally and internationally and brought the highest levels of artistry to the country. In 1918 the independent state of Lithuania was restored with a declaration of independence on February 16, and shortly thereafter, professional institutions of national art were founded in Vilnius and Kaunas. As the old capital, Vilnius again became the governmental seat of power. Occupied almost immediately by Poland, a situation that lasted until 1939, a provisional capital was established in Kaunas. Large estates formerly owned by Germans, Poles, and Russians were divided among the new citizens, and Lithuania began to assert its national identity. On December 31, 1920, the Lithuanian Art Creator's Society produced Verdi's *La Traviata* with great success, and in 1922 their theater was reorganized as the State Theater. Although the repertoire of both the opera and the ballet depended on standard French, German, Italian, and Russian works, the creations of Lithuanian composers were promoted. The conductors Juozas Tallat-Kelpša, Mykolas Bukša, and Vytautas Marijošius, the stage designer Mstislav Dobuzinsky, and the singers Veronika Podenaite, Vince Jonuškaite-Zauniene, Antanina Dambrauskaite, Vladislava Grigaitiene, Kipras Petrauskas, Juozas Mažeika, Antanas Kučingis, and Ipolitas Nauragis together created a national theater. Guest soloists included dal Monte, Chaliapin, Ohman, and Darsonval, as well as the conductors Cooper, Malko, Dobrovein, Coates, Wolff, and Annovazzi.

The occupation and forced incorporation of Lithuania into the Soviet Union in 1940 did not immediately result in major changes in the theatrical activities. During this time as well as during the Nazi occupation from 1941 to 1944, there was an emergence of new theaters. The Kaunas Operetta was founded, the State Opera was reestablished in Vilnius, and a musical company began productions in the Šiauliai Theater. By the summer of 1944, however, the occupation by the Red Army caused about thirty soloists, two-thirds of the ballet, and many actors and vocal teachers to leave for the West. All connections with European theaters and conservatories were terminated; indeed, all Western influences were eliminated. Ideological requirements were placed on all theatrical activity, and in the course of a few seasons, only old and politically acceptable productions were given. In 1948 the State Theater moved back to the capital of Vilnius, and from then until 1960 works by Soviet composers formed one-third of the opera repertoire and half of the ballets performed. In spite of the political influences on the theater's activity, it succeeded in remaining a remarkable center of national culture. With a repertoire of Mozart, nineteenth-century Italian operas, an occasional twentieth-century work by Gershwin or Prokoffiev, and over thirty operas and ballets by Lithuanian composers, the theater provided some balance.

Among the most distinguished theater performers were the conductors Rimas Geniušas, Vytautas Viržonis, and Jonas Akelsa; the directors Antanas Zauka, Juozas Grybauskas, Juozas Gustaitis, and Vlada Mikštaite; the sopranos Elena Saulevičiute and Elena Čiudakova; the tenor Valentinas Adamkevičius; the baritone Jonas Stasiūnas; and the bass Rimantas Siparis. Since the 1970s Lithuanian opera singers have been allowed to travel abroad again, and a number of young artists have won international competitions, including Nijole Ambrazaityte in Bucharest, V. Daunoras in Moscow and Toulouse, Vladimir Prudnikov in Athens, and I. Milkevičiūte in Budapest and Tokyo. The entire company made tours in thirteen different seasons between 1954 and 1990, including Bulgaria, Greece (1983 Athens Festival), Sweden, and Syria (Grand Prix of the eighth Bosra Art Festival). Opera stars such as Moser, Tomowa-Sintow, Bumbry, Vishnevskaya, King, Rossi-Lemeni, Quilico, Herlea, Nesterenko, Chauviré, Plitsetzkaya, and Besmertnova have performed on the Vilnius stage. In addition, the State Theater has hosted the Warsaw Chamber Opera and Grand Theater, the Slovak National Theater from Bratislava, and the opera and ballet troupes from Weimar and Erfurt.

Since 1974 the Lithuanian Opera has been housed in a new 1,142-seat theater which includes the latest in lighting and stage machinery and theatrical support services. The 1989–1990 season included 39 principal artists, an 80-voice choir, and an orchestra of 103 musicians. The entire theater company totals 704 people. Virgilijus Noreika has been the artistic and managing director since 1975; the chief conductor is Jonas Aleksa and the chief director is Eligijus Domarkas. Roughly 250 performances of thirty opera and ballet productions take place in the ten-month season beginning each September.

ACCESS: Vienuolio 1, 232600 Vilnius. Virgilijus Noreika, Artistic and Managing Director.

JONAS BRUVERIS
TRANS. LORETA KIRNAITE

Monaco

MONTE CARLO (28,000)

Opéra de Monte-Carlo

An independent principality since the thirteenth century, Monaco has a long tradition of music. The city of Monte Carlo was not founded until 1858, but it quickly became a social and economic center. The celebrated architect Charles Garnier designed the 600-seat Grand Theater in 1879, just four years after the Théâtre National de L'Opéra de Paris had opened. Roaul Gunsbourg, the French composer and impresario, directed the Opéra from 1893 to 1950. During his very first season, Gunsbourg adapted and produced the first staged performance of Berlioz's *La Damnation de Faust* (on February 18). The next season saw the posthumous premiere of Franck's *Hulda* (March 8), and Gunsbourg continued to be responsible for a number of historical premieres, including Massenet's *Le Jongleur de Notre-Dame* (February 18, 1902); Saint-Saën's *Hélène* (February 18, 1904) and *L'Ancêtre* (February 24, 1906); Massenet's *Thérèse* (February 7, 1907), *Don Quichotte* (February 24, 1910, with Feodor Chaliapin) and *Roma* (February 17, 1912); Fauré's *Pénélope* (March 4, 1913); Massenet's *Cléopâtre* (February 23, 1914) and *Amadis* (April 1, 1922); Puccini's *La Rondine (March 27, 1917,* with della Rizza and Schipa); Ravel's *L'Enfant et les Sortilèges* (March 21, 1925); Honegger's *Judith* (February 13, 1926); and Honegger/Ibert's *L'Aiglon* (March 11, 1937). Among the many famous artists who appeared over the years, Caruso, Melba, and Patti are, along with Chaliapin, perhaps the most notable. All operas are performed in the original language, and the company uses the outstanding National Symphony of Monte Carlo in the pit. With no permanent company, the roster of guest artists varies from season to season.

BIBLIOGRAPHY: Joelle Castallan, *Spécial Monte Carlo: Centenaire de la Salle Garnier (1879–1979)* (Paris, 1979). Thomas J. Walsh, *Monte Carlo Opera, 1879–1919* (Dublin, 1975).

ACCESS: Place du Casino, Monte Carlo. (33 93) 50 69 31; fax (33 93) 30 07 57. M. John Mordler, Director. Marie-Christine Forestier, Administrator.

[From materials supplied by the company]

New Zealand

WELLINGTON (328,163)

Wellington City Opera

Opera has played an important part in the cultural life of New Zealand since the middle of the nineteenth century when the country was still a colony of Great Britain. Lyster's Royal Italian and English Opera was performing widely as early as 1864, and the Pollard Opera Company was crucial in Rosina Buckman's early career. After World War I, J. C. Williamson managed opera tours with well-known singers. Donald Munrow founded the New Zealand Opera Company in 1954, a valiant effort that unfortunately did not succeed. A young company committed to the stagione concept, Wellington City Opera was formed in 1984 as a nonprofit, Charitable Trust company. Funded through a mixture of box office (62 percent), public monies (15 percent), corporate sponsors (11 percent), and private/unearned income (12 percent), the City Opera is dedicated to providing maximum opportunities to New Zealand artists. New Zealand has produced more internationally successful singers per capita than most countries, many of whom are among the world's finest. Beginning with Frances Alda and Rosina Buckman, and counting Kiri Te Kanawa and Donald McIntyre among current operatic favorites, this tiny country has produced more than its share of stars. A prime consideration regarding present and future productions is bringing experienced artists back to their country in principal roles to serve as models and inspirations for younger New Zealand singers. The company performs in the State Opera House, but rents it for the season as does any other performing arts organization. Some time in the future, a permanent home will become necessary.

The current budget exceeds a half million dollars, which supports two major productions each year in rather long runs, plus, during this season, a New Zealand International Festival of the Arts production of Wagner's *Die Meistersinger von*

Nürnberg. Based on this schedule, the company supports the projection of three major operas in future seasons. Wellington City Opera presently has an accumulated budget balance and is consolidating finances to accommodate any future contingencies. Young audiences are developed by subsidizing ticket prices. The repertoire is selected on the basis of wide appeal as well as indicated production costs, which means that only standard works with affordable casting and technical requirements are scheduled. It is hoped that the future growth of the company will permit more adventuresome programming.

BIBLIOGRAPHY: Phyllis Wilkins Brusey, *Ring Down the Curtain* (Wellington, 1973). David Fingleton, *Kiri Te Kanawa: A Biography* (London, 1982). Norman Harris, *Kiri: Music and a Maori Girl* (Sidney, 1966). Maurice Hurst, *Music and the Stage in New Zealand: A Century of Entertainment 1840–1943* (Auckland, 1946). Beryl Margaret Te Wiata, *Most Happy Fella: A Biography of Inia Te Wiata* (Wellington, 1976).

ACCESS: State Opera House, 109 Manners Street, Wellington. (64 04) 844434; fax (64 04) 843333. Gillian Manolin, General Manager.

[From materials supplied by the company]

Norway

OSLO (456,124)

Den Norske Opera

Norway is a constitutional monarchy and achieved its independence from Sweden in 1905. The capital and major seaport of the country is Oslo, known as Christiana until 1925 when it reverted to the name of the original (1047) settlement. The first recorded operas were presented toward the end of the eighteenth century, and various professional touring companies visited irregularly. The National Theater, which opened in 1899, produced some operas, but it was not until 1950 that the Norsk Operaselskap, founded by Jonas and Gunnar Brunvoll, provided a viable organization devoted to the production of operas. With a subsidy from the city of Oslo, the Brunvolls' company finally laid the groundwork for a permanent company, and in 1959 the company became Den Norske Opera with Kirsten Flagstad as the first general administrator. The inaugural season opened in February with Eugen d'Albert's *Tiefland*, the same opera in which Flagstad had made her Oslo debut at the National Theater on December 12, 1913, as Nuri. Her unexpected appearance in the Norwegian premiere, which was sung in Norwegian and was the only opera produced at the National Theater that season, marked the beginning of a long and distinguished career. Flagstad retired the next year due to ill health and Odd Grüner-Hegge, artistic director of the Oslo Philharmonic, took over the company. During the first decade of its existence the company built up a repertoire of some forty operas, and it continues to add works including operas by contemporary Norwegian composers. Although the company hires primarily native talent, guest conductors, producers, and singers have become a valued part of the programming.

BIBLIOGRAPHY: Oyvind Anker, *Christiana Theater's Repertoire, 1827–1899* (Oslo, 1956).

ACCESS: Folketeatret, Storgaten 23, 0184 Oslo 1. (47 2) 42 94 75; fax (47 2) 42 78 77. Bjorn E. Simensen, General Manager. Heinz Fricke, Music Director.

[From materials supplied by the company]

Poland

GDAŃSK (metro 1,411,000; city 760,000)

Państwowa Opera i Filharmonia Baltycka

[The Slavic settlement of Gyddanyzc dates back to the tenth century and has had a mixed Polish and German culture over the centuries. Its operatic history begins with a festive performance of Marco Scacchi's *Le nozze d'Amore e di Psyche* in 1646. As choirmaster for the Polish king, Scacchi was a leading figure in the musical life of Warsaw as well. Johann Meder's *Nero* was the first German opera produced in Danzig in November 1695. The city was under Prussian rule beginning in 1793, when Russia and Prussia divided Poland. The Danziger theater was opened in 1801, and operas were a part of the program. After World War I the city became the Free City of Danzig from 1918 to 1939 and enjoyed considerable internal autonomy. Between the world wars the resort of Sopot hosted open-air performances of opera, including Wagner's complete "Ring" cycle in 1939. With the invasion of Poland in 1939, Danzig fell under German control. All the theaters were destroyed during the war, along with a considerable portion of the city itself. Opera reappeared in 1949 at the Teatr Wybrzeze produced by the Studio Operowe. This organization formally united with the orchestra in 1953 to form the Panstwowa Opera i Filharmonia Baltycka.]

Professional opera was reborn in Gdańsk the week of March 23, 1950, with a performance of Tchaikovsky's *Eugene Onegin* in Polish conducted by Stanislaw Skrowaczewski, supported by the Filharmonia Baltycka, and cast with a group of promising young singers. The artistic director was Robert Satanowski, who currently holds the same position in Warsaw. Shortly thereafter, the Opera Studio was introduced, premiering with Stanislaw Moniuszko's *Straszny dwór* (*The Haunted Manor*) [which premiered in 1865]. In September 1950 Kazimierz Wilkomirski was appointed general manager of the combined organization, which was renamed the Opera Baltycka. The season opened with Mozart's *Le Nozze de Figaro*, starring Jerzy Podsiadke and Eugene Banaszcyk. Among the artists in the early years were Kinga Bródków, Katarzyn Chmieck, and Kazimierz Sandurski. By 1953 the season had increased to 125 performances, and the orchestra season was cut correspondingly. Wilkomirski conducted a new production of Moniuszko's famous *Halka*, which was directed by the retired tenor Kazimierz Czarnecki. Several new operas were added to the repertoire, including Puccini's *La Bohème* and Rossini's *Barber of Seville*.

Zygmunt Latoszewski returned to the company in February 1955 to conduct Tchaikovsky's *Queen of Spades*, and the next year he conducted Gounod's *Faust*. The success of Tadeusz Szeligowsky's *Bunt Zakow* was due to the excellent chorus. The year 1957 saw the union of the opera and the ballet, and both ensembles collaborated in productions of Eugen d'Albert's *Tiefland* and Mascagni's *Cavalleria rusticana*. The season also included an important premiere of Britten's *Peter Grimes*. That fall the company was invited to the second annual Invitational Festival in Warsaw. Jerzy Katlewicz became artistic director at the beginning of the 1961–1962 season. A new production of Gluck's *Orfeo ed Euridice*, starring Krystyn Szczepański and presented in February, was one of the highlights of the season. Borodin's *Prince Igor*, directed by Jerzy Goliński; Verdi's *Don Carlos*; and Waladislaw Zelenski's *Konrad Wallenrod* filled out the season of musical theater. During the remainder of the decade, Katlewicz mounted productions of Verdi's *Otello* and Puccini's *Turandot* before he left the company in 1968. His successor, Jerzy Procner, who was both a musician and an economist, opened with Verdi's *Il Troubador* followed by Massenet's *Don Quixote*, directed by Danuta Baduszkow. Ballet and symphony programs resumed their former luster under his leadership.

Zbigniew Chwedszuk became director in 1972 and produced Bizet's *Carmen* and Saint-Saëns's *Samson et Dalila*. Both productions starred the mezzo Stefani Toczyska, who would later perform at the Teatro alla Scala and the Metropolitan Opera Association in New York. As the program expanded it became clear that two orchestras were needed to maintain the level of excellence, and during the 1974–1975 season, plans were made to employ the newly trained musicians who were available. Chwedszuk, who remained as artistic director until 1981, produced a number of outstanding ballets as well as a memorable production of Donizetti's *La Favorite* which starred Stefani Toczyska and Floria Skulski. For the 1981–1982 season Wojceik Rajski assumed the directorship, and, although a satisfactory *Eugene Onegin* and *Halka* were produced, his real favorite was the symphony orchestra. Two seasons later, in 1983–1984, Januszow Przybylski took over as artistic director and remained active until 1989. During his tenure, Verdi's *Nabucco*, directed by Ryszarda Peryta in the settings of Andrzey Sadowski, toured Europe with great success. Other memorable productions include Donizetti's *Lucia di Lammermoor* and Verdi's *Macbeth* directed by Kari Vileniusa. In 1989 the opera company toured Switzerland, Denmark, and Germany with productions of Verdi's *Rigoletto* and Puccini's *Manon Lescaut*.

BIBLIOGRAPHY: *Almanach sceny polskiej*, 1959/60– . Anna Czekanowicz, ed., *Panstwowa Opera i Filharmonia Baltycka, 1945–1985* (Gdańsk, 1985). W. Kmicic-Mieleszyński, *Polska kultura muzyczna w Wolnym Mieście Gdańsku (1920–1939)* (Gdańsk, 1965). *Państwowa Opera i Filharmonia Baltycka w Gdańsku*... (Gdańsk, 1971).

ACCESS: Aleja Zwyciestwa 15, 80–219 Gdańsk. (48 58) 41 46 41/42/43; fax (48 58) 41 38 27. Wlodzimierz Nawotka, General Manager.

ANNA CZEKANOWICZ
TRANS. ALEX LINIECKI

KRAKÓW (metro 1,220,000; city 691,000)

Krakowski Teatr Muzyczny

One of the oldest Polish cities, Kraków is among the country's finest cultural and artistic centers. Its opera history begins with the founding of the first permanent opera company in 1787 by Jacek Kluszewski, who was the owner of the Kraków theater. By the 1820s many of the operas of Rossini and Mozart had been produced, and Polish works by Karol Kurpiński (*Jadwiga, Królowa Polska* and *Zamek na Czorsztynie*) and Józef Elsner (*Krøl Wiśliczanki*) were very popular. Due to frequent political changes, ongoing artistic organizations did not exist. Guest performances were the norm until Boleslaw Wallek-Walewski founded the opera in 1915. It functioned until 1924 and was revived from 1931 until the beginning of World War II. Between the world wars the city was associated with the new state of Poland, and musical life flourished. The Kraków Opera opened on September 1, 1931, and quickly became a focus of Polish musical life. Evolving out of the opera studio, which was founded in 1954, the Kraków Opera Company was officially founded in 1956. The original director was Robert Satanowski, who remained in Kraków until 1976, when he moved to Warsaw. It was recognized and supported by the government in 1958 as the Miejski Teatr Muzyczny–Opera i Operetka w Krakowie. Renamed the Krakowski Teatr Muzyczny in 1976, the company performs in a 918-seat theater.

BIBLIOGRAPHY: K. Michalowski, *Opery polskie* (Kraków, 1954).

ACCESS: Senacka 6, 31–002 Kraków. (48 12). Ewa Michnik, Director.

[From materials supplied by the company]

LODZ (metro 1,119,000; city 724,000)

Teatr Wielki W Lodzi

The history of opera in Lodz is similar to that of operas in many cities. A touring company performed the first works in the 1860s, and, except for a failed effort to found a local company in 1888, the public was forced to depend on guest performances until after World War II. Interest in a permanent ensemble was strong, however, and on October 18, 1954, the Society of Friends of Opera founded the Lodz Opera. For twelve years the company performed in two playhouses, the Teatr Jaracza and the Teatr Nowy, where thirty-six operas and ballets were produced under difficult circumstances. Persistence, patience, dedication, and, above all, high artistic standards finally bore fruit with the gala opening of the Teatr Wielki on January 19, 1967. Four local premieres celebrated the opening: Stanislaw Monieszko's *Halka* (the most popular Polish opera ever written received its one thousandth performance in Warsaw alone on October 8, 1935), Borodin's *Prince Igor*, Moniuszko's *Straszny dwór (The Haunted Manor)*, and Bizet's *Carmen*. *Straszny dwór* was the work that inaugurated the company in 1954, and it was received with such enthusiasm that a widespread commitment was made to ensure its permanent future. It is perhaps no accident that this particular opera has historically been involved with patriotism and politics, and the fact that Moniuszko was the primary representative of Polish nationalism guaranteed a sympathetic reception.

The new Lodz Opera is one of the largest opera houses in Europe and the second largest theater in Poland, second only to the Wielki Theater in Warsaw. The 1,300-seat theater contains the finest modern equipment available, including hydraulic lifts and turntables in the main stage. Acoustics are excellent and the public areas are most attractive and comfortable. The current repertoire includes a number of standard works such as *Rigoletto*, *La Traviata*, *La Bohème*, *Lohengrin*, and *Il Barbiere di Siviglia*, as well as Romuald Twardowski's *Tragedyja albo rzecz o Janie i Herodzie* (1969) and *Lord Jim* (1973), and Tadeusz Paciorkiewicz's *Romans gdański* (1968), all of which received their world premieres in Lodz. Paciorkiewicz had taught at the Lodz Conservatory (1949–1959) and was a local favorite. A number of operas have received their Polish premieres in Lodz, including Halvy's *La Juive*, Bellini's *Norma*, Boito's *Mephistofele*, Donizetti's *Lucia di Lammermoor*, and Mussorgsky's *Boris Godunov*. Paderewski's only opera, *Manru*, which received its 1901 premiere in German in Dresden, represents the company's commitment to Polish history.

Since its founding the company has been invited to perform throughout Europe, including houses in Austria, Finland, France, Germany, Greece, Hungary, Italy, the Netherlands, and Yugoslavia. A special occasion was the gala opening of the Teatro Vittorio Emanuelle in January 1968 with opera stars Fiorenza Cossotto and Maria Chiara. With productions of Stanislaw Moniuszko's *Halka* and *Straszny dwór*, the Lodz Opera began an artistic exchange with the Opéra de Lyon in France, a cooperative effort that hopefully will continue. With public support, the future of the company looks promising.

BIBLIOGRAPHY: T. Kaczyński, *Dzieje sceniczne 'Halki' Stanislawa Moniuszki* (Kraków, 1969).

ACCESS: Plac Dabrowskiego, 90–249 Lódź 1. (48 42) 33 99 60. Slawomir Pietras, Director.

ELZBIETA ADAMCZYK
TRANS. MARC ÄNDERS

POZNAŃ (metro 1,317,000; city 697,000)

Teatr Wielki

The city of Poznań was the first capital of the kingdom of Poland in the 900s. Annexed to Prussia in the second partition of the country in 1793 (two years before the country itself ceased to exist as a separate nation in 1795), Poznań remained under Prussian control until the end of World War I in 1918, when it became part of the new Polish republic. In the cultural struggle that permeated the arts during this period, Poznań's operas were produced by German companies. The Poznań Teatr Wielki, known as the Pegasus House because of the winged horse on the roof, was designed by the architect Max Littmann from Munich. Construction began in 1901 and the theater opened on September 30, 1910, offering German-language operas, operettas, and plays to the theatergoing public. When Poland regained its independence in 1918 there was strong sentiment for a reawakening of Polish culture. On August 31, 1919, Stanislaw Moniuszko's *Halka* (the most popular Polish opera ever composed) began the new history of one of the most important Polish music centers. Through September 1939, twelve world premieres of Polish operas and ballets, including Feliks Nowowiejski's *Legenda Baltyku* (November 28, 1924), and eighteen Polish premieres of foreign operas and operettas, including Janáček's *Jenufa* (1924), Strauss's *Ariadne auf Naxos* (1926), Puccini's *La Rondine* (1929), Mozart's *Così fan tutte* (1933), Borodin's *Prince Igor* (1934), Verdi's *Les Vêpres Siciliennes* (1935), and Handel's *Giulio Cesare* (1936) had taken place in the Pegasus House. Guest artists during this time included Ewa Brandowska-Turska, Mattia Battistini, Kazimiers Czarnecki, Adam Didur, Stanislaw Gruszczyński, Jan Kiepura, Toti dal Monte, Ada Sari, Wanda Wermińska, Stefan Belina-Skupiewski, and Józef Woliński.

On June 2, 1945, the Teatr Wielki in Poznań was the first opera house in Poland to start postwar activity. The next five years brought about the restoration of the standard national and international repertoire and included some forty local premieres. During the Bierdiajew years (1949–1954), the company mounted *Boris Godunov*, *Prince Igor*, and the Polish premiere of Rimsky-Korsakov's *Snow Maiden*. On January 22, 1950, the Teatr Wielki was nationalized and received the name Stanislaw Moniuszko. The company toured to Moscow, Leningrad, and Kiev in 1952, with outstanding success. Among the soloists during this period were Zofia Czepielówna, Antonina Kawecka, Barbara Kostrzewska, Halina Dudicz-Latoszewska, Jerzy Sergiusz Adamczewski, Franciszek Arno, Warclaw Domieniecki, Józef Katin, Aleksander Klonowski, Edmund Kossowski, Henryk Lukaszek, Józef Przada, Marian Wozniczko, and Józef Sendecki. Zdzislaw Górzyński returned as director (1954–1963) and greatly expanded the repertoire. Witold Rudziński's *Komendant Paryża* was given its world premiere (March 27, 1960), and Eugene Suchoń's *Krutniawa* and Menotti's *The Consul* received Polish premieres. *Die Freischütz*, *Lakmé*, Rózycki's

Pan Twardowski, *Der fliegende Holländer*, *Turandot*, *Rigoletto*, Paderewski's *Manru*, and *Il Barbiere di Siviglia* were all added to the schedule.

Satanowski replaced Górzyński in March 1963. He was the first director in Poland to produce Wagner's *Tannhäuser* and *Tristan und Isolde* after the war. He also was responsible for the Polish premieres of Shostakovitch's *Katerina Izmaylova*, Liebermann's *Die Schule der Frauen*, Ravel's *L'Enfant et les sortilèges*, Szokolay's *Blood Wedding*, and Mussorgsky's *Khovanschina*. Among the leading artists of his regime were Zdzislawa Donat, Alicja Dankowska, Aleksandra Imalska, Antonina Kawecka, Bozena Karlowska, Krystyna Pakulska, Janina Rozelówna, Barbara Zagorzanka, Jan Czekay, Albin Fechner, Józef Katin, Andrezej Kizewetter, Edward Kmiciewicz, Marian Kondella, Marian Kouba, Henryk Lukaszek, Wladyslaw Malczewski, Józef Przada, Bogdan Ratajczak, Stanislaw Romański, Józef Wegrzyn, and Slawomir Zerdzicki. One of the highlights of Jan Kulaszewicz's term as director of the company was the world premiere of Zbigniew Penherski's *Zmierzch Peryna* (*The Damnation of Peryn*) on October 6, 1974.

With the appointment of Mieczyslaw Dondajewski on April 1, 1978, the Teatr Wielki embarked on a new course. Dondajewski's intention was to create an opera house of great spectacles, based on coexistence and harmony of music and acting, choreography and scenography, under the direction of the conductor. According to his aesthetic, art lives only when it arouses strong emotions and inspires intensive thinking. The new director mounts very controversial productions arousing "creative agitation" and touching on the timeless problems of humanity as well as contemporary concerns. The audience should be deeply moved on leaving the theater, perhaps even indignant, but never indifferent. Dondajewski, along with a production team that includes stage director Ryszard Peryt and stage designer Andrzej Sadowski, has strongly influenced the artistic image of the Teatr Wielki. The direction they have chosen includes balancing the repertoire, continuing to produce standard works but in a manner that speaks to contemporary times. The productions have to satisfy the expectations of the audience while at the same time introducing certain tensions and emotions resulting either from the newness of the work or its uniqueness and, importantly, its unusual and unexpected contents. Currently the company employs fifty principal artists, a chorus of seventy, a ballet of forty, and an orchestra of eighty-six musicians. The season runs from September through June and includes an average of four premieres.

CHRONOLOGY OF DIRECTORS: Adam Dolzycki, 1919–1922. Piotr Stermmicz-Valcrociata, 1922–1929. Zygmunt Wojceichowski, 1929–1933. Zygmunt Latoszewski, 1933–1939. Zygmunt Wojciechowski, Zygmunt Latoszewski, and Zdzislaw Górzyński, 1945–1949. Walerian Bierdiajew, 1949–1954. Zdzislaw Górzyński, 1954–1963. Robert Satanowski, 1963–1969. Mieczyslaw Nowakowski, 1969–1972. Jan Kulaszewicz, 1972–1978, Mieczyslaw Dondajewski, 1978-present.

BIBLIOGRAPHY: H. Ehrenberg, *Geschichte des Theaters in Posen* (Posen, 1889). T.

Świtala, *Opera poznańska, 1919–1969* (Poznań, 1973). Jerzy Waldorff, *Opera Poznańska, 1919–1969* (Poznań, 1970).

ACCESS: Teatr Wielki, im. Stanislawa Moniuszki, ul. Fredry 9, 60–967 Poznań. (48 61) 52 82 91/52 44 78. Mieczyslaw Dondajewski, Dyrektor Naczelny i Artystyczny.

ROMUALD POLCZYNSKI
TRANS. KATARZYNA PETRYNIAK

WARSAW (metro 2,413,000; city 730,000)

Teatr Wielki

With a new production of Stanislaw Moniuszko's *Straszny dwór* (*The Haunted Manor*) on November 20, 1965, the Teatr Wielki again took its place as the leading opera house of Poland after a quarter century of reluctant silence. The building itself, which was constructed in 1833 from the design of the Italian architect Antonio Corazzi, numbers among the most important historical structures in Poland. The Teatr Wielki, or Grand Theater, is not only grand in name. Covering almost five acres with over five hundred thousand cubic meters of space, it is the largest theater ever built. The history of opera in Warsaw, however, begins much earlier than the construction of this particular house. Poland's capital city can boast of being one of the first cities north of the Alps to have a permanent opera theater. As early as 1628, King Wladyslaw IV engaged an Italian company for the Warsaw Hoftheater, and the following year a number of operas were produced. Under Wladyslaw's successors, however, this new form of theatrical art was largely ignored. Opera returned again to Warsaw when August, the elector of Saxony, was elected King August II of Poland in 1697. As elsewhere in Europe, the Italians dominated operatic events in Warsaw. King August brought his own company from Dresden, directed by Jacek Różycki; it was made up primarily of Italians. Their performances, which were initially given at the Royal Court, were soon attended by commoners. To fulfill this need, a sturdy wooden, thoroughly proper Opernhaus was erected in 1725; it was popularly known as the Operalnia. [The house was open to both members of the nobility and common citizens at no charge. The opera grew under the reign of August III (1733–1763), who provided large royal subsidies. The Operalnia was demolished in 1772.] The Dresden court ensemble visited Warsaw regularly between 1758 and 1762, including the prima donna Faustina Bordoni and her husband, the composer Adolf Hasse. [A number of Hasse's operas were performed in Warsaw, including the premieres of a new version of *Artaserse* on October 8, 1760, *Zenobia* on October 7, 1761, and a new version of *Sirone* for Carnival in 1763.]

The first Polish opera, Maciej Kamieński's *Nedza uszcześliwiona* (*Misery Made Happy*), was premiered on July 11, 1778. A number of Singspiels in Polish followed, among them Jan Stefani's beloved *Krakowiacy i Górale* (*The Cracovians and the Highlanders*). The Italian monopoly was gradually being threatened by the French opéra comique as French ensembles were invited. The repertoire was enriched with works by Gluck as well as Mozart Singspiels. Moreover, performances were now being given in a new structure built by the Italian architect Bonaventura Solari on Krasinski Square. This theater presented plays as well as opera, and it served both foreign and native ensembles. The next developments in the history of opera in Warsaw must be seen in a historical context. During the second half of the eighteenth century, Poland gradually lost its independence through a growing foreign interference in its national affairs, especially by Czarist Russia. The country was partitioned in 1772, 1793, and 1795 between Russia, Austria, and Prussia, and Poland completely disappeared as a separate nation in 1795. Only after the end of World War I did Poland regain her sovereignty.

Although they had a pro forma king in the person of Stanislaw August Poniatowski until 1795, the Polish people were threatened with the loss of their national identity during the more than 140 years in which they endured the oppression of foreign powers. All political, economic, and cultural life at this time was defined by the nationalistic struggle. While the Austrians were quite liberal in their cultural politics, the Prussians strictly enforced Germanization. The Russians, who had taken the Polish heartland with the capital of Warsaw, pursued a policy of Russianization on all fronts, encountering bitter resistance. Thus, opera in Warsaw for well over a century was not so much music theater as it was a place of resistance against a repressive and hated regime. Occupied first by the Prussians and then by Napoleon's troops, the artistic climate of the Grand Duchy of Warsaw expired under pressure. After Napoleon's defeat, the Congress of Vienna gave a large part of Poland, including the former capital of Warsaw, to Russia which made the territory a province under the absolute control of the czar.

In the new theater on Krasinski Square, a German influence joined that of the French and Italians. One of the first composers to write Polish operas, Józef Ksawery Elsner, who was born in Grottkau, Schlesien, and who was the teacher of Chopin, composed no fewer than twenty-five operas [*Krøl Lokietek* premiered on April 3, 1818] which were produced in Warsaw between 1800 and 1820. Also prominent at the time was the gifted conductor Karol Kurpiński, who also composed a number of operas [for example, *Zamek na Czorsztynie* premiered on May 11, 1819]. Kurpiński assumed the direction of the Krasinski Square theater in 1824, but the house was soon viewed as out-of-date and too small for the growing audience. It was decided to build a new, larger theater, and, after almost eight years of construction, the Teatr Wielki opened on February 24, 1833. From the beginning it had the character of a Polish national theater, an unrealistic designation in light of the Russian sensitivity to national movements following the 1831 insurrection which was clearly manifested in the mandated suppression of the Polish language and culture. All theaters, including the Teatr Wielki after 1833, remained among the few trustees of Polish culture until 1918. In the eyes of the populace the theaters fulfilled a national mission which was broader than a site for the muses; opera, and especially Polish opera, became a symbol of resistance.

Initially, the Teatr Wielki produced the same repertoire as the Krasinski. Inaugurating the new house with a Polish opera was not conceivable, so a gala production of Rossini was scheduled with an accompanying ball. Among the prominent artists of the time, especially in the new operas of Bellini [such as *La Sonnambula* on June 2, 1840, which was translated by Kurpiński] and Donizetti were Paolina Rivoli and Julian Dobrski. Although the Teatr Wielki was built with the resources of the Warsaw Civil Service, the real authority over the theater resided with the officials of the czar. With the element of loyalty always in question, the factor of hidden censorship prevented the appearance of new Polish operas. The repertoire featured the current works of the world theater, but even here patriotic signs appeared. Popular arias of Donizetti were given patriotic texts and became hits. [Tomasz Nidecki, who had succeeded Kurpiński as artistic director, was responsible for the first Polish performances of Bellini's *Norma* on May 8, 1845, and Flotow's *Martha* on July 20, 1850, among others.] The artistic level of the theater was substantially raised when the Italian conductor Giovanni (later Jan) Quattrini arrived. He enlarged the repertoire to include the newest operas of Verdi, Bizet, Gounod, and Meyerbeer. He can also be credited with developing young singers to the point where they could be gauged by international standards; and the theater itself enjoyed an international reputation. All the famous European singers who appeared in St. Petersburg also visited the Teatr Wielki in Warsaw. This resulted in numerous performances in which each role was sung in a different language. Jan Quattrini was also responsible for premiering the final four-act version of Stanislaw Moniuszko's *Halka* which, because of its musical qualities, achieved more than a blatant patriotic demonstration. [Paolina Rivoli was the younger sister of the Polish soprano Ludwika Rywacka, and she appeared in the Warsaw premiere of Halèvy's *La Juive* as well as in the world premiere of the final version of Moniuszko's *Halka* on January 1, 1858, partnered by Dobrski.] Today *Halka* is considered simply *the* Polish national opera.

Following new outbreaks of unrest at the beginning of 1861, the czarist authorities brought to Warsaw an Italian ensemble whose performances were generally boycotted resulting in a theater that was practically empty for the better part of a year. Between 1865 and 1873 most of the performances were in Italian, but on September 28, 1865, Moniuszko sent a new patriotic signal with his opera *Staszny dwór* which the Russian authorities promptly removed from the repertoire after three performances. Their prohibition could not stop Moniuszko's triumph in the long run. Between 1858 and 1872 he was the artistic director of the Polish opera with Quattrini who was responsible for the international repertoire, and his works were performed abroad. The Polish audience supported his works, ignoring to a great extent other operas that were frequented by members of the Russian occupation forces. Along with the contemporary works of Flotow, Spontini, Meyerbeer, and Halévy, the repertoire included Verdi's *Nabucco*, *Macbeth*, *Il Trovatore*, and *Ernani*. In many cases the performers were traveling foreign ensembles which used the resident chorus and orchestra. The soloists had been discharged after the premiere of *Straszny dwór*, but they had to be recalled in order to entice a broader public back to the theater to be entertained with operettas. Quickly, however, the Polish artists were again performing opera, such as Verdi's *Sila przeznaczenia* (*La forza del destino*), *Aida*, and *Don Carlos*, as well as Boito's *Mefistofele*.

Cesare Trombini was director of the Teatr Wielki from 1874 to 1881 and again from 1891 to 1898. During his tenure, *Lohengrin* (1879) was premiered in Warsaw, it was followed by *Tannhäuser* (1883) after his departure. Other novelties included Bizet's *Carmen*, Massenet's *Manon*, Mascagni's *Rycerskosc wiesniacza* (*Cavalleria rusticana*), and *Willidy* (*La Villi*), which was the theater's first Puccini production. Every effort was made to conform stylistically to the Italian vocal school. Famous guests included Gemma Bellincioni, Luisa Tetrazzini, Titta Ruffo, Enrico Caruso, and frequent visitor Mattia Battistini [engaged every year between 1894 and 1912, he made recordings in Warsaw in 1903], all of whom acted as role models. Marcella Sembrich and Alexander Brandrowski also appeared in their homeland, and Jean and Edouard de Reszke, who are probably the most famous Polish singers in operatic history, appeared for a brief engagement in 1893. Emil Mlynarski took over the Teatr Wielki toward the end of the century [1898–1903], and he was responsible for engaging emerging stars Janina Korolewicz and Salomea Krusceniski (Kruszelnicka) as well as Adam Didur. Economic difficulties marked the following years, and the theater was run by the artists themselves as well as by various impresarios, who never lasted very long. In spite of the circumstances there were some memorable productions, including Wagner's *Holender tulacz* (*Der fliegende Holländer*) and *Spiewacy norymberscy* (*Die Meistersinger von Nürnberg*) [on October 22, 1908], and Richard Strauss conducting his *Salome* [October 15, 1907].

In spite of the chronic economic difficulties between 1918 and 1939, when the subsidy was drastically reduced following Poland's independence, the Teatr Wielki—occasionally run again by the artists—generated a new impetus. Between 1917 and 1919 the Polish soprano Janina Korolewicz-Waydowa served as director of the Polish opera. In 1919 she was succeeded by the conductor Emil Mlynarski, whose enlightened directorship ushered in a golden age which lasted until 1929. A number of new Polish operas were premiered, and the repertoire was focused on the most important works of operatic literature. Numerous guests enriched the daily activities so that the organization never sank to simple routine. Karol Szymanowski's *Hagith* [1913] and *Krol Roger* [premiered on June 19, 1926] were produced, and, alongside works of Ravel [*L'Heure espagnol* in 1928] and Giordano, Mussorgsky's *Boris Godunov* and Beethoven's *Fidelio* [1919] were accorded Warsaw premieres. The German repertoire in particular was enriched with the reappearance of Wagner's earlier operas, and local premieres were mounted of *Trystan i Izolda*, *Parsifal*, *Zygfryd*, and *Zmiersch bogów* (*Götterdämmerung*). Among others, Grzegorz Fitelberg and Artur Rodzinski conducted as colleagues of Mlynarski. Ewa Bandrowska-Turska, Wanda Werminska, Ada Sari, and Ignacy Dygas were among the outstanding singers.

Things began to go downhill at the beginning of the 1930s with Mlynarski's departure. In order to lure the public, the schedule consisted predominately of operettas. The government eliminated the subsidy and leased the theater to entrepreneurs who produced at their own risk. Although Janina Korolewicz-Waydowa again served as director (1934–1936), the decline could not be stopped. Even guest appearances by the beloved tenor Jan Kiepura did not change the situation. Moreover, at the end of the decade the invasion of German troops again cost Poland her freedom. The final performance before the beginning of the war was Moniuszko's *Straszny dwór* on May 31, 1939. Shortly thereafter, in the fall, the Wielki Teatr became the victim of a German air raid. During the war the Poles were declared undesirables by the Nazi occupation forces, cultural activities were prohibited, and the opera had to comply. For a time, however, there was an official Polish ensemble in the German Theater der Stadt Warschau, which was allowed to perform German operettas in Polish between 1941 and 1944. As an exception, Humperdinck's *Jas i Malgosia* (*Hänsel und Gretel*) was performed.

During the initial postwar years, cultural activity took place under a new liberalization, but that quickly changed under the imposition of new political conditions. Moscow imposed a communist government that immediately determined what would be allowed in the area of culture, including the opera. For the time being, however, the people could enjoy their newly won freedom to the fullest. The first opera performances after 1945 were *Pajace* (*I Pagliacci*) and Moniuszko's *Verbum mobile* in a temporary theater which, until 1948, produced Mozart's *Uprowadzenie z Seraju* (*Die Entführung aus dem Serail*) along with Puccini's *Madama Butterfly*, Gounod's *Faust*, and Moniuszko's *Halka*. The resumption of normal performances of the Warsaw Opera was only possible when the 1,000-seat Roma-Saal, which was under the control of the diocese of Warsaw, was successfully refitted for this purpose. One of the pioneers of opera in Poland, Zygmunt Latoszewski, conducted the inaugural performance of Mozart's *Wesele Figara* (*Le Nozze di Figaro*). Numerous Polish operas were produced along with standards from the international repertoire. Wagnerian opera returned to the schedule with *Lohengrin* in 1953. The first *Halka* in the Roma-Saal, which was conducted by Zygmunt Latoszewski, created a sensation. The prominent Polish director Leon Schiller created a production that emphasized the powerful revolutionary nature of the libretto without relegating the musical score to the background. During the height of the Stalin era, little else was worth noting. The theater was rarely able to plan anything, following instead the directives from above, which led naturally to a paralyzing stagnation of the opera. Between 1949 and 1955 there were only two new productions. Zygmunt Latoszewski acted as director until 1954, followed by Walerian Bierdjajew who served until 1956.

Following the first great workers' rebellion in postwar Poland in 1956, Jerzy Semkow was appointed director of the Warsaw Opera (1959–1961) followed by Bohdan Wodiczko, who was hired to prepare the ensemble for its move back to the Teatr Wielki. His politically based repertoire, however, was criticized: Stravinsky's *Oedipus Rex*, Gluck's *Ifigenia na Taurydzie*, Honegger's *Judith*,

Nono's *Czerwony plaszcz* (*Intolleranza*), Dallapiccola's *Wiezien* (*Il prigioniero*), Ravel's *Daphnis i Chloe*, and various other works that were all much too distant from the historically traditional repertoire. Consequently, the conservative authorities removed Wodiczko, and Witold Rowicki was named artistic director of the newly opened Teatr Wielki. Completely destroyed except for the foundation and the facade, the Teatr Wielki was rebuilt relatively late. Today there is an entirely new theater behind Corazzi's magnificent facade; it has the largest stage possible in a normal opera house, over 2,000 seats but can accommodate 3,500 people; and a foyer and promenades with marble walls and chandeliers of Murano glass. The gala inauguration on November 20, 1965, featuring Moniuszko's *Straszny dwór* was broadcast throughout Europe via television. The production of Jerzy Merunowicz followed conventional paths, and the opera was conducted by Witold Rowicki, who would remain only a single season, to be followed by Zdzislaw Górzynski, himself to remain as artistic director only a few months. Within two months of the opening, eight other productions were mounted, some carried over from the Roma-Saal. In December 1967 the Warsaw Wielki Theater undertook its first foreign tour bringing *Halka*, *Straszny dwór*, *Carmen*, Stravinsky's *Oedipus Rex*, and Karol Szymanowski's *Harnasie* to the Bolshoi Theater in Moscow.

Jan Krenz became the artistic director beginning with the 1968–1969 season, and he conducted *Otello*, *Boris Godunov*, and *Elektra* (directed by Alexander Bardini) as well as an Italian-language *Lucia di Lammermoor* and *Tosca*. Krenz was succeeded by Antoni Wicherek in 1973, who was responsible for a number of contemporary works during his tenure of eight years: Penderecki's *Diably z Loudun*, Menotti's *The Consul*, and George Enescu's *Oedipus*. He also conducted a new production of *Tannhäuser*, with Hanna Lisowska as Elisabeth, and *Holender tulacz* (*Der fliegende Holländer*). Verdi's *Falstaff* was conducted by Kazimierz Kord in a new production by Regina Resnik. With the imposition of martial law following the strike of the independent Solidarity movement, the Teatr Wielki was paralyzed. At the beginning of the season Robert Satanowski took over both as artistic director and Intendant. Despite the adverse prevailing circumstances, he was able to restore stable conditions and to continue to expand and adjust the repertoire. Since the time of his administration, most of the operas are performed in their original language and foreign guests are invited to play certain roles. Alongside the Polish repertoire, program emphasis has also been on the classic Russian operas. The Teatr Wielki's productions of *Boris Godunov*, *Pikowaya Dama*, and *Prince Igor* appeared in many cities, including Jerusalem, Paris, Berlin, Brussels, Athens, and Vienna. There were also tours to Moscow, Dresden, Monte Carlo, and München featuring other operas.

The Chamber Opera of the Teatr Wielki produces contemporary works that are popular in Poland and also result in engagements abroad. For example, Zbigniew Rudzinski's *Manekiny* (*Dummies*) has evolved into a regular export piece. Another strength lies in the German repertoire with Beethoven's *Fidelio*, Mozart's *Die Entführung aus dem Serail*, and the Polish premiere of Alban

Berg's *Wozzeck* as typical examples. Special attention is given to the works of Richard Wagner. Following the return of *Der fliegende Holländer*, Satanowski produced *Der Ring des Nibelungen*, which he personally rehearsed and conducted. August Everding directed and Günther Schneider-Siemssen created the stage settings of what was the Polish premiere of the entire cycle. Polish singers performed alongside guest artists in what was for them an unfamiliar style; one, however, that they eventually mastered, including the difficulties of Wagner's German. Toward the end of the 1980s, when the ruling communist government resigned and a democratic political system replaced the dictatorship, there was no more meddling in cultural affairs. Now the pressing difficulties are of a financial nature. The government has no money, and no one knows who, in the final analysis, will support the Teatr Wielki. This is a question of a theater that has over one thousand employees, not counting the artistic personnel. A new era in the long history of the Teatr Wielki will have to be initiated. How opera without money was possible was demonstrated over two hundred years ago by the Warsaw Opera Kameralna, which did not have its own theater for many years and which was better known outside of Poland than within the country. In any case, that relatively small ensemble became a never to be forgotten institution in the cultural life of Warsaw. Regardless of what happens, one thing is certain: There will never be a Warsaw without opera.

CHRONOLOGY OF ARTISTIC DIRECTORS: Karol Kurpiński, 1833–1840. Tomasz Nidecki, 1840–1852. Ignacy Dobrzyński, 1852–1853. Jan Quattrini, 1853–1874. Stanislaw Moniuszko [Polish operas], 1858–1872. Cezar Trombini, 1874–1881. Adam Minchejmer, 1882–1890, with Józef Rebicek, 1882–1891. Cezar Trombini, 1891–1898. Emil Mlynarski, 1898–1903, with Vittorio Podesti, 1898–1907. Aleksander Rajchman, 1907–1909. Artists' Cooperative, 1909. Francesco Castelano, 1910. Sergiusz Metaxian, 1910. Pietro Cimini, 1910–1914. Aleksander Rajchman, 1914–1915. Piotr Maszynski, 1915. Artists' Cooperative, 1916–1917. Janina Korolewicz-Waydowa, 1917–1918. Employee Cooperative, 1918–1919. Emil Mlynarski, 1919–1929; Piotr Stermich-Valcrociata, 1928–1930. Adolf Poplawski, 1930–1931. Artists' Cooperative, 1931–1934. Janina Korolewicz-Waydowa, 1934–1936. Jerzy Mazaraki, 1936–1938. Artists' Cooperative, 1938. Adam Dolzycki and Ryszard Falkowski, 1938–1939. Eugeniusz Poreda and Kazimierz Poreda, 1945–1948. Witold Rudzinski, 1948–1949. Wiktor Bregy, 1949. Zdzislaw Górzński, 1949–1952. Zygmunt Latoszewski, 1952–1954. Walerian Bierdiajew, 1954–1956. Pawel Kruk, 1956–1957. Tydeusz Bursztynowicz, 1957–1959. Jerzy Semkov, 1959–1961. Bohdan Wodiczko, 1961–1965. Witold Wowicki, 1965–1966. Zdzislaw Górzyński, 1966–1968. Jan Krenz, 1968–1973. Antoni Wicherek, 1973–1980. Robert Satanowski, 1981–present.

BIBLIOGRAPHY: *Almanach sceny polskeij*, 1959/60– . Tomasz Blaszczyk, *Dyrygenci polscy i obey w Polsce dzialajacy w XIX i XX wieku* (Kraków, 1964). *Dwadzieścia piec lat opery Warszawskiej w Polsce Ludowej, 1945–1970* (Warszawa, 1970). Józef Kański, *Teatr Wielki w Warszawie* (Warszawa, 1965). Karol Michalowski, *Opery polskie* (Kraków, 1954). Henryka Secomska, *Repertuar Warzawakich Teatrow Rzadowych, 1863–1890* (Warszawa, 1971). Halina Swietkicka, *Reperuear Teatrow Warszawakich, 1832–1862* (Warszawa, 1968).

ACCESS: Plac Teatralny, 00–076 Warszawa. (48 22) 263 287/288; 263001. Robert Satanowski, Dyrektor.

CARL H. HILLER
TRANS. MARC ÄNDERS

WROCLAW (metro 1,119,000; city 724,000)

Opery Wroclaws

The introduction of opera to the city occurred in 1725 while the area was still part of the Hapsburg empire. Antonio Bioni and Daniel Gottlob Treu managed an Italian ensemble which presented the works of Alberti, Caldara, and Vivaldi as well as their own compositions. Bioni, for example, premiered nineteen of his operas in Breslau, beginning with *Armida al campo* (1726 in the Theater im Ballhause) and ending with *L'odio placato* in 1733. Treu contributed four of his operas, including *Astarto* in 1725 and *Don Chisciotte* in 1727. Breslau became a part of Prussia in 1742, and in 1782 the first real opera house was opened. The next significant operatic event was the appointment of the seventeen-year-old Carl Maria von Weber as conductor in 1804. An opera house designed by Karl Ferdinand Langhans, which was known as the Stadttheater from 1841 to 1933, opened on November 13, 1841, with Goethe's *Egmont*, and the theater quickly became a haven for the production of Wagnerian opera, beginning with *Tannhäuser* in 1852. Following considerable damage due to a fire, the house was rebuilt between 1865 and 1867; it burned down four years later and was again rebuilt. The original seating was in excess of 1,600; by 1940 the auditorium seating had been reduced to 1,129.

As a result of boundary changes following World War II, Breslau (now Wroclaw) became a part of Poland, and a gala performance of Stanislaw Moniuszko's *Halka* on September 8, 1945, initiated a tradition of Polish opera which continues to this day. The former Stadttheater was renamed the Państwowa Opera. The new government nationalized the theater in 1949, providing sufficient financial support so that company could be enlarged. Although special attention is paid to Polish works (Moniuszko, Noskowski, Nowowiejski, Zeleński, and Paderewski, among others), the repertoire includes most of the standard works of the nineteenth and twentieth centuries.

BIBLIOGRAPHY: *Opera Wroclawska, 1945–1965* (Wroclaw, 1966).

ACCESS: Państwowa Opera, Swidnicka 35, 50–066 Wroclaw. (48 71) 386 41. Wiktor Herzig, Dyrektor.

[From materials supplied by the company]

Portugal

LISBON (2,126,400)

Companhia de Opera do Teatro São Carlos

Opera flourished under the patronage of the Portuguese court during the eighteenth century. The Royal Palace Theater as well as the Teatro dos paços da Ribeira (opened on March 31, 1755), the Teatro do Bairro Alto, and the Teatro do Salitre catered to the interest primarily in Italian operas. The Teatro São Carlos opened on June 30, 1793, with Domenico Cimarosa's *La Ballerina amante*, a work that, appropriately enough, had premiered in Naples in 1782. Designed by José da Costa y Silva, the 1,100-seat house was a replica of the San Carlo in Naples, with five tiers, two balconies, and a gallery. In December of the following year, the first opera sung in Portuguese in the new house, Leal Moreira's *A Vingança da Cigana*, premiered. The theater prospered until shortly before World War I, hosted touring companies for several years, and then fell into disuse until it was reopened in 1940 with performances of Rui Coelho's *Dom João IV*. The national government assumed control of the house in 1946, and it quickly became the leading opera house in the country. João di Freitas Branco took over as director in 1970. It currently functions as one of the finest Italian opera houses outside Italy, and includes a sprinkling of French and German repertoire.

BIBLIOGRAPHY: Francisco da Fonseca Benevides, *O Real Theatro de S. Carlos de Lisboa*... (Lisboa, 1883); Francisco da Fonseca Benevides, *O Real Theatro de S. Carlos de Lisboa: Memorias, 1883–1902* (Lisboa, 1902). João de Freitas Branco et al., *O Theatro de San Carlos (1793–1956)* (Lisboa, 1956). Joachim José Marques, *Cronologia da opera em Portugal* (Lisboa, 1947).

ACCESS: Teatro São Carlos, Rua Serpa Pinto 9, 1200 Lisbon. (351 1) 346 8408/346 8610; fax (351 1) 37 17 38. João de Freitas Branco, Director.

[From materials supplied by the company]

Romania

BUCHAREST (1,975,808)

Opera Română (Romanian Opera)

Bucharest became the capital of Romania in 1861. However, the first opera house, Theatrum Vlahicum Bucharestini, opened in 1814, followed in short order by three other theaters. In 1852 the National Theater opened under the direction of Ion Wachmann, giving a focus to the growing cultural life of the city. The repertoire was primarily Italian, although the city itself was quite cosmopolitan. Although there were other companies, the Romanian Opera, which was originally founded in 1877 by George Stephanescu, proved to be the strongest. Following the war, the Romanian Lyric Opera Association produced an *Aida*, led by the composer Ion Nonna Otescu, at the National Theater in 1919, which was patronized by Queen Maria. This venture was so successful that the company was proclaimed a state institution, Opera Română, and was given a theater. This building was destroyed by bombs in 1944, and the new 1,100-seat Opera Română opened in 1953 with Tchaikovsky's *The Queen of Spades*. The new house is currently the major theater for opera.

BIBLIOGRAPHY: Octavian Cosma, *Opera romînaesca: Privire istorica asupra creatiei lirico-dramatice* (Bucureşti, 1962). Ioan Massoff, *Teatrul romînesc; privire istorica* (Bucureşti, 1961).

ACCESS: Blvd. Gheorghe Gheorghiu-Dej 70–72, Bucharest. (40 0) 15 79 39. Petre Brâncuşi, Director.

[From materials supplied by the company]

Republic of South Africa

Opera in South Africa, beginning at an amateur performance level, dates back to 1801. The first, rather primitive, experiences of operatic art were in the Cape, and in the nineteenth century the Cape already boasted an Opera House that catered to visiting ensembles. Local performances as well as productions of grand opera by touring international companies enjoyed good patronage. Thirty years later, with the discovery of gold on the Reef and the foundation of Johannesburg, an opera house—the Theatre Royal—was built, and operas such as *Faust* and *Il Trovatore* were performed, as well as works by Gilbert and Sullivan. Eleven years later a second opera house, the Standard Theatre, was inaugurated. In 1912 the Quinlan Opera Company toured South Africa and presented seasons in Cape Town and Johannesburg that included *Madama Butterfly*, *Faust*, *Lohengrin*, *Tannhäuser*, *Aida*, *Carmen*, and *La Fanciulla del West*. The Johannesburg Operatic and Dramatic Society was established in 1919 and John Connell, one of the founding members, in particular worked tirelessly to bring opera to the people. In the next two decades a number of Italian and German operas were added to the repertoire, and in 1948 Connell inquired about the possibility of a state subsidy, but without success. The next two years saw the production of seventeen operas, one of which, *Die Zauberflöte*, was performed in Afrikaans. From 1950 to 1955, several African theaters promoted opera and made it possible for audiences in Johannesburg, Cape Town, and Durban to hear some outstanding foreign singers. Amongst the visitors were Gigli, Infantino, Fortunati, Frazzoni, Rina Gigli, and the conductor Franco Ghione. The highlight of this period was the visit of the Piccola Scala.

The musical foundations, however, had been laid during the decades between the world wars. In 1926 the Sistine Singers toured South Africa, and one of their members, the tenor Giuseppe Paganelli, recognized the potential of the country and decided to settle in Cape Town. For the next eighteen years he taught singing at the South African College of Music and the University of Cape

Town (UCT). As early as 1929 he staged his first operatic production in the Opera House, and *The Barber of Seville* was enthusiastically received. Comments in the press at the time lamented the shortage of funds which made the training of future artists almost impossible. The next year Paganelli produced Donizetti's *Don Pasquale* with Albina Bini as Norina, and again there was great public and critical acclaim. The fledgling company moved to the Little Theatre in 1933 with Cimarosa's *Il Matrimonio Segreto*, which was a gala occasion with the governor-general of the Union of South Africa in attendance. The reservations concerning the training of singers would be addressed in 1946 with the appointment of Gregorio Fiasconaro as director of the UCT Opera School. By 1956 this young operatic ensemble was advanced enough to tour England with a repertoire of three operas, including Bartok's *Duke Bluebeard's Castle*, and Fiasconaro would become a fixture in opera productions throughout the country in the decades to come.

In 1956 the National Opera Association of South Africa was formed in Johannesburg. The South African Broadcasting Orchestra was engaged to support the productions, and the goals were twofold: to encourage indigenous opera and to provide professional opportunities for South African singers. A few months later the Opera Society of South Africa was formed to promote the performance of opera in Afrikaans. The following year the two organizations merged as the South Africa Opera Foundation, and for the next five years opera productions were controlled by the foundation, which received subsidies from the state, the provinces, and various city councils. An important development was the formation of the Eoan Group in Cape Town in 1933 by Helen Southern-Holt. This has been the most important cultural organization among the Coloured population. Since 1956, in line with other opera groups in the country, the Eoan Group received state and municipal grants. The group grew phenomenally and established a national reputation. Conductor Joseph Manca joined the group in 1943 [he retired in 1977] and in 1949 he presented the first full-length operetta, *A Slave in Araby*, assisted by the Cape Town Municipal Orchestra. By 1956 the company was ready to mount its first opera, *La Traviata* (in Italian), followed by four other works, all produced by Gregorio Fiasconaro. In a decision that heralded a new era in the development of the cultural life of the country, the South African Government decided to subsidize the performing arts in 1962. Five regional performing arts councils were founded in 1963 to promote opera, ballet, music, and drama in the four provinces of Transvaal, Cape, Natal, and the Orange Free State, as well as in South West Africa (Namibia). What had been a minor tributary of the South African way now offered new vistas for entrepreneurs, artists, and the general public. In 1965 the Eoan Group presented a six-opera season in the Cape Town City Hall and went on a second national tour. Opera seasons were also presented by Alessandro Rota in 1967 and 1969. In 1969 the Eoan Group inaugurated their own cultural center, the Joseph Stone Auditorium, in Athlone, and in 1975 the group visited Great Britain and appeared at the International Festival for Youth Orchestras in Aberdeen.

AMANDA BOTHA

CAPE TOWN (1,911,521)

Opera of the Cape Performing Arts Council (CAPAB)

The CAPAB Opera Company was founded in 1964 and presented its first production of Smetana's *The Bartered Bride* in February 1965 in the Alhambra Theatre. Although the house was later demolished, it would remain the company's primary site until 1970. The company had the advantage of casting singers from the established University of Cape Town Opera School and Company. Government policy at the time prevented the engagement of performers from the highly successful Eoan Group. [Prior to the founding of CAPAB Opera, all major operatic activity was generated either by the University Opera Company (founded by Erik Chisholm in 1951) or by the Eoan Group, and many of the country's finest musicians trace their beginnings to one of these two organizations.] In any case, this was a trial period of initial professional experience that would provide the basis of quality for South African opera in the future. The repertoire consisted of standard operatic fare such as *Il Barbiere di Siviglia*, *Carmen*, *Martha*, *La Bohème*, and *Così fan tutte*. In May 1971 the Nico Malan Opera House, a well-equipped theater complex, became the permanent home of CAPAB. Four to six operas in five languages are produced each season for some thirty-five to forty-five thousand spectators in a stagione format. Emphasis is on the standard German and Italian literature, with modern works only rarely produced. CAPAB, like the Performing Arts Council of Transvaal, is a fairly conservative operatic institution, introducing one new opera each season, albeit even then a standard selection.

CAPAB is primarily an indigenous company relying on South African singers, who are given permanent contracts. Guest artists are invited to join the company for a period of two or three seasons, again with fixed contracts. Initially the Cape Town Symphony Orchestra [founded in 1914] supported the productions. In 1971 David Tidboald founded the CAPAB Orchestra, and since its move to the 1,200-seat Nico Malan Opera House that same year, the company has enjoyed the benefit of a permanent musical and technical staff. The complex also houses complete shop facilities and rehearsal spaces. A permanent chorus was established in 1975 with the intention of promoting talented singers into the ranks of the ensemble. Financial support comes entirely from public funds. The current repertoire of the company encompasses some forty-five operas, of which eleven are by Verdi, five by Wagner, and four each by Mozart and Puccini. Some outstanding guest artists have included Leonie Rysanek, Walter Berry, Murray Dickie, Ingrid Bjoner, Nicolai Gedda, Jon Vickers, and Hermann Prey.

BIBLIOGRAPHY: Gregorio Fiasconaro, *I'd Do It Again* (Cape Town, 1982). Jaques P. Malan, ed., *South African Music Encyclopedia* (Cape Town, 1984). Desirée Talbot, *For the Love of Singing: Fifty Years of Opera at UCT* (Cape Town, 1978).

ACCESS: P.O. Box 4107, Cape Town 8000, Cape Province. (27 21) 21 5470. Murray Dickie, Artistic Director.

AMANDA BOTHA

JOHANNESBURG (1,609,408) and PRETORIA ((822,925)

Performing Arts Council of Transvaal (PACT)

With the advent of the four provincial arts councils in 1963, PACT Opera inherited a tradition of opera performed in the Transvaal and particularly in Johannesburg and Pretoria, which it had maintained and enhanced. The first operas presented were *Tosca* and *The Marriage of Figaro* in Afrikaans. For the first eighteen years of its existence, the Civic Theatre in Johannesburg and the Aula Theatre in Pretoria were used. In 1981 the State Theatre in Pretoria was inaugurated with a gala production of Verdi's *Otello*. An average of forty performances of four to six operas per year attracts the support of forty to fifty thousand opera lovers, a substantial total, as neither the Civic Theatre nor the new State Theatre seats many more than one thousand. The repertoire, performed in five languages, spans the literature from Mozart to contemporary works, including those of Benjamin Britten. Its roster includes internationally and locally renowned singers, conductors, directors, and designers. PACT is a fairly conservative operatic institution with a basic repertoire of standard works. Since 1981 it has introduced at least one or two new works each season. The choice is pragmatic and is based on cost and general audience appeal, with both repertoire and casting geared to pleasing potential patrons.

PACT Opera has sought to be an international opera company hosting foreign artists of various nationalities. Nearly all its casts have been cosmopolitan, including both South Africans and foreigners working side by side. In the beginning the company did not have a permanent professional orchestra, chorus, or staff. The original PACT Orchestra founded by Leo Quayle was replaced by the PACT Symphony Orchestra in 1976, and since 1988, PACT Opera has enjoyed the services of the National Orchestra. A permanent chorus was founded in 1980, and with the advent of the State Theatre in 1981, complete craft facilities, shops, and multiple rehearsal halls became available for the first time. Since 1966 the company has engaged a number of contract artists who have performed both leading and supporting roles and who form the core of the resident ensemble. The company depends primarily on public funding, although regular contributions come from both the private sector and individual patrons. The State Theatre also receives assistance from the State Theatre Opera Foundation and the Friends of the Opera. There are currently forty-one operas in the repertoire, including eleven by Verdi, five by Puccini, and three each by Mozart and Wagner. Among the artists who have appeared with the company are Giuseppe Campora, Norman Bailey, Renato Bruson, Tito Gobbi, Franco Tagliavini, Adriana Maliponte, Alfredo Kraus, Fiorenza Cossotto, Peter Glossop, Monserrat Caballé, Martina Arroyo, and Gilda Cruz-Romo.

BIBLIOGRAPHY: Stanley Peskin, *PACT Opera: The First Twenty-Five Years* (Pretoria, 1970).

ACCESS: P.O. Box 566, Pretoria 0001, Transvaal. (27 12) 322 1665; fax (27 12) 322 3913. Johan Maré, Opera General Manager. Neels Hansen, Opera Artistic Director.

AMANDA BOTHA

Spain

BARCELONA (223,444)

Consorci del Gran Teatre del Liceu

Although operas were known to have been presented in Barcelona during the eighteenth century, the importance of the art form in the social and musical life of the city begins with the opening of the Gran Teatre del Liceu on April 4, 1847. Designed by the architect Miquel Garriga i Roca, the 3,500-seat theater was one of the most famous and beautiful in the world. It was constructed by a group of citizens who formed the Liceu Filharmónic de Montesion to raise the necessary funds as the government was not willing to subsidize the project. When the theater was totally destroyed by fire in April 1861, one thousand shares were issued and it was immediately rebuilt to a design by José Oriol Mestres and inaugurated on April 20, 1862. Descendants of those shareholders retained rights to seating until December 1980, when the theater was reorganized under a consortium made up of representatives from the Generalitat of Catalunya, the Barcelona City Council, the Ministry of Culture, the Diputació of Barcelona, and the Association of Opera Box Owners of the Gran Teatre del Liceu. The 1980s marked the first time the theater had received any public subsidy, a recognition of the escalating cost of producing opera.

Considerable damage was done to the building in 1893 by an anarchist bomb attack during a performance of Rossini's *Guglielmo Tell*, but again the citizens of Barcelona rallied to repair it. As one of the most famous lyric theaters in the world, the Gran Teatre del Liceu has hosted the finest vocalists in Europe as well as leading conductors, designers, dancers, and choreographers. Gris, Picasso, Miró, and Dalí all painted sets for various productions. The house has presented such memorable events as the first European *Parsifal* outside Bayreuth and the Spanish debuts of Nijinsky and Anna Pavlova. Grandiose and cosmopolitan, it was a fitting location for the triumphant debut of Victoria de los Angeles in Mozart's *Le Nozze di Figaro* in 1945.

The opera season typically runs in December and January and includes some eight to ten operas. Prior to reorganization the house produced twenty works in a season, but this was reduced to sixteen in 1985–1986 (sixty performances) and further reduced in 1990–1991 (thirteen operas with sixty-five performances), and the projection for 1991–1992 is for one hundred performances of eight to ten works. The house expects a maximum audience of twenty-eight thousand for the 1991–1992 season. Under the new system, progress has been made toward the building of a permanent resident ensemble, ballet, chorus, and orchestra. Uwe Mund was appointed the official conductor in 1987 and entrusted with the job of building a quality company. There are plans to associate native artists with the company so that international stars can be brought in to completed productions essentially to highlight the season rather than serving as the entire operation, as was the case in the past. As one of the world's oldest continually operating theaters, the Consorci del Gran Teatre del Liceu has offered a varied program of ballets, concerts, operas, and recitals for almost 150 years, and with its new orientation it looks forward to a healthy and productive artistic future.

BIBLIOGRAPHY: Marcos Jesus Bertran, *El gran Teatre del Liceu de Barcelona: 1837–1930* (Barcelona, 1931). *Cien años del Liceo: 1847–1947* (Barcelona, 1948). Juan Mestres y Calvert, *El gran Teatro del Liceo visto por su empresario* (Barcelona, 1946). José Subirá, *La ópera en los teatros de Barcelona*, 2 vols. (Barcelona, 1960).

ACCESS: El gran Teatro del Liceu, C. Sant Pau, 1 bis, 08001 Barcelona. (34 3) 318 91 22, 318 91 73. Uwe Mund, Music Director.

[From materials supplied by the company]
TRANS. EVA BEAUDET

MADRID (3,123,713)

Asociación Amigos de la Opera de Madrid

Operas were being performed in Madrid as early as 1635, and by the end of the century, elaborate productions were being mounted for the court. Italian opera seria flourished under the patronage of Philip V, who brought the famous castrato Farinelli to Spain. Following Philip's death in 1746, Italian opera fell in and out of favor. Important theaters that produced opera at that time included the Teatro de los Caños del Peral and the Teatro del Príncipe. Ramón Carnicer's operas dominated the musical scene in Madrid during the first half of the nineteenth century, but after his death in 1855 the new zarzuela achieved unprecedented popularity. The birth of this typically Spanish music drama was signaled by the premiere of Rafael José María Hernando's *Colegialas y Soldados* on March 21, 1849, at the Teatro Comedia. Hernando's works, together with those of Gastambide (*La Mansajera* premiered on December 24, 1849, at the Teatro del Príncipe) and Francisco Asenjo Barbieri (*Gloria y Peluca* premiered on March

9, 1850, at the Teatro Variedades), entertained generations of theatergoers. By the end of the century as many as ten theaters in the capital were devoted exclusively to this Spanish art form. Two theaters, however, continued the traditions of Italian opera: the Royal Palace Theater, which was supported by Isabel II, and the Teatro Real, which opened on the site of the old Teatro de los Caños del Peral on November 19, 1850, with Donizetti's *La Favorita*. Until it closed in 1925, the Teatro Real was a bastion of Italian opera in Madrid. Royalty and society figures frequented performances of Rossini, Bellini, Donizetti and Verdi, the latter being a particular favorite. *La Forza del Destino* was given its Spanish premiere on February 21, 1863, only two weeks after its first Italian performance in Rome, and Verdi was in Madrid for the occasion.

The closure of the Teatro Real marked the end of an impressive musical era. One of the greatest European opera houses would remain silent for over forty years, leaving the capital of Spain without a showcase for major artistic events. The Friends of the Opera Association of Madrid was created in 1962 to address this problem. Its objective was the promotion of concerts and recitals, ballets, zarzuelas, and especially opera. Especially active during the Madrid opera season, the association also publishes books and other materials related to its mission, produces recordings, organizes contests, funds scholarships, and promotes musical research. The first season was organized in 1964 with a production of *Tosca* in the Zarzuela Theater. [Teatro Lirico Nacional La Zarzuela, Jovellanos 4, 28014 Madrid (34 1) 429 82 85; fax (34 1) 429 71 57.] That initial season also included *La Bohème*, *La Cenerentola*, *Il Trovatore*, *Don Giovanni*, *Faust*, and three popular zarzuelas. The Teatro Real reopened on October 13, 1966, with Frühbeck de Burgos conducting a performance of Beethoven's Ninth Symphony. Opera reappeared in the house with performances of Handel's *Giulio Cesare*. Since then the association has presented 143 works in 697 performances through the 1989–1990 season. The twenty-fifth anniversary season included productions of *Lulu*, *La Bohème*, *Die Entführung aus dem Serail*, *Adriana Lecouvreur*, Verdi's *Attila*, and *Les Contes d'Hoffmann*. The Teatro Real is currently being renovated and is scheduled to reopen as the new home of the Teatro Lírico Nacional.

BIBLIOGRAPHY: J. Borrell, *Sesenta años de musica, 1876–1936* (Madrid, 1945). M. Muñoz, *Historia del Teatro Real* (Madrid, 1946). Gaspar Gómez de la Serna, *Gracias y desgracias del Teatro Real* (Madrid, 1975). A. Martinez Olmedilla, *Los teatros de Madrid* (Madrid, 1947). José Subirá, *Historia y anecdotario del Teatro Real* (Madrid, 1949). José Subirá, *El teatro del Real Palacio* (Madrid, 1950).

ACCESS: Escuela Superior de Canto, Calle San Bernardo 24, 28015 Madrid. (34 1) 521 20 18). D. José Luis Martín de Bustamente, President.

[From materials supplied by the company]
TRANS. DELFINA SABOGAL-TORI

Sweden

STOCKHOLM (1,617,038)

Drottningholms Slottsteater

The story of the Drottningholm Palace Theater outside Stockholm is a fairy tale that includes a malicious queen, a king who is assassinated, and a theater that slept for 125 years only to be reawakened in 1921. Along with the famous Markgräfliches Opernhaus in Bayreuth, the Slottsteater is one of the world's best preserved theaters and dates from the 1700s. The original stage machinery works perfectly with ropes and pulleys, and scenery changes can be managed in a matter of seconds. Colors shift, locations are altered, and clouds disappear with all the charm of a magical toy box. The original theater had been finished in 1754, but it burned to the ground some eight years later. Queen Lovisa Ulrika, wife of Adolph Fredrik and sister of Frederick the Great, replaced the structure with a larger theater designed by Karl Fredrik Adelkrantz, which was built between 1764 and 1766. At that time Drottningholm was the royal summer palace and had no entertainment. The new theater with its thirty-five boxes and bedrooms quickly became a favorite of the touring French and Italian opera troupes. The architect had to use the simplest materials in construction; wood, papier-mâché, and plaster painted gold and trimmed with marble. Even today the salon and scenery look as they did over two hundred years ago: No fundamental restoration has been done to alter the original look. The theatrical fare of the time was relatively simple, but the productions were filled with dazzling scenic and acoustical effects.

When Queen Ulrika's only son, Gustaf III, became king in 1771, a brilliant era of literature and the arts flowered in Sweden. Gustaf authored a number of plays and poems and, indeed, was responsible for the plots of several Swedish operas. The country, however, suffered politically from rival factions, and the king forced his parliament to accept a new constitution. He believed in an informed despotism, and a number of his nobles conspired against him. His assassination at a masked ball in Stockholm on March 16, 1792, became the plot for Giuseppe Verdi's famous *Un ballo in maschera*. With his death, theatrical performances ceased, and over the years from 1800 until World War I the theater became a museum for art filled only by guests at garden parties and by the children of visiting royalty. Some 229 years after the Drottningholm Castle theater had slipped into obscurity, a civil servant by the name of Agne Beiger visited the castle and realized immediately that it represented a unique treasure. He worked tirelessly to promote the idea of restoring Queen Ulrika's legacy, as well as that of her son, and after a thorough reconstruction, the theater was ready for the public in 1922. The Kungliga Teatern (Royal Opera) in Stockholm gave occasional opera and ballet performances, but the potential of the neglected theater was yet to be realized. During the reconstruction it was thought that much of the original machinery would have to be replaced, but the old designs were found to work remarkably well. Scenery stage hands in the cellar could, by way of a remarkable winch system, quickly change the seven major beams; the five corkscrew-shaped cylinders could still make billows in the background; stones hitting stones sounded like horrendous thunder; and the rippling sailcloth, when turned, sounded like the wind. The old system triumphed over modern technology and even today has been copied. No other theater of that era can boast of anything like Drottningholm. The theater is in a wonderful class by itself, historically, architecturally, and technically.

For the first time in 1946 the management team was allowed to mount its own performances. For over two decades the theater had been touted as a museum curiosity; now, the administration looked for ways in which to make Drottningholm a Swedish institution. A search for young native talent was undertaken, and in 1947 Elisabeth Söderström made her debut at the palace theater. Little did the young artist know then that she would be designated head of that theater effective 1993. Gustaf Hilleström was artistic director from 1946 to 1967, and under his leadership the repertoire featured the dramas of Corneille, Racine, and Molière, as well as revivals of the operas of Uttini, Gluck, and Monsigny—repertoire of the 1700s and the 1940s. Little by little, Pergolesi, Scarlatti, and Cimarosa entered the repertoire, and the Royal Opera in Stockholm was encouraged to increase its commitment. Prominent conductors such as Sixten Ehrling, János Ferencsik, Albert Woolf, Sten Frykberg, Lamberto Gardelli, Raymond Leppard, Charles Farcombe, and Sergio Comissiona were engaged. The big international breakthrough came when Queen Elizabeth of England visited the theater in 1956, attracting other royalty and members of the world press.

In 1968 Bertil Bokstedt succeeded Hilleström and instituted a new artistic direction. Theatrical irony replaced historical resurrection, and outstanding producers from around the world were invited to Drottningholm to stage productions in a contemporary style. Götz Friedrich realized his conception of Mozart's *Così fan tutte*, and his colleagues produced other modern European realizations of both standards and historical revivals. Arnold Östman, the present artistic director, has had a slightly different concept since his appointment in 1980. The Swedish government provided a larger subsidy but with the provision that the performance schedule be reduced, thus making historical restorations a moot issue. Östman opted for a production concept that stressed original instrumentation with period instruments. Mozart's *Don Giovanni*, cast with young singers including Helena Döse, Anita Soldh, and Gösta Winbergh, was the first experiment in this concept, and it was an immediate success. Unfortunately, the producer, Göran Järvefelt, died, and the psychological realism he brought to the theater will be missed in future seasons. However, the works of Mozart in honor of the bicentennial (*Idomeneo* and *La Finta Giardiniera*) and a cycle of Gluck's operas, beginning with *Iphigenie en Tauride*, are projected at the core of the repertoire, and the productions of the Drottningholm Slottsteater will continue to make their mark on the international operatic scene through live performances, recordings, and broadcasts over Swedish Television.

BIBLIOGRAPHY: Margarete Baur-Heinhold, *Theater des Baroque: Festliches Bühnenspiel im 17. und 18. Jahrhundert* (München, 1966). Agna Beijer, *Drottningholms slottsteater på Lovisa Ulrikas och Gustaf IIIs tid* (Stockholm, 1981). Gustav Hilleström, *The Drottningholm Theatre: Past and Present* (Stockholm, 1980).

ACCESS: Drottningholms Teatermuseum, Box 27050, 102 51 Stockholm. (46 8) 665 1400; fax (46 8) 661 0194. Per Forsström, General Manager. Arnold Östman, Artistic Director.

LARS RING
TRANS. ASTRID SUNDELÖF

Kungliga Teatern (Royal Opera)

Credit for the founding of the Royal Opera in Stockholm belongs to King Gustaf III, who, upon assuming the throne, decided to create a Swedish national theater to stem the growing French influence on Swedish culture. He began with that most difficult of arts forms, the opera, without any soloists, chorus, or ballet under his command. In addition, no suitable theater for the production of opera was available. The one component that he did not lack was an orchestra, the Hofkapelle, which had served the royal family since 1526 and which to this day serves as the opera orchestra of the theater. On the strength of his position, in combination with an unusually high interest in and knowledge of the theater, he assembled an ensemble and engaged the Italian composer Francesco Uttini to write an opera based on a libretto by the Swedish author Johan Wellander. There was a dance hall in the old city next to the castle which was renovated into a theater. The French ensemble that was using the hall was dismissed by the king, and he furnished the small building sparingly for his opera. Thus, on January 18, 1773, the Royal Opera was initiated with the premiere of Uttini's *Thetis och Pelée*. [A portion of the opera was revived for the 150th anniversary of the Stockholm opera house on January 18, 1923.] Christoph Willibald Gluck was introduced to the Swedish public on November 25, 1773, with Uttini's arrangement of *Orfeo ed Euridice*, and shortly thereafter *Iphigenia in Aulis* [on December 29, 1778] and *Alceste* [on February 26, 1781] were both produced in the dance hall. Uttini's last opera, *Aline Drotning uti Golconda*, was premiered on January 11, 1776.

King Gustav III was well aware of the fact that unless a suitable theater could be built, his operatic dream would not be able to flourish. He therefore engaged the architect of the Drottningholm Slottsteater, Karl Fredrik Adelcrantz, to build an opera house in the vicinity of his castle. After nine seasons in the renovated dance hall, the ensemble moved into the new opera house which was built on the same site where the present house stands. The gala opening took place on September 30, 1782, with the premiere of Johann Gottlieb Naumann's *Cora och Alonzo*. [The opera was revived for the one hundredth anniversary of the theater.] The second premiere in the new house was Gluck's *Iphigenie auf Tauris* [on May 5, 1783]. This decade, the memorable Gustav era, signaled a golden age for the Swedish theater and musical life in general. Particularly notable were productions of Naumann's *Gustav Wasa* [which premiered on January 19, 1786], Johann Häffner's *Elektra* [which premiered at the palace on July 22, 1787, and was then performed at the Royal Theater on December 10], Georg Vogler's *Gustav Adolf och Ebbe Brahe* [which premiered on January 24, 1788], and Josef Martin Kraus's *Soliman den II* [which premiered on September 22, 1789; Kraus had succeeded Uttini as Hofkapellmeister]—all works that some two hundred years later are again in the repertoire. This glorious epoch ended tragically with the assassination of the king by conspiring nobles during a costume ball in the opera house on March 16, 1792. Following the death of Gustav III, the dance hall was torn down. His successor, King Gustav IV Adolf, was interested neither in opera nor in music, and everything that Gustav III had founded and supported came to an end, culminating with the closing of the opera house in 1806. The theater was empty until 1812, when it reopened. It remained active until 1891, when it was demolished to make way for the current structure.

The work of Mozart first appeared with the Swedish premiere of *Die Zauberflöte* [in Swedish on May 30, 1812], and all the composer's major operas had been produced by 1830. During this period, until 1825 when the theater burned down, the Arsenalsteater presented some fifty premieres of the lighter operas of such composers as Paisiello and Cimarosa, works that now grace the stage of the newly rediscovered Drottningholms Slottsteater. Jenny Lind is thought to have made her operatic debut in Stockholm in the premiere of Adolf Lindblad's *Frondörerna* on May 11, 1835. Both Verdi and Wagner were born in the year during which Mozart's *Don Giovanni* was premiered [December 6, 1813, in Swedish] in Stockholm. Decades would pass before the works of these masters were produced; initially, Verdi's *Macbeth* [April 29, 1852] and Wagner's *Rienzi* [June 5, 1865]. The operas of Adam, Auber, and Meyerbeer were popular, and Beethoven's *Fidelio* [April 14, 1832], Weber's *Die Freischütz* [June 21, 1863], and Bizet's *Carmen* [March 22, 1878] all found their way into the repertoire. During the 1880s a severe economic crisis gripped the nation and the government was forced to curtail the subsidy for the opera. At the same time there was strong support among the populace for a larger, modern opera house. The physical deterioration of the old Gustav Opera House made it imperative to replace it with a new structure. *Die Meistersinger von Nürnberg*, *The Tales of Hoffmann*, and *Otello* were the last premieres presented in the old house before the final performance on November 30, 1891.

In the interim period operas were performed in the 1,000-seat Nya Svenska Theater (which was destroyed by fire in 1925), which had a stage suitable for large productions. Among the twenty-five operas that were premiered in this house, *Die Walkühre*, *Falstaff*, *Hänsel und Gretel*, *Pagliacci*, *Manon*, and *The Bartered Bride* are among the most notable. The new 1,264-seat Royal Opera House was inaugurated on September 19, 1898, with portions of Franz Berwald's *Estrella de Soria* [which premiered on May 12, 1862]. Designed by Axel Anderberg, the theater exemplified the typical nineteenth-century opera house and was equipped with state-of-the-art stage machinery and fire protection devices. A major artistic achievement of the new theater was the production of the complete "Ring" cycle between March 14 and 20, 1907, in Swedish. Several years after the composer's performance ban expired in 1913, *Parsifal* was premiered in Stockholm on April 21, 1917. The operas of Puccini and Richard Strauss were added to the repertoire along with the works of native composers such as Wilhelm Stenhammar [*Tirfing* premiered in the new house on December 9, 1898, followed by *Das Fest auf Solhaug* on October 31, 1902] and Wilhelm Peterson-Berger [*Ran* premiered on May 20, 1903; *Arnjolt* premiered on April 13, 1910; and *Adils och Elisiv* premiered on February 27, 1927]. Since its premiere over eighty years ago, *Arnjolt* has become almost a national opera.

[Over the years a number of outstanding singers have made their debuts in the Royal Opera House, including Jussi Björling (1930), Julia Claussen (1903), Nanny Larsén-Todsen (1906), Oscar Ralf (1918), Set Svanholm (1930), Kirsten Thorberg (1924), and Gertrude Wettergren (1922); and after the war, Nicolai Gedda (1951), Berit Lindholm (1963), Kirsten Meyer (1952), and Birgit Nilsson (1946).] The current company includes 45 soloists, a 72-member chorus, an orchestra of 115 musicians, and some 700 administrative and technical support personnel. The season includes 240 performances split approximately into 70 percent opera and 30 percent ballet. Fifteen operas and six ballets are in the repertoire, which includes four new opera productions and two ballet premieres each season. The company also performs in both the Drottningholms Slottstheater and the Södra Teatern. Since the Second World War the company has undertaken a number of tours throughout Sweden and the world.

CHRONOLOGY OF GENERAL DIRECTORS (SINCE 1892): Axel Burén, 1892–1907. Artur Tiel, 1907–1908. Albert Ranft, 1908–1910. Hans von Stedingk, 1910–1919. Karl Axel Riben, 1919–1924. John Forsell, 1924–1939. Harald André, 1939–1949. Joel Berglund, 1949–1956. Set Svanholm, 1956–1963. Göran Gentele, 1963–1971. Bertil Bokstedt, 1971–1978. Folke Abenius, 1978–1984. Lars af Malmborg, 1984–1987. Eskil Hemberg, 1987–present.

BIBLIOGRAPHY: Klas Ralf, *Jubelboken Operan 200 år* (Stockholm, 1963). Klas Ralf,

Kungliga Teatern: Repertoar 1773-1973 (Stockholm, 1974). Alfred Rundberg, *Svensk operakonst: Kultur och form* (Stockholm, 1952). Ake Sällström, *Opera pa Stockholmsoperan* (Stockholm, 1977).

ACCESS: P.O. Box 16094, 103 22 Stockholm. (46 8) 22 17 40. Eskil Hemberg, General Manager; Gary Berkson, Music Director.

ERIK-GUSTAV RÖDIN
TRANS. MARC ÄNDERS

Switzerland

BERN (metro 932,577; city 135,500)

Stadttheater Bern

The first theater to host visiting ensembles in Bern was the Ballenhaus, which was built in 1678. A group of local citizens formed a limited corporation in 1776 in order to build a new theater and concert hall. Designed by Niklaus Sprüngli, the Hôtel de Musique was built between 1767 and 1769, but regular performances date only from 1800 when the French acting company St.-Gérand performed plays and operas in the theater. When the manager absconded with the receipts the very next year, St.-Gérand was replaced by a Germany company in 1803. Mozart's *Die Zauberflöte* was presented in the old theater in 1796, and *Don Giovanni* was presented in the Hôtel de Musique in 1812, followed by *Der Freischütz* in 1823 and *Fidelio* in 1836. The municipality of Bern began subsidizing the theater in 1837, and since that time the house has presented regular seasons with a permanent staff. The auditorium was renovated in 1838, and gas lighting was introduced in 1843. When Bern became the capital of the Swiss confederation in 1848, new emphasis was given to the theater. Verdi's *Attila* was produced in 1850, followed by Wagner's *Tannhäuser* in 1857. The first Swiss performance of Wagner's *Tristan und Isolde* took place on March 18, 1889. Humperdinck's *Hänsel und Gretel* was performed on February 27, 1895, and lit by the modern wonder of electricity.

Discussions began that same year about the need for a new theater, and the last performance in the old theater, Gounod's *Faust*, took place on April 6, 1900. [The theater was completely restored in 1981 as a historical monument.] The architect René von Wurstemberger was contracted in November 1897, and he proposed a Renaissance-style theater with an interior designed after the Opéra Comique in Paris. The new 940-seat Haus am Kornhausbrücke opened on September 25, 1903, with a gala performance of Wagner's *Tannhäuser* conducted by Paul Wolff. Some five years later, in April 1908, a gala production of *Der Ring des Nibelungen* was mounted. Only ten months after the Dresden premiere, Richard Strauss's *Der Rosenkavalier* was produced. Richard Strauss conducted his own *Elektra* and *Ariadne auf Naxos*, and Arthur Nikisch, assisted by the young Bruno Walter, conducted Wagner's operas and Hans Pfitzner's *Palestrina*. During the 1970s a number of contemporary works were produced, including the Swiss premiere of Jan Cikkers's *Spiel von Liebe und Tod* (1970) and *Auferstehung* (1978) and the European premieres of Rolf Liebermann's *Penelope* (1971) and Antonio Carlos Gomez's *Lo Schiavo*. The house also produced the German-language premieres of Rossini's *Mit List zum Ziel* (1972) and Donizetti's *Der überlistete Vater* (1975). The house was closed during the 1982–1983 and 1983–1984 seasons for extensive remodeling and rebuilding, and reopened on October 20, 1984, with a gala performance of *Tannhäuser*. The 1989–1990 season included productions of *Parsifal, Die lustigen Weiber von Windsor, Il Trovatore, Rusalka, Albert Herring,* Franz Schubert's *Alfonso und Estrella, Die Entführung aus dem Serail,* and *Eine Nacht in Venedig*. The current company employs forty-five soloists, a thirty-five-member chorus, and an orchestra of ninety-two musicians.

CHRONOLOGY OF DIRECTORS: Georg Kiedaich, 1903–1906. Alfred Stender-Stefani and Julius Bergmann, 1906–1908. Benno Koebke, 1908–1914. Albert Kehm, 1914–1920. Ludwig Peppler, 1920–1925. Hans Kauffmann, 1925–1931. Karl Lustig-Prean, 1931–1934. Hans Zimmermann, 1934–1937. Eugen Keller, 1937–1946. Ekkehard Kohlund, 1947–1953. Stephan Beinl, 1953–1958. Dr. Albert Nef, 1958–1959. Walter Oberer, 1960–1979. Wolfgang Zörner, 1979–1981. Edgar Kelling, 1981–1987. Philippe de Poros, 1987–1990. Edgar Kelling, 1990–1991. Elice Grauss, 1991–present.

BIBLIOGRAPHY: Peter Tschanz, ed., *Stadttheater Bern: Unser Theater* (Bern, 1984).

ACCESS: Nägeligasse 1, CH-3000 Bern 7. (41 31) 21 17 11; fax (41 31) 22 39 47. Edgar Kelling, Direktor.

[From materials supplied by the company]
TRANS. MARC ÄNDERS

GENEVA (371,356)

Grand Théâtre de Genève

Although the city of Geneva is geographically situated in a region where French, German, and Italian cultures meet, it has not played a historical role in the history of opera in Europe. Ironically, the modern history of the theater in Geneva begins with Jean-Jacques Rousseau's famous "Lettre à d'Alembert" in which he argued against the corrupting influences of the theater. Religious constraints and social conventions were potent forces of the day. The 800-seat Théâtre de Rosimond ("Foreigner's Barn") at the corner of the Place Neuve was built in 1766 and remained open for only two years before burning down in January 1768 after some 144 performances. André Grétry composed his first

French opera, *Isabelle et Gertrude*, in Geneva in 1767, and this work appears to be among the first operas performed in the city. The 940-seat (plus 160 standing room) Théâtre de Neuve designed by the architect Matthey opened on the same site on July 2, 1782. Initially, only plays were produced, but gradually, Mozart's operas as well as contemporary Italian works were performed. Without a permanent company, the city had to depend on visiting artists and touring ensembles primarily from Germany and Italy to keep their opera alive. A special event occurred in January 1850 when Marietta Alboni visited Geneva to perform Donizetti's *La Favorite* to enthusiastic audiences and rave reviews. A typical eighteenth-century house, the Théâtre de Neuve was active until its demolition in 1874, albeit without any particular artistic or musical distinction. That year the new Grand Théâtre de Genève was begun, a smaller version of the Palais Garnier in Paris designed by the architect Jacques-Elysée Goss that copied the facade of l'Opéra de Paris. Thanks to the legacy of the duke of Brunswick, the city of Geneva could afford a luxurious new theater, which seated 1,300 with standing room for another 100 people. When the new Grand Théâtre opened with Rossini's *Guglielmo Tell* on October 4, 1879, Geneva finally had a suitable home for a permanent company. A permanent chorus and ballet supported the guest artists during the opera season. Early premieres in the theater included Louis Lacombe's *Winkelried* on February 17, 1892, and Emil Jaques-Dalcroze's *Janie* on March 13, 1894, followed by *Sancho Panza* on December 13, 1897, and Louis Aubert's *La Forêt bleue* on January 7, 1913.

The auditorium and the stagehouse were completely destroyed by a fire during a performance of Wagner's *Die Walküre* on May 1, 1951. Between 1952 and 1962 performances took place under less than ideal circumstances in the Casino-Théâtre; the present 1,500-seat Grand Théâtre opened on December 10, 1962, with Verdi's *Don Carlos* in the original French version. Construction took a prolonged time because the first proposal for reconstruction was turned down after a referendum; a more expensive, revised proposal was later accepted. The new Grand Théâtre was inaugurated as a foundation subsidized by the city of Geneva. Under the direction of the architects Schopfer (Geneva) and Zavelani-Rossi (Milan), the foyer was restored in the original style of the Second Empire. Operating under a stagione system augmented by visits from other companies, which have included the English Opera Group and the Brno Opera, the company presents some eight operas and two ballets each season for a total of seventy-five to eighty performances. The audience reaches some one hundred thousand each season. The theater has never had its own orchestra, opting instead to use the renown Orchestre de la Suisse Romande [founded by the conductor Ernest Ansermet in his hometown in 1918, the same year he conducted the premiere of Stravinsky's *L'Histoire du soldat*] or occasionally the Orchestre de Chambre de Lausanne. Marcel Lamy was director from 1962 to 1965; Lamy was succeeded by Herbert Graf in 1965 who opened his first season with a stunning *Die Zauberflöte* conducted by Ansermet and featuring sets by Kokoscha; Graf was succeeded in 1973 by Jean-Claude Riber (1973 to 1980); and Hugues Gall has been the director from 1980 to the present.

BIBLIOGRAPHY: Roger de Candolle, *Histoire du théâtre de Genève* (Genève, 1978). Jean-Jacques Roth, *Grand théâtre de Genève: Operas—Moments d'exception* (Paris, 1987).

ACCESS: 11, Boulevard du Théâtre, CH-1211 Genève 11. (41 22) 21 23 18. Hugues R. Gall, General Director.

[From materials supplied by the company]
TRANS. RENÉE SCHMUKI AND EVA BEAUDET

LUZERN (311,761)

Stadttheater Luzern

In contrast to practically all other European countries, theaters in Switzerland never have been the domain of the aristocracy. In countries surrounding the oldest republic on the Continent, opera houses were founded and guided by men from the nobility, while the theaters in Swiss towns owed their origin to the Catholic church, on the one hand, and the citizens of Protestant towns, on the other. In Lucerne, the only relatively large town of Catholic Central Switzerland, the Jesuits played a leading role in both sacred and secular theater. From 1480 on, public plays in marketplaces, and later in courtyards and churches, paved the way for a 500-seat theater that was built by the Jesuits in 1740, the Comödienhaus. When the religious order was disbanded in 1773, the town took over the theater. Plans were discussed as early as 1812 to replace the old theater, and the last performance took place in 1834. Designed by Louis Pfyffer, the new theater on the river Reuss next to the Jesuit church was begun in 1837 and opened in 1839 with a performance of Schiller's *Wilhelm Tell*. The city of Lucern assumed control of the theater in 1840, and a number of renovations and expansions took place over the next one hundred years. The 558-seat house was completely renovated and improved between 1968 and 1970. It reopened on March 14, 1970, with a festive performance of Molière's *Die gelehrten Frauen*. This theater is the only one in Switzerland that is not dependent on a foundation, a joint-stock company, or a board of directors. Its director is responsible to one of the town councilors, and its funding comes from the town and the twenty-five surrounding communities, which are, in turn, provided with guest performances primarily by the "Opera Factory" and the Schweizer Gastspiel-Oper.

The Lucerne Stadttheater has, in recent years, taken part in the International Music Festival Lucerne. The world premiere of Kurt Schwertsik's *Der lange Weg zur grossen Mauer* was performed in Lucerne on May 14, 1975, and the theater has produced a number of Swiss premieres, including Verdi's *Die beiden Foscari* (1971), Menotti's *Help, Help, the Globolinks* (1971), Prokofiev's *Die Verlobung im Kloster* (1976), Donizetti's *Maria Stuarda* (1979), Shostakovich's

Die Nase (1979), Britten's *Owen Wingrave* (1987), and Henze's *Die englische Katze* (1988). The 1990–1991 season included productions of *Der Troubador, West Side Story, Eugene Onegin, Wiener Blut, Der Türke in Italien, Die Zauberflöte,* and *Die Entführung aus dem Serail.* The current company employs twenty-seven soloists, a sixteen-member chorus, and an orchestra.

BIBLIOGRAPHY: André Gottrau, ed., *Luzern und sein Theater: 150 Jahre Stadttheater* (Luzern, 1989).

ACCESS: Theaterstraße 2, CH-6002 Luzern. (41 41) 23 33 63; fax (41 41) 23 33 67. Horst Statkus, Direktor.

[From materials supplied by the company]
TRANS. MARC ÄNDERS

ZÜRICH (metro 1,141,494; city 360,000)

Opernhaus Zürich

As the largest city in Switzerland and the cultural capital of the German-speaking population, Zürich plays a major role in the arts of the country. At the center of musical life in the city is the Tonhalle Orchestra, which has been a professional organization since 1868. Prior to that time the orchestra played for opera productions in the Aktientheater from 1834 until it burned down in 1890. Built by the Viennese architects Ferdinand Fellner and Hermann Helmer, the Aktientheater opened on November 10, 1834, and was home to a number of visiting artists, including Wilhelmine Schröder-Devrient in 1843. As the center of Richard Wagner's activities during his Zürich exile, the composer conducted a number of operas during the 1850–1851 season, including *Der Freischütz, Die Weisse Dame, Norma, Don Giovanni, Die Zauberflöte,* and *Fidelio.* The first Swiss performance of *Der fliegende Holländer* took place in the Aktientheater on April 25, 1852. conducted by the composer. The fiftieth anniversary of the house was celebrated on November 1, 1884, and six years later the building was destroyed by fire on January 1, 1890.

So successful had the opera become that a new theater, the 1,100-seat Stadttheater, was built in 1890–1891, opening on September 30 with the first performance (Wagner's *Lohengrin*) taking place the next day. Wilhelm Furtwängler was hired in 1906, and the history of the Stadttheater from that time is rich in cultural highlights: The city hosted an international opera festival as early as 1909; the first authorized production of *Parsifal* outside Bayreuth (Wagner's personal ban expired on December 31, 1913, some thirty years after the composer's death) was in Zürich on April 13, 1913, after the Swiss copyright had expired; and the Darmstadt Opera under Felix Weingartner guested in 1917, the same season Arthur Nikisch conducted *Tristan und Isolde,* and Strauss conducted his *Elektra.* That fall Bruno Walter conducted Pfitzner's *Palestrina* in the composer's staging; Ferruccio Busoni, Paul Hindemith, Richard Strauss, Othmar Schoeck, Arthur Honegger, Frank Martin, and other famous composers exerted their influence in the musical development of the theater, which has always supported contemporary works. The world premieres of Berg's *Lulu* (two acts and fragments of the third act were performed on June 2, 1937), Hindemith's *Mathis der Mahler* (May 28, 1938), and the European premiere of Gershwin's *Porgy and Bess* (1945), as well as the initial staging of Schönberg's *Moses und Aron* (June 6, 1957) took place in Zürich. More recently, *Madame Bovary* by Heinrich Sutermeister, *Ein wahrer Held* (1975) by Giselher Klebe, and *Ein Engel kommt nach Babylon* and *Der Kirschgarten* by Rudolf Kelterborn all received premieres in the theater.

During the tenure of Claus Helmut Drese as director (1975–1986) the company produced a Monteverdi cycle in cooperation with Nikolaus Harnoncourt and Jean-Pierre Ponnelle. *L'Orfeo*, *L'Incoronazione di Poppea*, and *Il Ritorno d'Ulisse in Patria* were recorded on both film and compact disk, and the company toured the three productions in Germany, England, and La Scala in Italy for the two hundredth anniversary of that distinguished house. During the renovation and expansion of the theater from 1982 to 1984, the company maintained an "opera mobile program," performing on stage and in concert in a variety of different venues throughout Zürich. The house reopened on December 1, 1984, with Wagner's *Die Meistersinger von Nürnberg* and *Der Kirschgarten* commissioned from Rudolf Kelterborn especially for the occasion. The company currently employs 199 soloists including guests, a 50-member chorus, and an orchestra of 101 musicians.

CHRONOLOGY OF DIRECTORS: Paul Schroetter, 1891–1896. Ludwig Treutler, 1896–1898, Karl Skraup, 1898–1901. Alfred Reucker, 1901–1921. Paul Trede, 1921–1932. Karl Schmid-Bloss, 1932–1947. Hans Zimmermann, 1947–1956. Karl-Heinz Krahl, 1956–1960. Herbert Graf, 1960–1962. Emil Jucker, Werner Meyer, and Christian Vöchting, 1962–1964. Hermann Juch, 1964–1975. Claus Helmut Drese, 1975–1986. Christoph Groszer, 1986–1991. Alexander Pereira, 1991–present.

BIBLIOGRAPHY: Hans Erismann, *Das ging ja gut an: Geschichten und Geschichte des Opernhauses Zürich* (Zürich, 1984). Martin Hürlimann and Harry Olt, *Theater in Zürich: 125 Jahre Stadttheater* (Zürich, 1959). *150 Jahre Theater in Zürich* (Zürich, 1984).

ACCESS: Falkenstraße 1, CH-8008 Zürich. (41 1) 251 69 20. Christoph Groszer, Direktor.

MYRTHA SCHENKEL

Turkey

ANKARA (3,306,327)

Ankara Devlet Opera ve Balesi (The Ankara State Opera and Ballet)

Although Western opera is a major twentieth-century phenomenon in Turkey, the first recorded opera performance took place several centuries earlier in May 1797 in Topkapi Palace in Istanbul, given by a touring Italian company for the Sultan Selim III. It is known that ballet companies were invited to perform for royal weddings and feasts in the Ottoman Palace as early as the sixteenth century. Moreover, there was a tradition of offering closed performances of operas both in the royal palace and in various foreign embassies. Following the Ottoman Reformation, touring opera companies frequented Turkey and a number of new theaters were built to accommodate their productions. One of the earliest was the Bosko Theater in Pera, Istanbul, which was managed by and named after the famous comedian. Bosko realized the potential of opera, and provided translations so that the audiences could follow the plot of the new art form. One of his earliest productions was Donizetti's *Belisario* in 1842. The theater changed hands in 1844, and major renovations were undertaken to make it more suitable for opera. The new owner, Michael Naum, opened the house on December 29, 1844, with Donizetti's *Lucrezia Borgia*, which enjoyed considerable success. He had obtained a monopoly to stage operas in their original language, a privilege he enjoyed until 1867. This period was crucial to the development of opera in Turkey as the public was given the opportunity to hear international stars perform their favorite roles. Naum also commissioned a number of works, including Lombardi's *Giselda* and Giacomo Panizza's *Silistre*.

Following Naum's death and the destruction of his theater in the great fire of 1870, several other impresarios opened theaters to present opera. The works of Verdi, Offenbach, and Puccini were especially popular. All the theaters followed the prevailing Italian design with boxes circling the auditorium, and they were designed to hold up to 1,600 people. As a result of the popularity of Italian opera, a number of indigenous opera companies were founded. Dikran Çuhaciyan, Güllü Agop, Küçük Ismail, and Minakyan all had ensembles. The first Turkish opera composer was Dikran Çuhaciyan (1836–1898), whose output includes *Arif' in Hilesi* (1872), *Köse Kahya* (1874), and *Leblebici Horhor Aga* (1875). The Constitutional era was dominated by national operettas exemplified in the work of Vittorio Redaglia and Nurullah Şevket. Following World War I, Mustafa Kemal (Atatürk) headed a National Congress which met in Sivas in 1919. He was elected president of a provisional national government in 1920, and following the Treaty of Lausanne in 1923, the Republic of Turkey was founded. Kemal instituted a secular government and westernized the legal system. These changes created a social climate for the real beginning of modern opera, which dates from the founding of the Istanbul Operatic Society in 1930. By 1934 the Grand Opera Council was producing Verdi's *La Traviata*, and that same year President Kemal Atatürk adopted opera as another means to deepen his country's relationships with the West. To highlight an official visit of the shah of Iran in the capital, Atatürk commissioned the young composer Ahmet Adnan Saygun to prepare a Turkish opera based on his own theme, to be realized as a libretto by Münir Hayri Egeli. Time was short, there was a lack of both trained singers and orchestra personnel, and the rehearsals quickly degenerated into chaos. Only the personal intervention of Atatürk himself saved the production which, by the way, turned out to be a tremendous success. *Özsoy* marks a significant step forward for Turkish opera, as it convinced Atatürk to mandate the establishment of a State Academy of Music and Performing Arts, which was officially proclaimed on June 25, 1934.

As a constituent of the new academy, the Ankara State Conservatoire began in 1936, and a number of foreign artists were invited, including Paul Hindemith. Hindemith recommended the well-known producer Carl Ebert to head the new Department of Performing Arts, and Ebert began his work in the fall of 1936. Ismet Inönü succeeded Atatürk as president, and, with his support, Ebert assumed the direction of opera production in 1939. The first graduates of the new program gave their premiere performance in the Ankara Helkevi on June 21, 1940. Mozart's *Bastien and Bastienne* with Rabia Erler, Süleyman Alkan, and Ruhi Su, and the second act of Puccini's *Madama Butterfly* with Mesude Çaglayan, Necdet Demir, Süleyman Tamer, Orhan Günek, and Nuri Turkan were performed in Turkish, accompanied by the Presidential Philharmonic Orchestra. Within a year the students were advanced enough to perform a complete *Madama Butterfly*, assisted by professional artists including Nurullah Şevket Taşkiran and Semiha Berksoy, on June 12, 1942. These initial graduates of the program worked for the Preparatory Studio Stage until 1947, as there was still no independent opera company offering employment to singers.

Muhsin Ertugrul succeeded Ebert after the latter's contract was not renewed on March 31, 1947. The next year, on April 2, 1948, the new Great Theater (Büyük Tiyatro) building in Ankara opened with a festive performance of Ahmet

Adnan Saygun's unfinished opera *Kerem*. [Ebert left for the United States to become the director of the opera program at the University of Southern California (1949–56). As one of the organizers of the Glyndebourne Festival in 1934, he was artistic director there until 1939 and again from 1946 to 1959.] Cevat Mumduh Altar succeeded Ertugrul and managed both to strengthen the resident ensemble and to import more famous artists from the world's stages. During this period Turkish artists such as Leyla Gencer, who had studied at the conservatory with Elvira de Hidalgo, Orhan Günek, and Ferhan Onat, were beginning to make their artistic mark in Europe. Muhsin Ertugrul returned as general director in 1954 and pursued a policy of supporting provincial theaters throughout the country. Necil Kazim Akses was appointed general director in 1958, at a time when the managements of the opera and the theater were separated. Tours were mounted throughout Turkey, and especially to Istanbul, where the Istanbul City Opera was founded, a company which later became a constituent part of the Istanbul Devlet Opera ve Balesi (State Opera and Ballet). As the result of legislation that created the General Directorate of the State Opera and Ballet on July 14, 1970, the Ankara State Opera and Ballet and the Istanbul State Opera and Ballet became independent organizations. In 1983 the Izmir Devlet Opera ve Balesi (State Opera and Ballet) was founded under the same guidelines. The 1990–1991 repertoire included *Alayin Kizi* (*The Daughter of the Regiment*), *Carmen*, *Carmina Burana*, *Così fan tutte*, *Fiddler on the Roof*, *Italya'da Bir Türk* (*A Turk in Italy*), Moniuszko's *Perili Köşk* (*The Haunted Manor*), *Tosca*, *La Traviata*, *Il Trovatore*, Strauss's *Yarasa* (*The Bat*), Mozart's *Zaide*, and Ada's *Ali Baba ve Kirk Haramiler* (*Ali Baba and the Forty Thieves*).

CHRONOLOGY OF GENERAL DIRECTORS: Muhsin Ertugrul, 1948–1951; Cevat Mumduh Altar, 1951–1954; Mushin Ertugrul, 1954–1958; Necil Kazim Akses, 1958–1970; Erol Gömürgen, present.

ACCESS: State Opera and Ballet, Post. Kod 06850, Ulus-Ankara. (90 1) 145 3916. Erol Gömürgen, General Director.

[From materials supplied by the company]

ISTANBUL (5,842,985)

Istanbul Devlet Opera ve Balesi (The Instanbul State Opera and Ballet)

The origins of the Devlet Opera ve Balesi in Istanbul lie in the efforts of the Municipal Conservatory to produce operatic excerpts on March 28–29, 1959. Assisted by the Istanbul City Orchestra, which was directed by Cemal Reşit Rey and Demirhan Altug, the experiment was a success, and efforts were undertaken to establish an Istanbul City Opera. The first production was Puccini's *Tosca* in the Drama Theater at Tepebaşi on March 19, 1960. Staged by Aydin Gün and conducted by Kurt Eichorn, the production starred Leyla Gencer and Orhan Günek. In 1969 the company was taken under the umbrella of the General Directorate of the State Opera and Ballet in Ankara and named the Istanbul State

Opera and Ballet. With the opening of the Istanbul Culture Palace on April 12, 1969, the company had a new home, and Robert Wagner became the first general music director. The Culture Palace was severely damaged by fire on November 27, 1970, and until the complex was restored and reopened as the Atatürk Cultural Center in 1977, the company performed in the Maksim Stage and the San Cinema. During the thirty years since its inception, the company has produced some sixty-six operas and eight operettas, including seven works by Turkish composers. The current director is Mesut Iktu, and Renato Palumbo is the general music director. The 1990–1991 repertoire included Zemlinsky's *Bir Floransa Trajedisi (A Florentine Tragedy)*, *Bir Maskeli Balo (Masked Ball)*, *La Bohème*, *Carmina Burana*, Kalman's *Çardaş Prensesi*, *Maça Kizi (Queen of Spades)*, *Windsor'un Şen Kadinlari (The Merry Wives of Windsor)*, *Konsolos (The Consul)*, and operas by Rossini, Cimarosa, Thomas, and Richard Strauss.

ACCESS: Atatürk Kültür Merkezi, 80090 Taskim, Istanbul. (90 1) 151 5600. Mesut Iktu, Director. Renato Polumbo, Music Director.

[From materials supplied by the company]

IZMIR (2,317,829)

Izmir Devlet Opera ve Balesi (The Izmir State Opera and Ballet)

With the opening of the Izmir City Theater in 1946, a suitable home was available for the first time to host the visiting opera and operetta productions from Ankara. The success of the companies from Ankara and Istanbul led to the acquisition in 1979 of the former cinema and conference hall known as Elhamara. Public interest grew, and on July 27, 1982 a director was appointed to organize the local company. Its first performance as the Izmir State Opera and Ballet took place on October 21, 1982. The current director is Kirgiz Aray, and the general music director is Ercan Yenal. The general repertoire includes works by Donizetti, Lortzing, Puccini, Kalman, Pergolesi, Smetana, Menotti, Nicolai, Lehar, and Verdi.

ACCESS: Atatürk Kültür Merkezi, 80090 Taskim, Istanbul. (90 1) 151 5600. Mesut Iktu, Director. Renato Palumbo, Music Director.

[From information supplied by Asim Cem Konuralp, Ministry of Culture, Republic of Turkey]

TRANS. REHA KORMAN

Union of Soviet Socialist Republics

KIEV (city 2,587,000)

Taras Shevchenko Academic Opera and Ballet Theater

Founded in 862 Kiev was for a time the ancient capital of Russia. It became the capital of the Ukraine in 1934 and serves as the center of indigenous culture in the republic. The history of professional theatrical art in Kiev dates back to the early nineteenth century with the founding of the first drama company in 1804. The repertoire included plays as well as operas by Mozart and others. Guest artists were occasionally invited, and between 1863 and 1866 Ferdinand Berger's company performed a number of operas, including Verdi's *Ernani*, *Macbeth*, and *Il Trovatore*, Donizetti's *Lucia di Lammermoor*, Rossini's *Il Barbiere di Siviglia*, and Bellini's *Norma*. Local interest in musical performances was so high that the civic authorities decided to open an opera house in Kiev. With the completion of the City Theater in 1856, a suitable home for opera became a reality, and the founding of the Kiev Opera occurred a few years later when a permanent professional company was announced on October 25, 1867. The repertoire consisted of both Russian and Western Europe works, and included Dargomizhsky's *The Mermaid*, Glinka's *A Life for the Tsar*, Donizetti's *La Fille du Régiment*, and Verdi's *Rigoletto*. Peter Tchaikovsky soon became the company's favorite composer, and his *Oprichnik* was produced only eight months after its St. Petersburg premiere on April 24, 1874. This was followed by productions of *Eugene Onegin* in 1884, *Mazeppa* in 1886, and *Queen of Spades* in 1890, only days after the St. Petersburg premiere on December 19. The composer himself felt that the Kiev productions displayed greater professionalism and impact than those in Moscow or St. Petersburg. At the time, the company boasted such outstanding vocalists as O. Santagano-Gorchakova, M. Akramov, the tenor Alexander Dodonov, A. Bartsal, the tenor Dimitri Usatov (who discovered Feodor Chaliapin in 1893), V. Zarudna, M. Medvedev, and the bass

Fedor Stravinsky (father of Igor Stravinsky). Beginning in 1896 the Kiev Opera featured Chaliapin almost every season. The public was fortunate to have seen the great artist perform Boito's *Mefistofele* and Mussorgsky's *Boris Godunov*. The stage was blessed as well with such vocal stars as Mattia Battistini, Maria Gelevani di Tejada, Adelina Pdodvani, Lina Cavalieri, Yaroslava Korolevich-Vaidova, Titta Ruffo, Giuseppe Anselmi, Antonina Nezhdanova, Ivan Alchevsky, and Leonid Sobinov.

From the beginning there was strong support for native composers, and the opera quickly became a focus of Ukrainian musical life. The period between 1917 and 1925 was full of economic and political complications for the company. In 1926, however, the operas was granted the prestigious title of Academic Opera Company, and the ensemble regained its former luster. The composer Mykhaylo Verikivsky joined the company as a conductor and remained until 1928, when he was engaged at the opera in Kharkov. The Ukraine was always famous for its vocal talent, so it was only natural that the company embarked again on a program of artistic excellence. The soprano Oksana Petrusenko (beginning in 1934), Zoya Patorzhinsky, Mikhailo Romensky, Yuri Kyporenko-Damansky, the baritone Andriy Ivanov (beginning in 1934), Mikhailo Mikisha, and Boris Hmyria all contributed to the growing quality of the house. The well-known conductor Stefan Turchak was appointed director of the company in 1938, a post he retained until 1988. The new theater, which had been built in 1901, was renamed the Taras Shevchenko Theater in 1939. (Taras Shevchenko [1814–1861] was the Ukraine's most famous poet, and he led an unsuccessful attempt to win his country's independence from Russia in the 1840s.)

During World War II the company was evacuated to Ufa and Irkutsk, returning to Kiev in 1944. The city had suffered major damage during the war, and it would take decades to rebuilt it to match its former charm and beauty. The postwar repertoire featured the works of Prokofiev, Melikov, Khachaturian, Meitus, Dzerzhinsky, and Krein, along with the standard European eighteenth- and nineteenth-century operas. A renewed interest in Ukrainian compositions was highlighted by productions of Mykola Lysenko's classic *Taras Bul'ba* (1890; premiered in Kiev in December 1903), *Utoplennitsa* (*The Drowned Woman*, 1871–1883; premiered in Kharkov in 1885), *Aeneid* (1910; premiered in Kiev in 1911), and *Nich pid Rizdvo* (*Christmas Eve*, 1874; revised, 1877–1882; premiered in Kharkov in 1883). After finishing studies in Leipzig with Reinecke and Richter, Lysenko became an influential composer and Ukrainian patriot, and his works are revered as part of the Ukrainian national heritage. During this period the company commissioned leading native composers, including Mykhaylo Verikivsky whose *Batrachka* (*The Maid*) premiered in 1946; Konstantin Dankevich, whose controversial *Bogdan Khmelnitsky* premiered in Moscow on June 15, 1951, and had to be extensively revised before it was accepted; and Gerogi Maibrorda's *Taras Shevchenko*, which premiered in 1964.

In the late 1950s the company resumed touring throughout Europe. Bulgaria, Hungary, Rumania, and Yugoslavia all received the ensemble with great enthusiasm, further strengthening the artistic image which had steadily improved since the war. A new generation of singers appeared to sustain the traditions of the past, including Yelizaveta Chadvar, Andriy Kilot, Vasyl Tretyak, Mykola Vorulev, Ivan Patorzhinsky, Boris Hmyria, Yuri Hulayev, Dmytro Hnatiuk, Yevheniya Myroshina, as well as the mezzo Larissa Rudenko (1939–1970) and the baritone Andrej Ivanov (1934–1950), who were particular favorites of the public. Invited to participate in a number of international festivals, including those of Dresden, Wiesbaden, and Zagreb, the company has been able to project its image well beyond its own borders. Some outstanding singers have been members of the ensemble, including Stepan Fitsich, Volodymyr Hryshko, Anatoliy Kocherga, Yevdokiya Kolesnyk, Heorhiy Krasulya, Nadia Kudelya, Victoria Lukianets, Roman Maiboroda, Yevheniya Myrosh-Niocenko, Velantin Pivovarov, Iven Ponomarenko, Valentina Reka, Mykola Shepa, Cizcla Tsipola, Halina Tuftina, Lyudmila Yurchenko, and Lidiya Zabilyasta. Volodymyr Dranishnikov, Ariy Pezovsky, Veniamin Tolba, Illya Chistyakov, Volodymyr Yorish, Olexander Klimov, and Kostiantyn Simeonov have all conducted. The production tradition has included Mykola Smolych, Volodymyr Skliarenko, and Dmytro Smolych. Dmytro Hnatiuk continues that tradition today. The current repertoire includes some thirty domestic and foreign operas, and each season roughly two hundred ballet and opera performances are given.

BIBLIOGRAPHY: N. Herasimova-Persidska, *Mykhaylo Ivanovich Verikivsky* (Kiev, 1959). N. Shurova, *Mikhaylo Verikivsky* (Kiev, 1972). M. Stefanovich, *Kievsky derzhavny ordena Lenina teatr opery ta balety URSR imeni T. H. Shevchenka* (Kiev, 1960). O. S. Zinkevich, *Georgi Miaberoda* (Kiev, 1973).

ACCESS: 50 Volodymyrska Street, Kiev 252030; fax (7 44) 2255388. Volodymyr Kozhukhar, Chief Conductor. Dmytro Hnatink, Senior Stage Director.

VASYL TURKEVYCH

MOSCOW (city 8,967,000)

Bolshoi Opera Theater of the USSR

Moscow was founded in the middle of the twelfth century by Prince Yuri Dolgorki. Astride important trade routes, by the late fifteenth century it had grown into the most important Russian city. In 1547 Ivan IV was recognized as the first czar of all of Russia. The Romanov dynasty began in 1613 with Czar Michael Romanov, who reigned until 1645. Peter I began building a new capital, St. Petersburg (Leningrad), in 1703. His reign (1682–1725) fostered the introduction of Western ideas into the country. Moscow became the capital again after the revolution in 1918. One of the first Italian comic operas produced in Germany, Giovanni Ristori's *Calandro*, was also the first opera to be staged in Moscow on December 11, 1731, in a temporary theater built in the Kremlin for the occasion. The first permanent opera house opened in 1742. Reforms of Peter the Great finally opened the door to secular music in Russia. Various foreign artists visited Russia, including Giovanni Locatelli, who brought his opera company in 1757. These performances gave a strong impetus to native opera composers, who were very active in the second half of the century. A National Theater was formed in 1756 under Czarina Elizabeth and moved to its own opera house in 1763.

The Bolshoi Theater in Moscow traces its founding to March 28, 1776, when Prince Urusov was granted an imperial monopoly over all the theatrical performances in the city. Directed by Michael Maddox, the company performed ballets, operas, and plays in the Petrovsky Theater until it was destroyed by fire in October 1805. The government of Alexander I took direct control of the operation, and the company moved to the new Bolshoi Theater, which, in turn, burned down in 1812. Temporary quarters were used until the opening of the Bolshoi Petrovsky Theater on January 6, 1825. It was at this time that the composer Alexei Vertovsky, who had moved to Moscow in 1823, became associated with the Imperial Theater. His involvement lasted until 1860, and he played an important role in the development of opera in Russia. The magnificent new edifice designed by Mikhailov was one of the finest theaters in Europe at the time and produced a variety of international and national operas until it was destroyed by fire in 1853. Reopened on August 30, 1856, in its present design by Alberto Cavos, the 2,000-seat house was dedicated to ballet and opera and excelled in grandiose sets and staging. Actually, nothing remained of the original house except the outer walls and the facade, so Cavos was able to correct the original acoustic and visual deficiencies. The birth of Russian opera dates from the premiere of Glinka's *A Life for the Czar* in St. Petersburg on December 9, 1836. The opera first appeared at the Bolshoi in Moscow on September 19, 1842, conducted by Ivan Johannes, and it marks the beginning of a potent nationalism played out in the operatic figure of a tragic hero.

The Bolshoi was flourishing, but the government moved to place it under the control of Directorate of the Imperial Theaters in the capital of St. Petersburg. Premieres of major new works were now the exclusive province of the imperial city, and, to add insult to injury, the Bolshoi was leased to an Italian opera company in 1861, resulting in minimal performances of Russian works. The modern history of the Bolshoi begins with the public premiere of Tchaikovsky's *Eugene Onegin* on January 23, 1881, and the composer's *Mazeppa* on February 15, 1884, further strengthened the relationship. In 1882 Alexander III had ended the imperial monopoly that controlled all the theaters, and the Moscow Private Russian Opera was founded by Savva Mamontov in 1885, featuring high-caliber singers such as Vladimir Lossky, Pyotr Olenin, Nadezhda Salina, Feodor Chaliapin, and Elena Tsvetkova. In 1904 Sergey Zimin continued Mamontov's work with his own private company, which mounted unusual and experimental productions until 1924. Members of the original group premiered Rimsky-Korsakov's *Sadko* on January 7, 1898, in St. Petersburg after Czar Nicholas II had removed it from the Marinsky Opera schedule the previous year. At the same time the Bolshoi Theater was presenting the operas of Arensky, whose

Rafael premiered in Moscow on May 6, 1894; Rachmaninoff (who also conducted at the house); and Rimsky-Korsakoff, among other Russian composers. Now all the major works of Tchaikovsky, Borodin, Mussorgsky, and Rimsky-Korsakoff were given elaborate productions, usually shortly after their premieres in St. Petersburg. The company was nurturing outstanding singers during this period: Aleksandrova-Kochetova, Deisha-Sionitskaya, Donskoi, Khokhlov, Korsov, Lavrovskaya, Preobrazhenskaya, and Salina all graced the boards in a variety of roles.

By the turn of the century, the Bolshoi Theater was presenting most of the standard repertoire found elsewhere in Europe, but at the same time the company was devoting special attention to Russian opera. All the Rimsky-Korsakoff operas were produced, plus those of Dargomizhsky, Mussorgsky, and Rachmaninoff. The musical standards, both orchestral and vocal, reached new heights under Cooper, Rachmaninoff, and Suk. The roster of principal artists was studded with outstanding artists such as Alchevaky, Bagdanovich, Baklanov, Bonachich, Chaliapin, Grizunov, Nezhdanova, Petrov, Pirogov, Savransky, Sobinov, Stepanova, and Zruyeva. Realism in acting and singing matched the expectations of the times which were greatly influenced by the work of Stanislavsky.

The revolution led to widespread changes in the education of performers and in the production of opera, the latter due primarily to the new audiences, which, for the first time, had access to all the theatrical events. The Bolshoi reopened to this new audience on April 8, 1918, with excerpts from *Russlan and Ludmilla* by Glinka and *Sadko* by Rimsky-Korsakoff. Tenor Leonid Sobinov served as director of the Bolshoi, and two famous directors founded artistic groups, Stanislavski's Bolshoi Theater Opera Studio (later the Stanislavski Opera Theater) and Nemirovich-Danchenko's Moscow Arts Theater Music Studio (later the Nemirovich-Danchenko Music Theater). The two innovative programs were combined in 1941 as the Stanislavski-Nemirovich-Danchenko Musical Theater, which is now one of the leading opera companies in the country. The principal challenge was to create a new repertoire for a new society. In 1924 the first work by a Soviet composer, Yurovsky's *Trilby*, premiered at the Bolshoi, and early in 1927 Prokoffiev's *L'Amour des trois Oranges* followed the Leningrad Russian premiere of February 18, 1926. Shostakovich's *Lady Macbeth of Mtsensk* opened in Moscow only two days after the Leningrad premiere on January 22, 1934, with both productions in rehearsal at the same time, and Dzerzhinsky's *The Quiet Don* opened on January 8, 1936, a matter of weeks after the Leningrad premiere. Practically every season a new ballet or opera was produced in an ongoing attempt to define the parameters of the new Soviet style.

World War II seriously affected the company, as it did artistic activity in the cultures of all European countries. After the war, the Bolshoi promoted operas composed in Eastern Block countries, such as *The Bartered Bride*, *Duke Bluebeard's Castle*, and *Jenufa*; revived a number of national-subject works such as *Boris Godunov*; supported regional operas like Spendiarov's *Song of the Woods*; and premiered contemporary works such as Muradelli's *New October*, which explored new directions. Arkhipova, Atlantova, Eisen, Gulyayev, Mazurok, Milashkina, Nesterenko, Pyavko, Rudenko, Sotkilava, and Vedernikov, among others, have inherited the legacy of earlier vocal artists. The Bolshoi today remains the protector of tradition in the best sense. Historical works that are important to an understanding of the nation as well as standard repertoire operas are produced with an emphasis on artistic continuity. As the leading opera company in the Soviet Union, the Moscow Bolshoi remains a magnet for the finest conductors, designers, directors, and singers throughout the country. The theater was closed in June 1986 for extensive restoration, opening again in 1988. The 1989–1990 season included productions of *Werther*, *Eugene Onegin*, Rimsky-Korsakoff's *Mlada*, *Boris Godunov*, Tchaikovsky's *Yolanta* and *Mazeppa*, *Life for the Tsar*, and Verdi's *La Traviata* and *Un Ballo in Maschera*. The season ran from November through June and concluded with a tour to Covent Garden in London.

A highlight of the 1990–1991 season was the long-awaited tour to the United States. For the second time in the history of this heralded ensemble, a company of some 450 artists appeared in New York City at the new Metropolitan Opera House. Opening to sold-out houses on June 25, the Bolshoi presented a world premiere of a new production of Tchaikovsky's *Eugene Onegin*. [The first public premiere of the opera took place in Moscow on January 23, 1881. The first staged American premiere was at the Metropolitan Opera House on March 24, 1920. Sung in Italian, the production starred Claudia Muzio, Giuseppe DeLuca, and Giovanni Martinelli.] This represented the first time that the company had premiered a new production outside of the Soviet Union. *Onegin* was followed by Rimsky-Korsakoff's *Mlada* [premiered in St. Petersburg on November 1, 1892] featuring the ballet. The final production of the tour was an American stage premiere of Tchaikovsky's opera on the legend of Joan of Arc. *Orleanskaya Dyeva* (*The Maid of Orleans*) originally premiered in St. Petersburg on February 25, 1881. The Bolshoi revived the work after more than six decades of neglect, and presented the American stage premiere as a special treat for American audiences.

BIBLIOGRAPHY: Grigorii B. Bernandt, ed., *Slovar'oper* (Moscow, 1962). V. E. Cheshikhin, *Istoriya russkoy operï* (St. Petersburg, 1905). Abram A. Gozenpud, *Russkii opernyi teatr XIX veka 1836–56* (Leningrad, 1969). Abram A. Gozenpud, *Russkii opernyi teatr XIX veka 1857–72* (Leningrad, 1971). Abram A. Gozenpud, *Russkii sovetskiy opernyi teatr* (Leningrad, 1963). E. Grosheva, *Bol'shoy teatr v evo proshlom i nastoyashchem* (Moscow, 1962). B. A. Pokrovsky and Y. N. Grigorovich, *The Bolshoi: Opera and Ballet at the Greatest Theater in Russia* (New York, 1979). A. S. Rabinovich, *Russkaya opera do Glinka* (Moscow, 1948). B. Schwarz, *Music and Musical Life in Soviet Russia, 1917–70* (New York, 1972). A. Shaverdian, *Bol'shoy teatr Soyuza SSR* (Moscow, 1952). *Teatral'naia entisiklopediia* (Moscow, 1967).

ACCESS: Ploshchad Sverdlova 1, Sverdlov Square, Moscow. (7 95) 292 6534. Vladimir Kokonin, Director General. Aleksandr Lazarev, Artistic Director.

[From materials supplied by the company]

United Kingdom

BELFAST, NORTHERN IRELAND (metro 444,000; city 299,600)

Opera Northern Ireland

The capital of Northern Ireland was too small to support professional musicians during much of its history. The major house, the Theatre Royal, did not have a permanent orchestra until the middle of the nineteenth century. This was about the same time that touring opera companies began occasional visits to the city. With the opening of the Grand Opera House in 1895, an annual season of opera became possible and performances continued there until 1953 (except during World War II). The Carl Rosa Company played Belfast and, after the war, the Saddler's Wells Opera Company visited the province on a regular basis. Indigenous opera began in Northern Ireland in 1957 with the formation of the Grand Opera Society of Northern Ireland. The new company recruited a local amateur chorus which, together with local and guest professional artists, worked to produce an annual season of opera in Belfast. The next major development was in 1969 when, after twelve years of administration by enthusiastic and dedicated amateurs, the company appointed a full-time administrator and changed its name to the Northern Ireland Opera Trust (NIOT). A grant from the Arts Council was an important factor in this development.

NIOT presented annual seasons of opera in Belfast throughout the 1970s, when the social conditions in the city did not lend themselves to such work. Performances were given in many different kinds of theaters, movie houses, and church halls throughout Northern Ireland until, in 1980 with the refurbishment of the Grand Opera House, the company at last had a suitable home in which to perform. In 1984 the company was reorganized again when it merged with the Studio Opera Group, a local amateur company that had been founded in 1950 by Havelock Nelson. This new company was called Opera Northern Ireland (ONI). ONI is the only professional opera company in Northern Ireland and presents regular seasons in the Grand Opera House as well as throughout the province. As might be expected in a city whose musical strength was historically centered in choral music, ONI has a chorus that consists of the cream of local amateur singers. This chorus joins with the professional Ulster Symphony and principal singers who come to ONI as guest artists from companies in Europe and North America to give three productions a year in Belfast and one touring production. In addition, the company has developed a small educational program to introduce and discuss the company's work in schools throughout Northern Ireland. The current annual budget is in excess of $1.1 million, of which 65 percent is represented by a grant from the Arts Council of Northern Ireland. The remainder comes from box office receipts (18 percent) and sponsorship (17 percent). The company currently performs to audiences that average 90 percent capacity in the 1,000-seat Grand Opera House. The general manager is assisted by an administrator, a press officer, a technical manager, and an artistic director. All other artistic and technical personnel are contracted as necessary for each production.

ACCESS: 181A Stranmillis Road, Belfast BT9 5DU. (44 232) 381241; fax (44 232) 682709. Randall Shannon, General Manager. Kenneth Montgomery, Artistic Director.

[From materials supplied by the company]

CARDIFF, WALES (283,900)

Welsh National Opera

Cardiff, the capital of Wales and the largest city in the principality, is the home of most of the major Welsh cultural organizations, including three television stations, the Welsh Arts Council, the National Museum of Wales, the British Broadcasting Corporation Welsh Symphony Orchestra, and the Welsh National Opera itself. Music, especially choral music, has always been a part of the Welsh cultural tradition, and it is on this tradition, and on the principle of bringing opera to the general public rather than to a small and elitist audience, that the Welsh National Opera was founded.

Welsh National Opera (WNO) was founded in 1946 and has changed in the intervening years from an amateur company that hired professional soloists and engaged a professional orchestra to a fully professional company with a national and international touring program, many recording contracts and concert appearances, and a permanent base in Cardiff. WNO has no theater of its own, but performs in Cardiff at the New Theater, in Swansea at the Grand, and in the principal theaters of the other cities to which it tours: Liverpool, Manchester, Birmingham, Bristol, Southampton, Plymouth, Oxford, and London. Three seasons of performances are given each year, with at least one new production in each season. The company's funding is generated by ticket sales; grants from the Arts Council of Great Britain, the Welsh Council, and the councils of cities on tour; and sponsorship by companies and private organizations.

In 1943 the suggestion was put to Idioes Owen, a Cardiff singing teacher and conductor, that a grand opera company should be founded in Wales. It was not the first time that such a suggestion had been made: As early as 1890, a company called Welsh National Opera had taken two works by Joseph Parry on tour but had been forced to disband. The Cardiff Grand Opera Society, another precursor, had existed in the 1920s and 1930s, and there were other amateur operatic societies in Wales. On December 2, 1943, Idioes Owen was elected by a group of fellow musicians as musical director of a company that was first known as the Lyrian Grand Opera Company and immediately renamed Welsh National Opera. Most of the early chorus members were amateurs with full-time jobs. Victor Fleming was engaged to conduct the first performance, a concert at the Empire Theater, for which a free-lance orchestra was contracted. A permanent business manager, William Smith, joined the company, and the first staged performance, a double bill of *Cavalleria rusticana* and *I Pagliacci*, was put on at the Prince of Wales Theater, Cardiff, on April 15, 1946. This was followed by Gounod's *Faust*.

The first season was an artistic, if not a financial, success, and the company was able to plan a season for the following year with a new production of *Carmen*, conducted by Victor Fleming and produced by Norman Jones. Within the next three years, *La Traviata, Madama Butterfly, The Bartered Bride*, and *Les Contes d'Hoffmann* had also been produced. Charles Mackerras, now musical director, made his first appearance of a forty-year association with the company conducting the Offenbach opera. Such was the popular success of the first productions that applications poured in from people hoping to join the chorus. All were amateurs, coming from different walks of life, but all shared a love of singing. Many of those accepted were versed only in tonic sol-fa notation, and some could not read music at all. However, from the outset the chorus produced a very special quality of sound, not achieved by any other opera company. This occurred despite the fact that there were two choruses, one serving Cardiff and the other Swansea, and for both, the rehearsals were largely a matter of learning the music by rote. It was not until 1968 that the chorus became fully professional, and today it is regarded as one of the finest in the world.

For many years various professional orchestras around the country played for the company, until in 1970 a permanent orchestra named the Welsh Philharmonia was formed. Under the guidance of Richard Armstrong, music director from 1973 to 1986, and Brian McMaster, managing director, who came from English National Opera in 1976 where he had been controller of opera planning, WNO began to emerge as a major force in the operatic world. McMaster initiated a tradition of recruiting producers from European theaters, generating a series of exciting and controversial productions that included Ruth Berghaus's *Don Giovanni*, Göran Järvefeld's *Ring*, and the *Otello* and *Falstaff* productions of Peter Stein. Many other European producers, such as Harry Kupfer, Liviu Ciulei, and André Engel were to do their first work in Britain at the invitation of WNO. New works were commissioned from the Welsh composers Alun Hoddinott,

William Matthias, and John Metcalf. Reactions to these productions focused the attention of the general public on the theatrical aspects of opera and increased the international reputation of the company.

It was initially thought that the orchestra would appear regularly on the concert platform as well as fulfilling its operatic commitments. As the number of opera performances grew, however, fewer and fewer concert engagements were undertaken. In 1979 the orchestra was renamed the Orchestra of Welsh National Opera, which was felt to be more appropriate to its function. In recent years the orchestra's regular work has covered the major operatic repertory, ranging from Monteverdi to Tippett. The Wiesbaden May Festival 1986 featured WNO for the third time with Mozart's *Le Nozze di Figaro*. That same year saw the completion of the "Ring" cycle, a fitting finale to Richard Armstrong's thirteen-year appointment as music director. His tenure paralleled the growth of musical standards to international levels. The arrival of Sir Charles Mackerras as musical director in 1987 marked the start of a new era, beginning with a magnificent new production of *The Trojans*. A musicologist as well as a conductor, Mackerras introduced a number of authentic performance practices in addition to exploring the Czechoslovakian opera repertoire and the works of Richard Strauss.

In 1989 the orchestra and chorus of WNO performed the world premiere of George Lloyd's *The Vigil of Venus* at the Royal Festival Hall, conducted by the composer, the recording of which has been released by Decca. The orchestra continues to perform at concerts in Cardiff, London, and elsewhere, including foreign tours to Lisbon, Leipzig, the Dresden Festival and the Frankfurt am Main Festival. The year 1989 saw Peter Stein's production of *Falstaff* in New York and Milan, and the next year the company took *Falstaff* and *Salome* to Tokyo. A feature of the 1990 season was a Promenade Concert in which Sir Charles Mackerras presented a program of Czech music, repertoire that is now considered a particular specialty of the organization. Recent recordings for Decca and EMI include *Tristan und Isolde* and *Parsifal*; Richard Bonynge conducting *Hamlet, I Masnadieri, Rodelinda, Norma, Anna Bolena, Ernani*, and *Adriana Lecouvreur*; and most recently, Sir Charles Mackerras conducting *Osud* for the Delius Collection (series of recordings).

Although WNO has featured some of the world's most renowned singers, including Sutherland, Caballé, Pavarotti, and Söderström, the company has also launched the careers of a number of young artists. Among those who made early appearances are Dennis O'Neill, Thomas Allen, Pauline Tinsley, Forbes Robinson, Suzanne Murphy, Helen Field, Jeffery Lawton, Arthur Davies, Philip Joll, and Anne Evans. An association with the Cardiff Singer of the World Competition has also brought new talent into the company. Bryn Terfel, the winner of the Lieder Prize in 1989, has gone on to sing principal roles and make a number of recordings.

CHRONOLOGY OF MUSIC DIRECTORS: Charles Groves, 1961–1963. Bryan Balkwill, 1963–1967. James Lockhart, 1968–1973. Richard Armstrong, 1973–1986. Charles Mackerras, 1987–present.

ACCESS: John Street, Cardiff CF1 4SP. (44 222) 464666; fax (44 222) 489515. Brian McMaster, Managing Director. Charles Mackerras, Music Director.

SIMON REES

GLASGOW, SCOTLAND (city 760,000)

Scottish Opera

Glasgow achieved artistic preeminence over Edinburgh at the end of the nineteenth century and has since become the home of the Scottish National Orchestra, Scotland's one professional opera company, and the British Broadcasting Corporation Scotland and Scottish Television. Formal opera dates from 1877 when the Carl Rosa Company began scheduling annual visits, which lasted past the turn of the century. A local amateur company, the Glasgow Grand Opera Company, was formed in 1905 to support the visits of the Carl Rosa Company, and, on its own initiative it mounted such memorable productions as the first complete performance of Berlioz's *Les Troyens* in 1935. In an earlier move that would have later implications for an indigenous professional opera company, the Choral Union Orchestra and the Scottish Orchestra had merged in 1898, and, as the Scottish Orchestra, it quickly became the premier instrumental ensemble. In 1951, renamed the Scottish National Orchestra, it mounted a year-round schedule of concerts under the leadership of Karl Rankl, Hans Swarowsky, and Alexander Gibson. Gibson, who assumed the post of musical director and principal conductor, was the first Scot to head the orchestra. He was also intensely interested in opera.

In 1962 Gibson founded the Scottish Opera which, with the musical support of the Scottish National Orchestra, mounted productions of *Pelléas et Mélisande* and *Madama Butterfly*. The close association of the two organizations has continued, and the season has been expanded from a single week of six performances to a year-round operation. Beginning in 1967 they presented a number of operas, including *The Rake's Progress, Peter Grimes, Elegy for Young Lovers, Macbeth*, and Orr's *Hermiston*, all at the Edinburgh Festival. Peter Ebert joined the company as director of productions in 1963 and remained in that post until 1975. A complete performance of Wagner's *Der Ring des Nibelungen* was given in December 1971 at the King's Theatre. A number of Scottish composers have been commissioned beginning in 1972, and the company moved into a permanent home, the refurbished Theatre Royal (originally opened in 1867) in 1975. Promenade performances of opera, previously reserved for audiences in London, were initiated in 1976. The general policy of Scottish Opera has been to feature neglected masterpieces as well as contemporary small-scale works.

CHRONOLOGY OF GENERAL ADMINISTRATORS: Peter Hemmings, 1962–1977. Peter Ebert, 1977–1980. Jean Cox, 1980–present.

BIBLIOGRAPHY: George Bruce, *Festival in the North: The Story of the Edinburgh*

Festival (London, 1975). H. G. Farmer, *A History of Music in Scotland*, repr. ed. (London, 1970). C. Wilson, *Scottish Opera: The First Ten Years* (Glasgow, 1973).

ACCESS: 39 Elmbank Crescent, Glasgow G2 4Pt. (44 41) 248 4567; fax (44 41) 221 8812. Richard Mantle, Managing Director. John Mamceri, Music Director.

[From materials supplied by the company]

GLYNDEBOURNE, ENGLAND

Glyndebourne Festival Opera

Glyndebourne, the English county manor house and estate of John Christie has, since the opening of its opera house in 1934, become the site of one of the great summer opera festivals in the world. In 1931 Christie married Audrey Mildmay, a young operatic soprano who had recently lent some professional stature to one of the amateur opera productions held in his Sussex manor house. The new husband was an opera lover who had frequented the festivals in Bayreuth, Munich, and Salzburg, and the newspapers announced in 1933 that he was going to open his new opera house with operas by Mozart and Wagner. Following the advice of his wife, Christie had the intimate 311-seat theater designed with a suitable stage and a pit large enough for a small orchestra. The house was also provided with up-to-date lighting and technical equipment. Events in Nazi Germany provided the venture with the first-rate production team of conductor Fritz Busch from Dresden and producer Carl Ebert from Berlin. Having been given unconditional artistic control of the fledgling operation, Busch and Ebert proceeded to create a standard of performance and production unknown in Great Britain at the time. Supported by John Christie's wealth, unlimited rehearsal time, prompt attention to the minutest production details, and intense artistic work became possible in completely undisturbed surroundings. This formula, the result of one man's personal commitment, would be the basis for Glyndebourne's transformation into an international attraction.

The inaugural season opened with Mozart's *Le Nozze di Figaro* on May 28, 1934, followed by *Così fan tutte*. There were six performances of each opera within the two-week season, and after the third night, the house was sold out. Those who were fortunate enough to attend were treated to a first-rate performance, a lovely dinner and a walk in the garden during the now traditional long intermission, and the good fortune to be present at the creation of a premiere musical event. There were no real stars in those first two casts. The secret of success lay in the quality of the overall ensemble: voice, musicianship, acting, and physical appearance were all weighed in the selection of the principals, resulting in a company that included singers from America, Austria, Czechoslovakia, Finland, Germany, Great Britain, and Italy. Rudolf Bing joined the company as general manager for the second season, a position he held until he went to the Metropolitan Opera Association in 1949. Moran Caplat took over and served until Brian Dickie succeeded him in 1981. When Dickie left Glyndebourne in December 1988 to take up the post of general director of the Canadian Opera Company, Anthony Whitworth-Jones was appointed general administrator.

Basic production principles were articulated during the early years, and they played a major role in the evolution of the festival. Integrated productions featuring singing actors who were well rehearsed and who fit naturally into an ensemble concept thrilled and moved audiences in a theater that, although seating had been expanded to 600 by 1939, retained its intimate flavor. [The theater was expanded to 700 in 1953, and its current capacity is 800.] By this time the tradition was firmly established, but it would be more than ten years before the Festival Opera returned to normal following the disruptions of the war. During that time the estate housed evacuees rather than artists. It reopened in 1946 with the world premiere of Britten's *The Rape of Lucretia* produced by the English Opera Group (subsidized by Christie) and featuring the operatic debut of Kathleen Ferrier. Benjamin Britten, John Piper, and Eric Crozier had founded the English National Opera (ENO) that year to promote the composition and performance of new operas, and they, along with Peter Pears, went on to create the Aldeburgh Festival. On June 20, 1947, ENO premiered *Albert Herring* with Pears and Cross and conducted by Britten, and the same season Carl Ebert returned to produce a memorable *Orfeo ed Euridice* with Ferrier. Neither 1948 nor 1949 saw any productions at Glyndebourne, but the company did begin an association with the Edinburgh Festival, producing its operas from 1947 to 1951, from 1953 to 1955, and again in 1960. Audrey Christie was the prime founder of the Edinburgh Festival through the Glyndebourne Society, and, with Rudolf Bing as the first artistic director, succeeded in creating an opportunity for Glyndebourne to produce opera at the city of Edinburgh's expense. The Christie fortune could no longer support the dream of 1934.

The first of a number of guarantees from British industry helped to relieve the growing financial burdens in 1950, and the formation of the Glyndebourne Festival Society in 1951 established an annual subscription for tickets that endures to this day. The festival has become so popular that very few tickets are currently available outside subscription. The Christies were relieved of all financial responsibility in 1954 with the formation of the Glyndebourne Arts Trust which established an endowment to ensure future program improvements and cover any deficits. Of the original creators of the Festival Opera, Fritz Busch died in 1951, followed by Audrey Mildmay Christie in 1953 and John Christie in 1962. The retirement of Carl Ebert in 1964 meant that new blood would control the destiny of John Christie's dream. Sir George Christie, who had succeeded his father as chairman of Glyndebourne Productions Limited in 1958, took over the family responsibility for the artistic and financial details.

The formation of the Touring Company in 1968 permitted an extension of the festival repertoire to the larger provincial centers. Using the same costumes and scenery, these productions utilize younger, less experienced singers and serve as a testing ground for aspiring artists trained in the Glyndebourne tradition.

United Kingdom 223

Between 1934 and 1988 the Glyndebourne Festival Opera produced sixty-five operas by thirty-four composers, including five world premieres. The British Broadcasting Corporation televised thirty-eight productions, including two documentaries, one of which detailed the fiftieth anniversary celebration in 1984. Six operas are normally presented each season in a festival running from the third week of May to the second week of August. The world famous London Philharmonic has been the resident orchestra at Glyndebourne since 1964.

CHRONOLOGY OF GENERAL ADMINISTRATORS: Rudolf Bing, 1935–1949. Moran Caplat, 1949–1981. Brian Dickie, 1981–1988. Anthony Whitworth-Jones, 1988–present.

CHRONOLOGY OF MUSIC DIRECTORS: Fritz Busch, 1934–1951. Vittorio Gui, 1951–1963. John Pritchard, 1964–1977. Bernard Haitink, 1978–1979. Andrew Davis, 1980–present.

CHRONOLOGY OF PRODUCTION HEADS: Carl Ebert, 1934–1959. Günther Rennert, 1960–1968. Franco Enriquez, 1968–1971. John Cox, 1971–present.

BIBLIOGRAPHY: Wilfred Blunt, *John Christie of Glyndebourne* (London, 1968). *Glyndebourne Festival Programme Book: 1952–1988* (Glyndebourne, 1952–1988). John Higgins, ed., *Glyndebourne: A Celebration* (London, 1984). John Higgins, *The Making of an Opera: "Don Giovanni" at Glyndebourne* (London, 1978). Spike Hughes, *Glyndebourne: A History of the Festival Opera* (London, 1965, repr., 1981). John Julius Norwich, *50 Years of Glyndebourne* (London, 1985). Ira Nowinski, *A Season at Glyndebourne* (London, 1986).

ACCESS: Lewes East Sussex BN8 5UU. (44 273) 812321; fax (44 273) 812783. Anthony Whitworth-Jones, General Administrator. Peter Hall, Artistic Director. Andrew Davis, Musical Director.

[From materials supplied by the company]

LONDON, ENGLAND (metro 6,735,400; city 4,400,000)

English National Opera

The original company dates from the opening of the Sadler's Wells Theatre in 1931. The brainchild of Lilian Baylis, who dreamed of resurrecting the old Music House as an Old Vic for North London, the theater was home to the Vic-Wells Opera and Ballet from 1931 to 1934. Baylis had headed an appeal for reconstruction funds in 1927, and enough was raised to complete the project in 1930. The 1,548-seat theater opened on January 6, 1931, with Shakespeare's *Twelfth Night*, and opera and ballet initially alternated with the Bard. The Vic-Wells Opera Company had a standard repertoire of over two dozen operas, and that would grow appreciably until the Second World War. Baylis's aim was to offer performances of the highest possible standard at the lowest possible price, and for over fifty years the company has maintained this objective and brought opera into the center of British life. When the acting company decided to remain at the Old Vic, the company was renamed the Sadler's Wells Opera and Ballet

(1934); it performed in the refurbished house until the bombing of London, when the theater closed. Notable productions included Verdi's *Falstaff* and the British premiere of Mussorgsky's *Boris Godunov* in the original scoring. During the war the company toured a number of chamber productions directed by Tyrone Guthrie and gave short seasons at several London theaters, including the Princess Theater, where Joan Cross directed the last wartime season. Energetic regional touring was maintained until 1983, when the expansion of the four regional companies brought about a change of government policy for this London-based company.

The world premiere of Benjamin Britten's *Peter Grimes* on June 7, 1945, reopened the house to great acclaim. Produced by Eric Crozier and conducted by Reginald Goodall, the cast was headed by Peter Pears, Joan Cross, and Edith Coates. Back again in its old home, the company, now named the Sadler's Wells Opera, performed there with its sister, the Sadler's Wells Ballet, until 1968, when it made a permanent move to the London Coliseum. In 1948 Norman Tucker joined the company, injecting a new atmosphere and direction into a floundering enterprize, and new productions of Verdi, Janáček, and works by British composers were added to the repertoire. That same year the Arts Council of Great Britain was incorporated to administer public subsidies to artistic organizations. Its predecessor, the Council for the Encouragement of Music and the Arts, had provided funds for the company's wartime tours, and expectations were high that, at last, financial uncertainties would be over. A proposed merger with the Carl Rosa Company in the late 1950s unfortunately caused dissension in both organizations. In 1958 a substantial Arts Council grant to the Carl Rosa Company was withdrawn; Salder's Wells absorbed some of the personnel, and, with a performance of *Don Giovanni* on September 7, 1960, a historic company that had been founded in 1875 was disbanded. With renewed public and press support, the Sadler's Wells Opera now provided most of the provincial tours in Britain, indicating that there was a place for a stable company that produced opera in English throughout most of the year.

The local artistic outcome was that Stephen Arlen, who had succeeded Norman Tucker in 1966, moved the company to the Coliseum in 1968, opening with *La Traviata* on August 3 of that year. He also appointed Charles Mackerras as musical director (1970–1977). [Since Stephen Arlen moved the company in 1968, the Sadler's Wells Theatre has hosted other well-known opera companies from Great Britain and Europe. An attempt to build the New Sadler's Wells Opera failed, and the company was permanently disbanded in February 1989. Sadler's Wells Theatre can be contacted at telephone 01–278 6563; fax 01–837 0965.] Lord Harewood took over from Arlen in 1972. Originally built as a music hall in 1904, the 2,354-seat Coliseum is the largest theater in London. Because of the size of both the auditorium and the stage, many felt it was unsuitable for opera. However, productions of Wagner's "Ring" and Prokoffiev's *War and Peace* mollified the critics. The name of the company was changed to the English National Opera (ENO) in 1974, and the company continues its policy of hiring primarily British singers. To maintain high artistic standards, the permanent ensemble of principal singers, chorus, orchestra and technicians works regularly with guest artists. ENO performs all operas in English, believing that if opera is to be defined as drama through music, then it will reach its audience most directly in the language they understand.

In a newly established series of commissions from British composers, a new opera is presented every season. Most notable in recent years has been Harrison Birtwistle's *The Mask of Orpheus* in 1986. Stephen Oliver, Jonathan Harvey, John Buller, Robin Holloway, Mark-Anthony Turnage, and Judith Weir are scheduled for works in the future. In addition, the outreach and education unit, the Baylis Programme, develops future audiences and extends the appeal and accessibility of opera beyond the confines of the Coliseum to all sections of Britain's complex, multicultural society. The Contemporary Opera Studio encourages the writing of new opera with the participation of playwrights, novelists, poets, composers, producers and designers in an unprecedented combination of creative talent. ENO currently presents over two hundred performances of between eighteen and twenty works each season. Over a quarter of those attending have never before been to an opera. Moreover, additional millions enjoy ENO performances through radio and television broadcasts. In the summer of 1990 ENO accomplished a hugely successful tour of the Soviet Union, taking three operas—*Macbeth, The Turn of the Screw*, and Handel's *Xerxes*—to Kiev, Moscow, and Leningrad.

BIBLIOGRAPHY: Denis Arundel, *The Story of Sadler's Wells, 1683–1987* (London, 1978). R. Jarman, *A History of Sadler's Wells Opera* (London, 1974). M. Stapleton, *The Sadler's Wells Opera* (London, 1954).

ACCESS: London Coliseum, St. Martin's Lane. London WC2N 4ES (44 71) 836 0111; fax (44 71) 836 8379. Peter Jonas, General Director. Mark Elder, Music Director. David Pountney, Director of Productions. Sadler's Wells Theatre; (44 01) 278 6563; fax (44 01) 837 0965.

[From materials supplied by the company]

Royal Opera House Covent Garden

The Royal Opera House is a dominant landmark in one of London's busiest and most popular areas. The district takes its name from a convent garden that served the Catholic monks of Westminster until the dissolution of the monasteries in the sixteenth century. From the 1630s to the 1970s it was a thriving market, but for over 250 years a Covent Garden theater has provided various forms of theatrical entertainment. The present theater is the third to have stood upon the site; the first theater was built by the actor/manager John Rich. Rich had inherited one of the two sets of Letters Patent granted by King Charles II in 1661, at the time of the restoration of the monarchy. These Letters Patent allowed their owners sole rights to build theaters within the city of London and Westminster, to perform spoken drama, and to call their theaters Royal. The second set of Letters Patent attached to the Theatre Royal, Drury Lane, where a theater has stood on virtually the same site since 1663. The Theatre Royal, Covent Garden and the Theatre Royal, Drury Lane enjoyed a continuous state of rivalry until their fortunes took significantly differing courses during and after the Second World War.

John Rich, an energetic and resourceful manager, commissioned a new work from John Gay for his Lincoln's Inn Fields theater in 1728. Gay produced *The Beggar's Opera*, a pastiche on the popular Italian operas of the day, which provided a tremendous success. The financial rewards of this work allowed Rich to build a new and larger theater in Covent Garden, which at the time was a lively but not overly respectable area of London. Designed by Edward Shepherd, the first Theatre Royal, Covent Garden opened on December 7, 1732, with a performance of William Congreve's *The Way of the World*. The building was very small, measuring only one hundred by fifty feet, and had no street facade. It was built primarily as a house for drama, but eighteenth-century audiences expected a variety of entertainments, including music and dance. Not surprisingly, the first musical piece to be heard at Covent Garden was *The Beggar's Opera*, which was performed on December 16, 1732. Various specialty acts and ballad operas appeared until Rich engaged George Frideric Handel for three seasons of opera, from 1735 to 1737. Handel's company was distinguished and included Anna Strada del Po and the castrato Carestini. He produced *Ariodante* and *Alcina* (1735), *Atalanta* (1736), and *Arminio* and *Berenice* (1737), but the public taste for grand Italian opera was waning. Following the relative failure of these works, Handel devoted his energies to oratorio, many of which were written for Covent Garden or received their first performances there. Unfortunately, these seasons were financially disastrous for Handel, and he relinquished his connection with Covent Garden in 1752, having lost his entire private fortune there.

Following Handel's retirement, Italian opera was rarely heard at Covent Garden, but the popularity of English ballad operas continued. In 1760 Thomas Arne transferred from Drury Lane to Covent Garden. He was succeeded by Charles Dibdin and his son Thomas, whose operas *The Cabinet* and *Family Quarrels* were produced in 1802. Singers of note at this time included the tenor John Braham; Nancy Storace, who created the role of Susanna in Mozart's *Le Nozze di Figaro*; and Francesco Benucci, the first Mozart Figaro and the first Guglielmo in *Così fan tutte*, as well as the celebrated soprano Mrs. Billington. Despite this sporadic musical activity, the theater remained primarily a playhouse, and in 1803, two members of a famous theatrical family, John Philip Kemble and his sister, Mrs. Sarah Siddons, took joint shares in the management. An unexplained fire completely destroyed the theater on September 20, 1808. Work began immediately on a replacement, and on September 9, 1809, the second Theatre Royal, Covent Garden opened with Kemble as Macbeth and Mrs. Siddons as Lady Macbeth. The new theater was very different from its eighteenth-century predecessor. Designed by Robert Smirke, it had a long and imposing facade on Bow Street based on the Temple of Minerva in Athens, and was London's first public building in the neoclassical style. In an attempt to recoup some of the cost of rebuilding, the management introduced price increases which sparked off price riots; these proved to be the most prolonged in theater history.

In 1811 Henry Bishop was appointed musical director. Now remembered chiefly as the composer of "Home Sweet Home," Bishop was responsible for adapting most of Walter Scott's novels for the stage and for introducing a number of foreign operas in his own adaptations and arrangements. Mozart's *Don Giovanni* became *The Libertine*, with Charles Kemble, a notable actor, in the title role. In subsequent years Bishop performed similar operations on Rossini's *Il Barbiere di Siviglia* and Mozart's *Le Nozze di Figaro*. Charles Kemble succeeded his brother as manager of the theater and was responsible for dismissing Henry Bishop in 1824. Kemble invited Carl Maria von Weber to be music director and to compose an opera for Covent Garden. Weber came to London to supervise rehearsals and to conduct the premiere of *Oberon* on April 12, 1826, to an overwhelming success.

Covent Garden continued to house occasional performances of significance, although the main opera house in London since 1710 had been the King's Theatre in the Haymarket. This theater, known since the accession of Queen Victoria in 1837 as Her Majesty's Theatre, was to witness the greatest flowering of Romantic ballet and opera in the early nineteenth century. At Covent Garden, the unadulterated works of Rossini were gradually introduced, and in 1830 Maria Malibran made her debut. Malibran returned the following year in a company that included the German soprano Wilhelmina Schröder-Devrient, "The Queen of Tears." This season also saw Giuditta Pasta in her only Covent Garden appearance, in which she played Norma, the role she had created at the opera's premiere. The 1840s, however, saw a gradual decline in the fortunes of Covent Garden, and when the Theatres Act of 1843 effectively ended the Patent Theatres monopoly of spoken drama, it was not long before Covent Garden closed down. The company of singers at Her Majesty's Theatre, headed by music director Michael Costa, had also been experiencing difficulties with the management, and in 1846 plans were made to open a rival Italian opera house in London. A company headed by Giuseppe Persiani, husband of the soprano Fanny Persiani, and the music publishers Cramer, Beale and Co., purchased the lease of Covent Garden. The auditorium was completely remodeled to designs by Benedetto Albano, and the theater reopened on April 6, 1847, as the Royal Italian Opera with a performance of Rossini's *Semiramide*. Virtually the entire company of singers and musicians had transferred from Her Majesty's, and Covent Garden [under the leadership of Frederick Gye, who would serve as manager from 1849 to 1877] was firmly established as an opera house, and has remained so almost exclusively since that date.

As the theater's name suggests, Italian operas formed the bulk of the repertory, and in the first season there were performances of works by Bellini, Donizetti, Rossini, and two early works by Verdi—*I due Foscari* and *Ernani*—as well as

Mozart's *Don Giovanni* and *Le Nozze di Figaro*. French and German works were given but all were translated into Italian. Donizetti, Bellini, and Rossini dominated the repertory, with Meyerbeer and Verdi growing in popularity. In 1853 Berlioz conducted a single performance of *Benvenuto Cellini*; that same year, Verdi's *Rigoletto* was premiered at Covent Garden, with *Il Trovatore* and *La Traviata* following in successive seasons. Seasons given by the Royal Italian Opera lasted for approximately five months, from April until August. The theater continued to be used for concerts, mainly in the autumn months, and in the 1840s the French conductor/showman Louis Antoine Jullien introduced the first promenade concerts. The theater was also used for other events, and in 1856 it was leased to "Professor" J. H. Anderson, the self-styled "Wizard of the North," for a series of entertainments concluding with a grand bal masque. It was during this "disorderly bal masque," on March 5, 1856, that the second theater was burned down.

Despite considerable opposition, Gye determined to build a replacement theater, and work began on the present building in September 1857 to designs by Edward Barry. The friezes by Flaxman and Rossi that decorated the facade of the second theater were retrieved from the ruins and incorporated in the new facade. The auditorium is a fine example of a traditional late-nineteenth-century Italianate opera house with four semicircular tiers of boxes rising to a gallery. The color scheme has remained virtually unchanged, and the tiers are decorated with winged nymphs who increase in maturity as the levels descend. The theater opened on May 15, 1858, with Meyerbeer's *Les Huguenots*, with virtually the same company and repertory as before the fire. Giulia Grisi retired in 1861, and that same season her successor as reigning soprano, Adelina Patti, made her debut as Amina in *La Sonnambula*. Patti's roles that season included Lucia, Martha, Rosina, and Violetta, as well as Zerlina in a performance of *Don Giovanni* with Grisi singing Donna Anna. Patti appeared in a wide variety of roles and was the first London Aida and Juliette in Gounod's *Romeo et Juliette*. She also appeared regularly as Marguerite in Gounod's *Faust*, an extraordinarily popular opera, first given at Covent Garden in 1863 and performed in every season thereafter until 1911.

All operas continued to be given in Italian, including the first Wagner heard at Covent Garden. This was not until 1875, when *Lohengrin* was performed, with Ernest Nicolini as Lohengrin and Emma Albani as Elsa, and conducted by Auguste Vianesi. The next year *Tannhäuser* was presented; followed by *Der fliegende Holländer*, which was given as *Il vascello fantasma* in 1877. Gye retired in 1877 and was succeeded by his son Ernst, who was, by that time, Albani's husband. In 1881 Augustus Harris became manager and ushered in a golden age of singing at Covent Garden, offering a magnificent roster of singers, conductors, and performances of greater artistic integrity. Harris began to present operas in their original languages, with French operas in 1889 and German operas in 1892, the year that the word "Italian" was dropped from the name of the theater. During his first season the great Australian soprano Nellie Melba made her debut, and she was to reign supreme until her final farewell appearance in 1926. Singers that she appeared with regularly included Caruso, the de Reszkes, Maurel, and Scotti. Other singers appearing under Harris's management included Calvé, the Ravogli sisters, Eames, Plançon, and Francesco Tamagno.

Following Augustus Harris's retirement in 1896, seasons organized by the Grand Opera Syndicate continued much as before but with a gradual decline in artistic standards and initiative. However, a complete reversal occurred when Thomas Beecham began his association with Covent Garden in 1910. During his initial season Beecham introduced Richard Strauss's *Elektra* and revived many works by English composers, including Arthur Sullivan's *Ivanhoe* and Ethyl Smythe's *The Wreckers*. In his second season Beecham added Strauss's *Salome* to the repertory, and in 1913 he presented *Der Rosenkavalier*. The 1911 season also saw the first Covent Garden performances by Serge Diaghilev's Ballets Russes company. During the First World War the Royal Opera House was used mainly as a furniture repository, although some charity performances were given. [Beecham founded and personally guaranteed the Beecham Opera Company in October 1915, and the company evolved quickly and unexpectedly into a "grand opera" organization. His singers included some of the finest British artists, and the company continued with some memorable productions until it was forced into liquidation in December 1920.] Covent Garden reopened in 1919 with Beecham himself as lessee, but in 1920 he was declared bankrupt and did not appear at Covent Garden again until the 1930s.

Seasons continued much as before the war, with German opera in the ascendence. *Der Rosenkavalier* was given with casts that included Lotte Lehmann, Elisabeth Schumann, and Richard Mayr, and Frida Leider, Lauritz Melchoir, Rudolf Bockelmann, and Herbert Janssen appeared regularly. Italian opera was revitalized briefly by the appearances of Rosa Ponselle in *La Traviata, La Gioconda, Fedora,* and *Norma* between 1929 and 1932; by Eva Turner in a variety of roles, including her outstanding Turandot; and Beniamino Gigli in many of his most famous roles. Beecham returned in 1932, remaining as music director until 1939. The Staatsoper Dresden visited in 1936, bringing Richard Strauss to conduct performances of *Ariadne auf Naxos* and Karl Böhm to conduct four operas including *Der Rosenkavalier* and *Tristan und Isolde*. Beecham's last season at Covent Garden was in the summer of 1939; plans were issued for the 1940 season, only to be halted by the outbreak of the Second World War. During the war the Royal Opera House was leased to Mecca Cafés Ltd. for use as a dance hall, and provided much-needed solace to members of the armed forces on leave and to citizens of London. The theater resounded to the music of popular bands and saw the introduction of the jitterbug and jive from America.

There was a possibility that Mecca would be able to extend their lease at the end of the war and that the theater would remain a dance hall. Fortunately, thanks to the intervention of the music publishers Leslie Boosey and Ralph Hawkes, the theater was reclaimed for the lyric arts. [The Covent Garden Opera Trust was established which, in cooperation with the Arts Council of Great

Britain, articulated the goal of establishing Covent Garden as the British national center of opera and ballet.] David Webster was appointed general administrator in 1945 and began the task of reestablishing the theater as an opera house. Karl Rankl was appointed music director for the newly formed Covent Garden Opera Company and began work on establishing a company and repertory. The policy was that operas were to be given in English and that emphasis should be placed on encouraging British performers. The first performance by the company was a joint production with the Sadler's Wells Ballet of Purcell's *The Fairy Queen* in December 1946, followed on January 14, 1947, by a production of *Carmen*.

It soon became apparent that there would not be sufficient British and Commonwealth singers to fulfill the demands of an international opera house and, although many foreign singers, including Kirsten Flagstad, Elisabeth Schwartzkopf and Hans Hotter, were prepared to relearn their roles in English, the policy soon reverted to singing operas in the original language. Karl Rankl retired in 1951, having laid the foundations for a fine chorus and orchestra. The company benefited subsequently from working with, among others, Erich Kleiber, John Barbirolli, Clemens Krauss, and Rudolf Kempe. Maria Callas made her debut as Norma in 1952 and sang the heroine in Franco Zeffirelli's memorable *Tosca* with Tito Gobbi as Scarpia in 1964. That same year a young Australian soprano joined the company—Joan Sutherland, whose early roles included Clothilde to Callas's Norma. Her performances in Zeffirelli's *Lucia di Lammermoor* in 1959 launched her international career.

Rafael Kubelik succeeded Rankl in 1955 and pursued his aim of establishing a fine ensemble at Covent Garden. In 1957 Kubelik conducted performances in English of Berlioz's *The Trojans* with only one guest artist and an almost entirely British and Commonwealth cast that included Marie Collier, Joan Carlyle, John Vickers, Michael Langdon, and Forbes Robinson. Lucchino Visconti's production of *Don Carlos*, which was given in 1958 to celebrate the centenary of the Royal Opera House, featured Vickers, Brouwenstijn, Barbieri, Christoff, and Gobbi conducted by Carlo Maria Giulini. Following Kubelik's retirement in 1958 there was another interregnum until Georg Solti was appointed in 1961. Solti's declared ambition was to make Covent Garden the best opera house in the world, and during his ten years as music director, the Royal Opera House was the scene of many exciting musical events, including Zeffirelli's *Falstaff* with Geraint Evans conducted by Giulini in 1961, Sena Jurinac in *Fidelio* conducted by Klemperer, Visconti's productions of *Il Trovatore* in 1964 and *La Traviata* in 1967, Peter Hall's production of *Moses and Aaron* in 1965, and Jon Vicker's first *Peter Grimes* in 1969.

David Webster retired as general director in 1970. He had seen both companies receive Royal Charters, the Covent Garden Opera Company having become the Royal Opera in 1968. Webster was succeeded by John Tooley, who had been assistant general administrator since 1955. That same year Frederick Ashton retired as director of the Royal Ballet, and in 1971 Solti retired from the Royal Opera. Kenneth MacMillan was appointed to lead the ballet company and Colin

Davis became music director of The Royal Opera. The Colin Davis/John Tooley years saw many distinguished and exciting performances, including Kiri te Kanawa as the Countess in *Le Nozze di Figaro* in 1971, the Götz Friedrich production of the "Ring" cycle (1974–1978), and the British premiere of Berg's *Lulu*. Davis also led the company on tours to Milan (an exchange with the Teatro alla Scala in 1976), to the Far East in 1979, and to the Olympic Games in Los Angeles in 1984. John Tooley launched the Covent Garden Proms and pioneered the use of the Big Screen on the Piazza, giving a wider audience the opportunity to enjoy performances at a greatly reduced price or, in the case of the Big Screen, for free.

Colin Davis was the first to retire in 1984, to be followed by John Tooley in 1988. Bernard Haitink assumed the post of music director of the Royal Opera in 1986 at the same time that Jeremy Isaacs was appointed general director. Isaacs and Haitink are both determined that Covent Garden should retain its reputation as a "centre of excellence," and new productions have included the British premiere of *Un re in áscolta* and the first productions by the Royal Opera of *Prince Igor* and *The Cunning Little Vixen*. Revivals have included the return of Luciano Pavarotti in *L'Elisir d'Amore* and Placido Domingo in *Otello*. Haitink has led the orchestra out of the pit to give concerts on stage at the Opera House and in concert around the country. Jeremy Isaacs's first seasons have seen the introduction of fairly substantial ticket increases which was not universally applauded. As he endeavors to make audiences pay the market price for tickets, Isaacs is keen to establish new audiences. He has continued the use of the Big Screen on the Piazza and the Proms, pursued the possibility of increased television and radio broadcasts, and scheduled the company in open-air concert performances.

The Royal Opera House is now facing a major redevelopment which includes plans to improve backstage, rehearsal, and production facilities, as well as to provide new office accommodations. The auditorium will remain virtually unchanged except for the installation of air-conditioning, but spacious new foyer spaces will be provided in the Floral Hall adjacent to the theater and there will be an entrance via newly constructed porticos in the Piazza. This exciting prospect will mean the closure of the theater for up to three seasons, but Jeremy Isaacs is determined that it will provide the Royal Ballet and the Royal Opera with a theater that will take them proudly and magnificently into the twenty-first century. [Unfortunately the current economic climate has mandated some rethinking of the future of all of the arts in the United Kingdom. The Chairman of the Board of the Royal Opera House, Lord Sainsbury, announced his intention to step down in April 1991. His replacement, Angus Stirling, will have to cope with a continuing deficit as well as with reduced government funding for the proposed theatrical and commercial development of the Covent Garden market hall area. There is some question as to whether or not the ten new productions announced for the 1991–1992 season will in fact receive the requisite funding.]

CHRONOLOGY OF GENERAL ADMINISTRATORS: Sir David Webster, 1945–1970. Sir John Tooley, 1970–1988. Jeremy Isaacs, 1988–present.

CHRONOLOGY OF MUSIC DIRECTORS: Karl Rankl, 1946–1951. Rafael Kubelik, 1955–1958. Sir Georg Solti, 1961–1971. Sir Colin Davis, 1971–1986. Bernard Haitink, 1987–present.

BIBLIOGRAPHY: Frances Donaldson, *The Royal Opera House in the Twentieth Century* (London, 1985). Montague Haltrecht, *The Quiet Showman: Sir David Webster and the Royal Opera House* (London, 1975). *A History of the Royal Opera House: Covent Garden, 1732–1982* (London, 1983). Paul Robinson, *Solti* (Toronto, 1979). Harold Rosenthal, *Opera at Covent Garden: A Short History* (London, 1967). Harold Rosenthal, *Two Centuries of Opera at Covent Garden* (London, 1958).

ACCESS: Royal Opera House Covent Garden, London WC2E 9DD. (44 71) 240 1200; fax (44 71) 836 1762. Jeremy Isaacs, General Administrator. Bernard Haitink, Music Director.

FRANCESCA FRANCHI

United States of America

BALTIMORE, MARYLAND (metro 2,160,000; city 772,000)

Baltimore Opera Company

Although musical activities in Baltimore predate the American Revolution, Baltimore has never evolved into a center of the arts in America. As the first city in the country to establish an orchestra using public monies (1914), the Board of Estimate affirmed this commitment by appropriating $8,000 to launch the Baltimore Symphony Orchestra at its debut concert on February 11, 1916. Operatic activities began in 1932 in a workshop setting. In 1940 the Baltimore Civic Opera Company (BCOC) was founded by Eugene and Mary Martinet, and the company initially performed in the auditorium of the Maryland Casualty Company. The company was chartered in 1950, and its professional status dates from this time.

The Metropolitan Opera diva Rosa Ponselle formally associated herself with the company in 1951, and shortly thereafter was asked to join the Board of Directors. Prior to her association with BCOC, Ponselle was instrumental in the effort to fund the Baltimore Symphony Orchestra (BSO) as a full-time ensemble. In 1952 the company moved to the Lyric Theater. With a capacity of 2,456, the Lyric Theater was designed after the Leipzig Neues Gewandhaus and was completed in 1894. The name was shortened to Baltimore Opera Company (BOC) in 1961. In 1964 the Baltimore Symphony Orchestra negotiated "an enduring relationship with the [BOC]. . . . Although the Opera had previously utilized BSO musicians, this was the first time the entire orchestra was used in the pit." Ponselle was named artistic director, a position she held until June 1979. The company currently produces three or four standard nineteenth-century operas each season.

BIBLIOGRAPHY: *Baltimore Evening Sun and Baltimore News-Post* (1951, 1952, 1964). Kenneth S. Clark, *Baltimore: Cradle of Municipal Music* (Baltimore, 1941). *Opera News*.

Rosa Ponselle and James A. Drake, *Ponselle: A Singer's Life* (Garden City, NY, 1982). *Washington Post* (1951, 1952, 1964).

ACCESS: 527 North Charles Street, Baltimore, MD 21201-5030. (301) 727 0592; fax (301) 727-7854. Michael Harrison, General Director.

[From materials supplied by the company]

BOSTON, MASSACHUSETTS (metro 2,780,000; city 580,000)

Boston Lyric Opera Company

[Settled in 1630, Boston quickly became one of the cultural and educational centers of the United States, a distinction that it retains to this day. Unfortunately, due to the historical Puritan traditions, theater has never occupied the prominent place in Boston culture that it may deserve. Visiting companies provided most of the stage entertainment until the end of the nineteenth century. In 1883 the new Metropolitan Opera Association began its annual visits from New York, followed by the Chicago Opera Association in 1917. Purely local efforts came to naught until Boris Goldovsky's New England Opera Conservatory Opera Workshop opened for business in 1942. One of his protégées, Sarah Caldwell, formed the Boston Opera Group (BOG) in 1958; it was later renamed the Opera Company of Boston. BOG inaugurated its first season on January 29, 1959, in the Fine Arts Theatre, which was later known as the Little Opera House. The company moved to the refurbished Schubert Theatre on January 10, 1969, with the American premiere of the Bartok trilogy for the stage. With the demise of the Metropolitan Opera National Company in the spring of 1967, the Opera Company of Boston completed the tour with Alban Berg's *Lulu*. Famed for its world and American premieres, the Opera Company of Boston played an important role in the contemporary American operatic scene.]

In 1976 three opera companies in Boston—the New England Chamber Opera, New England Regional Opera, and Associate Artists Opera Company of New England—merged to form the Boston Lyric Opera (BLO). In the words of Randolph J. Fuller, president of the Boston Lyric's board from its inception to the present, the three companies had basically the same aims and were tired of "chasing the same dollar." When the boards of the three companies merged, Fuller and Ernest Triplett, who had been president and artistic director of the Associate Artists Company, took over the same positions with the new Boston Lyric Company. Partly in reaction to Sarah Caldwell's Opera Company of Boston, which used local singers only in the chorus of its large-scale productions, the new company was dedicated to presenting opera with singers from the New England area in English versions at affordable prices.

The New England Chamber Opera, which had been directed by Philip Morehead, had a special grant to present Mozart's *Zaide* at Wellesley College, and this became the Boston Lyric's first production. Conducted by Morehead, it was presented both at Wellesley and the Massachusetts College of Art in 1977 and was received enthusiastically by the local press and by *Opera News*. After producing Carl Orff's *Die Kluge*, the company found itself with insufficient funds and limited its activity the following season to presenting a benefit concert at Jordan Hall. Entitled "A Jenny Lind Evening," it featured Elizabeth Parcells, who had starred in *Zaide*, and made some money for the BLO. When Ernest Triplett, who had sung in the concert, resigned as artistic director and Philip Morehead left Boston to become chorus director at the Chicago Lyric Opera, the company entered a second phase in its history.

Characteristics noted in the first season of the BLO—unusual repertory, ingenious fund-raising ideas, and the constant search for better performing space—became more prominent as the company grew under John Balme, a British conductor and musicologist who was brought in from the San Diego Opera. Balme began his tenure as artistic director of the BLO in 1979 by conducting stylish performances of Verdi's *Un giorno di regno*, which were given in the modest auditorium of the Brookline High School. Balme's abilities as a first-rate conductor were immediately evident, as was his talent for putting together effective productions of unusual repertory using local singers, all on an extremely limited budget. Under Balme the company took a huge step forward in 1980 when it moved to the Boston University Theater and presented a season that included Mozart's *La Clemenza di Tito*, Menotti's *The Consul*, and Monteverdi's *L'Incoronazione di Poppea*. The Monteverdi was produced together with the noted early group Banchetto Musicale and became part of Boston's widely publicized Early Music Festival. BLO continued to expand in original ways, gaining funds and publicity in events that ranged from a performance for Gardner Museum patrons of Amherst Webber's *Fiorella*, an unknown comic opera that had once been put on at the museum by Mrs. Gardner, to presenting BLO singers in a free concert performance of Verdi's *Aida* for an audience of 15,000 on the Boston Esplanade.

The 1980–1981 season offered two performances each of Mozart's *The Abduction from the Seraglio*, Massenet's *Werther*, and Bellini's *Norma*. Again the casts were composed of Boston-based artists who had been singing regularly with the company, such as Patti Dell, D'Anna Fortunato, Anna Gabrieli, Priscilla Ganley, Valerie Walters, Richard Conrad, Ray DeVoll, Peter Elvins, Demetri Haitas, Robert Honeysucker, and James Maddalena. With *Norma* the company presented its first production in Italian. The following season was equally ambitious with productions of *Madama Butterfly, Ariadne auf Naxos*, and *Il Trovatore*, the last presented in a controversial staging that updated the work to the time of the Spanish Revolution. For the first time several of the leading singers were imported from New York. In the summer of 1982 Balme and the BLO launched their most ambitious project—complete concert performances of Wagner's "Ring" cycle. This undertaking was financed by the New York Wagner Society, and bus-loads of enthusiastic Wagnerians came from New York to Boston on four successive Sunday afternoons to cheer the performances. The venture was a resounding success with everyone but the local critics, who had become increasingly hostile to the BLO as the company became more ambitious. Several of the leading singers were brought from outside Boston, most notably the veteran tenor Ticho Parly as Siegfried and Roger Roloff, whose first Wotans were highly acclaimed, as was Balme's sensitive conducting of the remarkable free-lance orchestra recruited from Boston area musicians.

The BLO "Ring" generated so much enthusiasm that for the 1982–1983 season it was decided to present it in a fully staged production, first in Boston and then at the Beacon Theater in New York, with financial backing from patrons in both cities. This ambitious undertaking proved immensely successful, especially in New York, where it received glowing reviews in the *New York Times*. New Yorkers, who had not enjoyed performances of the "Ring" for many seasons, talked for years about this extraordinary production by the "spunky little Boston Lyric Opera." Ironically, the BLO's biggest triumph almost brought about its downfall. The promised financial backing did not materialize, and after the "Ring" performances the company found itself $450,000 in debt, forcing it to cancel the 1983–1984 season. John Balme resigned as general director, and the position was taken by Anne Ewers, who had staged both the "Ring" and *Madama Butterfly*. With the aid of the board and several singers, the new administration managed to retire the debt in the next two years. To help achieve this goal, a number of benefit concerts were given, with John Balme and the performers all donating their services, and Bostonians enjoyed such events as a concert performance of Meyerbeer's *Les Huguenots* in historic Trinity Church.

Clever ways were devised to attract a new public. When the film *Amadeus* appeared, the BLO presented a double bill of Mozart's *Impresario* and Salieri's *Prima la musica e poi le parole*. The 1985–1986 season began with a production of Handel's *Agrippina* to mark the bicentennial of the composer's birth and ended with a month-long citywide tribute to John McCormack, chaired by the mayor and the archbishop of Boston, to celebrate the Irish tenor's centennial year. This season also included a double bill of Poulenc's *La voix humaine* and Walton's *Façade*. In 1986–1987 the BLO began limiting its seasons to two productions, and presented *Rigoletto* and *The Rake's Progress*. The following year, in addition to giving Donizetti's *Maria Stuarda*, the company joined with the Theater of the Deaf to produce a signed performance of Britten's *The Turn of the Screw*. This was the first signed opera to be given in the United States, and it brought the company special grants to make opera accessible for the handicapped. The French consul general in Boston became the honorary chairman of the 1988–1989 season, which celebrated the bicentennial of the French Revolution with productions of Poulenc's *The Dialogues of the Carmelites* and a Massenet double bill of *The Portrait of Manon* and *Thérèse*. During this season Anne Ewers resigned as general director and John Balme gave up his position as artistic advisor and principal conductor to become general director of the Lake George Opera. Justin Moss, who had been development director at the Baltimore Opera Company, was named general manager, with Richard Gaddes, formerly of the Opera Theater of St. Louis, as artistic advisor and Stephen Lord as music director.

With these men at the helm, the company moved into the newly renovated Emerson Majestic Theatre for the 1989–1990 season. Planned by the previous administration, it included Patricia Craig in the title role of *Tosca*, concert performances of *Der fliegende Holländer* with Roger Roloff returning to sing the Dutchman and John Balme conducting for the last time with the company, and *La Traviata*, all given in the original language. The inadequate orchestra pit of the Emerson Majestic was renovated and vastly improved for the 1990–1991 season, which included Donizetti's *The Daughter of the Regiment*, Richard Strauss's *Ariadne auf Naxos* (featuring the splendid Deborah Voigt in the title role), and Marc Blitzstein's *Regina*. The Boston Lyric Opera now has a new image and different aims. It no longer promotes local singers or strives to produce opera in English, a tradition that began in Boston with Boris Goldovsky's New England Opera Theater. Instead, the BLO is another well-run regional company. It has a stronger financial basis than ever before, it has gained an imposing list of backers, and, after fifteen years of steady growth, it gives every indication of becoming Boston's most successful operatic organization.

BIBLIOGRAPHY: Cardell Bishop, *Boston National Opera Company and Boston Theatre Opera Company* (Santa Monica, CA, 1981). Quaintance Eaton, *The Boston Opera Company* (New York, 1965). *Opera News* (1976, 1982, 1985).

ACCESS: 811 Boylston Street, Boston, MA 02116–2601. (617) 267 1512; fax (617) 421 9835. Justin Moss, General Director.

PETER ELVINS

CENTRAL CITY, COLORADO (city est. 2,500)

Central City Opera

Founded in 1932, the Central City Opera Festival is one of America's oldest summer festivals. The opera company is really part of the history of Colorado, the history of Central City, and, more immediately, the history of the Opera House. With exception of a suspension for World War II (1942–1945) and for the 1982 season, programs have been mounted each year since the Victorian opera house was acquired by the University of Denver in 1931. It was partially restored and reopened under the sponsorship of the Central City Opera House Association. Performances take place in the 1878 building which was originally constructed by Cornish and Welsh miners. Seating 756 in historic hickory chairs, the edifice is a glorious reminder of the wealth of silver and gold deposits found around Central City. Three major operas in a six-week season, with an emphasis on American conductors, stage directors, and principal artists, provide visitors with an excellent opportunity to mix the arts with Rocky Mountain splendor (elevation, 8,450 feet). Offering only opera and operetta since 1976, the summer festival, through its Artist in Residence Program (now in its fourth year), is a major training ground for young artists. The company serves as an important regional center, giving all performances in English. Box office income in 1990 exceeded $717,000 with 98 percent attendance for the season. Subscriptions increased by 12 percent, making 1990 the most successful season in Central City Opera's history. Season performances as well as selected recitals were taped for later broadcast over KVOD-FM. Restoration of the Opera House, which was inaugurated several years ago with the replacement of the roof and the ceiling (with faithful reproductions of the original ceiling murals by San Francisco artist John Massman) and the installation of a state-of-the-art computerized lighting system, continues with the restoration of the hundred-year-old foundation.

BIBLIOGRAPHY: *Denver Post. Rocky Mountain News.*

ACCESS: Central City Opera House Assn., 621 17th Street, Suite 1601, Denver, CO 80293. (303) 292 6500; fax (303) 292 4958. John Moriarty, Artistic Director. Daniel Rule, General Manager.

[From materials supplied by the company]

CHAUTAUQUA, NEW YORK (city est. 4,700)

Chautauqua Opera Association

[Located in the rolling hills of southwest New York State and situated on the western shore of Chautauqua Lake, Chautauqua Institution was founded in 1874 by John Heyl Vincent and Lewis Miller. From its original mission of training Sunday-school teachers, the institution quickly expanded into adult education activities and cultural enrichment.] During the summer of 1926, Vladimir Rosing brought his American Opera Company from the Eastman School in Rochester to Chautauqua for a series of six productions in the Amphitheater which were sung in English. Rosing's work incorporated quite modern and radical theater ideas, and he believed in integrated productions. He also emphasized three objectives for the Rochester company, which would become a part of the heritage of opera at Chautauqua: the use of native singers, production of opera in the vernacular, and a fusion of music, dramatic expression, and production elements. The enthusiastic response of Chautauquans created momentum for a permanent company. A gift of $100,000 by Mrs. O. W. Norton in memory of her husband and daughter enabled the institution to build a multipurpose theater to house opera and other staged events. The original stagehouse was expanded in 1937, and a major restoration and renovation, including a new electrical system, lighting, and stage machinery was completed in 1984.

About this same time the Chautauqua Symphony Orchestra was assembled out of the remains of the New York Symphony. Albert Stoessel was officially appointed music director of the institution with both the opera and the symphony under his direct control. After the completion of the 1,367-seat Norton Memorial Hall, the Chautauqua Opera Association (COA) opened its first season with

Flowtow's *Martha* on July 19, 1929, conducted by Stoessel. Over the next sixty-two consecutive seasons the company would produce a total of 127 different operas, operettas, and musicals. Stoessel remained in control of the company until 1942. While conducting the New York Philharmonic on May 12, 1943, he collapsed before a shocked audience. The 1943 festival had already been planned and artists had been engaged. Alfredo Valenti, Stoessel's associate since 1929, took over as artistic director and remained in that position until his retirement after the 1958 season. Stoessel's death unfortunately precipitated the separation of the symphony orchestra and the opera, and a number of guest conductors would be brought in to handle the musical side of the productions. It was not until the appointment of Julius Rudel (then general director of the City Center Opera Company in New York) in 1958 with the title of music director that COA again had a conductor at the helm.

The summer of 1959 confirmed the rather momentous break with the past. Rudel, now in his first full season as general director, opened the season with Giannini's *Taming of the Shrew* followed in two weeks by Floyd's *Wuthering Heights*. In spite of a critically acclaimed season, Rudel was not rehired in 1960, and John Daggett Howell was appointed general director. Since the 1960s COA has produced mainly standard repertoire for an audience of summer residents. An important aspect of the company is the fact that it operates as one component of a total program. Because it is not an independent unit operating autonomously, budget, length of season, and choice of repertoire are all dependent on the overall aims and directions of the institution.

From the beginning, the chorus of the COA has played an important role in the production, and, indeed, many young professionals have graduated from its ranks into leading roles, including Rose Bampton. In 1964 the Ford Foundation awarded COA a grant of $100,000 a year for five years. In 1968 the Martha Baird Rockefeller Foundation funded an Apprentice Artist Program to offer training and performance opportunities for young professionals. This guaranteed the excellence of the resident chorus as well as providing for competent young singers who could assume leading roles in extra performances of scheduled productions.

CHRONOLOGY OF ARTISTIC DIRECTORS: Albert Stoessel, 1929–1943. Alfredo Valenti, 1943–1958. Julius Rudel, 1959. John Daggett Howell, 1960–1965. Leonard Treash, 1966–1980. Cynthia Auerbach, 1981–1987. Linda Jackson, 1987–present.

BIBLIOGRAPHY: *Chautauquan Daily*. Robert H. Cowden, *The Chautauqua Opera Association 1929–1958: An Interpretive History* (n.p., 1974). Gill Gallagher, *Opera at Chautauqua, 1928–1978* (Westfield, NY, 1979). T. Morrison, *Chautauqua: A Center for Education, Religion, and the Arts in America* (Chicago, 1974). Jeanette L. Wells, *A History of the Music Festival at Chautauqua Institution, 1874–1957* (Washington, DC, 1959).

ACCESS: Chautauqua Institution, P.O. Box 28, Chautauqua, NY 14722. (716) 357 6200. Linda Jackson, General Director.

ALFREDA LOCKE IRWIN

CHICAGO, ILLINOIS (metro 7,100,000; city 2,857,000)

Lyric Opera of Chicago

[Until 1909 opera in Chicago was provided by touring companies, including those of Henry Abbey, James Mapleson, the Metropolitan Opera Association, and the Italian Grand Opera Company of New York. In 1910 the Chicago Grand Opera Company was formed with Cleofonte Campanini as musical director. It endured as the Grand Opera Company (1913), the Chicago Opera Association (1915), and the Chicago Civic Opera (1921) until it was dissolved in 1932. Among notable productions was the world premiere of Prokofiev's *L'Amour des Trois Oranges* on December 30, 1921 conducted by the composer. Between 1933 and 1946, guest artists performed various operas again under the name of the Chicago Grand Opera Company.]

Lyric Opera was born of the vision and enthusiasm of a small group of people who believed that Chicago deserved a permanent opera company. The triumvirate of Carol Fox, Lawrence Kelly, and Nicola Rescigno presented two sold-out performances of *Don Giovanni* in February 1954 featuring Nicola Rossi-Lemeni and Eleanor Steber in the 3,563-seat Civic Opera House. So successful was this venture that the three formed the Lyric Guild and announced a three-week opera season for the fall of that year. Fox had convinced Maria Callas to make her American debut in *Norma*, so on November 1, 1954, with a cast that included Simionato, Picchi, and Rossi-Lemeni, the new company was born. The opening night triumph was followed by *La Traviata* on November 8 with Callas, Simionato, and Gobbi, and *Lucia di Lammermoor* with Callas and di Stefano on November 15. After an eight-year lapse, Chicago again had an opera company of its own. The initial season included productions of *Il Barbiere di Siviglia, La Bohème, Carmen, Tosca*, and the first full-scale mounting of Giannini's *The Taming of the Shrew*. Bidu Sayao, Eleanor Steber, and Thomas Stewart joined the other artists in star-studded casts, and the policy of engaging international artists, often from Europe, was instituted.

Tullio Serafin was engaged for the 1955 season, and Renata Tebaldi joined Maria Callas in simultaneous residence. The company mounted the American premieres of Monteverdi's *Il ballo delle ingrate* and de Banfield's *Lord Byron's Love Letter*. To sustain the company's momentum productions were borrowed from Rome, London, San Francisco, and New York. The next year the Lyric Theatre became Lyric Opera of Chicago. Lawrence Kelly and Nicola Rescigno left to found the Dallas Civic Opera, and Dimitri Mitropoulos and Georg Solti were engaged to conduct. The Lyric's Gala Concert was recorded by London Records, and the Women's Board was inaugurated and hosted the first opening night gala. Highlights of the 1950s included the $16,000 subsidy gift from the Italian government in 1958, the same year that Arthur Rodzinski conducted the Lyric's first *Tristan und Isolde*. *Falstaff* became the first company production broadcast over WBBM, also in 1958. And both Josef Krips and Georges Prêtre made their American debuts as conductors during the 1959 season.

The Ford Foundation subsidized the world premiere of Giannini's *The Harvest* in 1961. Two years later the season was expanded to eight weeks and, for the first time, a matinee performance (*Don Pasquale*) was presented especially for high school students. The year 1965 saw the season expanded another week, and Lyric Opera sponsored two special performances of *Madama Butterfly* by the University of Indiana Opera Workshop. Tito Gobbi, who had appeared in every Lyric Opera season but one since the company's beginning, made his directorial debut in, and sang the title role of, *Simon Boccanegra*. The season was expanded to ten weeks in 1966, which included a week of performances by the Metropolitan Opera National Company presenting Floyd's *Susannah*, Rossini's *La Cenerentola, Carmen*, and *Madama Butterfly*. Failure to arrive at a contract agreement with the Musician's Union caused the cancellation of the entire 1967 season, but an eventual settlement mediated by Mayor Richard Daley led to an eleven-week 1968 season.

The 1970s began with Birgit Nilsson returning to the Lyric after a nine-year absence in Giocomo Puccini's *Turandot*, a role she sang for the first time in America in the 1958 Chicago production. The Lyric Opera Center for American Artists was founded in 1973 and, for the first time, WFMT radio broadcast the entire season's opening night performances. The company hosted the fourth Verdi Congress in 1974, which was the first time the event had been held in the United States. Lord Harewood, managing director of the English National Opera, and Massimo Bogianckino, artistic director of the Teatro alla Scala, made major presentations. On the technical side, a new one-million-dollar computerized lighting system replaced the one that had served since 1929. The company finally received national radio coverage in 1977 with WFMT radio's syndication of the 1976 season, which was carried over 250 stations in the United States and Canada. Commissioned by the Lyric Opera, Penderecki's *Paradise Lost* received its world premiere in 1978 with the entire production traveling to Milan for a European premiere at La Scala. This was followed by a command performance for Pope John Paul II at the Vatican. A highlight of the 1979 season was the twenty-fifth anniversary production of *Faust* which was filmed and televised nationally as part of the Public Broadcasting System's "Great Performances" series. Carol Fox, Lyric Opera's founder and guiding light for twenty-seven years, resigned for reasons of ill health in January 1981. Following her death in July, Ardis Krainik, who had been with the company since 1954, was appointed general manager.

Anticipating the innovative directions she would follow throughout her tenure, the new general manager engaged Peter Sellars, who made his Lyric Opera debut directing a stunning *Mikado* in 1983. That same season the company combined forces with La Scala and the Royal Opera House Covent Garden to present a live telecast, *Tribute to Maria Callas*, on the sixtieth anniversary of the great diva's birth. The Lyric Opera Center for American Artists opened its second decade with an announcement of a composer-in-residence program with William Neil beginning work on an opera in-house. Joan Sutherland returned to Chicago after a ten-year absence in the 1985–1986 season Chicago premiere of *Anna Bolena*. In addition, the season saw the first appearance of English projected surtitles as an assist to the audience. The very next season Lyric Opera expanded the program to eight productions, and William Neil's *The Guilt of Lillian Sloan* was premiered at Northwestern University's Cahn Auditorium. Nine productions were scheduled for the 1987–1988 season. In particular, the season featured the Chicago premiere of Philip Glass's *Satyagraha*, which enjoyed seven sold-out performances. All productions were now enhanced with projected English titles.

As the 1980s drew to a close, Peter Sellars returned to direct a highly controversial modern version of *Tannhäuser*, and the eight-production 1988–1989 season closed on February 3 with box office sales at a historic 100.85 percent. The 1989–1990 season marked the thirty-fifth anniversary of the company, and the commission of a new opera to be presented in the 1992–1993 season was announced. William Bolcom's *Gold* composed in honor of the five hundredth anniversary of the discovery of the Americas by the Europeans will mark the Third World premiere, produced by the Lyric opera. In October 1989, General Director Krainik announced a major artistic initiative, "Toward the 21st Century," the first long-term commitment to modern opera to be announced by a leading opera company. The project, beginning in the 1990–1991 season and running to the year 2000, will include a number of new works as well as major revivals of significant twentieth-century operas deserving of more attention: Argento's *The Voyage of Edgar Allan Poe* (1990–1991), Barber's *Anthony and Cleopatra* and Prokoffiev's *The Gambler* (1991–1992), William Bolcom's *McTeague* and Debussy's *Pelléas et Mélisande* (1992–1993), and Berg's *Wozzeck* (1993–1994). In conjunction with this major initiative, the Lyric Opera Center for American Artists produced Weisgall's *Six Characters in Search of an Author* (June 1990), and composer-in-residence Bright Sheng is completing an as-yet untitled work to premiere in 1991 in the 906-seat Civic Theater.

BIBLIOGRAPHY: Claudia Cassidy, *Lyric Opera of Chicago* (Chicago, 1979). Ronald Davis, *Opera in Chicago* (New York, 1966). Edward C. Moore, *Forty Years of Opera in Chicago* (Chicago, 1930, repr., 1977). *Opera News*.

ACCESS: 20 N. Wacker Drive, Chicago, IL 60606–2801. (312) 332 2244; fax (312) 419 8345. Ardis Krainik, General Director.

[From materials supplied by the company]

CINCINNATI, OHIO (metro 1,410,000; city 390,000)

The Cincinnati Opera

As the first capital of the Northwest Territory (1790), Cincinnati was one of the oldest settlements in the American West. As the home of a large German-American population, it encouraged choral activities, and in 1894 the Cincinnati

Orchestra Association was founded with Mrs. William Howard Taft as president. Now the oldest summer opera festival in the United States, the Cincinnati Summer Opera Association was formed in 1920 by Ralph Lyford, head of the Cincinnati Conservatory of Music's Department of Opera, to produce outdoor opera at the local Zoological Gardens. Under his direction, *Martha* was produced on June 27 in the band shell, which had been enlarged with a new forestage. His dream of a resident opera company met with almost instant success, and local radio broadcasts began in 1923. The band shell faced a clubhouse which was a popular dining spot at the time, and a pavilion (later destroyed in 1972) was built to join the two structures, forming an outdoor theater that was open on three sides. With Fausto Cleva as music director (1934–1963), the association became so successful that outstanding international artists were engaged. In 1935 a roof was added to the outdoor pavilion, and in 1937 national radio broadcasts of the operas began over WLW-NBC. The year 1941 saw Grace Moore's first *Manon* and Risë Steven's first American Carmen and Mignon. Jeanette MacDonald sang her first *Faust* and *Romeo et Juliette* in 1945. Many of the casts during the war years were filled with Metropolitan Opera Association stars, including Ezio Pinza, Lawrence Tibbett, Giovanni Martinelli, Bidu Sayão, Zinka Milanov, and Astrid Varnay. In 1949 the Cincinnati Opera became part of the Institute of Fine Arts, and ten years later, when John Magro became general manager, the first year-round administrative staff was formed. The 1961 season featured Teresa Stratas as both Mimi and Musetta in two different performances of *La Bohème*.

Styrk Orwell became acting manager in 1964 (general manager, 1965–1972), and the next summer Martina Arroyo sang her first *Aida* and Beverly Sills and Norman Treigle undertook triple roles in *The Tales of Hoffmann*. Elisabeth Schwarzkopf sang her last Marshallin in *Der Rosenkavalier* in 1967. James de Blasis made his Cincinnati Opera debut directing his "Wild West" version of *The Elixir of Love* in 1968. The 1969 season was notable for Montserrat Caballé's performances of *Il Pirata* on crutches. In 1971 James Levine conducted *The Barber of Seville* with Roberta Peters as his last Zoo performance. In 1972 the operation moved to the Music Hall (built in 1875 with a capacity of 3,630, making it the country's second largest hall after the Met; it was completely remodeled in 1970–1971) opening with Norman Treigle as Mefistofele. The move, funded by opera patrons Mr. and Mrs. J. Ralph Corbett, meant a new orientation for the company as a constituent of a center for the performing arts which included the Cincinnati Symphony Orchestra and Pops, the May Festival, and the Cincinnati Ballet. James de Blasis assumed the position of general director the next season and instituted a number of new program directions. The Young American Artists Program was initiated in 1974, followed by the In-School Program (ECCO!) in 1975, the year that the name of the company was changed to the Cincinnati Opera. Designed for singers who have limited professional credits, Young American Artists offers performance experience at a top level. ECCO! annually presents 200 programs to over 40,000 children and adults in the four-state area of Ohio, Kentucky, Indiana, and West Virginia. In 1980 *La*

Traviata was performed as the first nonsummer series production, and ten years later in 1990 the company celebrated its seventieth anniversary, making it the nation's second oldest opera company.

With ticket prices ranging from $7 to $45, ticket income, other earned income, and private donations provide 54 percent of the budget. The remainder comes primarily from the Fine Arts Fund, public agencies, and grants. Average attendance was 99 percent in 1990.

BIBLIOGRAPHY: *Cincinnati Historical Society Bulletin. Opera News.*

ACCESS: 1241 Elm Street, Cincinnati, OH 45210–2291. (513) 621 1919. James de Blasis, Artistic Director. Paul Stuhlreyer III, Managing Director.

[From materials supplied by the company]

DALLAS, TEXAS (metro 3,100,000; city 1,058,000)

The Dallas Opera

[As one of the major cultural centers in the southwestern United States, Dallas has had a long and distinguished history. Until the Dallas Civic Opera was founded, however, grand opera performances were provided by touring companies such as the Metropolitan Opera Association, the Chicago Grand Opera and the San Carlo Touring Opera.] When Maria Callas walked onto the stage at the State Fair Music Hall in November 1957, the Dallas Opera was not thinking of world premieres. Founded by Lawrence Kelly and Nicola Rescigno eight months earlier, the stripling company—then known as the Dallas Civic Opera—had first to prove itself. Impossible as it may seem now, the Music Hall was a quarter empty on the night of Callas's inaugural concert; Dallas at that time had practically no operatic tradition, and the hall was too large and dilapidated. Kelly and Rescigno, both fresh from the Chicago Lyric Theatre, were proceeding mainly on hopes and promises. They followed the Callas concert with two performances of *L'Italiana in Algeri*, the first production of the Rossini comedy in this country for nearly forty years, designed and staged by the then little-known Franco Zeffirelli and featuring the great Italian mezzo Giulietta Simionato.

From the beginning, Kelly and Rescigno envisioned something bold and sophisticated, a revolutionary approach that would "get opera out of the warehouse" and bring forth its full musical and dramatic powers. Although they had their critics, during their very first Dallas season the two innovators demonstrated what they could do. Callas sang like a dream, and Zeffirelli's sumptuous mounting of *L'Italiana in Algeri*, lit by Broadway's Jean Rosenthal, established a new look in opera. It also showcased the American debuts of tenor Nicola Monti and bass Paolo Montarsolo. Callas returned in 1958 for her last Violetta anywhere in a Zeffirelli production of *La Traviata*. Opposite Jon Vickers in his American debut, the soprano scored another triumph in Cherubini's *Medea*. This became the standard by which the Dallas Opera was to measure everything else for years. Just hours before the first performance, Rudolf Bing telegraphed Callas that her contract with the Metropolitan Opera had been canceled, creating local hysteria. The diva received the news after a seven-hour, full-voice rehearsal, and then went on that evening to give the performance of her career. Brilliantly staged by Alexis Minotis off the Greek National Theater, the production traveled to Covent Garden, La Scala, and Epidaurus. Dallas audiences saw *Medea* once more in 1959.

During 1959 and 1960 Zeffirelli staged *Lucia di Lammermoor* with Callas, directed the first American production of Handel's *Alcina*, and designed a lavish *Don Giovanni*. He proved less successful with *Thaïs* in 1961, the company's first venture into the French repertoire. Teresa Berganza first sang in this country in a repeat of *L'Italiana in Algeri*, and Joan Sutherland made her American stage debut as Alcina, initiating the company's tradition of Baroque opera. She then joined Elisabeth Schwarzkopf and an all-star cast in the Zeffirelli *Don Giovanni*. Socialite Elsa Maxwell flew to Texas for the occasion, and left saying, "It's really incredible—the greatest opera in the world in a little town like Dallas." Sutherland's 1961 *Lucia* benefited from the U.S. debut of nineteen-year-old Placido Domingo in the role of Arturo. The local press said that Domingo's "instincts for opera mark him as a talent with a future to match." *Otello* in 1962 offered not only Mario Del Monaco in his finest role but also the operatic debut of the late theater director John Houseman. Monteverdi's *L'incoronazione di Poppea* the next season, in its American professional stage premiere, brought together Patrice Munsel (Poppea) and Ramon Vinay (Nero), plus three Italians in their American debuts: soprano Lydia Marimpietri, mezzo Bianca Berini, and stage director Luciana Novaro. *Un ballo in maschera*, with its assassination theme, was scheduled for the evening of November 22, 1963, the day that President John F. Kennedy was shot in Dallas. The performance was postponed until the following evening. "No one could remember the words," a chorister later recalled. "We had words written on gloves, fans, masks, every possible, available space.... We were all in such a cloud. That was probably the most difficult performance we ever had to get through."

Financial problems reduced the number of operas in 1964 to two: Giuseppe Di Stefano partnered Marimpietri in *Madama Butterfly*, and *Samson et Dalila* paired Del Monaco with Belgian mezzo Rita Gorr. Stage director Carlo Maestrini, interpreting Saint-Saëns's score realistically, saw that Dagon's temple was spectacularly wrecked. The orgy scene was given such intensity that it produced blushes as well as cheers. Renata Tebaldi brought her Tosca to the company in 1965, followed by Montserrat Caballé's American stage debut as Violetta. "I think the first notes I heard out of Caballé's mouth turned me on like nothing else," a Dallas Opera executive later remembered. "You could hear from her a pianissimo that went all the way to the back row of the balcony. It was incredible!" Peter Glossop was heard in a stunning *Rigoletto* in 1966, joined by Margherita Rinaldi, Carlo Bergonzi, and Gilda Cruz-Romo making her U.S. debut in the small role of Giovanna. Gwyneth Jones triumphed as Lady Macbeth in her first American appearance, aided by sets and costumes by Peter J. Hall, who had initially worked with the company as Zeffirelli's assistant. Caballé came back for a *Nozze di Figaro* to remember; she sang the Countess like a goddess, partnered by Graziella Sciutti as a definitive Susanna. Rescigno persuaded Kelly to revive *Medea* with the legendary Magda Olivero in her long overdue American debut. The distinguished Italian soprano took three months to work on the role before agreeing to sing it. Her Medea was different from Callas's, but she proved a sensation, later returning for *Fedora, Il tabarro*, and *Tosca*, all to immense acclaim.

Kelly and Rescigno brought Ellis Rabb from the legitimate theater in 1968 to turn Offenbach's *Orpheus in the Underworld* into a charming soufflé, full of style and humor, with two choruses and two corps de ballet. Not all the company's innovations worked, although the record has been remarkable. A single-set *Aida*, staged by Rabb in 1969, stands as a notable failure. "None of us really understood what he [Rabb] was trying to do," a chorister said. The 1970 *Carmina Burana* staged by Bertrand Castelli, who had done *Hair* on Broadway a short time before, was a disaster. "I'm going to attempt a sort of liberation," Castelli said, and his rehearsals became a "love-in." That year financial difficulties reached an all-time high, necessitating a thorough reorganization of the company's finances. The 1971 *Fidelio* was the Dallas Opera's first foray into the German repertoire, with Austrian soprano (now mezzo-soprano) Helga Dernesch making her American debut and Australia's Charles Mackerras as guest conductor, another first. The Music Hall was completely remodeled in 1972, although the acoustics still left much to be desired. Certainly smaller scale works such as Purcell's *Dido and Aeneas*, which opened the season following the renovation, remained problematic. However, Spanish tenor Alfredo Kraus arrived for *Werther* that year, giving the company's French repertoire a new lease on life; Dallas was later to see his first performances of Hoffmann, Gerald, and Roméo. In his debut season Kraus also sang Edgardo in *Lucia di Lammermoor*, with Dutch coloratura soprano Cristina Deutekom as the heroine and the Royal Opera House Covent Garden's John Copley making his American debut as director. Critic John Ardoin called it "quite the most splendid *Lucia* in my experience."

Andrea Chénier in 1973 was built around Jon Vickers, who sang the title role with ringing tones and a deep sense of character. *Chénier* was the last of the company's productions seen by Larry Kelly, who died of cancer in September 1974. Most of the general director's duties then fell on the shoulders of Nicola Rescigno. The season opened that autumn under a pall: Kelly had counted on hearing Beverly Sills sing her first *Lucrezia Borgia* for him, but the soprano discovered a malignancy and was forced to withdraw for surgery. After rehearsals had already begun, Leyla Gencer flew in to replace her. Marilyn Horne arrived that year for the first *Mignon* of her career, which was conducted and staged by Sarah Caldwell. In tandem with Krauss, the 1974 American debut of Kelly's last major discovery, Italian soprano Elena Mauti-Nunziata, ensured a brilliant *I Puritani*. Renata Scotto sang her initial *Anna Bolena* with the Dallas Opera in 1975, and her first *Manon Lescaut* four years later. However, the biggest event of 1975 was the company's entrance into the Wagnerian arena with inspired performances of *Tristan und Isolde*. The cast featured Vickers, Oklahoma-born Roberta Knie, and English mezzo Josephine Veasey. Franz-Paul Decker was borrowed from Montreal to conduct, and the Dallas Symphony responded beautifully to the challenge.

The company gave Handel's *Samson* its first American staged performances in 1976, with Vickers and Maureen Forrester. Beverly Sills finally appeared with the company in *La Traviata*, unfortunately not under the best of circumstances, and Knie was heard as a youthful, vocally splendid Salome. In July 1977 Plato Karayanis came aboard as general director, freeing Maestro Rescigno to devote more time to conducting. Originally a singer, Karayanis decided early in his career to concentrate on opera management. He arrived in Dallas determined to build the company's audience base, lengthen its list of subscribers, increase corporate support, and expand the repertoire, all of which he achieved. Douglas Moore's *Ballade of Baby Doe* in 1978 marked the Dallas Opera's first attempt at an American work. Other English-language operas would follow, such as Britten's *Peter Grimes* in a shattering 1980 production and Stravinsky's *The Rake's Progress*, staged in 1983 with the David Hockney sets and costumes. French works, notably the 1977 Krauss/Jeannette Pilou *Manon* and *Les pêcheurs de perles* in 1979 with Kraus and Richard Stilwell, have been mounted beautifully.

Dallas continued to make successful forays into German operas, such as *Der fliegende Holländer*, for which Franz-Paul Decker returned to conduct the outstanding British trio of Norman Bailey, Josephine Barstow, and Alberto Remedios. Between 1981 and 1985 the company produced the four operas of Wagner's "Ring" cycle, which was begun with a glorious *Walküre* conducted by Berislav Klobucar. The Yugoslavian maestro also led the 1982 *Rosenkavalier*, with Swedish soprano Elisabeth Söderström as a magnificent Marschallin. Another German-language work, *Die Zauberflöte*, marked the final installment in the company's presentation of the major Mozart operas. The Dallas Opera has not neglected the Italian repertoire, long the company's mainstay. Bellini's *I Capuleti e i Montecchi* was a bel canto joy in 1977, Frederica von Stade sang *La Cenerentola* in 1979, a dazzling new production of *Turandot* was unveiled in 1980, *Lucia* returned with Kraus and Ruth Welting in 1982, and *La fanciulla del West* was effectively produced in 1986. In a class by itself was the first American staging of a Vivaldi opera; starring Marilyn Horne and conducted by Nicola Rescigno, the 1980 production of *Orlando Furioso* was one of the brightest pages in the Dallas Opera's history.

In 1982 the company added a fourth performance of each of its operas, and introduced a spring season in 1984. Over the next four years, chamber opera classics such as *The Medium, The Rape of Lucretia, La favola d'Orfeo, Die Entführung aus dem Serail*, and *Il turco in Italia* were heard in the intimacy of the downtown Majestic Theatre. In 1988, after years of planning, the Dallas Opera (TDO) celebrated another milestone—the world premiere of a major contemporary work. Dominick Argento's *The Aspern Papers*, written for Frederica von Stade, brought a major international cast to Dallas in November 1988. A new production of *Cavalleria Rusticana/I Pagliacci* highlighted the 1989 season, and fulfilled a dream of Nicola Rescigno to bring this popular double bill to Dallas with a definitive Santuzza—the Dallas Opera debut of Giovanna Casolla. The 1990–1991 season brought the centennial performances of Borodin's *Prince Igor*, as well as a new production of *Hänsel und Gretel*, and expanded the opera season to five productions for the first time in the history of TDO. Plans are beginning for a new opera facility in Dallas by the year 2000, and the company is looking forward to many more dreams to be fulfilled in a home of its own.

BIBLIOGRAPHY: *Dallas Morning News. Dallas Times-Herald. Opera News.*

ACCESS: 1925 Elm Street, Suite 400, Dallas, TX 75201–4513. (214) 979 0123; fax (214) 754 0529. Plato Karayanis, General Director.

RONALD L. DAVIS

DENVER, COLORADO (metro 1,620,902; city 492,365)

Opera Colorado

The capital city of Colorado was founded in 1858 primarily to support the gold and silver mines in the nearby Rocky Mountains. In the beginning the state's economy was driven by a series of mining booms. Enormous wealth was generated in the mining industry, and Horace A. W. Tabor was a symbol of this era. Called the "Silver King," he built magnificent buildings in both Leadville and Denver and became a U.S. senator. The Tabor Opera House was one of his legacies, and it opened in all its magnificence in 1881 with a performance of Wallace's *Maritana* starring Emma Abbott. Until Tabor's financial ruin in 1893, the house featured many of the leading opera singers of the era. The Denver Grand Opera Company produced local opera from 1915 until 1951, followed in turn by the Greater Denver Opera Company (1955–1958) and the Denver Lyric Theatre (1958 through the 1970s). The Denver Opera Repertory Company attempted to carry on local traditions and was succeeded by Opera Colorado which, organized in 1981 with Nathaniel Merrill as general director, opened at the 2,650-seat Boettcher Concert Hall in 1983 with Puccini's *La Bohème* and Verdi's *Otello*, featuring international casts. The Boettcher Concert Hall is part of the center for the performing arts, opened in 1978, which includes the 2,400-seat Auditorium Theater built in 1908 and the Helen Bonfils Theatre Complex.

ACCESS: 695 South Colorado Blvd., Suite 20, Denver, CO 80222. (303) 778 6464. Nathaniel Merrill, General Director.

[From materials supplied by the company]

DETROIT, MICHIGAN (metro 4,400,000; city 1,065,000)

Michigan Opera Theatre

Never known as a cultural center since its founding in 1701, Detroit made a major commitment to opera when it began hosting an annual visit of the Metropolitan Opera Association sponsored by the now defunct Detroit Grand Opera Association. These visits were discontinued in 1985. The popular Overture to Opera series, which toured hundreds of schools and community centers statewide, was an educational component of the Association. Created by David DiChiera, the success of this series laid the groundwork for the establishment of Michigan's own professional opera company which launched its first season at Detroit's historic landmark theatre, the Music Hall, in 1971. That first season saw an eclectic mix of opera and musical theatre—Puccini's *La Rondine* and Andrew Lloyd Webber's *Joseph and the Amazing Technicolor Dreamcoat*—which would forge the company's programming path for future seasons. Michigan Opera Theatre (MOT), cited by the Detroit media as "one of the city's three cultural jewels" is the state of Michigan's premier opera company and serves as a statewide cultural resource committed to producing the very best professional productions from the grand opera, operetta, musical theater, and grand classical ballet repertory. By 1973, the presence of MOT served as a catalyst for the establishment of the Music Hall Center for the Performing Arts, a center devoted to the presentation of dance, music, and theatre.

In 1985 MOT's administrative offices moved and theater venues changed to accommodate the company's expanding artistic needs. The 2,100-seat Fisher Theatre, located in the historic Fisher Building designed by Albert Kahn, was chosen as the site of MOT's fall season of three productions. An additional grand opera production each spring had been scheduled in the Metropolitan Opera Association's touring venue, the 4,300-seat Masonic Temple, which was launched with Joan Sutherland in *Anna Bolena*. When the Met's visit was discontinued, MOT introduced its Spring Grand Opera Series at the Masonic Temple as a counterpart to the fall series at the Fisher, bringing the season to six full productions. In the tradition of major European houses, MOT expanded its programming with performances of classical ballet. Many of these productions are now coordinated with the Dayton Opera Association and Opera Pacific. This allows for a further improvement and expansion of the highly successful young artist residency program, the touring program, and production of National Opera which have included the North American premiere of the Armenian National Opera, *Anoush* by Tigranian, and the American premiere of the Polish Opera, *The Haunted Castle*, by Stanislaw Moniuszko. [Moniuszko was the primary representative of Polish nationalism, and his opera *Halka* is the most popular Polish opera ever composed.]

As a nonprofit company, MOT derives its annual income from a variety of sources including ticket sales, private/corporate/foundation donations, state and federal agencies, and special fund-raising events coordinated by dedicated volunteers. With a budget that exceeds $5 million, the company has remained deficit-free for the past seven seasons. Governed by a forty-member board of directors, the day-to-day operations are handled by a professional staff of thirty-five. Michigan Opera Theatre's long-term strategic plan calls for a permanent opera house, and in 1988 the board of directors agreed to purchase the Grand Circus Theater, a former movie palace in the heart of the old theater district. After renovation and expansion, it will, in conjunction with the Music Hall Center, fully house the company's activities.

ACCESS: 6519 Second Avenue, Detroit, MI 48202. (313) 874 7850; fax (313) 871 7213. David DiChiera, General Director.

REBECCA HAPPEL

FORT WORTH, TEXAS (metro 2,974,805; city 385,164)

Fort Worth Opera Association

Fort Worth began its existence as a small military outpost in 1849. Its first opera house, Evans Hall, was built in 1876, and the Fort Worth Opera House (1883) accommodated touring opera companies for a number of years. Founded in 1946, the Fort Worth Opera is the oldest continuously operating opera company in Texas. The Fort Worth Opera Association, as it was then known, was incorporated on May 28, 1946, by Eloise Snyder, Betty Spain, and Jeanne Axtell Walker. Snyder, a former New York City opera soprano, sang Violetta in the company's first production at the Will Rogers Auditorium on November 25, 1946, opposite Eugene Conley. Over its first decade of existence, the company mounted from one to four well-received productions a season under the baton of Walter Herbert, Karl Kritz, and Geoffrey Hobday. With the 1955–1956 season, the leadership passed to Rudolph Kruger, a distinguished student of such renowned European conductors as Felix Weingartner and Josef Krips. Kruger was to remain the leading spirit of the company as artistic director, general manager, and conductor for the following twenty-eight years. During his tenure, the Fort Worth Opera concentrated on works in the standard repertoire, accessible but musically sophisticated comic operas, and occasional novelties, primarily employing young singers of demonstrated promise. Kruger's discerning taste led him to engage numerous young singers over the years who subsequently became famous in the opera world. Beverly Sills sang her first Galatea in Offenbach's seldom-performed opéra bouffe; she sang her first Lucia with the company in 1968 and also appeared as Constanza in the *Abduction from the Seraglio*. At the age of twenty-one, Placido Domingo sang Edgardo in the 1962 *Lucia di Lammermoor*, his first major role in the United States. Ruth Welting made her debut in 1971 as Rosina. Mingled with these triumphs were such notable performances as Jerome Hines as Boris Godunov and James McCracken as Otello. Moreover, few audience members are likely to forget the farewell performances of Lily Pons as Lucia in an English-language production in which she sang the original Italian.

In 1964 the Fort Worth Opera received a $100,000 grant from the Ford Foundation to expand the season to four productions. This was followed in 1972 by further Ford grants totaling over $105,000 designed to put the company on a current fiscal basis. During the 1970s the company was very successful in attracting foundation support and selling tickets, so it had the enviable record of a balanced budget for seventeen consecutive seasons from 1963 through 1980. With the retirement of Kruger in 1982, a decision was made to move the Forth Worth Opera to a higher level. The company mounted its own productions of *The Pearl Fishers, Aida*, and Steven Paulus's *The Postman Always Rings Twice*. In spite of enthusiastic reviews and gratifying attention from the international opera world, significantly increased attendance did not materialize. This lack of audience support, coupled with a failure to attract new financial sources, resulted in a significant budget deficit. In 1986 the opera was forced to cut back to three productions, but fortunately, renewed public support enabled the company to retire most if its deficit of $600,000.

Through the vicissitudes of recent years, the Fort Worth Opera has continued to offer extensive outreach and education programs. Founded the year after the company itself, the Opera Guild sponsors a traveling ensemble, the Southwest Opera Theater, and the annual Opera Ball, as well as a host of other fund-raising activities. The Southwest Opera Theater has brought outreach opera to many thousands of elementary and junior high school students since the first production of Menotti's *The Old Maid and the Thief*. Since 1977 the Opera Preview programs have sought to educate a wider audience. And Fort Worth participates in the mixed arts festivals sponsored by the Arts Council of Fort Worth. Under the current directorship of J. Mario Ramos, the company continues to mount three highly professional productions each season. For the immediate future all productions are given in the 400-seat Scott Theater, an intimate setting that most effectively utilizes talented young singing actors. Plans are already being made to move into a new location in the renovated art deco Will Rogers Memorial Auditorium, which should be a pleasure after the cavernous 3,054-seat Tarrant County Convention Center.

BIBLIOGRAPHY: *Fort Worth Star-Telegram*.

ACCESS: 3505 West Lancaster, Fort Worth, TX 76017. (817) 731 0833. J. Mario Ramos, General Director.

PARKS CAMPBELL

HONOLULU, HAWAII (metro 762,565)

Hawaii Opera Theater

Although Hawaii was a kingdom nominally ruled by dark-skinned royalty until 1893, it had a considerable community of whites accustomed to Western art and music. Indeed, the Hawaiian royal family itself had a well-developed taste for European culture. In 1854 local amateurs performed Donizetti's *Daughter of the Regiment* at the Varieties Theatre; in 1861 scenes from Verdi's *Il Trovatore* and von Flotow's *Martha* were presented at the Royal Hawaiian Theatre. King Kamehameha V was involved in the staging of this production, and it is even possible that Queen Emma sang a minor role in it. Visits by professional companies to early Hawaii were undertaken with caution: An expensive sea voyage during which the players could not expect to earn income made visiting Honolulu a considerable financial risk. The Gayton Combination Company performed Sullivan's *H.M.S. Pinafore* in 1880, only two years after the operetta's premiere in London, and this was by no means the first professional troupe to visit the islands. Local amateurs presented the operetta the following year after a smallpox epidemic had caused a delay of several months in the performance. It was one of the first performances in the new Music Hall.

Other professional groups included the Montague-Turner Opera Company, which visited Honolulu in 1885. Over a two-week period it presented scenes from operas with the help of local musicians. The fashionable audiences that came to hear and see them frequently included Hawaiian royalty. The company probably consisted entirely of Charles H. Turner, a tenor; his wife, soprano Annis Montague Turner (1846–1920); and a trunkful of costumes. Annis Turner, the remarkable daughter of the early lay missionaries to Hawaii, Amos Star and Juliette Montague Cooke, returned to Hawaii to live for a time after her husband's death. She coached local singers and sang the role of Leonora in Verdi's *Il Trovatore* on the occasion of the opening of the new Hawaiian Opera House in 1896. Her expertise and practical experience were also of considerable use to local amateurs when, a few years later, she coached the singers and sang the title roles in Wallace's *Maritana* (1903) and Bizet's *Carmen* (1904). Honolulu audiences were shocked when women of the chorus appeared onstage smoking cigarettes in *Carmen*.

Traveling opera companies visited Honolulu in 1913, 1915, and 1916 (the Lambardi, Bevani, and De Folco companies, respectively), presenting at least twenty complete operas in more than seventy total performances. The Lambardi Company brought its own costumes, scenery, properties, stagehands, and musicians; the De Folco Company even brought its corps de ballet of six dancers. De Folco was so financially strapped at the end of its Honolulu season that it hardly made it back to the mainland. After this time traveling companies avoided Hawaii. After 1916 opera performances were practically nonexistent until 1928–1929, when a short-lived local company that was formed to present amateur productions, the Honolulu Opera Association, produced von Flowtow's *Martha*, Balfe's *Bohemian Girl*, and Sullivan's *Sorcerer*. During the 1930s and 1940s the Honolulu Symphony's music director, the Englishman Fritz Hart, conducted several Gilbert and Sullivan productions with local amateurs. The most outstanding opera production during this time, however, was Puccini's *Madama Butterfly* with Ululani Robertson, a singer of Hawaiian descent, as Cio-Cio-San, a role that had won her considerable acclaim around 1930 in Europe. Robertson and a tenor, Tandy MacKenzie, who were both part Hawaiian, had modest careers in opera, the latter both in Europe and the United States. The first Asian to win a major role in a Honolulu musical stage production was local Korean-American soprano Florence Ahn, who sang the title role in the 1946 production of Sullivan's *Patience*.

The organization known today as Hawaii Opera Theater (HOT) was immediately preceded by productions mounted by an amateur group, the Civic Light Opera Association, which was active in 1952–1957, and a number of ambitious productions at the University of Hawaii at Manoa in the late 1940s and early 1950s by students under the direction of music faculty members Norman Rian and Richard Vine. Hawaii Opera theater, known then as the Opera Festival, began in 1961 with the presentation of *Madama Butterfly*, a perennial favorite in Hawaii, with its large Japanese minority. Another opera that was presented repeatedly because of its appeal to Asians was Puccini's *Turandot*. A difficult production for even a major opera house, the latter was successfully produced in 1969, 1977, and 1988.

It is no accident that HOT was founded shortly after Hawaii achieved statehood. The 1960s were a period of dynamism in the Islands. The Honolulu Symphony Orchestra made significant improvements in its performance levels and by 1967 was, for the first time, fully professional, with all the players belonging to the Musician's Union. HOT was at first a part of the Honolulu Symphony Society, the administrative arm of the symphony, and received its present name in 1969. From the beginning, its productions were distinguished from earlier efforts in Honolulu by an emphasis on total professionalism. The company brought in "name" singers for principal roles. Metroplitan Opera star Dorothy Kirsten, near the end of her career, took part in *La Bohème* (1967) and returned to perform *Tosca* (1971) and *La Fanciulla del West* (1976). Roberta Peters thrilled audiences with her Gilda in the 1975 production of *Rigoletto*. In 1965 a concert version of one of the Opera Festival offerings, Bizet's *Carmen*, was presented on the island of Maui, and in later years complete productions would sometimes be taken to one of the neighbor islands. Outreach performances were also presented to school children from 1965 to 1980, a project sponsored by the Symphony Women's Association until the 1980 Symphony/HOT split.

By 1969 HOT had achieved enough status to manage its own budget and fundraising drives. As the result of steady growth and conflicting logistics, HOT separated from the symphony in 1980 and became an independent organization. Outstanding productions since that time include the 1983 production of *Eugene Onegin* staged by Frank Corsaro, who used Stanislavski's 1922 Moscow laboratory production as a model. For its twenty-fifth anniversary celebration in 1985, HOT commissioned Maurice Palinski to build some two hundred costumes designed by Richard Gullicksen for its production of Mozart's *Magic Flute* set in an imaginery ancient Oceania. The 1986 production of Stravinsky's *Rake's Progress* with David Hockney's sets and costumes rented from the San Francisco

Opera was superlative. Supertitles in English appeared for the first time in 1987. Moreover, the 1990 *Così fan tutte* (renamed in Hawaiian *Pela no ho'i wahine*), set in nineteenth-century Honolulu, was even more successful than the *Magic Flute* in its use of Hawaiian mise-en-scène.

After the demolition of the 1,250-seat Hawaiian Opera House in 1917, Honolulu was without a suitable hall until the completion of the Mackinley High School Auditorium in 1928. In 1965 concert and opera performances were moved to the newly completed 2,100-seat Blaisdell Concert Hall in the Honolulu Arts Center, where HOT and the symphony share seasons. Since 1976 HOT has presented three performances of three operas each season. By the 1987–1988 season, its budget had grown to over $800,000. With the majority of seasons earning a budget surplus, the company is enjoying a period of excellent management and this, coupled with attractive productions, has meant a thriving HOT. Opera seems to have won a secure place in Hawaii's cultural life, one that promises to continue to please its audience, which, like the state's population, is made up of people of exceedingly diverse background and ethnic origin.

CHRONOLOGY OF ARTISTIC DIRECTORS: George Barati, 1961–1967; Robert LaMarchina, 1967–1978; Donald Johanos, 1978–1982; Beebe Freitas, 1982–1989; Marshall W. Turkin, 1989–present.

CHRONOLOGY OF EXECUTIVE DIRECTORS: Alice Taylor Glessner, 1980–1983; Rosanne Cribley, 1983–1988; Marshall W. Turkin, 1988–present.

BIBLIOGRAPHY: Dale E. Hall, *A History of the Honolulu Symphony Society and Hawaii Opera Theater* (in progress). *Honolulu Advertiser*. *Honolulu Star Bulletin*.

ACCESS: 987 Waimanu Street, Honolulu, HI 96814. (808) 521 6537. Marshall W. Turkin, Executive Director.

DALE E. HALL

HOUSTON, TEXAS (metro 3,100,000; city 1,716,000)

Houston Grand Opera

Touring companies began to bring opera to Houston shortly after the Civil War, and the Metropolitan Opera Association played the Winnie Davis Auditorium in 1901 and 1905. The Chicago Opera Association performed in the old City Auditorium beginning in 1919. Later, the San Carlo Opera Company and Charles Wagner's touring company had short seasons in the Music Hall, but the formation of a local opera company had to wait until Walter Herbert left the New Orleans Opera Association with the hope of building something similar in Houston. Mrs. Louis G. Lobit signed him to a contract, and the Houston Grand Opera (HGO) was chartered on August 6, 1955, with Walter Herbert as music director. By September 8, HGO had a Board of Directors headed by Mrs. Lobit as well as an Opera Guild headed by Mrs. William W. Bland. On an initial budget of $40,000, the first season featured two performances of *Salome* with Brenda Lewis and Frederick Jagel and two performances of *Madama Butterfly* with Eugene Conley and Nancy Swinford Blackburn, a member of the HGO Board, as Butterfly. The first artistic milestone was the 1958 *Elektra* with Inge Brokh, Regina Resnik, and Norman Treigel, directed by Herbert Graf. In 1959 Herbert initiated a program of contemporary operas in local theaters with Menotti's *Consul* and Weill's *Street Scene*. Richard Tucker's first Calaf in *Turandot* in 1960 could not stave off near bankruptcy, and the company was rescued by the Houston Endowment and the Anderson Foundation.

An outreach Opera-in-the-Schools program extended the company's base of support, and the next five seasons saw the Houston debuts of Jerome Hines, Richard Cassilly, Sherrill Milnes, James McCracken, Jon Vickers, Cornell MacNeil, and Jess Thomas. The latter two starred in the company's final season (1965) in the old Music Hall. HGO closed its first decade with the opening of Jones Hall for the Performing Arts in 1966, featuring Richard Tucker and Gabriella Tucci in *Aida*. About this same time the Houston Symphony Orchestra was associated with the opera productions, and all aspects of the final product—sets, costumes, direction, and singers—showed a marked qualitative improvement. HGO was coming of age. The next season was notable for Placido Domingo's Houston debut in *Faust* followed by Don José in *Carmen*. Audiences were also treated to their first contemporary opera, Henze's *The Young Lord*, perhaps the finest complete production of the Herbert years. The year 1969 signaled a time of change as Herbert negotiated a move to San Diego while at the same time renewing his Houston contract through 1971. David Gockley left his post at New York's Lincoln Center in 1970 to become business manager. The next year he became associate director, and in 1972 he replaced Herbert as general director—clearly the right individual in the right place at the right time. Houston's economy was booming, and Gockley had a long list of ideas to try out.

Gockley's first year as general director featured the new "American Series" which showcased young American artists singing in English. A free Spring Opera Festival was also inaugurated in the Miller Outdoor Theater in Hermann Park. In 1973 Carlisle Floyd's *Of Mice and Men* as well as the American premiere of Vaughan Williams's *Hugh the Drover* had world premieres. A generous grant from the Moody Foundation underwrote HGO's touring subsidiary, the Texas Opera Theater, in 1974, and the list of world premieres continued with Pasatieri's *The Seagull*. Joplin's *Treemonisha* received its first fully staged professional performances in 1975, followed by a national tour, a Broadway run, and a Deutsche Grammophon (DGG) recording. In 1976 HGO's *Porgy and Bess* was on Broadway (which received Tony and Grammy awards) followed by a recording (which was awarded the Grand Prix du Disque) and a European tour. Filling out a remarkable five years, the Houston Opera Studio, HGO's young artist training program which was operated jointly with the University of Houston, was founded in 1977 under the direction of David Gockley and resident composer Carlisle Floyd.

Another important step was achieved in 1979 when Tenneco Corporation agreed to sponsor nationwide radio broadcasts of Houston Grand Opera productions. This same season John DeMain was appointed music director. The year 1980 saw the initial Prima Donna (later, Great Artist) Series with recitals by Renato Scotto and Mirella Freni. The Twenty-fifth Anniversary Gala Concert in 1981 featured Placido Domingo and Renato Scotto, and the company presented its second Carlisle Floyd world premiere, *Willie Stark*, staged by Harold Prince in Jones Hall. The production was broadcast nationwide as part of the Public Broadcasting System's "Great Performance" series. HGO (along with the New York City Opera) became the first American company to use Surtitles for all foreign-language productions in 1984, the same year in which ground was finally broken for the opera's new home, the Wortham Theater Center. The next season, Houston Grand Opera was honored with the National Institute of Music Theater Award.

The Wortham Theater Center, the $70 million home of the Houston Grand Opera and the Houston Ballet, formally opened in October 1987 with the triple repertory of *Aida*, the world premiere of *Nixon in China*, and *The Abduction from the Seraglio*, an artistic event of national and international importance. On July 8, 1988, the opera world was treated to the world premiere of *The Making of the Representative for Planet 8* by Philip Glass and Doris Lessing in a co-commission project with three European companies. The 1989–1990 season began with a celebration of four centuries of British opera, including the world premiere of Sir Michael Tippett's *New Year*. With a budget of almost $12 million for the 1988–1989 season, HGO mounts eight major productions (68 performances) featuring internationally known and celebrated artists in a repertory format: fall, winter, and spring. Texas Opera Theater gives over 250 performances annually, and total attendance in 1987–1988 for all HGO activities was 127,698. As one of the most active and progressive major opera companies in North America, HGO has become something of a role model for innovation, top-quality programming and cooperative undertakings with other production and media organizations.

ACCESS: 510 Preston Street, Houston, TX 77002. (713) 546 0200; fax (713) 247 0906. David Gockley, General Director.

SCOTT HEUMANN

LOUISVILLE, KENTUCKY (metro 906,152; city 298,451)

Kentucky Opera

Kentucky Opera, or the State Opera of Kentucky, was founded in 1952 in Louisville by Moritz von Bomhard. A native of Germany who had become a U.S. citizen, von Bomhard masterminded the entire operation. He had vast experience in conducting, and in the early days he designed the sets, trained the singers and chorus, directed the staging and, until 1970, even designed the opera brochures. Operas were presented in the Columbia Auditorium, which lacked an orchestra pit, until the 1963–1964 season when the company moved to the Brown Theatre (1,400 seats). After a major restoration, it was renamed the Macauley Theatre. In the 1950s five operas were commissioned by Kentucky Opera and given their world premieres. In addition to the standard opera repertoire, Bomhard always presented one opera a year that was new to his audience. Stravinsky's *Oedipus Rex*, Britten's *Peter Grimes*, and Jánaček's *Jenufa* were most successful, as was his first Wagnerian opera, *The Flying Dutchman*. He never repeated an opera more than once in five years, and managed to do a Mozart opera once a year. Four operas were presented yearly. Bomhard retired in 1982 and Thomson Smillie became general director. A native of Glasgow, Scotland, Smillie had worked for Scottish Opera for twelve years, in addition to being artistic director of the Wexford Festival Opera of Ireland. He left the Opera Company of Boston and was available when the Kentucky Opera was searching for a replacement for Bomhard. Mary Ann Krebs was appointed executive director in 1983.

The opening of the Kentucky Center for the Arts in the 1981–1982 season presented a real challenge to the company. The 2,400-seat Robert S. Whitney Hall was considerably larger than the Macauley, and the 620-seat Moritz von Bomhard Hall was really suited only for small scale productions. Kentucky Opera elected to produce grand operas such as Verdi's *Aida* in the Whitney, operettas such as *The Merry Widow* at the Macauley, and chamber operas such as Britten's *Albert Herring* in the Bomhard. Eighty-two different operas have been produced since the initial season in 1952, including George Antheil's *The Wish* [world premiere on April 2, 1955], Peggy Glanville-Hicks's *The Transposed Heads* [world premiere on March 27, 1954], Philip Glass's *The Fall of the House of Usher*, and Nicolas Nabokov's *The Holy Devil*. [Nabokov's opera was a world premiere on April 18, 1958. The revised version was premiered by the Oper der Stadt Köln in Germany as *Der Tod des Grigori Rasputin* on November 27, 1959.] The Louisville Orchestra plays for performances in all three theaters. An active outreach program, Opera-Go-Round, gives over one hundred performances statewide to over 51,000 students annually.

Kentucky Opera is run by a board of fifty-seven members. Additional social and fund-raising activities are undertaken by the Kentucky Opera Guild. A professional office staff of twelve manages development, finance, marketing, and public affairs, and a production staff of the same size handles the rehearsals and performances. Kentucky Opera is financed by ticket sales, corporate and individual sponsors, the National Endowment for the Arts, the National Endowment for the Humanities, the Kentucky Arts Council, and the Greater Louisville Fund for the Arts. From an initial budget of some $10,000, Kentucky Opera now operates on a budget of more than $2 million annually with ticket income and other earned income covering 23 percent of the budget. Single ticket prices for the 1988–1989 season ranged from $8 to $35.

ACCESS: 631 South Fifth Street, Louisville, KY 40202–2201. (502) 584 4500; fax (502) 584 7484. Thomson Smillie, General Director. Mary Ann Krebs, Executive Director.

[From materials supplied by the company]

MIAMI, FLORIDA (metro 1,625,781; city 346,865)

Greater Miami Opera

As a reflection of its status as a continuing outpost of New York City with regard to its classical music orientation, the Opera Guild of Greater Miami was founded by Arturo di Filippi in 1941. The first thirty seasons featured guest artists in a limited number of performances not only directed by Anthony Stivanello but also supported by his huge storehouse of sets and costumes in New York. The 1974 season with Robert Herman as general manager set the stage for a bold new direction which featured talented designers and directors creating new productions. Twelve years later, in 1985, Robert Heuer was appointed general manager. Performances since 1951 have alternated between the Dade County Auditorium and the Miami Beach Auditorium, neither of which is technically or acoustically appropriate for grand opera. Current seasons feature four standard repertory selections with international stars.

BIBLIOGRAPHY: Robert Herman and Mary Voelz Chandler, *The Greater Miami Opera: From Shoestring to Showpiece, 1941–1985* (Miami, 1985).

ACCESS: 1200 Coral Way, Miami, FL 33145–2980. (305) 854 1643; fax (305) 856 1042. Robert M. Heuer, General Manager. Willie Anthony Waters, Artistic Director.

[From materials supplied by the company]

MINNEAPOLIS and ST. PAUL, MINNESOTA (combined metro 2,113,533; cities 370,951 and 270,230)

The Minnesota Opera

A spirit of rivalry has always existed between the Twin Cities of Minneapolis and St. Paul, Minnesota, which straddle the banks of the Mississippi River. The state capitol is in St. Paul, while Minneapolis hosts the main campus of the University of Minnesota, an original land grant university. Both cities have long been rich in culture, owing in part to a nationally admired program of corporate philanthropy. The Minnesota Orchestra, whose home base is Orchestra Hall in Minneapolis, also has a St. Paul season. Similarly, the St. Paul Chamber Orchestra, whose hall is the exquisite Ordway Music Theater, reciprocates with a Minneapolis series. St. Paul's Schubert Club recently celebrated its one hundredth birthday as a recital impresario, while Minneapolis's Tyrone Guthrie Theater, the nation's largest regional theater, is approaching its thirtieth anniversary.

For forty years (1945–1986) New York's Metropolitan Opera Association played the university's Northrop Auditorium (seating capacity 4,000) as a part of its annual spring tour, which was discontinued after the 1986 season. These seven days in May constituted a sold-out festival attracting visitors from all the surrounding states, and was always a herald of spring. While the "Met" was satisfying the local thirst for conventional opera, there remained a need for an alternative style of opera production. In 1963 Minneapolis's Walker Art Center launched the Center Opera Company and gave it a home in the adjacent Guthrie Theater. Its first general manager was John Ludwig. Together with Phillip Brunelle, Eric Stokes, and Wesley Balk, Ludwig created an ensemble that developed an immediate national reputation for originality and irreverence. After a few years, the Walker Art Center spun off the company, which then became known as the Minnesota Opera.

The company's mission ever since has remained ambitious. In addition to its annual season of four main stage productions, its New Music Theater Ensemble, which explores experimental works, has a season of its own. Its summer Broadway musical presentation has become a July tradition, and the company's annual Midwest Tour has brought thirty-five productions to over 450,000 people in more than two hundred cities since its 1979 inception. It is one of only three such touring companies in the nation. Between the main stage, the ensemble, and the tour, the company has no fewer than thirty-two world premieres to its credit. Many of those operas retain their appeal and continue to be mounted today. The most recent premiere was *Frankenstein, the Modern Prometheus* by Libby Larson, a Minneapolis resident, in 1990. In 1992 the company will stage the world premiere of *Kaguya: the Girl from the Towers of the Moon*, by Robert Moran and Michael John LaChiusa, which will probably be held in the renovated State Theater in the heart of Minneapolis's thriving downtown.

In 1978 the St. Paul Opera Association, which had been producing opera in a more traditional vein, merged with the Minnesota Opera, which in 1985 became a constituent in the Ordway Music Theater, where most of its main-stage productions are mounted. With offices, costume shops, warehouse, rehearsal and studio space in the new Opera Center, which is situated on Minneapolis's historic waterfront, the company enjoys a true presence in both Minneapolis and St. Paul. The move to the state-of-the-art Opera Center has enabled the company to construct many of its own sets, props, and costumes for all four of its divisions. Following the merger, the company survived a period of growing pains to become a significant part of Twin Cities's culture. Under Kevin Smith, its general director since 1981, the company has taken on a sense of security and dependability. With a deficit under control and an annual budget of $4.2 million, the Minnesota Opera produces twenty-one performances during its main season, which runs from October through May. Its income is equally earned and contributed. Half of its audience is between the ages of eighteen and forty-four; another 28 percent is over fifty-five.

Among names most associated with the Minnesota Opera is composer Dominick Argento, a Minneapolis resident and professor of music at the University of Minnesota. He has enjoyed six commissions or premieres there: *The Masque of Angels, The Voyage of Edgar Allen Poe, Miss Havisham's Wedding Night, Casanova's Homecoming*, and *Postcard from Morocco*. His *Water Bird Talk, The Boor*, and *The Aspen Papers* also have been produced locally. Argento was a member of the Center Opera's original artistic team, and remains on the company's board of directors. In 1989 Smith named George Manahan as the company's principal conductor, a post new to the Minnesota Opera. While the company does not employ its own full-time orchestra, this area is blessed with a surplus of highly talented musicians. Budgetary constraints and pit dimensions limit the size of the orchestra, but Manahan has been well received. He is responsible for half the company's repertoire, and guest conductors are invited for the balance of the season. The company's Broadway Musical series began in 1986 and has been produced in cooperation with the Ordway, although that arrangement and venue may change in subsequent seasons. Rogers and Hammerstein and Kern and Hammerstein have dominated, but Lerner and Loewe's *My Fair Lady*, shared with the Houston Grand Opera, was the most recent production. The summer musical with its sold-out houses is a substantial source of revenue for the company.

ACCESS: Park Square Court, 400 Sibley Street, Suite 20, St. Paul, MN 55101–1901. (612) 333 2700. Kevin Smith, General Director.

PHILLIP GAINSLEY

NEW ORLEANS, LOUISIANA (metro 1,150,000; city 515,000)

New Orleans Opera Association

New Orleans enjoys a rich and varied operatic history dating from the late eighteenth century when, in 1796, Gretry's *Sylvain* was sung at the Théâtre St. Pierre. By 1819 with the opening of the second Théâtre d'Orléans, a tradition had been established; resident troupes recruited in France performed in repertoire during the winter months, and the new scores that were then in vogue in Paris were demanded by a discriminating audience. The annual season at the Orléans was supplemented by performances at several other theaters and by visits from touring companies from Havana. With its opening in 1859, the French Opera House replaced the old Théâtre d'Orléans as the center of operatic life. The annals of these two theaters contain the first U.S. performances of dozens of major and minor scores, mainly of the Italian and French repertoire.

After the French Opera House was destroyed by fire on December 4, 1919, New Orleans was left without a suitable theater in which an annual opera season could be produced. Instead, for almost a quarter century it relied on brief visits from Fortune Gallo's San Carlo Opera, and the touring Chicago and Metropolitan Opera Association companies to fill the operatic void. Determined to reestablish opera on a permanent basis, a group of music lovers led by Walter L. Loubat (1885–1945) drew up a charter creating the New Orleans Opera House Association (February 18, 1943) and planned an inaugural summer season of open-air performances—"Opera under the Stars"—in the City Park stadium. An opening bill of *Cavalleria Rusticana/I Pagliacci* (June 11–12, 1943) was followed by three other works. Amelio Colantoni served as artistic director; former Metropolitan Opera conductor Louis Hasselmans was recruited from nearby Louisiana State University's faculty; and Lelia Haller, a New Orleanian who had danced with the Paris Opera ballet, began the training of a resident corps de ballet. The initial season scored a success, but the ever-present threat of evening showers in semitropical New Orleans prompted a move indoors that fall. The 1943–1944 winter season used the concert hall of the City's Municipal Auditorium; it would remain the opera's home for the following thirty years. For its second season the association also contracted for a permanent general director/conductor.

Walter Herbert, a distinguished German musician and conductor, began an eleven-year association as general director in October 1943. Herbert was conscious of the need to build slowly. To develop audience support, and in recognition of the city's Latin roots, the repertoire initially reflected a cautious approach, with a dependence on popular French opera scores interspersed within the standard Verdi and Puccini catalogue. However, Herbert's vision looked ahead to a day when unfamiliar works might also become acceptable. His abrupt departure in 1954 left many of his plans unrealized [see Houston Grand Opera], but during his tenure as general director he presented the first local staging of Menotti's *The Old Maid and the Thief*, Strauss's *Der Rosenkavalier*, and a double bill of *Salome* with Stravinsky's *Petrouchka*. Other operas heard during those years, which have been staged only rarely in New Orleans, were *Samson et Dalila, Otello, Tristan und Isolde, Andrea Chénier, Don Pasquale*, and *La Gioconda*. The roster of leading singers appearing with the association between 1943 and 1954, included Albanese, de los Angeles, Flagstad, Milanov, Sayão, and Varnay, as well as Björling, Mario Lanza (in his only operatic stage appearances), London, Pinza, Tibbett, Vinay, and Warren. Friction between Herbert and certain board members led to his termination in June 1954.

The board named as its next music director and associate conductor Renato Cellini (1912–1967), who was then at the Metropolitan Opera. In addition to his duties and coaching at the "Met," Cellini had conducted several complete recordings for RCA Victor. At the same time the Opera Association settled on veteran Armando Agnini (1884–1960) as its principal stage director, that post having been filled most recently by William Wymetal and various guest directors. Cellini's inaugural work, *La Bohème* (October 7–9, 1954), was the first of seven productions continuing the season of seven or eight works which had been standard since the mid-1940s. Recognizing the need for developing and training young singers, and allowing them opportunities for onstage experience, Cellini immediately made plans for a summer season to launch the Experimental Opera Theatre of America (EOTA) in June 1955. EOTA functioned thereafter in 1956, and from 1958 to 1960. Although its repertoire largely reflected that of the parent company, a few novelties were offered during these seasons—*Amelia Goes to the Ball*, *The Beggar's Opera*, *The Consul*, *The Bartered Bride*, and the first local staging of the complete *Trittico*.

Highlights of the Cellini years included the first New Orleans staging of Strauss's *Elektra*, Verdi's *Falstaff*, Puccini's *Manon Lescaut* and *Turandot*, and Carlisle Floyd's *Susannah*. Revivals of operas that had not been played in New Orleans for many years included *Boris Gudonov*, *L'Amore dei tre Re*, *La Cenerentola*, *Norma*, and *Werther*. As in previous seasons, the roster of guest artists imported for leading roles included the names of many leading artists. Despite growing competition for stars, these ten seasons saw the New Orleans debuts of Bible, Borkh, Curtin, della Casa, Nordmo-Loevberg, Raskin, Sills, Stevens, and Udovick, and of Alva, Cassily, Campora, Christoff, Domingo, Gedda, Konya, MacNeil, Quilico, Siepi, Tozzi, and Valletti. Young artists at the start of their careers who appeared in EOTA productions included Mignon Dunn, Enrico di Giuseppe, John McCurdy, John Reardon, Joseph Rouleau, Andre Turp, and Margarita Zambrana.

Poor health forced the retirement of Cellini in 1964. The following spring the association appointed Knud Andersson as music director and resident conductor. Knud Andersson, who began his New Orleans career as chorus director in October 1953 during Walter Herbert's tenure, occasionally led performances during the regular season as well as summer EOTA productions, most notably the first New Orleans staging of Floyd's *Susannah* (1962). At the same time the board created a production team by naming Arthur Cosenza its resident stage director. Cosenza had first appeared with the association in supporting roles during the 1953–1954 season. Following Armando Agnini's death in March 1960, Cosenza had increasingly functioned in the role of stage director while maintaining his faculty connection with Loyola University of the South, where he supervised the Opera Workshop. In the fall of 1970 Cosenza was named general director, a position he continues to hold.

A highlight of these fifteen seasons was the celebration, in 1966–1967, of the association's twenty-fifth anniversary, a gala season that featured new productions of *Faust*, the first New Orleans staging of *Macbeth*, Domingo and Caballé in *Il Trovatore*, *Der fliegende Holländer*, a virtually uncut mounting of *Lucia di Lammermoor* starring Joan Sutherland, and Tito Capobianco's inventive production of *Les Contes d'Hoffmann*, featuring Beverly Sills, John Alexander, and Norman Treigle. Other notable productions between 1964 and 1979 included the world premiere of Carlisle Floyd's *Markheim* (March 31, 1966), with Norman Treigle, the first New Orleans stagings of Strauss's *Arabella* and *Ariadne auf Naxos* and Verdi's *Atilla* and *Nabucco*; and revivals of *La Sonnambula*, *Werther*, *Louise*, *Les Pêcheurs de Perles*, *La Fille du régiment*, *Ernani*, *Fidelio*, and *Die Walküre*.

In 1973 the association launched a series of revivals of French grand operas, works that had been standard repertory pieces at the old French Opera House prior to 1919 but that had not been played for several generations. Among these were Halévy's *La Juive* (1973), Massenet's *Hérodiade* (1975), Meyerbeer's *Les*

Huguenots (1975), and Donizetti's *La Favorite* (1976). Major singers heard for the first time during this period were Björner, Cruz-Romo, Deutekom, Elias, Gencer, Hunter, Kabaivanska, Lear, Maliponte, Meier, Nilsson, Rankin, Ricciarelli, Sighele, Tinsley, Tucci, Watson, and Zeani, and Corena, Diaz, Elvira, McCracken, Morris, Paskalis, Plishka, Taddei, Vickers, and Ward. A summer season in 1966 by the Repertory Opera Theatre, featuring young singers, harkened back to Cellini's EOTA of the 1950s. However, the idea did not survive the season, and there was a gradual contraction in the number of works offered during the regular season as well, from eight operas (1964–1965 to 1968–1969), to seven and then six (1970–1971 to 1976–1977), and finally to five (1977–1978 to 1981–1982). Later there was still further erosion to the present schedule of four operas, each staged on two evenings.

Almost from its inception in 1943 the Opera Association had staged its regular season in the concert hall, whose most serious drawbacks were variable acoustics and the lack of a sunken orchestra pit. Work had gone on for some time in acquiring and clearing land for a new cultural center adjacent to the existing auditorium; midway in its 1972–1973 season, the association was able to relocate to the new 2,713-seat Theatre for the Performing Arts, which had opened on January 9 with a dedicatory concert by the New Orleans Philharmonic Symphony Orchestra. A time-worn production of *Madama Butterfly* was the first work offered by the Opera Association. However, with its next production that spring, Massenet's *Thaïs*, the association presented a stage picture worthy of its new surroundings. The new theater has served the Opera Association well despite occasional technical problems.

Knud Andersson retired at the end of the 1978–1979 season, and the post of music director/resident conductor has remained unfilled. The past decade has seen a reduction in the number of operas offered, although the association has experimented with three rather than two stagings of each work. Recent seasons have offered two operas each fall followed by a single work after the Mardi Gras. Operas staged for the first time this decade included *Adriana Lecouvreur*, *La Fanciulla del West*, and *I Lombardi*. Guest artist rosters again featured some of the finest international stars available.

For many years the association maintained its own studios for the construction and storage of props and scenery. This operation was greatly expanded in January 1984 with the dedication of the H. Lloyd Hawkins Scenic Studio. Since that time productions have been shared on a rental basis with other regional opera companies. Beginning with an opening night *Aida* (October 1984), supertitles were introduced, initially with only moderate success. In its almost half-century of operation, the association has seen a number of local artists grow from supporting roles to national and international careers, most notably Norman Treigle. There is every indication that the New Orleans Opera Association will continue to provide first-class regional opera in all its dimensions.

ACCESS: 333 St. Charles Avenue, Suite 907, New Orleans, LA 70130. (504) 529 2278. Arthur G. Cosenza, General Director.

JACK BELSOM

NEW YORK CITY, NEW YORK (metro 9,600,000; city 7,552,000)

Metropolitan Opera Association

New York City, as the cultural center of the United States, is a major home of the nation's music industry as well as a showcase for national and international artists and organizations. Opera of consequence first opened in New York on November 29, 1825, when Manuel García and his ensemble of eight singers, accompanied by a local orchestra of twenty-four, presented *Il Barbiere di Siviglia* in the first of nearly eighty performances of seven operas. After a number of unsuccessful attempts to establish a permanent house, including the Astor Place Opera House, which opened in 1847, the Academy of Music opened its doors on October 2, 1854. An indication of its problems can be seen in the change of management that it experienced every season for the next twenty-four years. Access to choice seating was restricted and thus, in 1880, a group of wealthy businessmen, who were unable to gain accommodation to box seats at the Academy of Music, decided to build a newer and bigger opera house. The Metropolitan Opera House, at 39th Street and Broadway, opened on October 22, 1883, with Gounod's *Faust* and a cast including Christine Nilsson and Italo Campanini. The company, which has the longest continuous existence of any opera organization in the United States, was originally organized by the American impresario Henry E. Abbey. A generous spender, he gave New York very grand opera, with musicians and costumes all imported. When the company reached a deficit of almost $600,000 in 1884, his contract was not renewed.

During the Met's first season, everything (including *Lohengrin*) was sung in Italian, but from 1884 until 1891 all performances were given in German, including Lilli Lehmann's 1885 debut as Carmen. After Abbey the Met stockholders looked for someone with a stronger musical background and engaged the conductor Leopold Damrosch, a friend of both Liszt and Wagner, to run the company. After only three months Damrosch died, and Edmund Stanton, secretary to the board of directors, became manager. He brought in the conductor Anton Seidl, a protege of Wagner, as music director. Seidl introduced both *Die Meistersinger* and *Tristan und Isolde* to America, and in one week he conducted a complete cycle of Wagner's *Der Ring des Nibelungen*. The German era at the Metropolitan ended with the 1890–1891 season, when Henry Abbey returned to run the company with John R. Schoeffel and Maurice Grau. Opening night was Gounod's *Roméo et Juliette* in its first New York performance in French. Emma Eames and Jean de Reszke sang the title roles and Edouard de Reszke was Friar Laurent.

In August 1892 fire destroyed most of the interior of the opera house, and there was no opera until the rebuilt and redecorated Met opened on November 27, 1893, with cream-colored walls and, for the first time, electric light. It was a season that saw the Met debuts of Nellie Melba, Emma Calvé, and Pol Plançon. The following season brought Francesco Tamagno as Otello and Victor Maurel as Iago, the roles they had created at the work's premiere at the Teatro alla Scala in 1887. Just a few weeks before the opening of the 1896–1897 season, Abbey died and Maurice Grau was named manager. The 1897–1898 season was canceled while the company was reorganized, and Grau assembled an unparalleled roster of artists for 1898–1899: Lilli Lehmann returning for her final season, the de Reszkes, Nellie Melba, Marcella Sembrich, Emma Eames, Ernestine Schumann-Heink, and conductor Franz Schalk. Grau ran the company through the 1902–1903 season, a period that saw the debuts of Milka Ternina, Johanna Gadski, Marcel Journet, Antonio Scotti, Louise Homer, and conductor Alfred Herz, but Grau's most lasting legacy was his long but successful negotiation which brought Enrico Caruso to the Met on the opening night of the 1903–1904 season.

That opening night also introduced the auditorium as it would be known until the last performances there in 1966. Redesigned by the firm of Carrere and Hastings, it contained an enormous sunburst chandelier dominating the gilded waffle-grid ceiling which was alive with paintings of musical putti, ornate box fronts and walls decorated in maroon and gold, and the elaborate proscenium arch with the names of Gluck, Mozart, Beethoven, Gounod, Wagner, and Verdi carved at the top. The curtain, however, was not yet the remembered gold, but red. Heinrich Conried took over as manager of the Met in 1903, but the most important event of the season was the opening night (November 23) performance of *Rigoletto* in which the thirty-year-old Enrico Caruso made his American debut as the Duke. He went on to sing five of his most popular roles that season—Radames, Cavaradossi, Rodolfo, Canio, and Nemorino, as well as Alfredo and Edgardo. He sang every opening night thereafter until his death in 1921 (except for 1906 when he deferred to the American debut of Geraldine Farrar). The 1903–1904 season was also the season during which Conried presented the first staged performance outside of Bayreuth of Wagner's *Parsifal*, in spite of the composer's stipulation that the work not be performed anywhere but Bayreuth for its first fifty years. The resulting furor culminated in an ultimately unsuccessful law suit brought against the Met by the composer's widow, Cosima. A further uproar broke out in 1906–1907 when Conried presented the American premiere of Richard Strauss's erotic opera *Salome*. The single performance created such a scandal that the work went unheard at the Met again until 1933–1934. Conried's final season, 1907–1908, brought the debuts of Russian bass Feodor Chaliapin and Austrian conductor Gustav Mahler, who went on to conduct forty-nine performances with the company in New York and on tour.

The 1908–1909 season ushered in the beginning of Giulio Gatti-Casazza's twenty-seven-year reign, a record unlikely ever to be matched. Gatti brought Arturo Toscanini with him from La Scala, and Toscanini led the opening night *Aida*, which featured the debut of Emmy Destinn. In December 1910 Toscanini led the world premiere of Puccini's *La Fanciulla del West* with the composer in attendance. While never officially given the title, Toscanini was in effect music director of the Met until his departure in April 1915. He conducted 459 performances during his seven seasons, including the American premiere of

Boris Godunov. As a replacement for Toscanini, Gatti-Casazza turned to the Viennese conductor Artur Bodansky, who made his debut with *Götterdämmerung* in November 1915 and went on to conduct for twenty-four years at the Met, conducting more performances at the old house than any other conductor. Additional debuts during this period include those of Luisa Tetrazzini, Frieda Hempel, Lucrezia Bori, Giovanni Martinelli, Claudia Muzio, and Maria Jeritza.

During this rich musical period, Gatti-Casazza was making improvements both in the company's finances and in the opera house itself. He continued to bring great singers from abroad and to introduce great American singers, among them Rosa Ponselle, Rose Bampton, Grace Moore, and Lawrence Tibbett. Repertory ranged from the American premiere of *Turandot, Jenufa*, and *Simon Boccanegra* to the world premiere of Puccini's triple bill *Il Trittico*. The 1929–1930 season opened successfully with *Manon*, featuring Lucrezia Bori, Beniamino Gigli, and Giuseppe De Luca. The next day the stock market crashed, but the company was not immediately affected. By 1932–1933, the effects of the Depression resulted in a drastic cut in the number of productions and a 10 percent pay cut for the singers. However, a new source of revenue appeared, which was to have an increasing importance for the company in the future—radio broadcasting. The National Broadcasting Company offered to pay to transmit opera from the Met, and the 1931 Christmas Day matinee of *Hänsel und Gretel* became the first complete opera broadcast from the Met. In 1932–1933 the Metropolitan launched a campaign to raise $300,000, an effort that succeeded in large part as a result of the participation of the new and rapidly growing radio audience. This broadcast and fund-raising campaign really marked the beginning of the Met's prominence as a national opera company.

The 1934–1935 season marked Gatti-Casazza's twenty-seventh and final year as general manager, and just as Grau's legacy was the then little-known Italian tenor, Enrico Caruso, so Gatti's legacy was an obscure Norwegian soprano, Kirsten Flagstad, whose unheralded debut as Sieglinde in the matinee broadcast of *Die Walküre* was the beginning of her legendary career and stage partnership with Danish tenor Lauritz Melchoir, who had joined the company as Tannhäuser in 1926. Only days after becoming general manager in 1935, Herbert Witherspoon died, and his assistant, Edward Johnson, a tenor for thirteen years with the Metropolitan, was named to succeed him. Johnson led the Met for fifteen years, including the difficult post-Depression and war years. He was strongly supported by Mrs. August Belmont, the first woman to join the company's board of directors. Belmont founded the Metropolitan Opera Guild in 1935 to aid in fund-raising and educational projects and the Metropolitan Opera National Council in 1952 to broaden the company's reach throughout the nation.

Edward Johnson was an active recruiter of talent, and during his administration he introduced many singers to Metropolitan audiences, including Zinka Milanov, Bidu Sayão, Jarmila Novotna, Astrid Varnay, Ljuba Welitsch, Jussi Bjoerling, Giuseppe Di Stefano, Alexander Kipnis, Martial Singher, and Ferrucio Tagliavini. He also brought in many great American artists, including Dorothy Kirsten,

Regina Resnik, Eleanor Steber, Risë Stevens, Helen Traubel, Blanche Thebom, Jerome Hines, Charles Kullman, Robert Merrill, Jan Peerce, Richard Tucker, and Leonard Warren. By the early 1940s, due to the war in Europe, the Metropolitan found itself with one of its strongest conducting rosters: Bruno Walter, Sir Thomas Beecham, Erich Leinsdorf, George Szell, and following the war, Fritz Reiner and Fritz Busch. The postwar years saw the first new "Ring" cycle at the Met since 1913–1914 (and one that was to remain in production for nearly thirty years as well), and the Metropolitan Opera premieres of Mozart's *Die Entführung aus dem Serail* (1946), Benjamin Britten's *Peter Grimes* (1948), and Mussorgsky's *Khovanshchina* (1950).

The Austrian-born opera impresario Rudolf Bing, manager of the Glyndebourne Festival Opera and creator of the Edinburgh Festival, succeeded Johnson in 1950–1951, and his first opening night was representative of his new approach of viewing opera as a theatrical art form, for which he brought in the world's leading theatrical designers and directors. He engaged Margaret Webster to direct and Rolf Gérard to design the first new production of Verdi's *Don Carlo* at the Metropolitan since 1922–1923, a performance that also featured the debuts of Cesare Siepi as King Phillip, Fedora Barbieri as Eboli, and Lucine Amara as the Celestial Voice. Johann Strauss's *Die Fledermaus*, which had not been heard at the Met since 1905–1906, became one of the company's biggest hits ever during Bing's inaugural season. Among the directors engaged were Peter Brook, Tyrone Guthrie, Alfred Lunt, Joseph Mankiewiecz, José Quintero, Franco Zeffirelli, Cyril Ritchard, Nathaniel Merrill, Paul-Emile Deiber, Otto Schenk, and Louis Barrault. Designers included Cecil Beaton, Eugene Berman, Beni Montresor, Franco Zeffirelli, Günther Schneider-Siemssen, Robert O'Hearn, Oliver Messel, Marc Chagall, and Boris Aronson.

The roster of singers and conductors that Bing brought to the Metropolitan is a virtually complete listing of the world's great singers during that period. Among them were Marian Anderson, Maria Callas, Eileen Farrell, Renata Tebaldi, Anna Moffo, Grace Bumbry, Shirley Verrett, Birgit Nilsson, Teresa Stratas, Joan Sutherland, Leonie Rysanek, Elisabeth Schwarzkopf, Renata Scotto, Mirella Freni, Montserrat Caballé, Marilyn Horne, Régine Crespin, Elisabeth Söderström, Fiorenza Cossotto, Christa Ludwig, Frederica von Stade, Carlo Bergonzi, Franco Corelli, Mario Del Monaco, Placido Domingo, Nicolai Gedda, James McCracken, Luciano Pavarotti, Jon Vickers, Tito Gobbi, George London, Cornell MacNeil, Sherrill Milnes, Hans Hotter, and Nicolai Ghiaurov. Conductors included Claudio Abbado, Ernest Ansermet, Leonard Bernstein, Karl Böhm, Colin Davis, Josef Krips, Lorin Maazel, Zubin Mehta, Dimitri Mitropoulos, Thomas Schippers, Georg Solti, Leopold Stokowski, Christoph von Dohnanyi, Herbert von Karajan, and, in June 1971, the young American conductor, James Levine, who eventually became the company's artistic director.

Among the historic events of the Bing years was the creation of the Metropolitan Opera National Company, a touring organization created to provide opportunities for young singers to refine their craft, and the company's first tour outside the United States and Canada since 1909–1910, when the Met went to Paris at the end of the 1965–1966 season, following an emotional farewell to the old Metropolitan Opera House on April 16, 1966. September 16, 1966, marked the fulfillment of a dream almost as old as the company itself: the opening of the new opera house at Lincoln Center with the world premiere of Samuel Barber's *Anthony and Cleopatra* performed by a nearly all-American cast. The season's nine new productions featured the highly acclaimed Met premiere of Richard Strauss's *Die Frau ohne Schatten* and a second world premiere, Marvin David Levy's *Mourning Becomes Electra* [premiere March 17, 1976]. At the end of the season the Metropolitan inaugurated a series of free concert opera performances in the parks of the five boroughs of New York City, which in later seasons would also include performances in Nassau County and New Jersey.

After twenty-two seasons at the helm, Bing (now Sir Rudolf) retired and introduced his successor, Göran Gentele, general manager of the Kurgliga Teatern (Royal Opera) Stockholm, to the New York public at his farewell gala on April 22, 1972. In a tragic echo of the appointment of Herbert Witherspoon in 1935, Gentele was killed in an automobile accident during a vacation in Sardinia in July 1972. He had been general manager of the Met for only eighteen days. Schuyler G. Chapin, assistant to Gentele, was named acting general manager and, along with music director Rafael Kubelik, set out to carry on with the plans made by his predecessor. Opening night was a new production of *Carmen* conducted by Leonard Bernstein, with Marilyn Horne as Carmen and James McCracken as Don José. Two innovations proceeded as conceived by Gentele: the American performer Danny Kaye acted as master of ceremonies for the first "Look-In," an informal program designed to introduce children to opera, and the "Mini-Met," a program to present smaller scale works than would be appropriate at the big house, opened at the Forum Theatre, a part of Lincoln Center's Vivian Beaumont Theatre, with Maurice Ohana's *Syllabaire pour Phèdre*, Purcell's *Dido and Aeneas*, and Virgil Thompson's *Four Saints in Three Acts*. The 1973–1974 season saw the Metroplitan Opera premiere of Berlioz's epic *Les Troyens* conducted by maestro Kubelik in his Met debut. The English stage director John Dexter made his company debut with the Met premiere of Verdi's *I Vespri Sicilliani*. The following season brought the American premiere of Benjamin Britten's *Death in Venice*, a new production of Mussorgsky's *Boris Godunov* using the composer's original orchestration, the debut of Beverly Sills in the Met premiere of Rossini's *The Siege of Corinth*, and the Metropolitan's three-week tour of Japan.

Chapin left following the end of the 1975–1976 season, and the company was then run by a triumvirate of Anthony Bliss as executive director (he became general manager in 1981), James Levine as music director, and John Dexter as director of production. During the next few seasons many new works were added to the repertory: in 1976–1977, Poulenc's *Dialogues of the Carmelites* and Berg's *Lulu*. At the end of the season the company established itself as a national presence on television. The first "Live from the Met" telecast, *La Bohème* with

Renata Scotto, Luciano Pavarotti, and James Levine conducting, took place on March 15, 1977. Over fifty telecasts have been broadcast in this series; in 1978–1979, Britten's *Billy Budd*; in 1979–1980, Kurt Weill and Bertolt Brecht's *Rise and Fall of the City of Mahagony*; and in 1980–1981 the triple bill *Parade*, consisting of Satie's ballet *Parade*, and the two one-act operas, Poulenc's *Les Mamelles de Tiresias* and Ravel's *L'Enfant et les Sortileges*, directed by John Dexter and designed, in his Met debut, by the English artist David Hockney. The 1981–1982 season featured another triple bill, this time of Stravinsky's *Le Rossignol, Le Sacre du Printemps*, and *Oedipus Rex*, as well as a new production of *La Bohème*, marking the return of director and designer Franco Zeffirelli to the Metropolitan. Mozart's *Idomeneo* received its Met premiere in 1982–1983.

The Metropolitan celebrated its one hundredth anniversary in 1983–1984 with a gala all-day concert on October 22, the exact day of the company's first performance in 1883. The four-hour matinee and the five-hour evening performance were televised live. The centennial season opened with the first revival of Berlioz's *Les Troyens* since its premiere in 1973, and also featured the first Handel opera ever given at the Met, *Rinaldo*, with Marilyn Horne in the title role and Samuel Ramey in his Met debut. The 1984–1985 season brought the Met premieres of Mozart's *La Clemenza di Tito* and George Gershwin's *Porgy and Bess* in honor of the fiftieth anniversary of the work's first performance. Anthony Bliss retired at the close of the season after nearly forty years of association with the company, and was succeeded by Bruce Crawford, who became general manager designate in September 1985 and general manager in January 1986.

The opening night of Crawford's first full season featured a new production of *Die Walküre*, the initial work of a completely new "Ring" cycle which would be completed during 1988–1989. New productions of *Die Fledermaus* and *Turandot* opened during 1986–1987, and the Met reentered the field of commercial recording with a complete "Ring" cycle for Deutsche Grammophon conducted by James Levine, a project that would take four years to complete. Highlights of the 1988–1989 season included Met premieres of Handel's *Giulio Cesare* and Schoenberg's *Erwartung* as well as a matinee broadcast of Wagner's "Ring" cycle which aired on four consecutive Sundays in April 1989.

Bruce Crawford announced his resignation effective at the end of the 1988–1989 season, and Hugh Southern, acting chairman of the National Endowment for the Arts, was appointed general manager on November 1, 1989. Highlighted by five new productions and three complete "Ring" cycles, the 1989–1990 season was capped by the largest opera telecast in American television history: the Met's complete "Ring" cycle broadcast on four consecutive evenings in prime time on the Public Broadcasting Service in June 1990. Southern resigned at the end of the season, and John Volpe, an assistant manager of the Metropolitan for ten years, was named general manager.

BIBLIOGRAPHY: F. P. Fellers, *The Metropolitan Opera on Record: A Discography of the Commercial Recordings* (Westport, CT, 1984). Irving Kolodin, *The Metropolitan*

Opera (New York, 1966). Julius Mattfield, *A Hundred Years of Grand Opera in New York: 1825–1925* (New York, 1927; repr., 1976). Martin Mayer, *The Met: One Hundred Years of Grand Opera* (New York, 1983). William H. Seltsam, *Metropolitan Opera Annals*, 4 vols. (New York, 1947, 1957, 1967, 1977) (vol. 4 by Mary Ellis Peltz and Gerald Fitzgerald).

ACCESS: Metropolitan Opera Association, Lincoln Center, New York, NY 10023. (212) 799 3100; fax (212) 870 4520. Joseph Volpe, General Director.

[From materials supplied by the company]

New York City Opera

Early in the 1940s both Mayor Fiorello La Guardia and members of the New York City Council supported the need for a permanent home for artists who might rehearse and give quality performances in New York City at reasonable prices. The old Mecca Temple had defaulted to the city. Released by the Board of Estimate, the building became the home of the City Center of Music and Drama, Inc., and was formally inaugurated by Arthur Rodzinski and the New York Philharmonic on December 11, 1943. Lawrence Tibbett was the guest artist, which may have been an omen for the all-American opera company which was to evolve. Originally founded as the City Center Opera Company, and the first group to become a permanent member of a conglomerate that would soon include the New York City Ballet and four other companies, the New York City Opera (NYCO) opened at the City Center Theater on February 21, 1944, with *Tosca*. From its inception NYCO was determined to become New York's "other company." Unable to employ singers with international reputations, it was forced to build a company of its own, and without the resources to finance grandiose and glittering productions, it chose to concentrate on little-known and unknown operas, showcase American composers, and undertake risky world premieres. The company has been highly successful over the years in all these ventures and thus has been able to avoid unnecessary direct competition with its famous neighbor, the Metropolitan Opera Company Association.

Since its inception, more than 2,100 singers—99 percent of them American—have been given opportunities to perform in imaginative productions of repertoire ranging from contemporary works to historical rarities and traditional favorites. During the 1940s and 1950s under the batons of Laszlo Halász (1944–1951), Josef Rosenstock (1952–1955), Erich Leinsdorf (1956–1957), and Julius Rudel (1957–1979), the company's roster was headed by such talents as Donald Gramm, Cornell MacNeil, Regina Resnick, Beverly Sills, Norman Treigle, and Shirley Varrett. The following decades saw the emergence of a new generation of young Americans, artists like Samuel Ramey, Sherrill Milnes, Tatiana Troyanos, Faith Esham, and Carol Vaness, who are now involved in major national and international careers. Unique among major North American companies today, City Opera has a roster of some 130 principal artists which remains constant throughout an entire season of seventeen to twenty different productions. This gives young talent the chance to work as part of an ensemble, doing small roles one night and major roles the next. As a champion of young American singers of promise (approximately twenty-five make company debuts annually), City Opera employs performers of abundant talent but often limited professional experience. The ensemble concept is designed to address this need.

This "strong commitment to the principle of true ensemble opera" really began with the appointment of Julius Rudel as general director. Rudel had started as a musical assistant with the company in 1943 and was well acquainted with all the artists and staff. By the 1956–1957 season the company was insolvent, and there was a good chance that the board of directors would close down the company for good. With the support of his colleagues, Rudel was given the challenge of resurrecting the company, and he remained as general director through the 1978–1979 season. One of the high points of his tenure was the move from the old Mecca Temple on 55th Street to the New York State Theater at Lincoln Center, which City Center leased on January 1, 1966, for a period of fifty years. Rudel's tenure was marked by an expansion of the repertoire, continued emphasis on American artists, integrated productions that stressed theatrical as well as musical values, and strong support for American composers.

When Rudel resigned to pursue a variety of conducting interests, Beverly Sills began a ten-year tenure on July 1, 1979, under circumstances that were remarkably similar to those that had faced Rudel years earlier. There was a major accumulated deficit, union negotiations were strained, and the company's resources were stretched to the breaking point to cover all the obligations that it faced. Under Sills's leadership, however, the total budget more than doubled, from $11.3 million in 1979 to $26.1 million in 1989. The number of performance weeks increased from twenty-one to twenty-six, performances increased from 142 to 186, administrative staff grew from twenty-eight to fifty-five; and contributed income more than doubled from $4.4 million to $11 million. Attendance grew by 160,000 and subscriptions grew by almost 18,000.

In its forty-five seasons, the company has staged 205 different works, including 23 world premieres, 18 New York premieres, 12 New York stage premieres, 8 American premieres (both continents), 5 U.S. premieres, 1 North American premiere, and 1 U.S. stage premiere. The company's repertoire extends beyond the realm of opera to Bernstein's *Candide*, Sondheim's *Sweeny Todd*, and Romberg's *The Desert Song*. Moreover, in 1986 a Spring Musical Comedy Season was initiated to revive the great American Broadway tradition with such favorites as *Brigadoon, South Pacific, The Music Man*, and *The Pajama Game*. In addition, City Opera's National Company tours a single work from the standard repertoire, and since 1980 has played to over 500,000 people in 104 cities in thirty-seven states plus Canada. Given the breadth of the repertoire, the length of the season, and the imposing roster of American artists, the New York City Opera has a strong claim to the disputed title of "American Opera Company." Another young American, Christopher Keene, was appointed general director of the company in March 1989. As the first recipient of the Julius Rudel Award (1969–1971), Keene shares a long association with NYCO both as a performer and as an administrator. A leading interpreter of contemporary music, Keene conducted the American premiere of Glass's *Satyagraha* and Albert Riemann's *Melusine* and the German premiere of Henze's *We Come to the River*, as well as the world premieres of Floyd's *Bilby's Doll*, Menotti's *The Hero* and *Tamu-Tamu*, Pasatieri's *Inez de Castro*, and Villa-Lobos's *Yerma*.

BIBLIOGRAPHY: *Opera. Opera News. New York Times*. Beverly Sills and Lawrence Linderman, *Beverly: An Autobiography* (New York, 1987). Martin L. Sokol, *The New York City Opera* (New York, 1981).

ACCESS: New York State Theater, Lincoln Center, New York, NY 10023. (212) 870 5600; fax (212) 724 1120. Christopher Keene, General Director.

[From materials supplied by the company]

OMAHA, NEBRASKA (metro 569,614; city 314,225)

Opera/Omaha

[A number of theaters were home to musical events in nineteenth-century Omaha. Redick's Opera House, the Grand Opera House, and Boyd's Opera House all preceded the Orpheum Theater, an early-1900s masterpiece which was completely restored in 1975 and now serves as the home of both Opera/Omaha and the Omaha Symphony.] Opera/Omaha was founded in 1958 as the Omaha Civic Opera Society by a small group of dedicated opera lovers. The company was inaugurated on January 19, 1959, with a performance of *Madama Butterfly* held in the Joslyn Art Museum auditorium. During the early years (1959–1967) the company was a small, poorly funded community organization using local singers and board members who helped out in the productions. Glynn Ross, who later built the Seattle Opera into a major organization, directed a number of the early productions. Beginning in 1968, major stars including Brent Ellis, Jean Fenn, Dorothy Kirsten, Carol Neblett, Louis Quilico, Samuel Ramey, Regina Resnik, and Frederica Van Stade were hired to build the audience base. At that point the company was using the uninviting 2,400-seat Omaha Civic Auditorium which required amplification so that the voices could reach the back of the house.

The name was changed to Omaha Opera Company in 1972, and Jonathan Dudley was hired as the first general director in 1974. The newly restored Orpheum Theater was opened by Beverly Sills in *Lucia di Lammermoor* in 1975 with completely sold-out performances. The budget had grown, but so had the deficit, and the company mounted its first auction, a major fund-raising event which has been held annually ever since. Mary Roberts was hired as general director in 1980, and during her tenure, Opera/Omaha has tripled its budget and achieved national and international recognition. By 1982 the deficits had been retired and the company was showing a small surplus. Under her leadership the board of directors articulated the company's mission. The first purpose is ''to make opera available to the greater Omaha community by mounting full-scale, high quality productions... and the second is to increase audiences for opera through comprehensive educational and touring programs." The company was recently honored with a National Endowment for the Arts (N.E.A.) Challenge Grant on the basis of the educational programs.

The current season consists of two innovative works and one experimental opera in the Fall Festival season followed by two standard repertory main-stage works during the winter. Operas are performed in the original language with surtitles. The 1990 Fall Festival season in the Witherspoon Concert Hall in the Joslyn Art Museum included Donizetti's *Maria Padilla*, the American premiere of John Casken's *The Golem*, and Angelina Reaux in *Stranger Here Myself*, followed by main-stage productions in the Orpheum Theater of *The Magic Flute, Carousel*, and *Il Trovatore*. The resident Opera Ensemble tours throughout the region. Opera/Omaha operates on a budget of $2.0 million and receives public funds from the N.E.A. and the Nebraska Arts Council as well as monies from United Arts Omaha.

ACCESS: P.O. Box 807 DTS, Omaha, NE 68101–2101. (402) 346 4398. Mary Robert, General Director. John DeMain, Music Director.

[From materials supplied by the company]

PHILADELPHIA, PENNSYLVANIA (metro 4,800,000; city 1,606,000)

Opera Company of Philadelphia

Philadelphia commands a prominent place in American cultural and political history. Founded by William Penn in 1681, Philadelphia played a major geographical and political role in the formation of the United States and was, for many years, the country's largest city. Now ranked fifth in size, Philadelphia and the surrounding metropolitan area boasts a population of more than 4.7 million residents. The largest freshwater port in the world, Philadelphia retains a small-town atmosphere with its many parks and tree-shaded streets. Known in colonial times as the "Athens of the West," Philadelphia has been a center of operatic activity for more than 150 years. Unlike Chicago, San Francisco, or New York, until recently Philadelphia never had a single company that dominated its operatic life. In fact, the company with the longest record of performance in Philadelphia is the Metropolitan Opera Association, which appeared regularly between 1899 and 1961. The "Met," which performed as many as twenty times a season at the Academy of Music, accustomed Philadelphia to star-laden performances but, at the same time, stifled the emergence of a strong local company. To this day, many Philadelphians prefer to travel to New York for their opera.

The history of opera in Philadelphia is, more or less, the story of a succession of local companies that began ambitiously and then, after overstretching their resources, folded or survived through merger. Most performed at the Academy of Music which, although now the home of the Philadelphia Orchestra, was inaugurated as an opera house in 1857 with a production of *Il Trovatore*. [The

2,900-seat Academy of Music was built by Napoleon Le Brun based on the design of La Scala in Milan. At the time it was the finest opera house in the United States, and its beautiful interior and excellent acoustics make it the equivalent of any music hall in the country today.] Oscar Hammerstein built another opera house on North Broad Street (which is now a shell awaiting restoration) where he presented operatic seasons between 1908 and 1911. [The legendary battles between Hammerstein and the Met are well chronicled in Vincent Sheean's biography of the impresario.] From 1910 to 1915, a joint venture between Philadelphia and Chicago brought star-studded casts to both cities. After that, several attempts to establish a resident company failed.

For the next twenty years, a string of companies carrying diverse names like the Philadelphia Civic Opera, the Philadelphia Grand Opera, and the Pennsylvania Grand Opera, emerged but did not last. During the Depression years, two new companies sprang into existence: the Philadelphia La Scala Company under Giuseppe Bamboschek, and the Civic Grand Opera. The two merged in 1955 to form the Grand Opera under the direction of Antony Terracciano. A year later, Aurelio Fabiani brought the NBC Opera to the Academy of Music. The success of that venture led Fabiani to found the Lyric Opera Company. Now, as so often, Philadelphia had two companies competing for star singers, funding, and the allegiance of audiences. Fabiani, a colorful impresario with a flamboyant style, began his career as concertmaster of the Chicago Civic Opera and then made a fortune promoting wrestling events. Before creating the Lyric, Fabiani brought to Philadelphia tennis stars, midget auto racers, and ice skaters, as well as sopranos and wrestlers. In the same night, Fabiani presented Renata Tebaldi in concert and presided over a wrestling match between Antonio "Dropkick" Rocco and John "Adonis" Valentine. In his management of the Lyric, Fabiani brought musical knowledge and an impresario's talent for exploiting his product. In addition to Tebaldi, he presented Corelli, Milanov, di Stefano, Pavarotti, and Caballé. The Grand countered with Nilsson, del Monaco, Tucker, and Tagliavini.

Despite the starry casts, productions—especially the Grand's—proved ill-rehearsed. "Both companies," later wrote James Felton in the *Evening Bulletin*, "were glorified booking agencies, importing star singers when they could, leaving other elements almost to chance . . . orchestra, chorus, scenery, stage direction." There was talk of merger between the Grand and the Lyric for several years. In March 1962 the two boards voted to create the Philadelphia Opera. Less than a month later, the merger came apart when disgruntled board members of the Grand formed the Philadelphia Civic Opera. The Philadelphia Opera was dissolved before it had presented a single performance, and the Grand and Lyric were back in business.

In 1973 Fabiani died and Terracciano retired. Before his death, Fabiani was replaced by William Warden, who was then ousted for a new team of Ian Strasfogel and Eleanor Morrison which lasted less than a season. As the Lyric floundered, the Grand was suddenly faced with a revolt of its orchestra and chorus. Then Governor Milton Shapp stepped in and used his good offices to bring pressure for a merger, and he put together a package of support for a new company that included money from the city, the state arts council, and local foundations. After months of negotiation and maneuvering, the two sides came together on March 24, 1975, to sign the agreement. It was soon discovered that the Grand brought along a deficit of more than $200,000 that posed a financial threat to a new company with a budget of little more than $.5 million. Carl Suppa, the Lyric's promoter and choral director, became the company's artistic director. Max M. Leon, the director of the Grand, was named the company's general manager.

The Opera Company of Philadelphia (OCP) began its first season of six productions with *Faust* in September 1975. The company's first two seasons had some exciting moments. Renata Scotto's *Anna Bolena* and the world premiere of Gian Carlo Menotti's *The Hero* were among them. But the weakest elements of the Grand and Lyric seemed to be in control. Most of the stars from the past had either retired or were no longer available. Production values remained low. Casting and conducting proved erratic. The amateurish chorus and underrehearsed orchestra added little luster to the company's image. After a disastrous production of *Cavalleria Rusticana* and *I Pagliacci* in 1976, the company's board took decisive action and removed the general director and artistic director. A search led to Edward Corn, director of planning at the Metropolitan Opera. In the spring of 1977 Corn was brought in as the company's manager with Julius Rudel as artistic director.

Corn put OCP on a new course. He envisioned Philadelphia as a center for regional opera, emphasizing American singers, opera in English, and repertory that embraced American musical theater. To realize his goals, Corn brought in a youthful staff. He also raised the company's artistic standards. With Rudel's help, he made casting more consistent, improved the orchestra, and paid more attention to production values. Corn revamped the company but also began an ambitious series of outreach programs. He collaborated with the Eugene O'Neill Theatre Center in Connecticut to create new operatic works. He launched an intensive educational program, expanded the summer concerts in city parks, and tried to reach out to Philadelphia's large black community. In December 1978 OCP produced the premiere of *Rumpelstiltskin* by John Gardner and Joseph Baber, and six months later it inaugurated a summer festival in the outdoor theater at Longwood Gardens. Then, in 1980, just as his programs were in place, Corn left Philadelphia to become director of the National Endowment for the Arts opera program.

Ironically, Margaret Anne Everitt, who had been brought in by Ed Corn to be the OCP's director of planning, was appointed his successor. She quickly redefined the company. In her first season she canceled the summer festival, reduced productions from six to five, and cut back outreach programs. Everitt aimed to turn the Opera Company of Philadelphia into a major international company. In 1981 she ended OCP's association with Julius Rudel and took over artistic control. Everitt assumed her duties just as the company was finalizing plans for an international voice competition with Luciano Pavarotti. She saw the tenor as the OCP's entree into prominence and exploited his popularity to raise money to televise performances featuring the tenor and winners of the competition. Pavarotti appeared with the first group of prizewinners in productions of *La Bohème* and *L'Elisir d'Amore* in 1982. A telecast of *La Bohème* attracted the largest opera audience in the history of television and won an Emmy Award as the best classical telecast of the season. Subsequent competitions in 1985 and 1988 introduced more singers and resulted in telecasts of *Un ballo in maschera*, the Verdi Requiem, a highlights version of *La Bohème*, and *Luisa Miller*. Among the singers brought to prominence by the competition are Denes Gulyas, Mary Jane Johnson, Muccia Focile, Susan Dunn, Paata Burchuladze, Fiamma Izzo d'Amico, Anna Caterina Antonacci, and Kallen Esperian.

Everitt introduced a number of conductors, directors, and designers to Philadelphia audiences. She nurtured the conducting careers of Francesco Siciliani and Steven Mercurio and engaged Toby Robertson and Gray Veredon to stage their first opera productions. Among the designers she brought to Philadelphia were Franco Colavecchia and illustrator Gil Lesser. Michael Korn, OCP's associate conductor, raised the standards of the chorus and orchestra and also conducted operas by Britten, Handel, and Rossini. Everitt's list of accomplishments include a series of *Faust* operas by Gounod, Berlioz, and Boito, starring James Morris and Burchuladze; a *Pique Dame* staged by Gian Carlo Menotti, in which Régine Crespin sang the Countess for the first time in her career; and a double bill of *Dido and Aeneas* and *Oedipus Rex* which introduced Jessye Norman to American opera audiences. Everitt enlarged OCP's repertory with productions of Dvořák's *Rusalka*, Britten's *Death in Venice* and *Peter Grimes*, Janáček's *The Cunning Little Vixen*, Handel's *Ariodante*, Menotti's *The Saint of Bleeker Street*, and Rossini's *Mosè* and *La Gazza Ladra*.

The major setback of Everitt's tenure came on March 31, 1989, when the discovery of a crack in a ceiling support beam forced the sudden closing of the Academy of Music only hours before the premieres of a new production of *L'Elisir d'Amore* starring Pavarotti and prizewinners of OCP's third international voice competition. The company was forced to move its productions of Donizetti's opera and Verdi's *Luisa Miller* to other performance spaces. The resulting costs added significantly to the company's deficit. Subscribers, disgruntled by the inconveniences, failed to renew their subscriptions. Ticket sales fell for the 1989–1990 season of operas by Handel, Menotti, and Rossini. In mid season, the OCP's board forced Everitt's resignation. Jane Grey Nemeth, the director of the Pavarotti competition, became Everitt's acting replacement. Effective March 4, 1991, Robert B. Driver was appointed general director of the Opera Company of Philadelphia.

CHRONOLOGY OF DIRECTORS: Max M. Leon, General Manager, and Carl Suppa, Artistic Director, 1975–1976; Edward Corn, General Manager, 1977–1980; Julius Rudel, Artistic Advisor, 1977–1981; Margaret Anne Everitt, General Director 1980–1990; Jane

Grey Nemeth, Acting General Director, 1990–1991; Robert B. Driver, General Director, 1991–present.

ACCESS: 1500 Market Street, 26th Floor, Center Square, East Tower, Philadelphia, PA 19102. (215) 732 5814; fax (215) 790 1104. Robert B. Driver, General Director.

ROBERT BAXTER

PITTSBURGH, PENNSYLVANIA (metro 2,263,894; city 423,938)

Pittsburgh Opera

Pittsburgh is unique among America's leading metropolitan centers. The city lies in the juncture of the East Coast, the Midwest, Canada, and the South. While there is, to a degree, competition from major arts organizations in Cleveland and Philadelphia, Pittsburgh's cultural groups are committed to providing their large tri-state area (Pennsylvania, Ohio, and West Virginia) with sophisticated theater, music, dance, and opera. The "Steel City's" operatic history can be traced back to 1838 when Francis Wemyss treated Pittsburghers to their first opera, Rossini's *Il Barbiere di Siviglia*. It was just the first note of a glorious musical heritage. Despite the fact that the city could only count on isolated concerts and touring productions, many preeminent stars of the operatic stage did come and enrich the city's cultural life: Adelina Patti, Lilli Lehmann, the deReszke brothers, Ernestine Schumann-Heink, and Frieda Hemple. Local historians boast of their native daughter, Louise Homer. Furthermore, Victor Herbert lived in the Shadeyside area from 1898 to 1904.

With the arrival of the twentieth century, Pittsburgh was able to claim an important place in the operatic life of America. Again, audiences were treated to the finest vocal artists of the day: Francis Alda, Titta Ruffo, Beniamino Gigli, Feodor Chaliapin, and Lucrezia Bori. The German Opera Company arrived in 1923 for a four-day Wagner Festival at the Schenley Theatre. *Die Meistersinger von Nürnberg* starred Friedrich Schorr and Alexander Kipnis. Again, however, these events were not available on a regular schedule or as part of a traditional music season. Several ambitious Pittsburgh women decided to change all that— and with it, the cultural history of the region.

In the autumn of 1939, Mrs. John A. Byerly, Mrs. Robert Wickersham, Mrs. Winthrop L. Collings, Carolyn Hunt Mahaffey, and Mrs. Roland Pease, all members of the Tuesday Music Club, gathered their own resources and produced Pittsburgh's first home-based opera. They chose Gilbert and Sullivan's *Iolanthe*. Rehearsals were held in Byerly's game room. They ambitiously raised funds; recruited professional and amateur singers; engaged a young local musician, Anthony Caputo, to conduct; and sold tickets. Local critics were enthusiastic and encouraged the fledgling company to make plans for future seasons. With a clear vision and great faith, this same core of women founded the Pittsburgh Opera Society. On Friday, March 15, 1940, their inaugural season opened with Offenbach's *Les Contes d'Hoffmann*. The site was Carnegie Music Hall. Caputo conducted once again. The season continued with *Le Nozze di Figaro* and *Eugene Onegin*. These last two operas were conducted by Vladimir Bakaleinikoff, assistant conductor of the Pittsburgh Symphony. A new era in Pittsburgh's cultural life had taken its bow.

In 1942 another member of the Pittsburgh Symphony, Richard Karp, took the reins of the young opera company. The new director was a Viennese violinist who had conducted opera in Europe. As with many great European talents of that time, Karp fled to America to escape the renewed threat of oppression and war. He insisted on an all-professional company and his debut was celebrated with performances of *Don Pasquale* on the lawn of the Hotel Schenley, at the Clairton Lions Club, and at the Stephen Foster Memorial. Karp created glamour and notoriety in a very short time. He took his company to its new home in the Syria Mosque and entertained the city with exciting productions and superstars. Gladys Swarthout, Eleanor Steber, Roberta Peters, Leonard Warren, Ramon Vinay, Salvatore Baccaloni, Bidu Sayão, Victoria de los Angeles, Robert Merrill, Richard Tucker, Licia Albanese, Marjorie Lawrence, and Norman Treigle all sang for enthusiastic audiences. His seasons boasted Birgit Nilsson in *Turandot* with a young Tito Capobianco directing, Renata Scotto in *Madama Butterfly*, Monserrat Caballé in *La Bohème* and *Il Trovatore*, James McCracken in *Otello*, and Beverly Sills in *Lucia di Lammermoor*.

Growth had become synonymous with Pittsburgh Opera. As Karp enhanced both the repertory and the roster of artists, the budget followed close behind. The need for increased financial support became essential. In 1947 the Women's Association was organized and became a major source of additional income. The group later renamed itself the Woman's Auxiliary and is still a viable contributor to Pittsburgh Opera. A new home was also found. The beautifully renovated Loews Penn Theatre in downtown Pittsburgh was rechristened Heinz Hall, and the opera made its debut there in 1971 with Verdi's *Aida*. Away from the theater, Karp was said to be a warm and gentle man. In the pit, however, he engaged in heated debates with his orchestra. Pittsburgh lore has it that he even turned to his audiences during performances to remonstrate to them about their lack of etiquette in the theater. Nonetheless, the maestro was easily Pittsburgh Opera's greatest fan and promoter. It is conceded that without him, there might not be a Pittsburgh Opera. Karp's dynamic leadership came to an end in 1977 when he lost his final battle with cancer.

The next few years were unsettled. Karp's daughter, Barbara, took over the company. She had worked as a stage director for New York City Opera and for her father in Pittsburgh. As an artist, she was considered innovative and brilliant. However, her relationship with the opera's management was strained. After two seasons of mixed reviews and frustration, she resigned. The company's forty-first season opened with a new artistic director, James de Blasis, who was also director of the Cincinnati Opera. He was a graduate of Pittsburgh's Carnegie-Mellon University and founded that institute's opera workshop. He had been a stage director for Pittsburgh Opera as well as other local performing arts groups.

Eventually, Cincinnati Opera found the situation unworkable and de Blasis resigned his Pittsburgh post in 1982.

Tito Capobianco was not a stranger to Pittsburgh when he arrived in 1983 as the new general director. He had staged his first production for the company in 1963 and was a regular guest during Karps's administration. Capobianco was also acquainted with the geographical region and its opera public, having been director of Cincinnati's Summer Opera Festival and cocreator of the Opera Department at the Philadephia Music Academy. It was fortuitous for Pittsburgh that he had just resigned the general directorship of the San Diego Opera. With him came a renewed enthusiasm, vigor, and drive. Capobianco is a native of Argentina, and was named, in fact, after his father's favorite singer, Tito Schipa. He has been one of the leading stage directors in opera since his 1954 debut at the Teatro Argentino in La Plata with *I Pagliacci*. Capobianco productions have been noted for innovation and carefully detailed insight. His collaborations at the New York City Opera during the 1970s were hailed as landmarks in opera history and many of them are revived there on a regular basis.

Together with his new board of directors, Capobianco established new goals and long-range plans for Pittsburgh Opera. The performance schedule was modified to move opening nights from Thursday to Saturday and to include a Sunday family matinee series. OpTrans, simultaneous English translations projected above the stage, was introduced. He also formed the Pittsburgh Opera Orchestra which provided independence from any other orchestra or musical organization in the city. Previously, the opera had depended on the Pittsburgh Symphony to provide musicians. Guest artists have continued to thrill Pittsburgh Opera audiences, such as José Carreras, Agnes Baltsa, Ghena Dimitrova, Renata Scotto, Joan Sutherland, Grace Bumbry, Sherrill Milnes, Vladimir Atlantov, Giuseppe Giacomini, Vladimir Popov, Maureen Forrester, Sylvia Sass, Rosalind Plowright, Johanna Meier, and Justino Diaz. Capobianco's custom is to present young talent with brilliant futures to tantalize an eager public. Among them have been Richard Leech, Frances Ginsberg, John Cheek, Harry Dworchak, Rockwell Blake, Faith Esham, and Marilyn Zschau. The company's repertory has been enhanced with Pittsburgh premieres of Verdi's *Macbeth*, Thomas's *Hamlet*, Strauss's *Elektra*, and Boito's *Mefistofele*, plus the first American fully-staged production of Verdi's *La Battaglia di Legnano*.

The crowning glory of the 1980s was Pittsburgh Opera's beautiful, and permanent, new home: the Benedum Center for the Performing Arts. The Stanley Theater, built in 1928 as a vaudeville and movie house, was acquired by the Pittsburgh Trust for Cultural Resources in 1984. It was painstakingly restored to its original splendor and updated with additions to include important rehearsal space and dressing rooms. The stage was expanded, becoming the third largest performance space in the United States. Limitations at the Syria Mosque and Heinz Hall restricted sets to backdrops, painted flies, and simple props. The company could now import exciting state-of-the-art productions from other major opera companies and mount its own new works. Grand opening festivities celebrating the new Benedum Center included a gala concert by Luciano Pavarotti and Puccini's *Turandot* starring Dame Gwenyth Jones.

Under Capobianco's guidance, the company formed the Pittsburgh Opera Center in 1985. The program was designed to provide young artists on the brink of professional careers with valuable training and performance opportunities. Many have since appeared with the company in regular season productions and in important houses throughout the United States and Europe. In 1990 the center took a great step forward, joining resources with Duquesne University to create Pittsburgh Opera Center at Duquesne. As the twenty-first century approaches, Pittsburgh Opera looks ahead with new ambitions. In a sense, the philosophy behind the opera still reflects the spirit of that first *Iolanthe*: Every performance is just a beginning.

ACCESS: 711 Penn Ave., 8th Floor, Pittsburgh, PA 15222–3407. (412) 281 0912; fax (412) 281 4324. Tito Capobianco, General Director.

TIMOTHY B. DUNN

PORTLAND, OREGON (metro 1,242,594; city 366,383)

Portland Opera

Situated at the northern head of Oregon's Willamette Valley and at the juncture of the Willamette and Columbia rivers, Portland has long been the major metropolitan center of the region. Now, as trade increases with the Pacific Rim countries, the city is fast becoming a major international center. The city of Portland can date its first exposure to legitimate operatic productions as long ago as 1867, when the Bianchi Opera Company, a touring troupe employing five singers with piano accompaniment, presented seven evenings of complete operas in Portland's Oro Fino Theatre. Early in its musical history, Portland attempted, with varying degrees of success, to build its own first-rate opera company. An outstanding example, established in 1917, bore the same title as the present company—the Portland Opera Association. Its organizer was an Italian of vast operatic experience, Roberto Corruccini, who served as musical director and conductor for a variety of musical works, many of which the city had never seen before. The company disbanded when he died in 1923.

The present Portland Opera, which was established in 1950 under the title of Portland Civic Opera Association, began in the summer of that year with a production in Washington Park of Verdi's *Aida*, under the baton of Ariel Rubstein. In 1957 the Civic Opera was reorganized. By ordinance, the city of Portland authorized support of the Theatre Arts Opera Association through the Bureau of Parks and Public Recreation. Most of the performances of the Portland Civic and Theatre Arts Opera companies were given in high school auditoriums and at the Oriental Theatre. The Theatre Arts group continued until 1964, when it too was reorganized and incorporated as the present Portland Opera Association.

Since 1969 the renovated 3,000-seat Portland Civic Auditorium has been Portland Opera's permanent home.

From 1964 to 1966 the organization's general director and conductor was Henry Holt. At his departure, the baton was passed to Herbert Weiskopf, and after his death in 1970 it went to Stefan Minde, whose tenure extended through the 1983–1984 season. The company was restructured in 1982 with the appointment of Robert Bailey, who, as general director, continues to serve as chief operating officer for all administrative and artistic matters. Under his guidance Portland Opera has earned a national reputation for artistic excellence. The company is now ranked among the top 20 of the 105 opera companies in the United States, even though Portland ranks only thirty-fourth in population size. In 1984 the Portland Opera adopted the use of projected English translations, a revolutionary means of enhancing the theatrical experience of operas sung in a foreign language. In that same year the Portland Opera Orchestra was established as separate and independent from the Oregon Symphony. Both the Portland Opera Orchestra and the Portland Opera Chorus are composed of local, professional musicians whose performances are consistently praised.

In recent years the Portland Opera has performed under the batons of such renowned maestros as Imre Pallo, John Crosby, Anton Coppola, John De Main, Bruno Aprea, Joseph Rescigno, Stewart Robertson, Tamas Pal, and Richard Woitach. James DePreist, music director of the Oregon Symphony, made his opera debut conducting the Portland Opera Orchestra in the Portland premiere of *Andrea Chénier* in 1988. In November 1989 the legendary Luciano Pavarotti appeared in concert with the Portland Opera Orchestra conducted by Leone Magiera. Many prominent artists have appeared on Portland Opera's main stage, including Marcello Giordani, Ruth Ann Swenson, Tracy Dahl, Donnie Ray Albert, James McCracken, Cheryl Parrish, Judy Kaye, Maureen O'Flynn, Jon Garrison, Jozsef Gregor, Jerome Hines, James Johnson, and Giuseppe Giacomini.

Portland Opera received national attention in 1990 for the world premiere of *Lucy's Lapses*, the opera's first commissioned work. Previously, Portland Opera staged the world premiere of Herrmann's *Wuthering Heights* (1982) and the American premiere of Krenek's *Life of Orestes* (1975). The company's Scenic Studio and Costume Shop contribute to the company's professional stature. The credit line, "Sets and costumes constructed by the Portland Opera, Portland, Oregon," appears with increasing frequency in opera programs across the United States. Rentals to other companies are an important source of revenue and reinforce Portland Opera's prominence on the national creative scene. Five new productions have been designed and built in the past five seasons—*Aida, Don Giovanni, The Magic Flute, Der Rosenkavalier*, and *The Marriage of Figaro*.

New productions are not limited to the main stage. The Portland Opera's Community Outreach and Education efforts have expanded dramatically in recent years. The Portland Opera Players, a young touring company, books shows throughout the western United States and Canada. In addition to offering classes and opera previews, this arm of the Portland Opera has aimed specifically at younger opera audiences with three shows—"The Three Little Pigs," "The Seven Dwarfs," and "What Kind of Music is That?"—comprised of updated lyrics to standard operatic and musical theater scores. The 1989–1990 season attendance at Community Outreach and Education performances exceeded sixty thousand at some 205 events.

Since 1980 Portland Opera has held the annual Eleanor Lieber Auditions for Young Singers. Each year these auditions draw participants from Oregon, Idaho, Washington, Montana, and Alaska who compete for cash awards to further their musical studies. The Country Classic—Portland Opera's major benefit—has become the premiere equestrian competition in the Northwest United States. Now in its seventeenth year, the event has evolved into a three-day outdoor festival on the rolling banks of the Willamette River. Hundreds of volunteers plan and organize this extraordinary fund-raising event.

For the past three years, ambitious Annual Fund Campaign goals have been set and achieved. A new production sponsorship program has successfully attracted national corporate sponsors, among them Citicorp, AT&T, and American Express. Other major sponsors include First Interstate Bank, the Chiles Foundation, Louisiana Pacific, PG&E, Mentor Graphics Foundation, Albertson's, US West, and Benjamin Franklin Savings & Loan. In February 1989 the Portland Opera was awarded an $800,000 Fred Meyer Charitable Trust Challenge Grant and a coveted $150,000 Challenge II Grant from the National Endowment for the Arts. During Portland Opera's 1989–1990 silver anniversary season, record-setting numbers were recorded in subscribers, audience attendance, and funds raised, and ticket sales climbed over the $1 million mark for the first time. With a FY 1990 budget of $3.2 million, Portland Opera planned a 1990–1991 season of four operas and one musical in eighteen performances.

ACCESS: 1516 SW Alder, Portland, OR 97205. (503) 241 1407; fax (503) 241 4212. Robert Bailey, General Director.

JAMES FULLAN

RICHMOND, VIRGINIA (metro 632,015; city 219,214)

The Virginia Opera

The Virginia Opera (VO) was conceived as a regional effort that could serve the needs of the entire state, offering performance excellence as well as outreach activities and audience development. Organized in 1975 by founding president Edythe C. Harrison, the Virginia Opera has expanded its original programming in Hampton Roads to sixteen performances of four mainstage productions in addition to instituting a four-production series in Richmond. Known and respected nationwide for the identification and presentation of the finest young American singers, the company supports a variety of education and outreach programs. The Curriculum Program relates and integrates specific operas with schools' humanities subjects, "Buffa" and "One Pig Puppet Show" present in-school introduction-to-opera presentations, and special student matinee performances of full operas are offered throughout the state. Coupled with an Old Dominion University course on the season's operas, a Resident Artist Program, and WHRO-FM broadcasts, almost 1.5 million people are reached annually through education and outreach.

The Virginia Opera's dynamic growth and expansion of services in its fifteen years has produced a year-round company functioning statewide with an annual budget in excess of $2 million. Local, state, and federal grants, along with Business Consortium for Arts Support and private donations have all supported this impressive growth. VO's American premiere production of Thea Musgrave's *Mary, Queen of Scots* was first presented at the Norfolk Center Theater in 1978 and then remounted at the New York City Opera in 1981, bringing national attention. The British debut of the Virginia Opera's production of *A Christmas Carol* (premiered December 1979 in Virginia), presented by the Royal Opera at the Sadlers Wells Theater in December 1981, was an unqualified success. The world premiere of Musgrave's *Harriet, the Woman called Moses* in 1985 extended the company's image internationally. National Public Radio and British Broadcasting Corporation broadcasts have further introduced VO to opera lovers worldwide. The company's recording of *Mary, Queen of Scots* was nominated for the prestigious Koussevitzky Award, and *A Christmas Carol* was shown in Great Britain to an estimated audience of more than one million viewers in December 1982. Under the leadership of general director Peter Mark, the company's 1989–1990 season featured Verdi's *Il Trovatore*, Offenbach's *Tales of Hoffmann*, Britten's *Turn of the Screw*, and Rossini's *The Barber of Seville*. Three of the operas utilized subtitles in English for instant understanding.

ACCESS: P.O. Box 625, Norfolk, VA 23501. (804) 627 9545. Peter Mark, General Director. 422 East Franklin Street, Richmond, VA 23219–2226. (804) 644 8168; fax (804) 644 0415. Vaughan Scott, Executive Director.

[From materials supplied by the company]

SAINT LOUIS, MISSOURI (metro 2,356,460; city 453,085)

Opera Theatre of Saint Louis

[Founded in 1764 by French-Canadians, St. Louis has had, since the Philharmonic Orchestra was founded in 1838, a thriving musical culture. If one uses the founding date of the St. Louis Choral Society (1880) which gave a number of concerts with orchestra, the St. Louis Symphony is the second oldest orchestra in the United States. A local company had produced grand opera as early as 1830, but touring companies, including Maurice Strakosch's venture and the New Orleans French Opera Company, gave most of the productions during the nineteenth century. A complete "Ring" cycle conducted by Anton Seidl was given in 1889, and the Metropolitan Opera Association, as well as companies from Boston, Chicago, and Philadelphia, presented opera at the beginning of the twentieth century. The St. Louis Municipal Opera Theatre, which was founded in 1919, has had a distinguished record of summer seasons in the park.]

The Opera Theatre of Saint Louis was founded by Richard Gaddes in the spring of 1976 and flourished under his leadership until 1985. Now under the aegis of Charles MacKay and Colin Graham, the company celebrated its fifteenth anniversary in 1990 with a twenty-four-performance main season featuring new productions of *Peter Grimes, The Marriage of Figaro, The Daughter of the Regiment*, and *The Devil and Kate*, which have achieved an impressive 96.5 percent sale of house capacity. At a time when many companies have freely admitted the "museum" quality of their mainstream repertory, critics and operagoers have praised the Opera Theatre for its imaginative productions of adventurous works. As a leading regional company it attempts to explore "cutting edge" concepts and directions. The company attempts to nurture young American artists, giving them the opportunity to work with internationally known conductors, directors, and designers. Singers of the caliber of Ashley Putnam, Sheri Greenawald, Sylvia McNair, Jerry Hadley, Thomas Hampson, Vinson Cole, and Kallen Esperian made frequent appearances with Opera Theatre at the beginning of their careers, and now flourish throughout the opera world.

The company presents only new productions in the main season at the 950-seat Loretto-Hilton Center, productions that are marked by a spirit of risk and daring—mixing old with new and familiar with innovative—which has formed the company's distinctive identity. The spring season in May and June is noted for its attractive festival atmosphere. All productions are sung in English and are accompanied by members of the St. Louis Symphony. Among recent highlights are the first appearance of an American company performing an American opera (Stephen Paulus's *The Postman Always Rings Twice*) at the 1983 Edinburgh Festival, the first appearance (1988) of an American regional company in Japan, and the first production of a Japanese opera by an American Company in Japan (*Joruri*). In fifteen seasons the company has presented thirteen American premieres and six world premieres. Despite the enormous cost of producing new works, the overall budget, which has grown from $139,000 to $3 million, has never accumulated a deficit.

BIBLIOGRAPHY: W.G.B. Carson, *St. Louis Goes to the Opera: 1837–1941* (St. Louis, 1946). C. V. Clifford, *St. Louis' Fabulous Municipal Theatre: Fifty Seasons of Summer Musicals* (Louisiana, MO, 1970).

ACCESS: P.O. Box 13148, St. Louis, MO 63119–9990. (314) 961 0171; fax (314) 961 7463. Charles MacKay, General Director. Colin Graham, Artistic Director.

MAGGIE STEARNS

SAN DIEGO, CALIFORNIA (metro 2,100,000; city 1,156,000)

San Diego Opera

[Although a major metropolitan area in its own right, as well as being one of the oldest cities on the West Coast, San Diego has traditionally suffered in a cultural sense from its proximity to Los Angeles. In addition, the lack of an industrial base and a dedicated group of wealthy, civic-minded citizens have both contributed to the difficulties involved in funding and solidifying major musical organizations such as a symphony orchestra and an opera company. Prior to World War II, major music events were primarily given by touring artists and organizations. Although the San Diego Civic Grand Opera Association produced French and Italian operas between 1919 and 1932, a major community involvement had to wait for the formation of the San Diego Opera in 1950.] San Diego Opera was founded by a group of dedicated volunteers as a presenter of visiting opera companies, including San Francisco Opera. In May 1965 San Diego Opera became a producing company in its own right with its first production of *La Bohème*. For its first twenty-two seasons, the company was headed by Walter Herbert, who had also been active in Houston (1955–1971) and New Orleans (1943–1954). Drawing on strategies that had served him well before, Herbert aggressively ventured onto new ground, including the American premiere of Henze's *Der junge Lord* in his second season. He also attracted guaranteed box office stars such as Placido Domingo, Beverly Sills, and Norman Treigle. Upon his unexpected death in 1975 leadership was assumed by Tito Capobianco, who served as general director for eight seasons. Capobianco continued Herbert's aggressive tactics, launching a monumental annual Verdi Festival that offered the first American productions of some of the lesser known works. Excessive costs and limited local support combined to doom Capobianco's visions for San Diego, and in 1983 he left to take charge of the Pittsburgh Opera. Australian-born Ian Campbell, formerly assistant artistic administrator of the Metropolitan Opera Association, took over the company and is the current general director. Realizing the risks inherent in productions that were dependent on visiting stars, Campbell moved toward casts that were dependent on younger emerging performers. With deficits under control, the new general director now has the option to gradually expand both the number of performances and productions.

The 1990–1991 season called for the production of five grand operas at the Civic Theatre during a season that runs from January to May. International season operas are sung in their original language, with English translations projected above the stage. The FY budget of $5.3 million is funded at 48 percent through ticket sales. Current artistic goals call for the presentation of at least one twentieth-century opera and one new production each season, and these initiatives are the basis for the National Endowment for the Arts Challenge Grant of $400,000 that was awarded to San Diego Opera in February 1989. San Diego reaches an audience of some two hundred thousand people each year through its productions, special events, community outreach—the Opera Ensemble, which is now in its fourth year, features six young professional singers and an accompanist who present operatic programs to schools, community groups, and opera guilds during a ten- to twelve-week period in the fall—and radio broadcasts. Average ticket sales have stood at 94 percent of available seating, and that figure is improving.

ACCESS: P.O. Box 988, San Diego, CA 92112–0988. (619) 232 7636; fax (619) 231 6915. Ian D. Campbell, General Director.

[From materials supplied by the company]

SAN FRANCISCO, CALIFORNIA (metro 3,300,000; city 756,000)

San Francisco Opera

Although San Francisco has dropped to fourth place in population among California cities (behind Los Angeles, San Diego, and San José), it was and remains California's premiere cultural center in terms of the classical art forms. Beginning with the gold rush days of the 1840s, San Francisco rapidly took on the economic and social characteristics of the much older East Coast metropolitan centers. *The New Grove Dictionary of American Music* points out that between Bellini's *La Sonnambula* in 1851 "and the great earthquake and fire of 18 April 1906, nearly 5,000 operatic performances were given by more than 20 troupes in 26 different theaters." Intense musical activity flourished everywhere. Resident companies, as well as the touring troupes of Max Strakosch, J. H. Mapleson, Maurice Grau, the American National Opera Company, and the Metropolitan Opera Company Association, played to sold-out houses. Caruso and Fremstad's performance of *Carmen* on April 17, 1906, preceded the great earthquake by a matter of hours. Following the earthquake and resulting devastating fire which destroyed most of the theaters and performance venues, musical life was slow to recover.

Touring opera companies filled the gap while the social and cultural fabric was healing. Gaetano Merola (1881–1953), who had served as an assistant conductor with the Metropolitan Opera in 1899, visited San Francisco as a conductor for the W. A. Edwards International Grand Opera Company in 1909. He conducted San Carlo Opera Company productions on tour in San Francisco between 1918 and 1922. With support from the city's large Italian community, he produced three operas at Stanford University's football stadium during June 1922, and the success of this venture led to the formation of the San Francisco Opera, whose inaugural performance of *La Bohème* on September 26, 1923 at the Civic Auditorium he conducted. As general director of the San Francisco Opera for thirty seasons, he produced a repertoire of standard works from the European repertoire cast with well-known singers from the "Met."

A continuing effort to find suitable homes for the San Francisco Symphony Orchestra (founded 1911) and the opera culminated in the 3,252-seat War Memorial Opera House and the Veterans Building, which included a concert hall. Puccini's *Tosca* with Claudia Muzio inaugurated the opera house on October 15, 1932. Merola conducted and the National Broadcasting Corporation broadcast the first act. That first season in the new house included, among other productions, *Lucia di Lammermoor* with Pons, *Die Meistersinger von Nürnberg* with Schorr and Pinza, and *Faust* with Queena Mario. The autumn seasons were filled with as many as fourteen operas, all crammed in before November, when the singers had to be in New York for the opening of the "Met" season. Merola died while conducting "Un bel di" from *Madama Butterfly* at the Stern Grove Summer Music Festival on the afternoon of August 30, 1953, and Kurt Herbert Adler was named artistic director in November. Appointed chorus master by Merola in 1943, the Viennese-born conductor had moved up to the post of assistant to the general director. Following three very successful seasons, Adler's title was augmented to artistic and musical director, and then, in 1957, he became general director, the title last held by Merola. Until his retirement at the end of 1981 Adler aggressively built one of the finest opera companies in North America, indeed perhaps in the world.

The main autumn seasons were lengthened, and the number of performances was increased. By scouring the opera world actively for talent, Adler managed to eliminate the past dependence on Metropolitan Opera artists. Marilyn Horne, Leona Mitchell, Leontyne Price, and Jess Thomas all debuted under Adler, and Boris Christoff, Geraint Evans, Sena Jurinac, Birgit Nilsson, Luciano Pavarotti, Leone Rysanek, and Elisabeth Schwarzkopf all made their American opera debuts with the San Francisco Opera. Adler was responsible for the American stage premieres of (among others) Berlioz' *Les Troyens*, Honegger's *Jeanne d'Arc*, Janáček's *The Makropulos Affair*, Orff's *Carmina Burana*, Poulenc's *Dialogues des Carmélites*, and Schuller's *The Visitation*. He also substantially increased the company's involvement in programs for young artists. The San Francisco Opera Auditions started in 1954. The Merola Opera Program, established in 1957, selects approximately twenty singers for a ten-week period of study, individual coaching, master classes, and two complete opera productions with orchestra. Culminating with the Grand Finals, the Merola participants perform to a capacity audience in the War Memorial Opera House with full orchestral accompaniment. This program recently expanded to include apprentice coaches who seek to develop their skills in the special art of vocal coaching.

In 1967, with the assistance of a grant from the National Endowment for the Arts, Western Opera Theater (WOT) was born with the mission of taking full-length productions of opera in English to communities where live opera is a rarity. Since the first season WOT has presented thirty-five operas in over fifteen hundred performances, reaching nearly two million people in twenty-seven states. In March 1987 WOT became the first American opera company to tour in the People's Republic of China. Through their subsequent visits to China and Japan, Western Opera Theater has become the most active opera company in the Pacific

Rim. Created in 1974 to provide live operatic entertainment wherever people might gather, Brown Bag Opera appears in a wide variety of locations, from shopping malls to schools, city parks, retirement homes, hospitals and the San Francisco International Airport. Formerly the San Francisco Affiliate Artists–Opera Program, founded in 1977, the Adler Fellowship Program is a performance-oriented residency providing individualized, advanced training as well as roles in special productions and in the company's international seasons. Up to eleven fellows are on salary during the program's eleven-month contract period. Under the guidance of the San Francisco Opera staff, Adler Fellows are directed toward roles of increasing importance in future seasons of the San Francisco Opera. Moreover, launched with the world premiere of John Harbison's *Winter's Tale* in August 1979, the American Opera Project was designed as an innovative approach to identifying and previewing new works by American composers for presentation by major American opera companies. It provides a process through which a new opera can be tested and evaluated before it reaches its final form and, eventually, full-scale production. The ultimate goal of the American Opera Project is to expand the number of contemporary American works currently in the repertoire. Finally, the Summer Opera Festival (which has since been canceled) was initiated in 1980.

The War Memorial Opera House was expanded when the backstage addition was completed in June 1979. The extra support space, including storage facilities, held administrative offices, a ballet room, and a new chorus room. With the completion of the Louise M. Davies Symphony Hall in 1980, musicians who performed with both the symphony and the opera had to chose an affiliation, and thus a permanent San Francisco Opera Orchestra was born. Prior to Adler's retirement, the new Zellerbach Rehearsal Wing went into use in the fall of 1981. Including a rehearsal room with a full-size stage and orchestra pit, rehearsals with chorus and orchestra were now possible outside the Opera House for the first time. Canadian-born Terence A. McEwen was Adler's successor in 1982. As a former executive with London Records, McEwen was well positioned in the musical world, and he used his numerous contacts to continue to assemble stellar casts. Among his major triumphs was a new production of Wagner's *Der Ring des Nibelungen* and the American premiere of Tippett's *The Midsummer Marriage*. He was also responsible for bringing all the educational and outreach programs developed by Kurt Adler under the umbrella of the San Francisco Opera Center. Illness forced the early retirement of McEwen, and, on July 1, 1988, Iranian-born Lofti Mansouri, former general director of the Canadian Opera Company in Toronto, became the fourth general director of the San Francisco Opera.

BIBLIOGRAPHY: Arthur Bloomfield, *1922–1978: The San Francisco Opera* (Sausalito, CA, 1978). Lawrence Estavan, ed., *W.P.A. Project 10677: The History of Opera in San Francisco* (San Francisco, 1938). Lofti Mansouri, "A 'First' in Canada: The Story of the Launching of the New Canadian Opera Company Ensemble," *Opera Canada*, Summer 1980.

ACCESS: War Memorial Opera House, 301 Van Ness Avenue, San Francisco, CA 94102–4509. (415) 861 4008; fax (415) 621 7508. Lofti Mansouri, General Director.

[From materials supplied by the company]

SANTA FE, NEW MEXICO (city 48,953)

The Santa Fe Opera

As the center of the northernmost expansion of Hispanic influences in North America, Santa Fe served as the headquarters of the Spanish conquistadors. When economic leadership passed to Albuquerque early in the twentieth century, Santa Fe remained an active cultural center in the area. In addition to native American and regional expressions, professional art music began when John Crosby founded the Opera Association of New Mexico—later renamed the Santa Fe Opera—in 1956. In December of that year the Santa Fe Opera was incorporated under the leadership of Crosby as general director with a dedicated group of local business and social leaders as directors of the new nonprofit enterprise. An unusual, open-air, redwood theater with 480 seats was constructed. A reflecting pool separated the audience from the orchestra pit and the stage. Opening night, July 3, 1957, featured Puccini's *Madama Butterfly* to a sold-out house. By the end of the season, eight weeks later, an audience of more than twelve thousand people would account for sales of 90 percent capacity.

From the beginning, a unique artistic profile emerged that continues to this day, bringing the company international fame. Featuring a mix of familiar fare with revivals of rarely performed operas such as Stravinsky's *The Rake's Progress* and world premieres (Marvin David Levy's *The Tower* in 1957), Santa Fe Opera attracts a diverse and highly discriminating public. The casts are young, American, and exceptional actors. The smaller roles and chorus parts are taken by singers yet in school who come to Santa Fe to take part in the company's Apprentice Program to have the opportunity to learn from and work with experienced professionals. Each production is a total artistic entity with sets, costumes, lighting, and cast designed to complement each other for the highest theatrical effect. By the second season the full company had grown from 67 to 89, and the theater capacity was increased to 750. During its fifth season in 1961 the company, then numbering 180, toured Europe performing Douglas Moore's *The Ballad of Baby Doe* and Stravinsky's *Persephone* and *Oedipus Rex*, with the composer conducting the latter in Berlin and Belgrade. The company had an international triumph at the height of the cold war.

The first ten seasons were marked by constant growth and experimentation, but the second decade was ushered in by a disaster. Early in the morning of Thursday, July 27, 1967, fire broke out in the theater, and the intense redwood blaze consumed sets, costumes, musical instruments, and musical scores—everything was lost. Almost immediately, plans were made to rebuild. Igor Stravinsky agreed to serve as honorary chairman of a National Emergency Committee to rebuild the Santa Fe Opera. Before it was over, $2.4 million would be needed to complete the building and open the twelfth season. Commanding a 360-degree panorama of breathtaking scenery, the new Opera Theater is a distinctly Southwestern creation. Seating 1,773 and standing 150, the last row of seats is only ninety feet from the edge of the stage. The stage itself, open at the rear, is covered by a roof of nearly a quarter-acre that cantilevers out to thirty-six feet above the tenth row in the audience.

Today the Santa Fe Opera has a company of nearly five hundred at the height of the summer season, making it Santa Fe's second largest nongovernmental employer. Principal singers, primarily American, are drawn from every corner of the world. New Zealand soprano Dame Kiri Te Kanawa made her American operatic debut at Santa Fe, as did the Dutch conductor Edo de Waart. The orchestra is drawn from other leading opera companies, symphony orchestras, and conservatories. The corps de ballet is also assembled from companies across the nation. Stage directors, set and costume designers, and musical staff come from the major opera houses of New York, San Francisco, London, Stockholm, Stuttgart, and scores of others. The sense of ensemble that is Santa Fe is shared by audience and performers alike.

One of Crosby's founding principles for the company was to offer American artists the opportunity to gain experience in their own country. The Apprentice Program for Singers permitted, for the first time, outstanding students from leading colleges, universities, and conservatories to work alongside professionals in the disciplines necessary for a career in music. The roster of graduates includes Judith Blegen, Michael Devlin, Brent Ellis, Faith Esham, Sherrill Milnes, Leona Mitchell, Ashley Putnam, Samuel Ramey, John Stewart, Patricia Wise, and many others. In 1965 a similar training program was begun for Apprentice Technicians. Talented students of design, direction, lighting, costume, and set construction were given the opportunity to work side by side with the opera staff. Participants in both programs are selected by national auditions: 45 of 1,000 are accepted each season for the Singer's Program; 50 of the 600 applicants to the Technicians Program are invited to come to Santa Fe. Each season, two Monday evenings are devoted to Apprentice Concerts—the culminating artistic work of these talented apprentices.

In its first thirty seasons, the Santa Fe Opera has presented ninety-one different operas, thirty-four of which have been world premieres [including Luciano Berio's *Opera* which premiered on August 12, 1970; John Eatons's *The Tempest* which premiered on July 27, 1985; Carlisle Floyd's *Wuthering Heights*, which premiered on July 16, 1958, and was revised in 1959; George Rochberg's *The Confidence Man*, which premiered on July 31, 1982; and Heitor Villa-Lobos's *Yerma*] or American premieres [including Alban Berg's *Lulu*, five operas of Hans Werner Henze, Paul Hindemith's *Cardillas*, Krzystof Penderecki's *The Devils of Loudun*, Aribert Riemann's *Melusine*, Nino Rota's *The Italian Straw Hat*, and Richard Strauss's *Daphne*]. Another twenty-seven were rarely performed works. Equally important have been the professional stage premieres of works heard previously in America only in concert form or in student performances. Works by Britten, Janáček, Schoenberg, Strauss, Stravinsky, and Zemlinsky were seen for the first time in the New Mexico hills. The audience has increased to more than seventy thousand persons attending almost forty performances. The budget has grown to the $6 million range, with earned income averaging 50 percent of that figure.

BIBLIOGRAPHY: Eleanor Scott, *The First Twenty Years of the Santa Fe Opera* (Albuquerque, NM, 1976).

ACCESS: P.O. Box 2408, Santa Fe, NM 87504-2408. (505) 982 3851; fax (505) 989 7012. John O. Crosby, General Director. Philip Semark, Executive Director.

[From materials supplied by the company]

SEATTLE, WASHINGTON (metro 1,700,000; city 535,000)

Seattle Opera

Although several theaters (Squire's Opera House in 1879 and Frye's Opera House in 1884) had been built in Seattle shortly after its founding in 1851, they hosted primarily vaudeville and light entertainment. The Metropolitan Opera Association's touring company performed the first opera, *Carmen*, in Seattle in November 1899, featuring the legendary Emma Calvé. A local company, the Standard Grand Opera Company of Seattle, was founded in 1914. The next local effort, the Northwest Grand Opera Association, started mounting productions with guest artists in 1951 and is considered a direct forerunner of Seattle Opera, along with the Festival Opera and the Western Opera Companies. In 1962, the Century 21 World's Fair in Seattle left the city a significant legacy, both in the physical grounds of the Seattle Center and in the city's new spirit of confidence and pride. On those grounds, and from that spirit, Seattle Opera was born—one of the first permanent residents of the new 3,000-seat Seattle Opera House.

Under general director Glynn Ross, the fledgling company's initial season in 1964 consisted of two performances of *Carmen* and two performances of *Tosca*. By 1966 the company's season had grown to include five operas, and soon Seattle Opera had earned the highest per capita opera attendance rate of any opera company in the nation. In the summer of 1974 Seattle Opera garnered international recognition by presenting Richard Wagner's complete four-opera "Ring" cycle for the first time. Over the decade, visitors from all fifty states and from twenty-seven foreign countries came to Seattle specifically to attend performances of the "Ring." Declining ticket sales which forced the reduction in the number of performances of each opera mandated a review of company goals and policies. In 1983 Speight Jenkins was appointed the general director of the company, and the board of trustees joined in a commitment to raise the artistic level of Seattle Opera productions. That effort has proved enormously successful: Under Jenkin's leadership, the company has achieved an unprecedented level of quality. When, in the summer of 1986, the company introduced a new production of the "Ring," critical reviews were extremely favorable. Although costs have risen substantially, the company has achieved a balanced budget, and financial planning and fiscal caution are viewed as an integral part of the company's ability to survive. The mission statement addresses both artistic and budgetary concerns: "Seattle Opera strives to make a significant contribution to the artistic vitality of the Pacific Northwest by presenting important operas in production that are both musically accomplished and theatrically compelling. By reaching for the most demanding artistic standards, the company seeks to expand the audience for opera and maintain an international reputation for artistic excellence, while exercising a fiscal responsibility that earns the confidence of corporate and individual donors without whose support this work would not be possible." Audiences have responded, trends were reversed, and subscription sales reached a rate of 90 percent in the 1987–1988 season. This, coupled with a series of sold-out productions, suggests a possible increase in the number of performances, allowing for another subscription series. Ticket revenue now accounts for 41 percent of the budget, with festival donations (19 percent) and the sustaining fund (24 percent) covering another 43 percent.

Each Seattle Opera season consists of five different productions spanning the months from September to May. Seasons typically include operas from several different schools of music, usually in at least three different languages. The series is composed of at least one standard repertoire (popular) opera and one work that has either not been performed in Seattle before, or that, for some other reason, is considered unusual and interesting. An attempt is also made to produce the masterpieces of the twentieth century as well as new works of promise. Each production is presented with two different casts—a "gold" cast or well-known singers, and a "silver" cast of younger, less well-known singers or singers performing a given role for the first time. Recognizing that the United States now produces the best trained singing actors in the world, casting relies heavily on American artists in prominent roles. The orchestra is made up of members of the Seattle Symphony Orchestra who are employed jointly under a contract that is renewed every two years. The Seattle Opera Chorus is made up of thirty-six part-time professionals who are joined by a volunteer auxiliary chorus for large productions. In addition to the opera season, since 1975 Seattle Opera has offered a special attraction during the summer. Known as the Festival, this summer attraction always consisted of two complete performances of Wagner's four-opera *Ring of the Nibelungen* until 1985. Although future plans include frequent presentations of the "Ring," it is expected that other special programs will be presented in alternate summers.

BIBLIOGRAPHY: M. Salem, *Organizational Survival in the Performing Arts: The Making of the Seattle Opera* (New York, 1976). *Seattle Opera at 24: A Company Profile* (Seattle 1989).

ACCESS: P.O. Box 9248, Seattle, WA 98109–9248. (206) 443 4700; fax (206) 443 2533. Speight Jenkins, General Director.

[From materials supplied by the company]

VIENNA, VIRGINIA

Wolf Trap Opera Company

Wolf Trap Farm Park for the Performing Arts was opened in 1971 by the U.S. Department of the Interior on a gift of land received from Catherine Filene Schouse in 1956. Schouse had wished to create an environment where young artists with talent and promise could be heard, seen, and taught the demands of a professional career in the performing arts. Wolf Trap Opera Company has become Wolf Trap's most enduring and successful fulfillment of that goal as one of America's outstanding career-entry programs for young singers. Today approximately fifteen singers are chosen from over four hundred applicants annually to participate as members of the company in a ten-week residency. The Wolf Trap Opera Company was originally conceived as a summer training program not only for opera singers, but for dancers, actors, and instrumentalists as well, with a streamlining of the company's focus by 1973 toward emerging opera singers. Opera administrator and stage director Francis Rizzo headed the Wolf Trap Opera Company from 1973 to 1978, overseeing and participating in the company's annual tour of young artists and the selection of repertoire. During these years, the company offered fully staged productions both in the 6,800-seat Filene Center (modeled after the amphitheater at Saratoga Springs, New York) and in the auditorium of the Madeira School in McLean, Virginia.

In addition to evolving its philosophy at this time, the company also presented the world premieres of Pasatieri's *Il Signor Deluso* [premiered on July 7, 1974] and Stephen Douglas Burton's *The Duchess of Malfi*; the U.S. premiere of Busoni's *Doktor Faust* (1925); the local premiere of Prokofiev's *War and Peace*; and major revivals of such contemporary American operas as Robert Ward's *The Crucible*, Menotti's *The Saint of Bleeker Street*, and Vittorio Giannini's *The Taming of the Shrew*. Many singers who are well established internationally profited from summer residencies at Wolf Trap. The artistic leadership of conductor/director Sarah Caldwell during the 1980 season featured the American premiere of Heinrich Marschner's *Der Vampyr*. Met conductor Richard Voitach, previous director of the San Francisco Opera Center's Western Opera, began a seven-year association as music director in 1981. Stage director Adelaide Bishop joined him as artistic director for the 1981 and 1982 seasons.

Beginning in 1982 the company began to schedule productions in the newly opened 350-seat Barns of Wolf Trap, allowing the resident young artists to experience the full gamut of performing in the most intimate of circumstances. Highlights of these seasons include the local premieres of Blitzstein's *Regina* and Donizetti's *L'Ajo nell'Imbarazzo*. Francis Rizzo rejoined the company as artistic consultant in 1985, and since that time Wolf Trap Opera has produced major revivals of Britten's *A Midsummer Night's Dream* and *The Rape of Lucretia*, and Argento's *Postcard from Morocco*. One of the Wolf Trap Opera Company's primary goals is precisely to discover and foster the finest operatic talent in the United States, and a broad overview of the success stories from the inception of the company in 1971 to the present would fill many pages. A glance at the Metropolitan Opera Association's 1987–1988 roster alone gives a good indication of this: Faith Esham, Barbara Kilduff, Elizabeth Knighton, Dawn Upshaw, Linda Zoghby, Diane Kesling, Meredith Parsons, Margaret Wray, Rockwell Blake, Allan Glassman, Chris Merritt, Stanford Olsen, Neil Rosenheim, Neil Wilson, David Bernard, Stephen Dickson, David Hamilton, Norman Andersson, John Cheek, James Courtney, and Alan Held. From a moderate budget in its earlier years, the company projected $600,000 in 1991 and in excess of $1.25 million in the year 2000. If the success ratio of its alumni continues, the budget will be a small price to pay for significantly enriching the rosters of opera organizations worldwide.

ACCESS: Wolf Trap Foundation, 1624 Trap Road, Vienna, VA 22182. (703) 255 1900. Peter Russell, Administrative Director.

[From materials provided by the company]

WASHINGTON, D.C. (metro 3,100,000; city 639,000)

The Washington Opera

Washington, D.C., capital of the United States and center of a metropolitan area of about 3 million people, is ranked as the fifteenth largest city in the United States and lacks both the population and the industrial presence that support opera more lavishly in such cities as New York, Chicago, San Francisco, and Houston. Its primary industry is government. The "board of directors" of that industry, the U.S. Congress, was long reluctant to spend tax money on the arts and, when it finally decided to do so, preferred to send most of the money back home to where the voters were (the District of Columbia has no voting representative in Congress). This makes Washington different from world capitals such as Vienna, Berlin, Paris, and Moscow, where opera is lavishly supported by governments that are convinced of its special value as a cultural showpiece. Several efforts to establish a permanent opera company in Washington failed before the Opera Society of Washington (the original name of the Washington Opera) was founded in 1956, and the city's special climate for arts support has dictated that the major resident company should be "interesting" rather than "imposing"—that it should become noted for its discovery of young talent, its fresh repertoire, and its innovative production ideas rather than such budget-driven characteristics as million-dollar sets, a world-class orchestra, and a high proportion of international star singers on its roster. Nevertheless, it has managed, both in its early years and in the last decade, to generate quite a few memorable productions, including important world and American premieres.

The first operatic activity in the Washington area was that of visiting companies, mostly companies based in Philadelphia in the first half of the nineteenth century, and the Metropolitan Opera Association beginning in 1872. Local opera companies started and failed in the late nineteenth century, and after World War I, some began to survive for a while. [Several theaters, including Albaugh's Opera House (1884) and the Lafayette Square Opera House (1890), were built specifically to encourage local opera.] The Washington Community Opera was founded in 1918 and lasted a decade, changing its name midway to the Washington National Opera Association. The National Negro Opera Company, which performed in several cities, had its headquarters in Washington from the 1940s until 1962, and the Washington Civic Opera, which was subsidized by the city government, gave noteworthy free performances for about a quarter-century beginning in the 1950s. The area now has two small but interesting regional companies: the Prince George's Opera (based in Maryland) and the Opera Theatre of Northern Virginia.

There are also three small companies of more than regional interest. The Wolf Trap Opera Company, which is based at Wolf Trap Farm Park (a federally owned park facility in Vienna, Virginia, which is dedicated to the performing arts) recruits its ensemble afresh each year in nationwide auditions for young singers and presents three productions plus a gala concert each summer. Two chamber-sized productions are given in the Barn of Wolf Trap, a small, acoustically exquisite facility housed in two renovated eighteenth-century barns. A larger-scaled production (usually with sets and costumes from such companies as the Metropolitan Opera, Royal Opera House, Covent Garden, or Glyndebourne Festival Opera) is given in the Filene Center, a partly outdoor facility with amplified sound and a seating capacity of over 6,000. The Wolf Trap Company (thanks largely to the recruiting skills of artistic advisor Francis Rizzo) consistently finds young American singers who are destined for distinguished international careers. Rizzo is also a key figure in the Washington Concert Opera, the city's newest company, which each year produces two relatively unfamiliar operas (such as *Werther, The Pearl Fishers*, and *Lucrezia Borgia*) in concert performances with international casts, typically to capacity audiences in the 1,500-seat Lisner Auditorium on the campus of the George Washington University. The Summer Opera Theatre, which performs in the Nartke Theatre on the campus of the Catholic University of America, presents two productions, which are usually of high quality, each July.

In its earliest years, the Washington Opera was particularly notable for its premiere performances, including the world premieres of two operas by Ginastera: *Bomarzo* [premiered on May 16, 1967, the opera was originally scheduled for August 9 at the Teatro Colón but was removed from the schedule due to pressure from the Argentine government, which protested the explicit sexual violence] and *Beatrix Cenci* [commissioned by the Opera Society of Washington, it premiered on September 19, 1971]; Paul Hindemith's ballet *The Demon*; the revised version of Samuel Barber's *Vanessa* [in 1964, the premiere was at the Metropolitan Opera on January 15, 1958]; and Gian Carlo Menotti's *Maria Golovin* [which premiered on August 20, 1958]. American premieres included some operas from the remote past, such as Monteverdi's *Il Ritorno d'Ulisse in patria*, Cavalli's *L'Ormindo*, Haydn's *L'infedelta delussa*, and Berlioz's *Beatrice et Benedict*, as well as operas of the twentieth century: Delius's *Koanga* and *A Village Romeo and Juliet*, Schoenberg's *Erwartung* in its first American staged performance, and the first American performance by a professional company of Hindemith's *The Long Christmas Dinner* [conducted by the composer]. Artists who went on to distinguished careers after singing with this company in its early years included John Reardon, Donald Gramm, John Alexander, Judith Raskin, Benita Valente, Patricia Brooks, Shirley Verrett, George Shirley, Justino Diaz, Alan Titus, and Judith Blegen. The company's only world (or American) premiere in the 1980s was generated by its longstanding association with Gian Carlo Menotti: His opera *Goya* was given its first performance at the John F. Kennedy Center for the Performing Arts on November 15, 1986, with Placido Domingo in the title role and Rafael Frubeck de Burgos conducting. In the 1980s the Washington Opera has welcomed a number of new operas by American composers after they were "market-tested" by other companies, notably Dominick Argento's *The Aspern Papers* and Stephen Paulus's *The Postman Always Rings Twice*. In the late 1980s there were unconfirmed reports that the company had commissioned a new opera on the life and death of Marilyn Monroe, but this project apparently was canceled.

The Washington Opera's association with Gian Carlo Menotti dates back to its first season, 1956–1957, when one if its two productions was a Menotti double bill (without the composer's participation): *The Old Maid and the Thief* and *The Unicorn, the Gorgon and the Manticore*. He first worked with the company in 1965 as stage director for his *Maria Golovin* and returned to direct *The Medium* (a production recorded by CBS Masterworks) and *Amahl and the Night Visitors*. In the 1980s, the collaboration intensified, with Menotti directing outstanding productions both of his own work and of other composers' operas at a rate of approximately one per season. Since the 1979–1980 season, which represented a major turning point for the company, it has become customary for the Washington Opera to offer one pre-nineteenth-century opera and one modern (usually American) opera among its seven or eight productions each season. Several of the modern operas have been Menotti's works under his own direction. Three of these productions originated with the Washington Opera: *The Medium* and *The Telephone* (1983), *Goya* (1986), and *The Consul* (1988). *The Saint of Bleecker Street* was scheduled for 1991 in a production originated by Menotti at the Spoleto Festival, USA, of which he is the founder and artistic director.

These productions have been among the company's most memorable, and the double feature of *The Medium* and *The Telephone* was its most successful production of the 1980s. Besides playing to capacity audiences in Washington for two seasons, it was invited to the Edinburgh Festival in 1984, the 1985 Israel Festival, and the 1986 Spoleto Festival in Melbourne, Australia. Much of the acclaim was inspired by the brilliantly dramatic performance of Beverly Evans in the title role of *The Medium* and the comic expertise of Sheryl Woods in *The Telephone*. Also noteworthy was the work of designer Zack Brown—witty in

The Telephone and dramatically evocative in *The Medium*. However, the star of this show was unquestionably Menotti, a stage director who is completely attuned to his own artistic creation. In other seasons, he showed similar sensitivity to the work of other composers. Perhaps his most successful effort of this kind in Washington was the company's 1981 *La Bohème*, a vintage production that was also enhanced by the performances of a near-ideal cast (Jerry Hadley, Sheri Greenawald, Richard Stilwell, and Janice Hall), the emotive and aptly styled conducting of John Maurceri, and, again, the designs of Zack Brown, who had become the company's resident designer. The Menotti touch also gave distinction to the Washington Opera productions of *La Cenerentola* (1982), *Eugene Onegin* (1985), and *Tosca* (1988).

In the company's enterprising Opera Society years, when performances were given in the Lisner Auditorium, the president and a prime source of creative ideas as well as financial support was Hobart Spalding. The music director, Paul Callaway, was well established in the city's musical life as the organist and choirmaster at the (Episcopal) Cathedral Church of St. Peter and St. Paul since 1939. Callaway conducted all the company's productions until the U.S. staged premiere of *Erwartung* (CBS Masterworks released Stravinsky's 1962 performance of *Oedipus Rex*), and he continued to conduct frequently through the 1974–1975 season. By then the company had moved into the 2,200-seat Kennedy Center Opera House (where it opened in 1971 with the world premiere of Ginastera's *Beatrix Cenci* with Julius Rudel conducting), and it was under the direction of Ian Strasfogel, who also staged several productions: *Mahagony* and *The Rake's Progress* (1972–1973); *Macbeth*, *Il Ritorno d'Ulisse*, and *Il Tabarro* (1973–1974); and *Salome* (1974–1975). [A protégé of Walter Felsenstein and a specialist in contemporary works, Strasfogel produced Luciano Berio's *Passaggio* (1968) and Roger Sessions' *Montezuma* (1982).]

George London, who had been one of the great bass-baritones of his generation, became the general director of the company in 1975, by which time its season had expanded from two productions per year in the Lisner Auditorium to three at the Kennedy Center. [That same year London staged the first complete English-language *The Ring of the Nibelungen* in America (Seattle).] London changed the company's name from the Opera Society of Washington to the Washington Opera, hired Gary Fifield as the managing director, and began to develop ambitious long-range plans for the company as well as for the Gramma Fisher Foundation. These plans were aborted when London suffered a stroke in 1977. Fifield, as managing director, asked Rizzo to assist him as artistic administrator, expecting that London would recover and return to the company. London never did; he lived until 1985 but was permanently incapacitated. Rizzo who stayed with the company for the next ten years, had been artistic administrator of Wolf Trap since 1973 and earlier had been an associate of Gian Carlo Menotti as a personal assistant and later as American manager of the Spoleto Festival. Together, he and Fifield nursed the company through three challenging seasons, beginning with 1977–1978, and following London's plans as much as possible. In these years and on through much of the 1980s, the company drew on much of the talent Rizzo had uncovered earlier, particularly during his tenure at Wolf Trap, including such singers as Rockwell Blake, Janice Hall, J. Patrick Raftery, Allan Glassman, and Elizabeth Knighton; conductors John Mauceri and Cal Stewart Kellogg, and designer Zack Brown. Rizzo, as a longstanding friend of Menotti, persuaded him to direct the 1981 *La Bohème*. This was not Menotti's first work with the company, but it was the beginning of a long, close, new association. All the people named above and others, particularly director Peter Mark Schifter, contributed distinctively to the company's special flavor in the 1980s, but Menotti's presence is in many ways the most significant.

Two other interlocked elements impacted on the company at this time to launch it on the course it was to follow through the 1980s and into the 1990s. One was the opening of the Terrace Theater, a 500-seat jewel of an auditorium on the upper level of the Kennedy Center. Its acoustics and sight lines were ideal for intimate opera productions, although its seating capacity implied perennial cash-flow problems. At that time the Kennedy Center's executive Director of Performing Arts was Martin Feinstein who had been associated with Sol Hurok for about a quarter-century, had been an ardent opera fan since his school days, and had been a would-be opera impresario for much of his life. To give the public a spectacular view of the Terrace Theater's potentials, Feinstein invented a temporary company, the Kennedy Center Summer Opera, to present four chamber opera productions there in the summer of 1979 with the Kennedy Center financing the venture. The Kennedy Center Summer Opera was actually the Wasington Opera in the thinnest possible disguise, and this experimental season showed the company's potential more clearly, or at least with more focus, than anything it had done previously. Many elements associated with the intimate Terrace ambiance can be seen in the company's earlier history, but they came to permeate its work in the 1980s. These include an emphasis on theatrical as well as musical values, ingenuity in compensating for limited budgets, and the use of young American singers with acting skills as well developed as their voices. Bright, imaginative staging (with intense attention to small details) was particularly important in that small house, where the audience is almost in the middle of the action. However, this ideal has also been realized frequently in the larger houses where the company works.

A second sequel to the summer season was the appointment of Feinstein in 1980 as general director of the Washington Opera and a consequent escalation of activities: a bigger budget, more performances of more productions, and a quantum leap in the public attention given to the company and its new general director. Feinstein was building on smaller but solid foundations; Fifield had kept the company solvent and Rizzo had held it to high artistic standards. The 1979–1980 season had included a *Cendrillon* with Frederica von Stade, Ruth Welting, Maureen Forrester, and John Reardon; a *Traviata* with Catherine Malfitano, and a *Lucia* with Ashley Putnam and John Mauceri (who became the company's music director in January 1980) conducting. However, the scope of

Feinstein's ambitions was considerably larger, perhaps larger than the Washington community could or would support. The 1980–1981 season was something like a manifesto of the company's agenda for the decade: production in two theaters and escalation on all fronts. There were seven productions (forty-four performances), including a memorable *Madama Butterfly*, a fine production of the rarely seen *L'Amore dei Tre Re*, and four productions in the Terrace Theater, which had now become a part of the company's routine operations. This compared with four productions (sixteen performances) in the 1979–1980 subscription season. The Terrace Theater made the difference, with four productions (thirty-two performances) in its first subscription season. It must be remembered, of course, that each Terrace performance represents only about five hundred tickets sold—a fact that ultimately made opera impractical in that auditorium.

The level of activity remained at seven productions per season through 1984–1985, when there were seventy-two performances attended by 59,963 people. The company's budget had been $317,000 in fiscal year 1964–1965 and $2 million in 1979–1980, the year before Feinstein's appointment. By 1983–1984 it had risen to $5.34 million. Then economics caught up with aspirations: The 1985–1986 budget dropped to $4.8 million; two Terrace productions were canceled that season, and the number of performances for the remaining five productions was only forty-seven. There was a comeback in 1986–1987 when the number of productions went up to a rather contrived eight including a "guest production" of *Il Matrimonio segreto* imported bodily, with sets, costumes, conductor, stage director, and singers, from the Cologne Opera. The Cologne Opera's four performances raised that season's total to 7,655 in the Terrace Theater. This is a record that is likely to stand for quite a while, since the company abandoned the Terrace Theater the following season and moved its small productions into the Kennedy Center's Eisenhower Theater, a hall used mostly for spoken theater but acoustically excellent for music. Its sight lines and acoustics are not as good as those in the Terrace, but it holds more than twice as many people. This means that the 1987–1988 total of sixty-seven performances did not imply a loss of ticket sales, but they were only 83 percent of the company's enlarged capacity. For 1988–1989 the number of performances was scaled down to fifty-five; attendance dropped to 83,000, but that represented 99 percent of capacity.

In the years since then, ticket sales have been at or within a percentage point of capacity—sometimes actually going up to 101 percent through the resale of tickets returned as a charitable contribution. Budget escalation has also continued, to $7.5 million in 1989–1990 and a projected $8.7 million in 1990–1991. The number of performances has stabilized at or around fifty-five per season, and ticket income in 1989–1990 was 61 percent of the budget. With contributions accounting for the other 39 percent, this is an exceptionally high percentage of earned income, a fact of which the company is very proud. Given the special circumstances confronting opera in Washington, the Washington Opera may continue to grow in size, but slowly, at least for the foreseeable future.

CHRONOLOGY OF GENERAL DIRECTORS: Day Thorpe, 1956–1960. Bliss Hebert, 1961–1963. Paul Callaway (Musical Director), 1963–1967. Richard R. Pearlman, 1968–1970. Frank Marchlenski (Business Manager), 1970–1972. Ian Strasfogel, 1972–1975. George London (Acting Directors—Gary Fifield and Francis Rizzo, 1977–1979), 1976–1979. Martin Feinstein, 1980–present.

BIBLIOGRAPHY: Brendan Gill, *The John F. Kennedy Center for the Performing Arts* (New York, 1981). Nora London, *Aria for George* (New York, 1987).

ACCESS: Kennedy Center, Washington, DC 20566. (202) 416 7890. Martin Feinstein, General Director.

JOSEPH McLELLAN

Yugoslavia

BELGRADE (774,000)

Opera Narodnog Pozorista u Beogradu (Belgrade National Opera)

[Prior to its unification after World War I, portions of modern Yugoslavia were divided among several powers. When Austria-Hungary, Bulgaria, and the Ottoman Empire signed the armistice in 1918, the Allied principle of self-determination fanned the flames of nationalism once again. Austria, Czechoslovakia, and Hungary emerged as independent countries out of the old Austro-Hungarian Empire, and Allied diplomats formed Yugoslavia by adding Serbia to portions of Austria-Hungary, Bulgaria, and Montenegro. The result is that the country is still divided into six regions on the basis of old political and cultural boundaries. What we are seeing at the beginning of the 1990s is the resurfacing of old loyalties and configurations, and political events are having an affect on the cultural life of the nation.]

Few countries in Europe have such a variety of artistic traditions. A united kingdom, the kingdom of the Serbs, Croats, and Slovenes, was officially proclaimed on December 1, 1918, and a constitution was adopted in 1921 that provided for a constitutional monarchy. The new King Alexander dissolved Parliament in January 1929, and the country's name was changed to Yugoslavia. The 1931 constitution was supposed to restore democratic government, but political parties could not operate and on October 9, 1934, Alexander was assassinated. Amid continuing political turmoil, Yugoslavia joined the Axis Powers on March 25, 1941. After World War II, Josip Broz [Tito] and the National Front coalition won the November 1945 election. On November 29, 1945, the new parliament declared Yugoslavia a republic, and King Peter II was formally deposed in March 1947. Since the establishment of the new republic, Yugoslavia has supported nine opera houses with permanent companies.

Belgrade, the capital and largest city, lies on the banks of the Danube River, the most important waterway in Yugoslavia. The modern city dates from 1866, when it was freed from the Turks and became the capital of the independent Kingdom of Serbia. Although opera performances had occurred earlier, the 891-seat National Theater was built in 1868. Strongly influenced by the tides of nineteenth-century Romantic nationalism, Belgrade became increasingly open to Western cultural influences. When the Zagreb Opera visited in 1911 there was a surge of interest in establishing a local company, and a permanent company was formed in 1919 with Stanislav Bibičke appointed director and conductor. The company evolved to another level of achievement in the decade after 1924 under the leadership of Stevan Hristić, who was the first director (1923) of the Belgrade Philharmonic. Hristić was responsible for the first generation of native singers, and he brought a number of talented foreign artists to the capital including Chaliapin and Destinn. For the most part, operatic activities were suspended during World War II,and the National Theater was bombed. Operatic activity commenced again in 1945 with *Eugene Onegin* conducted by Oskar Danon. Since then the company has undertaken a number of tours and released various recordings.

CHRONOLOGY OF DIRECTORS: Stanislav Bibičke, 1919–1923. Stevan Hristić, 1924–1934. Oscar Danon, 1944–1963. Djordje Djurdjevic, 1964–present.

BIBLIOGRAPHY: J. Andreis, D. Cvetko and S. Djurić-Klajn, *Historijski razvoj muzičke kulture u Jugoslaviji* (Zagreb, 1962). M. Djoković, ed., *Jedan vek Narodnog pozorišta u Beogradu, 1868–1969* (Belgrade, 1968).

ACCESS: National Theater, Francuska 3, 11000 Belgrade. (38 11) 626 566; (38 11) 628–640/645.

[From materials supplied by the company]

ZAGREB (566,000)

Opera of the Hrvatsko Narodno Kazalište (Croatian National Opera)

As the second largest city in Yugoslavia, Zagreb supports a major symphony orchestra with its own home (1851-seat Vatroslav Lisinski Concert Hall built in 1973) as well as the Croat National Theater. The Vatroslav Lisinski complex has two halls, seating 1851 and 313 respectively. Historically the city did not experience any strong Austrian or Italian influences. Italian opera companies began to frequent the city during the 1820s with the eventual result of growing tensions between Croatian nationalists and the pro-German/Hungarian establishment toward the middle of the century. The first Croatian opera, *Ljubav i Zloba* by Lisinski, was performed by amateurs on March 28, 1846, and revived some twenty-five years later. Offenbach's *Daphnis et Chloé* was produced in Croatian in 1868, two years before the founding of a permanent opera company. The city's musical life benefitted greatly from the arrival of Ivan Zajc, the first professional Croatian musician, in 1870. He was the first Zagreb opera director, and he also directed his attention to building a competent orchestra. The first

Croatian national opera, Zajc's *Nikola Šubic Zrinski*, premiered on November 4, 1876. This work was revived for the inauguration of the new 850-seat National Theater on October 14, 1895.

Under the leadership of Stjepan Miletić, general manager of the Croatian Theater, the Zagreb Opera Orchestra began to give regular symphony concerts, and in 1920 members of the orchestra founded the Zagreb Philharmonic. The opera itself continued to thrive and directed considerable energies toward encouraging and supporting native composers. One of the first successful Serbo-Croatian folk operas, Baranović's *Striženo-Košeno*, premiered on May 4, 1932. In addition, a delightful Croatian comic opera, Gotovac's *Ero s Onoga svijeta*, opened on November 2, 1935. The company suspended formal activities during World War II, and since its revival has attempted to produce a varied repertoire while still affirming its national heritage.

BIBLIOGRAPHY: J. Andris, *Music in Croatia* (Zagreb, 1974). *Enciklopedija Hrvatskogs Narodnoga Kazalists u Zagrebu 1894–1969* (Zagreb, 1969). *Sto godina opere: Hrvatsko Narodno Kazalište* (Zagreb, 1971). L. Županovič, *Vatroslav Lisinski* (Zagreb, 1969). (Also see entries for Belgrade.)

ACCESS: Hrvatsko Narodno Kazalište, TRG Marsala Tita 15, 41000 Zagreb. (38 41) 447 100. Vladimir Benic, Director. Jasna Juric, Administrator.

[From materials supplied by the company]

Appendix: Additional Opera Companies

Belgium

ANTWERP (1,587,450)

Vlaamse Kameropera

BIBLIOGRAPHY: André Pols, *Vijftig jaar vlaamsche opera* (Antwerp, 1943). L. Sanders, *Onderzoek opera en publiek te Antwerpen* (Antwerp, 1974). Renaat Verbruggen, *Koninklijke Vlaamse Oper Antwerpen Gedenk-Klanken, 1893–1963* (Antwerp, 1965).

ACCESS: Centrumtheater, Pastorijstr. 23, B–2008 Antwerp. (33 3) 235 20 27. Walter Proost, Director.

GHENT (1,328,779)

Opera voor Vlaandern

Bibliography: Guy Verriest, *Het Lyrisch Toneel te Gent van de Oorsprong af tot op Heden* (Gent, 1964).

ACCESS: Schouwburgstr. 3, B-9000 Ghent. (32 91) 25 33 77/23 02 84. Eric De Meester, General Manager. Silveer Van den Broeck, Music Director.

LIÈGE (200,312)

Opera Royal de Wallonie

ACCESS: Lyric Centre, 1, rue des Dominicains, B-4000 Liège. (32 41) 235 910.

Egypt

CAIRO (6,325,000)

Egyptian Opera House

The Khedive of Egypt, Ismail Pasha, commissioned the Italians Avoscani and Rossi to build a grand opera house to celebrate the opening of the Suez Canal. He had hoped to convince Giuseppe Verdi to compose a piece for the festivities, but, instead of a new work, a production of *Rigoletto* conducted by Emmanuele Muzio inaugurated the new house on November 1, 1869. The composer was willing, however, to undertake a new opera with the stipulation that he be allowed sufficient time for its completion. *Aida* premiered in the new Cairo opera house on December 24, 1871 conducted by Giovanni Bottesini. Thereafter, operas were produced regularly with visiting artists predominating until 1961 when the first Arabic production, *The Merry Widow*, was mounted. The magnificent structure was completely destroyed by fire on October 28, 1971. With generous financial assistance from the Japanese government, a replacement theater was begun in 1985 and completed on March 31, 1988.

ACCESS: Shari' et Tahrir, Geziro, Cairo. (20 2) 42 05 94/95.

France

AIX-EN-PROVENCE

Aix-en-Provence International Festival

The festival was founded in 1948 by André Bigonnet and Gabriel Dussurget. Most of the performances take place in a 1,700-seat open-air theater. Hans Rosbaud was the principal conductor from its inception until 1959. The tenure of Bernard Lefort (1973 until 1980, Théâtre National de L'Opéra de Paris) was notable for its fine productions.

ACCESS: Aix-en-Provence International Festival, Palais de l'Ancien Archêveché, F-13100 Aix-en-Provence. (33 42) 231120, fax (33 42) 96126. Louis Erlo, Directeur Artistique.

Additional Opera Companies

BORDEAUX (2,723,600)

Opéra de Bordeaux

Designed by Victor Louis, the splendid 1,158-seat Grand Théâtre, which opened in 1780, remains one of the landmark theaters in France. Damaged during the revolution, the building was completely restored in 1799. Modernized just prior to World War II, the theater now hosts symphony concerts and chamber music as well as operas, operettas, and the annual Mal Musical de Bordeaux.

BIBLIOGRAPHY: Jean Latreyte, *Le Grand Théâtre de Bordeaux*. (Bordeaux, 1977).

ACCESS: Grand Théâtre Municipal, Place de la Comédie, F-33074 Bordeaux Cedex. (33 56) 90 91 60. Gerard Boireau, Directeur Artistique.

LILLE (metro 1,200,000; city 175,000)

Opéra de Lille

As the French hub connecting with the new tunnel under the English Channel, Lille will become a major center for the new national high-speed rail network. The opera currently performs in the 1,310-seat Opéra Municipal, but there is some talk of relocating in the new 175-acre business district named Euralille which will house the new train station, a communications complex, a world-trade center, as well as hotels and apartments.

ACCESS: Théâtre de l'Opéra, 2, rue des Bons Enfants, F-59800 Lille. (33 20) 559306.

TOULOUSE (metro 410,393; city 181,985)

Théâtre du Capitole

An ancient city, Toulouse was founded by the Romans in the second century B.C. Its distinguished musical history dates back to the troubadours, and its university, established in 1229 by Pope Innocent III, is the second oldest in France. The original Théâtre du Capitole was built in 1736 and opened on May 11, 1737. Its name derived from the twelve elected counsels, the Capitouls, who administered the city and thus owned the theater. The present 1,550-seat house launched its first season in 1923, and after a complete renovation in 1950 still serves as the home of the Toulouse opera company.

BIBLIOGRAPHY: Auguste Rivière and Alain Jouffray, *Le Théâtre du Capitole 1542–1977* (Toulouse, 1978).

ACCESS: Place du Capitole, F-31000 Toulouse. (33 61) 23 21 25. Jacques Doucet, Directeur Artistique. Robert Goaze, Directeur Général.

Germany

BIELEFELD (305,600)

Bühnen der Stadt Bielefeld

The 775-seat Stadttheater designed by Baurat Sehring opened on April 3, 1904, with Schiller's *Die Jungfrau von Orleans*.

ACCESS: Stadttheater, Niederwall 27, 4800 Bielefeld. (49 521) 51 24 89. Heiner Bruns; Intendant. Rainer Koch; Generalmusikdirector.

BONN (295,748)

Oper der Stadt Bonn

An 896-seat theater which opened on May 5, 1965 with a production of *Oresteia* by Aeschylus.

ACCESS: Am Boselagerhof 1, 5300 Bonn 1. (49 228) 7 28 12 00. Jean-Claude Riber, Generalintendant. Dennis Russell Davies, Generalmusikdirektor.

BRAUNSCHWEIG (252,200)

Staatstheater/Großes Haus Braunschweig

The 900-seat Großes Haus was originally opened in 1861. Largely destroyed in World War II, it reopened on December 25, 1948 with a gala performance of Mozart's *Don Giovanni*. Major construction is currently underway on the Großes Haus.

BIBLIOGRAPHY: Heinrich Sievers, *250 Jahre Braunschweigische Staatstheater* (Brunswick, 1941).

Access: Staatstheater, Am Theater, 3300 Braunschweig. (49 531) 4 84 27 01. Mario Krüger, Generalintendant.

BREMEN (546,794)

Theater am Goetheplatz

A 989-seat theater, which opened on August 27, 1950, was built on the site of the destroyed Bremen Schauspielhaus.

ACCESS: Theater am Goetheplatz, 2800 Bremen. (49 421) 36 53 2 11. Tobias Richter, Generalintendant.

KIEL (24,000)

Bühnen der Landeshauptstadt

Although operatic activity in the city can be traced back to the middle of the eighteenth century, the opening of the Stadttheater in 1841 marks the beginning of professional opera. A new 984-seat Stadttheater was opened in 1907 and was destroyed at the end of the war in 1944. The company moved to the old Schauspielhaus (which was renamed the Neues Stadttheater) from 1945 to 1953. During this time the Stadttheater was rebuilt, and it reopened on June 21, 1953.

BIBLIOGRAPHY: W. Danielsen, *Hundert Jahre Kieler Theater, 1841–1944* (Kiel, 1961).

ACCESS: Opernhaus am Kleinen Kiel, 2300 Kiel 1. (49 431) 9 01 28 92. Peter Dannenberg, Generalintendant.

KREFELD/MÖNCHENGLADBACH (488,000)

Vereinigte Städtische Bühnen

This unified company performs in theaters in both cities. The original Krefeld Theater on Rheinstraße was destroyed during World War II. A replacement was built on the same site and opened with Wagner's *Lohengrin* on October 7, 1952. The current theater designed by Graubner opened on January 12, 1963 with Mozart's *Don Giovanni* Mönchengladbach has two theaters both of which have been used for opera. The 753-seat Schauspielhaus, designed by Paul Stohrer, opened on September 10, 1959 with Wagner's *Die Meistersinger von Nürnberg*. The 811-seat Opernhaus, which opened in October 1930 with von Weber's *Der Freischütz*, was completely renovated and reopened on November 29, 1984 with Alban Berg's *Lulu*. The 1990–1991 repertoire included Henze's *Elegie für junge Liebende, Così fan tutte, Adriana auf Naxos*, Millöcker's *Der Bettelstudent, Ein Maskenball*, Janáček's *Katja Kabanowa*, and Jean-Philippe Rameau's *Platäas Hochzeit*.

ACCESS: Theaterplatz, 4150 Krefeld. (49 2151) 8 05 1 12; fax: (49 2151) 2 82 95. Hindenburgstraße 73, 4050 Mönchengladbach. (49 2166) 4 43 95; fax (49 2166) 42 01 10. Eike Gramss; Generalintendant.

MÜNCHEN (1,233,9990)

Staatstheater am Gärtnerplatz

BIBLIOGRAPHY: *100 Jahre Theater am Gärtnerplatz München* (München, 1965).

ACCESS: Gärtnerplatz 3, 8000 München 5. (49 89) 20 241 10; fax (49 89) 20 241 237. Hellmuth Matiasek, Intendant.

WUPPERTAL (381,000)

Opernhaus

The 851-seat opera house opened on October 14, 1956, with Hindemith's *Mathis der Maler*.

ACCESS: Opernhaus, Spinnstraße 4, 5600 Wuppertal 2. (49 202) 5 63 53 40; fax (49 202) 55 47 65. Peter Gülke, Generalmusikdirektor.

Iceland

REYKJAVÍK (metro 141, 938)

Iceland Opera

The rebuilt 505-seat Gamla Bió opened on January 9, 1982 with a gala performance of Johann Strauss's *Der Zigeunerbaron*.

ACCESS: Gamla Bió, Ingólfsstraeti, 121 Reykjavík. (354 1) 91 27033. Gardar Cortes, Director.

Italy

CATANIA (370,6790

Teatro Massimo Bellini

ACCESS: Via Perrotta 12, I-95100 Catania. (39 95) 321 020; fax (39 95) 321 830. Maria Francesca Siciliani, Direttore Artistico.

SPOLETO

Festival dei Due Mondi (Festival of Two Worlds)

Founded by the composer Gian Carlo Menotti in 1958, the festival utilizes four performance sites including the Teatro Nuovo, the Teatro Caio Melisso, the Piazza del Duomo, and the San Niccolo Cloister.

ACCESS: Via del Duomo 7, Spoleto. (39 743) 28100.

Additional Opera Companies

Mexico

MÉXICO, D.F. (10,355,347)

Opera Nacional

ACCESS: Ave Hidalgo 1–3er, Piso, C. P., 06050 México, D.F. (90 5) 512 50 81. Enrique Diemecke, Director.

Netherlands

AMSTERDAM (694,888)

De Nederlandse Opera

The Nederlandsche Opera, which dates its founding from 1941, performed a variety of repertoire in the Stadsschouwburg until the company was reorganized. Renamed the Nieuwe Nederlandse Opera in 1965, it was directed by Maurice Huismann, who was succeeded by Michael Gielen in 1973. Gielen's successor was Jan van Vlimen, who has evolved a limited repertoire that features the works of Mozart, Verdi, Wagner, and early-twentieth-century masterpieces. A new 1,594-seat Town Hall Music Theater was inaugurated on September 23, 1986.

BIBLIOGRAPHY: Ban Albach, *Het Huis Op Het Plein* (Amsterdam, 1957). S. A. M. Bottenheim, *De Opera in Nederland* (Amsterdam, 1946).

ACCESS: Waterlooplein 22, 1011 PG Amsterdam. (31 20) 551 89 22; fax (31 20) 832 350. Jan van Vlijmen, General Director. Juus Mostart, Artistic Director.

Spain

SEVILLE (1,550, 492)

Teatro de la Maestranza

Founded well before the birth of Christ, Seville has a long and distinguished musical history. Italian opera was very popular during the nineteenth century filling such theaters as the Anfiteatro and the 3,000-seat Teatro de San Fernando which both featured early performances of Verdi's operas. Productions continued with renowned guest artists until World War I after which support for the opera rapidly declined. With the economic resurgence of the 1980s, plans were formulated for a magnificent new 1,774-seat opera house designed by Aurelio del

Pozo and Luis Marín de Terán. Construction began in 1986 and after five years and an investment of forty million dollars, the world's newest opera house opened on May 10, 1991 with gala performances of operatic excerpts featuring Aragall, Berganza, Caballe, Carreras, Domingo, Krauss, and Lorengar. Placido Domingo has been appointed Artistic Director for the 1992 season, and he has announced a series of twelve productions showcasing such companies as the Metropolitan Opera (Verdi's *Un ballo in maschera*), La Scala, the Magio Musicale Fiorentino, and the Dresden Opera.

ACCESS: Teatro de la Maestranza. Placido Domingo, Artistic Advisor.

Sweden

GÖTEBORG

Stora Theatern Kungsparken

The city of Göteborg inaugurated a new 615-seat theater in 1859. It was renamed the Stora Theatre in 1880, when its productions included ballet and operetta for the first time. Operas became a prominent feature of the repertoire beginning in 1920.

ACCESS: Kungsparken, Box 53 116, 40015 Göteborg. (46 31) 17 47 45; fax (46 31) 13 11 35. Eskil Hemberg, Director. Sven-Olof Eliasson, Artistic Director.

Switzerland

BASEL (190,854)

Stadttheater Basel

The original Stadttheater was built in 1834. Completely renovated between 1873 and 1875, it was severely damaged by fire in 1904. Rebuilt, it reopened on September 20, 1909, and served the company until the new 1,015-seat Große Bühne opened on October 3, 1975. The current company employs 49 soloists, a 45-member chorus, and an orchestra of 168 musicians.

BIBLIOGRAPHY: Fritz Weiss, *Das Basler Stadttheater, 1834–1934*. (Basel, 1934).

ACCESS: Elisabethenstraße 16, CH-4051 Basel. (41 61) 22 11 30; fax (41 61) 22 19 90. Frank Baumbauer, Director. Michael Boder, Music Director.

Union of Soviet Socialist Republics

LENINGRAD (5,020,000)

Kirov Opera House

The Bolshoi Theater which opened to the public in 1783 (rebuilt in 1836) remained the principal opera house in Kiev until the 1,780-seat Maryinsky Theater opened in 1860. Following the revolution, the house became the State Academic Theater of Opera and Ballet and premiered a number of new Soviet operas. In 1935 it was renamed the Kirov Opera and Ballet Theater and has specialized in traditional repertoire and productions since then.
ACCESS; 1 Teatralnaya Ploschad, 190000 Leningrad. (7 812) 216 1211. Maxim Educardovich Kristin, General Director. Yuri Temirkanov, Artistic Director.

United States of America

HARTFORD (metro 726,144; city 136,392)

Connecticut Opera

All performances take place in the Horace Bushnell Memorial Hall (seating 3,277) which was built in 1930. Connecticut Opera was founded in 1942 as the Connecticut Opera Association.
ACCESS: 226 Farmington Avenue, Hartford, CT 06105. (203) 527-0713; fax (203) 293-1715. George D. Osborne, General Director.

TULSA (metro 689,434; city 360,919)

Tulsa Opera

Incorporated in 1898, Tulsa's serious involvement in classical music began with the inaugural concert of the Tulsa Philharmonic Orchestra in 1948. The Tulsa Opera originated that same year as the Tulsa Opera Club, and became Tulsa Opera, Inc., in 1953. The season, which usually includes three productions, features international stars, and it exists as a feature of the social calendar. Both the symphony and the opera perform in the 2,450-seat Chapman Music Hall, a constituent of the Performing Arts Center, a multihall complex that opened in 1977.
BIBLIOGRAPHY: M. H. Markham, ed., *Tulsa Opera. Inc., Dec. 4, 1948– March 17, 1973* (Tulsa, 1974).
ACCESS: 1610 South Boulder, Tulsa, OK 74119-4479. (918) 582-4035. Myrna Ruffner, General Manager. Nicholas Muni, Artistic Director.

Venezuela

CARACAS (1,044,851)

Opera de Caracas

The company has moved from the Teatro Municipal to the new 1,500-seat Complejo "Teresa Carreno," which was inaugurated in 1981.

ACCESS: Complejo "Teresa Carreno," Plaza Morelos, Caracas. (58 2) 572 9446. Elias Perez Borjas, Director.

Chronology of Foundings for Opera Companies Profiled

Very few companies in this list have an absolute founding date. Almost all have predecessors of one kind or another; announced plans, appointment of governing boards and artistic or musical directors, guaranteed funding, completion of buildings, inaugural performances—all these factors and more reflect on founding dates. In addition, interruptions of seasons, changes of names, and a move to new and more spacious quarters all impact on what may not be considered an official beginning. All the dates listed below have been selected for important and valid historical reasons, but, by the same token, many of them are arguable on artistic, political, or cultural grounds.

Paris	Théâtre National de L'Opéra de Paris	1673
Hamburg	Hamburgische Staatsoper	1678
Leipzig	Opernhaus	1693
Vienna	Wiener Staatsoper	1708
Palermo	Teatro Massimo	1726
London	Royal Opera House Covent Garden	1732
Naples	Real Teatro di San Carlo	1737
Berlin	Deutsche Staatsoper Berlin (Unter den Linden)	1742
Mannheim	Nationaltheater	1742
Copenhagen	Det Kongelige Teater og Kapel	1748
Stuttgart	Staatstheater Stuttgart	1750
München	Bayerische Staatsoper	1753
Turin	Teatro Regio di Torino	1753
Bologna	Teatro Comunale di Bologna	1763
Kassel	Staatstheater	1764

Stockholm	Kungliga Teatern (Royal Opera)	1773
Moscow	Bolshoi Opera Theater of the USSR	1776
Milan	Teatro alla Scala	1778
Kraków	Krakowski Teatr Muzyczny	1787
Marseille	Opéra de Marseille	1787
Venice	Teatro La Fenice di Venezia	1792
Rouen	Théâtre des Arts	1793
Gdańsk	Państwowa Opera i Filharmonia Baltycka	1801
Trieste	Teatro Giuseppe Verdi	1801
Linz	Landestheater Linz	1803
Karlsruhe	Badisches Staatstheater	1810
Hannover	Niedersächsische Staatstheater	1818
Darmstadt	Staatstheater	1819
Strasbourg	Opéra du Rhin	1821
Genoa	Teatro Carlo Felice	1828
Parma	Teatro Regio	1829
Lyon	Opéra Grand Théâtre	1831
Nürnberg	Städtische Bühnen	1833
Warsaw	Teatr Wielki	1833
Zurich	Opernhaus Zürich	1834
Bern	Stadttheater Bern	1837
Budapest	Magyar Állami Operaház	1837
Luzern	Stadttheater Luzern	1839
Dresden	Staatsoper Dresden (Semperoper)	1841
Wroclaw	Opery Wroclaws	1841
Barcelona	Consorci del Gran Teatre del Liceu	1847
Bucharest	Romanian Opera	1852
Brussels	Théâtre Royal de la Monnaie	1856
Santiago	Opera del Teatro Municipal	1857
Florence	Teatro Comunale di Firenze	1862
Augsburg	Städtische Bühnen	1867
Kiev	Taras Shevchenko Opera and Ballet Theater	1867
Tartu	Teatre Vanemuine	1870
Bayreuth	Bayreuther Festspiele	1876
Genèva	Grand Théâtre de Genève	1879
Monte Carlo	Opéra de Monte-Carlo	1879
Rome	Teatro dell'Opera	1880
Frankfurt am Main	Städtische Bühnen	1880

Prague	Národní Divadlo Prague (Prague National Theater)	1881
Brno	Janáček's Opera Brno	1882
New York	Metropolitan Opera Association	1883
Nice	Opéra de Nice	1885
Essen	Theater und Philharmonie Essen	1892
Zagreb	Opera of the Hrvatsko Narodno Kazalište (Croatian National Opera)	1895
Vienna	Wiener Volksoper	1898
Graz	Vereinigte Bühnen	1899
Köln	Opera der Stadt Köln	1902
Dortmund	Städtische Bühnen	1904
Vilnius	Lietuvos Operos ir Baleto teatras	1906
Buenos Aires	Teatro Colón	1908
Rio de Janeiro	Teatro Municipal	1909
Poznań	Teatr Wielki	1910
Berlin	Deutsche Oper Berlin	1912
Savonlinna	Savonlinna Opera Festival	1912
Verona	Arena di Verona	1913
Helsinki	Finnish National Opera	1914
Belgrade	Opera Narodnog Pozorista u Beogradu (Belgrade National Opera)	1919
Nancy	Opéra de Nancy et de Lorraine	1919
Bratislava	Slovenskí Národné (Slovak National Theater)	1920
Cincinnati	The Cincinnati Opera	1920
Salzburg	Salzburger Festspiele	1920
Sofia	Sofiyska Narodna Opera (Sofia National Opera)	1921
Stockholm	Drottningholms Slottsteater	1921
San Francisco	San Francisco Opera	1923
Chautauqua	Chautauqua Opera Association	1929
London	English National Opera	1931
Central City	Central City Opera	1932
Glyndebourne	Glyndebourne Festival Opera	1934
Athens	National Opera of Greece	1939
Baltimore	Baltimore Opera Company	1940
Pittsburgh	Pittsburgh Opera	1940
Miami	Greater Miami Opera	1941
Ankara	Ankara Devlet Opera ve Balesi (Ankara State Opera and Ballet)	1942

New Orleans	New Orleans Opera Association	1943
New York	New York City Opera	1944
Bregenz	Bregenzer Festspiele	1946
Cardiff	Welsh National Opera	1946
Fort Worth	Fort Worth Opera Association	1946
Lisbon	Companhia de Opera do Teatro Sao Carlos	1946
Berlin	Komische Oper	1947
Tel Aviv	The New Israeli Opera	1947
Sofia	State Musical Theater "Stefan Makedonski"	1948
Oslo	Den Norske Opera	1950
Portland	Portland Opera	1950
Wexford	Wexford Festival Opera	1951
Louisville	Kentucky Opera	1952
Bejing	Central Opera Theater	1953
Lodz	Teatr Wielki W Lodzi	1954
Wellington	Wellington City Opera	1954
Chicago	Lyric Opera of Chicago	1954
Houston	Houston Grand Opera	1955
Düsseldorf-Duisburg	Deutsche Oper am Rhein	1956
Shanghai	Shanghai Opera House	1956
Sydney	The Australian Opera	1956
Washington, D.C.	The Washington Opera	1956
Belfast	Opera Northern Ireland	1957
Dallas	The Dallas Opera	1957
Santa Fe	The Santa Fe Opera	1957
Toronto	Canadian Opera Company	1958
Vancouver	Vancouver Opera	1958
Omaha	Opera/Omaha	1959
Istanbul	Istanbul Devlet Opera ve Balesi (Istanbul State Opera and Ballet)	1960
Honolulu	Hawaii Opera Theater	1961
Glasgow	Scottish Opera	1962
Madrid	Asociación Amigos de la Opera de Madrid	1962
Edmonton	Edmonton Opera	1963
Johannesburg and Pretoria	Performing Arts Council of Transvaal (PACT)	1963
Cape Town	Opera of the Cape Performing Arts Council (CAPAB)	1964
Seattle	Seattle Opera	1964

San Diego	San Diego Opera	1965
Ottawa	National Arts Centre/Centre national des arts	1969
Detroit	Michigan Opera Theatre	1971
Vienna, Virginia	Wolf Trap Opera Company	1973
Philadelphia	Opera Company of Philadelphia	1975
Richmond	The Virginia Opera	1975
Adelaide	The State Opera of South Australia	1976
Boston	Boston Lyric Opera Company	1976
Saint Louis	Opera Theatre of Saint Louis	1976
Melbourne	Victoria State Opera	1977
Montréal	L'Opéra de Montréal	1980
Denver	Opera Colorado	1981
Tokyo	The Japan Opera Foundation (Nihon Opera Shinkokai)	1981
Izmir	Izmir Devlet Opera ve Balesi (The Izmir State Opera and Ballet)	1982

Selected Annotated Bibliography

During the course of compiling this book of profiles, a limited number of titles surfaced that proved to be of enormous help in confronting the historical, aesthetic, cultural, and artistic mysteries surrounding the world's opera companies. The mere fact that no single volume assembles so much information about so many organizations created a variety of problems relating to accuracy, objectivity, and completeness. Therefore, I was determined to root out the most available as well as the most accurate publications so that any interested reader who wished to pursue a particular company further would have some suggestions at hand concerning just where to look to do that. The major sources of additional information concerning specific companies will be found at the end of the profile in question. *Die Musik in Geschichte und Gegenwart: Allgemeine Enzyklopädie der Musik*, ed. Friedrich Blume, (Kassel, 1949–1979); *Enciclopedia dello spettacolo*, eds. Silvio d'Amico and Francesco Savio (Roma, 1954–1966); *The New Grove Dictionary of American Music*, ed. Stanley Sadie (London, 1986); and *The New Grove Dictionary of Music and Musicians*, eds. H. Wiley Hitchcock and Stanley Sadie (London, 1980) are all excellent general references. However, the titles listed below will, in many cases, touch on areas that these do not cover.

This selected bibliography has been kept deliberately short, and I have tried to include titles that are readily available in both North America and Europe. There are literally hundreds of books about theaters and opera companies. Indeed, a bibliography of these materials is sorely needed, but my intent was to provide resources for the general reader. These are related titles that will provide additional information if desired.

Aloi, Roberto. *Architetture per lo spettacolo.* Milano: Ulrico Hoepli, 1958.

    Technical information on approximately one hundred theaters worldwide. An important survey of facilities after World War II.

Beranek, Leo L. *Music, Acoustics and Architecture.* New York: John Wiley and Sons, Inc., 1962.

    Authored by a renowned partner in a major acoustical consulting firm, a large portion of this book is devoted to a brief description of fifty-four concert halls and opera houses worldwide, including the Teatro Colón in Buenos Aires, the

Vienna Staatsoper, the Paris Opéra, the old Metropolitan Opera House, the Bayreuth Festspielhaus, the Royal Opera House Covent Garden, and the Teatro alla Scala.

Bertz-Dostal, Helga. *Oper im Fernsehen.* 2 vols. Wien: Verlag und Druck Minor, 1970.

Production details including conductors of 1,646 television productions between 1936 and 1970. The record of efforts to make opera available to a wider audience.

Blyth, Alan, ed. *Opera on Record.* 3 vols. London: Hutchinson and Co., 1979; New York: Beaufort Books, 1983; Dover, NH: Longwood Press, 1984.

Volume 1 includes opera discographies of twenty-two composers; volume 2 includes twenty-four composers; and volume 3 includes sixteen composers. The discographies are all compiled by Malcolm Walker.

Bontinck-Küffel, Irmgard, ed. *Opern auf Schallplatten, 1900–1962: Ein historischer Katalog.* Wien: Universal Edition A.G., 1974.

A welcome list of some outstanding, long-forgotten performances.

Burian, Karel Vladimir. *Světová operní divalda.* Praha, Czechoslovakia: Suraphon, 1973.

Short profiles of 149 theaters throughout the world.

Celletti, Rodolfo. *Il Teatro d'opera in disc.* Milano: Rizzoli, 1976.

An attempt to catalog all complete opera recordings with both original and reissue numbers.

Celletti, Rodolfo, ed. *Le grandi voci: Dizionaria critico-biografico dei cantanti con Discografia Operistica.* Roma: Istituto per la Collaborazione Culturale, 1964.

Biographies of over three hundred noted opera singers, each of which has an extensive operatic bibliography compiled by Raffaele Vegeto and John B. Richards. A very useful source for release dating from the early years of the industry to the early 1960s.

Cowden, Robert H., comp. *Concert and Opera Conductors: A Bibliography of Biographical Materials.* Westport, CT: Greenwood Press, 1987.

Comprehensive bibliographies of 1,249 conductors. In addition, 55 collective works on conductors are annotated, as well as 169 related books. Seven major biographical dictionaries and encyclopedias plus ten important periodicals are cross-indexed. There is a separate index to conductors found in the 7th edition, (1984) of *Baker's Biographical Dictionary of Musicians*, edited by Nicolas Slonimsky.

Cowden, Robert H., comp. *Concert and Opera Singers: A Bibliography of Biographical Materials.* Westport, CT: Greenwood Press, 1985.

Comprehensive bibliographies of 720 singers. In addition, 120 collective works on singers are annotated as well as 154 related books. Ten major biographical dictionaries and encyclopedias and nine periodicals are cross-indexed. There is a separate index to singers found in the new *Grove Dictionary of Music and Musicians* (1980), edited by Stanley Sadie. [A second revised and expanded edition is in preparation at this time.]

Selected Annotated Bibliography

Dace, Walter. *National Theaters in the Larger German and Austrian Cities.* New York: Richards Rosen Press, 1980.

Important information on the theaters in Linz, Nürnberg, Stuttgart, Düsseldorf, Frankfurt am Main, Köln, München, Wien, Hamburg, and West Berlin. Lists theater collections and research institutes.

Dräger Gerhard, ed. *Deutsches Bühnen Jahrbuch: Das Große Adreßbuch für Bühne-Film-Funk-und Fernsehen.* Hamburg: Genossenschaft Deutscher Bühnen-Angehörigen, 1990

Indispensable handbook for theaters and personnel in Austria, Germany, and Switzerland. The major German-language theaters abroad are included. The ninety-nine editions of this publication provide an invaluable resource for the history of the German theater.

Farkas, Andrew. *Opera and Concert Singers: An Annotated International Bibliography of Books and Pamphlets.* New York: Garland Publishing, 1985.

Autobiographies, biographies, and studies of 796 singers, a total that includes cross references to multisubject monographs. Important for Slavic artists and for mention of published translations and other editions of biographies and autobiographies.

Gammond, Peter. *Illustrated Encyclopedia of Recorded Opera.* New York: Harmony Books, 1979.

Primarily a listing of long-playing (LP) recordings, multiple entries are often noted. Complete operas, abridged versions, highlights, and excerpts are listed for 155 composers from Adolphe Adam to Riccardo Zandoni.

Gammond, Peter. *Opera on Compact Disk: A Critical Guide to the Best Recordings.* New York: Harmony Books, 1987.

The author began as editor of *Gramophone Record Review* in 1966, so there is a great deal of experience behind his evaluations. This volume includes the vocal works of some sixty-eight composers from Johann Sebastian Bach to Hugo Wolf. The extensive annotations reveal the author's opinion of the best recordings.

Gishford, Anthony, ed. *Grand Opera: The Story of the World's Leading Opera Houses and Personalities.* New York: Viking Press, 1972.

La Scala, La Fenice, San Carlo, and Regio in Italy; L'Opéra, L'Opéra Louis XV, Monte Carlo, Toulouse (Le Capitole), and Bordeaux (Grand Théâtre) in France; Berlin (Deutsche Oper, Staatsoper, and Komische Oper), Dresden, Munich (Cuvilliés-Theater and Nationaltheater), Bayreuth, and Hamburg in Germany; Barcelona in Spain; Vienna Staatsoper in Austria; Prague National Theater in Czechoslovakia; Covent Garden, Glyndebourne, and The Maltings, Snape, in England; Stockholm's Royal Opera and Drottningholm Theater in Sweden; Leningrad's Kirov Theater and Moscow's Bolshoi in the Soviet Union; the Met, Chicago's Civic Opera, and San Francisco in the United States; El Teatro Colón in Buenos Aires, Argentina; and the Sydney Opera House in Australia.

Gray, Michael, and Gerald D. Gibson. *Bibliography of Discographies.* Volume I, Classical Music, 1925–1975. New York: R. R. Boker, 1977.

This comprehensive listing includes books, monographs, articles, and portions of articles that include a discography. It is the most comprehensive and scholarly work of its kind to date in any language. There are 3,307 entries arranged by subject with most helpful annotations. The authors were responsible for citations in the *Association for Recorded Sound Collections Journal* (1967–).

Harris, Kenn. *Opera Recordings: A Critical Guide*. New York: Drake Publishers, 1973.

Lists all available recordings of the seventy-six operas included from Cilea's *Adriana Lecouvreur* to Mozart's *Die Zauberflöte*. The index lists major opera companies, orchestras, singers, and conductors.

Holmes, John L. *Conductors on Record*. Westport, CT: Greenwood Press, 1982.

This labor of love includes 78-rpms and LPs up to the year 1977 with no attempt to be comprehensive. There are short biographies of over 2,000 conductors.

Hughes, Spike [Patrick Cairns]. *Great Opera Houses: A Traveler's Guide to Their History and Traditions*. London: Weidenfeld and Nicolson, 1956.

Prinzregententheater and the Theater am Gärtnerplatz in Munich; Staatsoper and Volksoper in Vienna; La Fenice in Venice; La Scala in Milan; Teatro Regio in Parma; Teatro della Pergola and Teatro comunale in Florence; Teatro dell'Opera in Rome; San Carlo and Teatro di Corte in Naples; Teatro Massimo and Teatro Politeama in Palermo; Teatro Massimo Bellini in Catania; Teatro Carlo Felice in Genoa; Teatro Regio in Turin; Théâtre de l'Opéra and Opéra-Comique in Paris; and Covent Garden in London.

Jäger, Stefan, ed. *Das Atlantisbuch der Dirigenten eine Enzyklopädie*. Zürich: Atlantis Musikbuck Verlag AG, 1985.

Covering 783 conductors, the extensive material on sixty-nine major figures makes this the outstanding book of its kind presently available.

Kesting, Jürgen. *Die Grossen Sänger*. 3 vols. Düsseldorf: Classen Verlag GmbH, 1986.

The most comprehensive history of the classical vocal arts currently available. The emphasis is on the nineteenth and twentieth centuries organized by country and vocal classification. Recordings are mentioned where appropriate.

Krause, Ernest. *Die Grossen Opernbühnen Europas*. Kassel: Bärenreiter-Verlag, 1966.

Pictures and brief descriptions of theaters in Berlin (Staatsoper, Komische Oper, and Deutsche Oper), Vienna (Staatsoper), Milan (Teatro alla Scala), Rome (Teatro dell'Opera), Venice (Teatro La Fenice), Paris (Grand Opéra and Opéra Comique), London (Covent Garden Opera and Sadler's Wells Theatre) Glyndebourne (Festival Theatre), Moscow (Bolchoi and Stanislawski-Nemirowitsch-Dantschenko-Music Theater), Leningrad (Kirov), Prague (Národni Divadlo), Budapest (Magyar Állami Operaház), Sofia (Narodna Opera), Warsaw (Teatr Wielki), Stockholm (Kungliga Teatern), Zurich (Opernhaus), Barcelona (Gran Teatro de Liceo), Munich (Nationaltheater), Dresden (Großes Haus), Stuttgart (Württembergische Staatsoper), Hamburg (Staatsoper), Frankfurt/am Main (Städtische Bühnen), Köln (Bühnen der Stadt), Düsseldorf (Deutsche Oper am Rhein), Leipzig (Städtische Theater), Bayreuth (Festspielhaus), Salzburg (Festspielhaus), and Halle.

Selected Annotated Bibliography 325

Kutsch, Karl-Josef, and Leo Riemens. *Großes Sängerlexikon*. 2 volcs. Bern: A. Francke Verlag AG, 1987.

An absolutely monumental work which includes biographies of 6,965 singers who performed over the past four hundred years. Many entries contain references to recordings. Volume 2 has an appendix of 2,334 operas and 376 operettas with statistics about their premieres, including casting for the important works. The earlier editions (1962, 1966, and 1969 in English; 1979 [supplement], and 1982) are subsumed in this edition.

Loewenberg, Alfred. *Annals of Opera 1597–1940*. 3rd rev. ed. Totowa, NJ: Rowman and Littlefield, 1978.

The basic scholarly source for determining opera premiere dates and location. A continuation of this seminal work was being edited by Harold Rosental prior to his death. Volume 2 (1940–1988) was scheduled for publication in May 1991. It will also update the performance listing of the earlier editions.

Marco, Guy A. *Opera: A Research and Information Guide*. New York: Garland Publishing, 1984.

Includes sections on all conceivable topics related to opera except for performers. When used in conjunction with the fourth edition of Duckels (*Music Reference and Research Materials: An Annotated Bibliography*, New York, 1988), multiple paths for further research are indicated.

Meyers, Kurtz, comp. and ed. *Index to Record Reviews*. 5 vols. Boston: G. K. Hall and Co., 1978–1980.

"Based on material originally published in *Notes, the Quarterly Journal of the Music Library Association* between 1949 and 1977." This invaluable source indexes fifty English-language periodicals.

Meyers, Kurtz, and Richard S. Hill. *Index to Record Reviews, 1978–1983* Boston: G. K. Hall, 1985.

Continues the previous volume.

Mordden, Ethan. *A Guide to Opera Recordings*. New York: Oxford University Press, 1987.

Includes examples from the early years of the recording industry to the 1980s. A very enlightening personal journey through the "highways and byways," which includes underground recordings as well.

Pride, Leo B., ed. *International Theater Directory: A World Directory of the Theater and Performing Arts*. New York: Simon and Schuster, 1973.

A general reference to theaters in 107 countries and territories around the world. Information is restricted to current address and seating capacity.

Schubert, Hannelore. *The Modern Theater: Architecture, State Design, Lighting*. Trans. J. C. Palmes. New York: Praeger Publishers, 1971; original edition; Stuttgart, 1971.

Theaters constructed following World War II in countries including Canada, Poland, the United States, plus over forty theaters in Austria, Germany, and Switzerland.

Steiger, Franz. *Opernlexikon*. 9 vols. plus 2 supplements. Tutzing: Verlegt bei Hans Schneider, 1977–1983.

Another massive compilation of factual chronological data about opera premieres.

Zielske, Harald. *Deutsche Theaterbauten bis zum Zweiten Weltkrieg: Typologisch-historische Dokumentation einer Baugattung*. Berlin: Selbstverlad der Gesellschaft für Theatergeschichte, 1971.

Important information concerning a number of theaters destroyed during World War II. Excellent bibliography.

Index

Page references in bold refer to main entries.

Adelaide, **4–5**
Adler, Kurt Herbert, 287–88
Aix-en-Provence, **306**
Aix-en-Provence International Festival, 306
Amsterdam, **311**
Ankara, **206–8**
Antwerp, **305**
Arena di Verona, **158**
Argento, Dominick, 259–60
Athens, **126**
Augsburg, **73**
Australian Opera, 7–10

Badisches Staatstheater, 107–9
Baltimore, **233–34**
Barbaia, Domenico, 147
Barcelona, **191–92**
Basel, **312**
Bastide, Paul, 71
Bayerische Staatsoper, 119–23
Bayreuth, **73–75**
Bayreuther Festspiele, 73–75
Beecham, Thomas, 229
Beijing, **43–44**
Belfast, **216–17**
Belgrade, **301–2**
Berlin, **75–92**
Bern, **200–201**

Bielefeld, **307–8**
Bing, Rudolf, 78, 267–68
Böhm, Johann Heinrich, 111
Bohnen, Michael, 79
Bologna, **138–39**
Bolshoi Opera Theater, 212–15
Bonn, **308**
Bordeaux, **306–7**
Boston, **234–37**
Bratislava, **46–48**
Braunschweig, **308**
Bregenz, **11–12**
Bregenzer Festspiele, 11–12
Bremen, **308**
Breslau. *See* Wroclaw
Brno, **48–49**
Brussels, **22–24**
Bucharest, **185**
Budapest, **127–31**
Buenos Aires, **1–3**

Cairo, **306**
Canadian Opera Company, 36–39
Cantania, **310**
Cape Town, **188–89**
Capobianco, Tito, 279–80, 285
Caracas, **314**
Cardiff, **217–20**
Central City, **237–38**

Central City Opera, 237–38
Chautauqua, **238–39**
Chautauqua Opera Association, 238–39
Chicago, **240–42**
Cincinnati, **242–44**
Connecticut Opera. *See* Hartford
Copenhagen, **53–54**
Corn, Edward, 275
Cosenza, Arthur, 262–63
Covent Garden. *See* Royal Opera House Covent Garden
Crosby, John, 289–90

Dallas, **244–48**
Danzig. *See* Gdańsk
Darmstadt, **92–94**
Den Norske Opera, 168–69
Denver, **248**
Detroit, **249–50**
Deutsche Oper am Rhein, 98–100
Deutsche Oper Berlin, 75–83
Deutsche Staatsoper Berlin, 83–89
Dortmund, **94–96**
Dresden, **96–98**
Drottningholms Slottsteater, 194–96
Düsseldorf-Duisburg, **98–100**

Ebert, Carl, 78, 80, 207–8, 221
Edmonton, **31–32**
Edmonton Opera, 31–32
Egyptian Opera House. *See* Cairo
Elizabethan Theatre Trust, 8
English National Opera, 223–25
Eoan Group, 187
Erkel, Ferenc, 127–28
Essen, **100**

Feinstein, Martin, 298–99
Felsenstein, Walter, 89–92
Festival dei Due Mondi. *See* Spoleto
Festival Ottawa, 35–36
Flagstad, Kirsten, 169
Florence, **139–42**
Fort Worth, **250–51**
Fox, Carol, 240–41
Frankfurt am Main, **100–101**
Friedrich, Götz, 82–83
Fujiwara Opera, 159

Gatti-Casazza, Giulio, 265–66
Gdańsk, **170–72**
Geiger-Torel, Herman, 37
Geneva, **201–3**
Genoa, **142–43**
Ghent, **305**
Glasgow, **220–21**
Glyndebourne, **221–23**
Glyndebourne Festival Opera, 221–23
Gockley, David, 255–56
Göteborg, **312**
Gran Teatre del Liceu, 191–92
Grand Théâtre. *See* Bordeaux
Graz, **12–13**
Gregor, Hans, 77, 90
Gunsbourg, Roaul, 164

Hamburg, **101–5**
Handel, George Frideric, 226
Hannover, **105–7**
Hartford, **313**
Hartmann, Georg, 77
Hawaii Opera Theater. *See* Honolulu
Helsinki, **57–59**
Herbert, Walter, 254–55, 261, 285
Honolulu, **251–54**
Houston, **254–56**

Iceland Opera. *See* Reykjavík
Israel National Opera, 136
Istanbul, **208–9**
Izmir, **209**

Janáček's Opera Brno, 48–49
Johannesburg, **189–90**
Jommelli, Nicoló

Karajan, Herbert von, 18
Karlsruhe, **107–9**
Karp, Richard, 278
Kassel, **109**
Kelly, Lawrence, 240, 244–46
Kentucky Opera. *See* Louisville
Kiel, **309**
Kiev, **210–12**
Kirov Opera House. *See* Leningrad
Köln, **110–16**
Komische Oper, 89–92

Kongelige Teater og Kapel, 53–54
Kraków, **172**
Krefield/Mönchengladbach, **309**
Kruger, Rudolph, 250
Kungliga teatern, 196–99

Leipzig, **116–17**
Leitner, Ferdinand, 125
Leningrad, **313**
Liebermann, Rolf, 68, 103–4
Liège, **305**
Lietuvos Operos ir Baleto teatras, 161–63
Lille, **307**
Lindenoper. *See* Deutsche Staatsoper Berlin
Linz, **13–14**
Lisbon, **184**
Lodz, **172–73**
London, **223–32**
London, George, 297
L'Opéra de Montreal, 32–33
Louisville, **256–57**
Luzern, **203–4**
Lyon, **61**
Lyric Opera. *See* Chicago
Lysenko, Mykola, 211

Mackerras, Charles, 219
Madrid, **192–93**
Maggio Musicale Fiorentino, 140–42
Magyar Állami Operaház, 127–31
Mahler, Gustav, 17–18, 103
Mannheim, **117–19**
Marseille, **62–64**
Melbourne, **5–7**
Menotti, Gian Carlo, 296–97
Merola, Gaetano, 286–87
Metropolitan Opera, 264–70
Metropolitan Opera National Company, 267
México, D. F., **311**
Meyerbeer, Giacomo, 85
Miami, **258**
Michigan Opera Theater. *See* Detroit
Milan, **143–46**
Minneapolis/St. Paul, **258–60**
Minnesota Opera. *See* Minneapolis/St. Paul

Monte Carlo, **164–65**
Montréal, **32–33**
Mortier, Gérard, 24, 68
Moscow, **212–15**
Mozart, Wolfgang Amadeus, 14–16, 119, 143
München, **119–23**
Münchner Opern-Festspiele, 120

Nancy, **64–65**
Naples, **146–48**
Národní Divadlo Prague, 49–52
Nationaltheater, 117–19
Nederlandse Opera. *See* Amsterdam
New Orleans, **260–63**
New York City, **264–72**
New York City Opera, 270–72
Nice, **65–66**
Niedersächsische Staatstheater, 105–7
Nihon Opera Kyokai, 160
Nihon Opera Shinkokai, 159–60
Nürnberg, **123–24**

Omaha, **272–73**
Opera Colorado. *See* Denver
Opéra de Monte-Carlo, 164–65
Opéra de Nancy et de Lorraine, 64–65
Opera del Teatro Municipal, 41–42
Opéra der Marseille, 62–64
Opéra du Rhin, 70–72
Opéra Grand Théâtre, 61
Opera Nacional. *See* México, D. F.
Opera Narodnog Pozorista u Beogradu. *See* Belgrade
Opera Northern Ireland, 216–17
Opera Româna, 185
Opera Royal de Wallonie, 305
Opera voor Vlaandern, 305
Opera Unter den Linden. *See* Deutsche Staatsoper Berlin
Oslo, **168–69**
Ottawa, **33–36**
Ottawa, National Arts Centre, 33–36

Palermo, **148–51**
Państwowa Opera i Filharmonia Baltycka, 170–72
Paris, **66–69**

Parma, **151–54**
Philadelphia, **273–77**
Pittsburgh, **277–80**
Pollini, Bernhard, 103
Portland, **280–82**
Poznań, **174–76**
Prague, **49–52**
Pretoria, **189–90**

Real Teatro di San Carlo, 146–48
Rennert, Günther, 103
Reykjavík, **310**
Richmond, **282–83**
Rio de Janeiro, **25–26**
Rizzo, Francis, 293, 297–98
Rome, **154–55**
Ross, Glynn, 291
Rouché, Jacques, 68
Rouen, **69–70**
Royal Opera House Covent Garden, 225–32
Rudel, Julius, 271

Sadler's Wells Opera, 223–24
Saint Louis, **283–84**
Salzburg, **14–16**
Salzburger Festspiele, 14–16
San Diego, **285–86**
San Francisco, **286–89**
Santa Fe, **289–91**
Santiago, **41–42**
Savonlinna, **59–60**
Savonlinna Opera Festival, 58, 59–60
Scottish Opera, 220–21
Seattle, **291–92**
Seefehlner, Egon, 81
Sellner Gustav Rudolf, 80
Semperoper. *See* Dresden
Seville, **311–12**
Shanghai, **45**
Shanghai Opera House, 45
Slovenské Národné Divadlo, 46–48
Sofia, **27–30**
Sofiyska Narodna Opera, 27–28
Solti, Georg, 68, 230
Spohr, Louis, 109
Spoleto, **309**

Staatstheater am Gärtnerplatz (München), 308
Stanislavsky-Nemirovich-Danchenko Musical Theater, 214
State Musical Theater "Stefan Makedonski," 28–30
State Opera of South Australia, 4–5
Stockholm, **194–99**
Stora Theatern Kungsparken. *See* Göteborg
St. Petersburg. *See* Leningrad
Strasbourg, **70–72**
Strauss, Richard, 97–98
Stuttgart, **124–25**
Sydney, **7–10**

Talvela, Martti, 59
Taras Shevchenko Academic Opera, 210–12
Tartu, **55–56**
Tchaikovsky, Peter, 210, 213
Teatre Vanemuine, 55–56
Teatro alla Scala, 143–46
Teatro Carlo Felice, 142–43
Teatro Colón, 1–3
Teatro Communale di Bologna, 138–39
Teatro Communale di Firenze, 139–42
Teatro de la Maestranza. *See* Seville
Teatro Giuseppe Verdi, 155
Teatro La Fenice di Venezia, 157–58
Teatro Lirico Nacional, 193
Teatro Massimo, 148–51
Teatro Massimo Bellini. *See* Cantania
Teatro Municipal, 25–26
Teatro Regio di Parma, 151–54
Teatro Regio di Torino, 156–57
Teatro São Carlos, 184
Tel Aviv, **136–37**
Terrasson, René, 72
Théâtre du Capitole. *See* Toulouse
Théâtre National de L'Opéra de Paris, 66–69
Théâtre Royal de la Monnaie, 22–24
Tietjen, Heinz, 74, 78–80
Tokyo, **159–60**
Toronto, **36–39**
Toscanini, Arturo, 145, 265
Toulouse, **307**

Index 331

Trieste, **155**
Tulsa, **313**
Turin, **156–57**

Ukraine, 210–12

Vancouver, **39–40**
Vancouver Opera, 39–40
Venice, **157–58**
Verdi, Giuseppe, 144
Verona, **158**
Victoria State Opera, 5–7
Vic-Wells Opera Company, 223
Vienna, **16–21**
Vienna (Va.), **293–94**
Vilnius, **161–63**
Virginia Opera. *See* Richmond
Vlaamse Kameropera, 305

Wagner, Richard, 73–75, 120, 292
Walter, Bruno, 78
Warsaw, **176–83**
Washington, D.C., **294–300**
Webster, David, 230
Wellington, **166–67**
Welsh National Opera, 217–20
Wexford, **132–35**
Wexford Festival Opera, 132–35
Wiener Staatsoper, 16–20
Wiener Volksoper, 20–22
Wolf Trap Opera Company, 293–94
Wroclaw, **183**
Wuppertal, **310**

Zagreb, **302–3**
Zeffirelli, Franco, 244–45
Zürich, **204–5**

About the Editor and Contributors

ELZBIETA ADAMCZYK is a Dramaturg with the Teatr Wielki w Lodzi in Lodz, Poland.

ROBERT BAXTER is the critic for the *Daily Sunday Courier-Post* in Cherry Hill, New Jersey.

JACK BELSOM is Archivist of the New Orleans Opera Association, a correspondent for *Opera* magazine, and a contributor to *The New Grove Dictionary of Opera*.

AMANDA BOTHA is a journalist, public relations consultant, and producer of television documentaries in Cape Town, South Africa.

JONAS BRUVERIS is the Dramaturg and Consultant of the Lietuvos Operos ir Baleto teatras in Vilnius, Lithuania.

PARKS CAMPBELL is associated with the Fort Worth Opera Association, Texas.

ANTHONY CLARKE is Communications Administrator for the Australian Opera in Surry Hills, Australia.

ROBERT H. COWDEN is Professor of Music at San José State University. He is the compiler of *Concert and Opera Singers: A Bibliography of Biographical Materials*, *Concert and Opera Conductors: A Bibliography of Biographical Materials*, *Instrumental Virtuosi: A Bibliography of Biographical Materials* (Greenwood Press, 1985, 1987, and 1989 respectively). Dr. Cowden has also translated several operas as well as authored numerous articles and reviews published in *Arts in Society*, *MLA Notes*, *The NATS Bulletin*, *Opera*, *The Opera Journal*, *Performing Arts Review*, and *Theatre Design and Technology*. He is presently working on a bibliography of biographical materials about vocalists in the commercial and entertainment fields as well as a revised and expanded edition of his bibliography of concert and opera singers.

ANNA CZEKANOWICZ is the Chief Dramaturg of the Państwowa Opera i Filharmonia Baltycka in Gdańsk, Poland.

RONALD L. DAVIS is a Professor at Southern Methodist University and has authored *A History of Opera in the American West* and *Opera in Chicago: A Social and Cultural History 1850–1965*.

JOAN DRIEDGER is a Public Relations Consultant for Vancouver Opera in British Columbia, Canada.

TIMOTHY B. DUNN is Director of Public Relations of the Pittsburgh Opera, Pennsylvania.

PAVEL ECKSTEIN is a noted Czech musicologist and the Senior Advisor to the General Manager of the National Theater Prague, Czechoslovakia.

PETER ELVINS is a free-lance writer and a member of the ensemble of the Boston Lyric Opera Company, Massachusetts.

IAN FOX is the music critic of the *Sunday Tribune* in Dublin and the Irish correspondent for *Opera*.

FRANCESCA FRANCHI is the Archivist for the Royal Opera House, Convent Garden, London, England.

OTTO FRITZ is the former Assistant Director of the Volksoper in Vienna, Austria.

JAMES FULLAN is Public Relations Manager of the Portland Opera, Oregon.

PHILLIP GAINSLEY is an attorney-at-law and a supporter of the Minnesota Opera, Minneapolis, Minnesota.

HANS-JOCHEN GENZEL is the Chief Dramaturg of the Komische Opera, Berlin, Germany.

JULIUS GYERMEK is the Chief Dramaturg and an Opera Producer for the Slovak National Theater in Bratislava, Czechoslovakia.

MANFRED HAEDLER is the Chief Dramaturg of the Deutsche Staatsoper Berlin, Germany.

DALE E. HALL is a Professor at the University of Hawaii at Manoa and was a contributor to *Symphony Orchestras of the United States: Selected Profiles*.

SABINE HAMMER is an Opera Dramaturg with the Niedersächsische Statstheater in Hannover, Germany.

REBECCA HAPPEL is Director of Press and Public Relations with the Michigan Opera Theater, Detroit, Michigan.

KALLE HEIN is the Dramaturg of the Theatre Vanemuine in Tartu, Estonia.

About the Editor and Contributors

SCOTT HEUMANN is the Artistic Administrator and Dramaturg of the Houston Grand Opera, Texas.

CARL H. HILLER is a music journalist who regularly contributes to *Opernwelt* and is the author of *Vom Quatermarkt zum Offenbachplatz: 400 Jahre Musiktheater in Köln*.

SHI HONG–E is the Director of the Shanghai Opera House in Shanghai, People's Republic of China.

ALFREDA LOCKE IRWIN is the official Historian of Chautauqua Institution, New York.

ROUMYANA KARAKOSTOVA is the Repertoire Director of the Musical Theater "Stefan Makedonski" in Sofia, Bulgaria.

MARK KRISTMANSON is the Production Coordinator for the National Arts Centre Festival Opera in Ottawa, Ontario, Canada.

LIU LIAN–CHI is the Director of the Central Opera Theatre in Beijing, People's Republic of China.

SUSANNE LITZEL is with the Public Relations Department of the Hamburgische Staatsoper, Germany.

JOSEPH McLELLAN is a free-lance writer in the Washington, D.C., area.

ALEX MATTALIA is journalist, music historian, and coauthor of *Marseille notre Opéra 1787–1919, 1924–1987. Petite Histoire et Grands Événements*.

UBALDO MIRABELLI is the General Manager of the Teatro Massimo in Palermo, Italy.

SONJA MÜLLER-EISOLD is the music critic for the *Westfälischen Rundschau*, and Music Historian at the Hochschule für Musik in Detmold.

LEENA NIVANKA is press officer for the Finnish National Opera in Helsinki.

ROMUALD POLCZYNSKI is Editor-in-Chief of the *Poznan Daily Express* as well as the historian for the Teatr Wielki in Poznan, Poland.

SIMON REES is the Publications Editor for the Welsh National Opera in Cardiff, Wales, Great Britain.

LARS RING is Assistant to the General Manager of Drottningsholms Slottsteater and music critic for the *Svenska Dagbladet* in Stockholm, Sweden.

ERIK-GUSTAV RÖDIN is the Assistant to the General Manager of the Kungliga Teatern in Stockholm, Sweden.

CURT A. ROESLER is the Dramatic Advisor of the Deutsche Oper Berlin, Germany.

MYRTHA SCHENKEL is the Assistant to the Director of the Opernhaus Zürich, Switzerland.

ULRICH SCHERZER is a Dramaturg for the Landestheater Linz, Austria.

VINCENZO RAFFAELE SEGRETO represents the General Manager of the Teatro Regio in Parma, Italy.

MAGGIE STEARNS is the Press Representative of the Opera Theater of Saint Louis, Missouri.

VASYL TURKEVYCH is the Senior Literary Consultant of the Kiev Opera and Ballet Theater, USSR.

NÓRA WELLMANN is the Archivist for the Hungarian State Opera in Budapest, Hungary.

ANGELIKA WORSEG is a member of the Publicity Department of the Bregenzer Festspiele in Austria.